W9-BFO-105

LABOR MARKET ECONOMICS

SAUL D. HOFFMAN
University of Delaware

PRENTICE-HALL, INC., Englewood Cliffs, New Jersey 07632

Library of Congress Cataloging-in-Publication Data

Hoffman, Saul D., (Date)
Labor market economics.

Includes index.
1. Labor economics. I. Title.
HD4901.H63 1986 331 85-12106
ISBN 0-13-517855-X

Editorial/production supervision and
interior design: Nancy Fillmore, Joan McCulley, and Mary Bardoni
Cover design: Ben Santora
Manufacturing buyer: Ed O'Dougherty

Printed in the United States of America

10 9 8 7 6 5 4 3 2 1

ISBN 0-13-517855-X 01

Prentice-Hall International (UK) Limited, *London*
Prentice-Hall of Australia Pty. Limited, *Sydney*
Prentice-Hall Canada Inc., *Toronto*
Prentice-Hall Hispanoamericana, S.A., *Mexico*
Prentice-Hall of India Private Limited, *New Delhi*
Prentice-Hall of Japan, Inc., *Tokyo*
Prentice-Hall of Southeast Asia Pte. Ltd., *Singapore*
Editora Prentice-Hall do Brasil, Ltda., *Rio de Janeiro*
Whitehall Books Limited, *Wellington, New Zealand*

FOR SUSAN AND JAKE

Contents

Preface

This text is intended for a one-semester course in labor economics. It draws on two relatively new developments in labor market analysis. The first of these is the regular application of economic theory to labor market behavior, an approach squarely in line with the main body of research in labor economics over the past decade or two. Economic theory is not used as a straitjacket, but as a guide and an organizing principle. I hope that I have managed to communicate in this text the idea that economic theory is a very valuable tool for considering labor market issues—an opinion that was, I am glad to say, strengthened by the act of writing this book. The book is neoclassical in perspective, but not, I hope, dogmatically so. There is considerable coverage of alternative approaches and new ideas.

The second development is the enormous increase in empirical knowledge about labor market behavior and labor market outcomes. I have drawn on that material throughout the book; it figures especially prominently in the chapters on human capital, labor market discrimination, income distribution, and unemployment. I have also tried to be honest about the weaknesses in that empirical literature. In several cases, there are reasonably extensive discussions of the relevant research methodology. It is important for students to see not only *what* is known, but also *how* it is known.

Labor economics is well known for its direct application to many contemporary public policy issues. That, indeed, is one of the things that makes labor economics enjoyable to teach and popular among students. Those applications are covered here in two ways. First, several of the issues that are too broad for a short "applications discussion" have been given regular status in the text. An extensive discussion of minimum wage legislation, drawing on the findings of the Minimum Wage Study Commission, appears in Chapter 3. Chapter 4 contains an in-depth treatment of two labor supply issues: (1) the labor supply effects of the welfare system, including the findings of the negative income tax experiments; and (2) the supply-side arguments concerning the possible effects of income taxes on labor supply. The discussion of the effects of unemployment insurance on unemployment is treated similarly.

Second, distinct "applications sections" are sprinkled throughout virtually all of the chapters. In a sense, "applications" is an inappropriate description for these sections. They are not just straightforward empirical examples that "prove" the theory or brief discussions of relevant policy implications. Rather, they more often extend the theoretical argument, apply the theoretical perspective to something new or something a bit more complex. I hope they might breathe more vitality into the theory and enable students to see the theoretical ideas more clearly.

This course assumes that students have had an introductory course in microeconomics; previous exposure to macroeconomics would be helpful, but is not essential. I have deliberately pitched the level of difficulty of this text about a half a notch below that of comparable texts. I have tried to be realistic about which graphical presentations are truly accessible (at reasonable cost) to students with only a limited background in economics. (I teach both the principles course and intermediate microeconomics in addition to labor economics, so I have some firsthand experience.) Instructors will notice that, for example, the presentation of long-run labor demand in Chapter 3, individual labor supply decisions in Chapters 4 and 5, and of compensating differentials in Chapter 8 are not quite as "rigorous" as they might be. I firmly believe it is only the complexity of the presentation that has been reduced; there is nothing simple about the ideas. Appendices to Chapters 3, 4, and 5 do present the standard graphical analyses for those instructors who wish to teach at that level.

No project of this length can be accomplished single-handedly, and I feel fortunate to have gotten good advice from many people. Together they transformed the process of writing a textbook into a genuine learning experience. I want to give special thanks to three people who helped me frequently and often at great length: Charles Link of the University of Delaware, John McDermott of the University of South Carolina, and Greg J. Duncan of the University of Michigan's Institute for Social Research. Their ideas and encouragement were invaluable.

Among the many others who graciously read drafts of some of the chapters and contributed good advice were Ken Koford, Bert Levin, Jeff Miller, Larry Seidman, and Jim Thornton, all of the University of Delaware; Lisa Ehrlich, now of the FTC; and Arthur Schwartz of the University of Michigan's Institute of Labor and Industrial Relations. I also want to thank

Jack E. Adams of the University of Arkansas at Little Rock, James F. Ragan of Kansas State University, Barbara B. Reagan of Southern Methodist University, and Donna E. Shea of Bentley College, all of whom offered useful comments in their capacity as official Prentice-Hall reviewers.

Credit must also go to the students I have taught at the University of Delaware over the past seven years. They are, I suspect, quite unaware of their contribution, but collectively they had an impact. There is no substitute for the kind of feedback they provided.

No one could ask for a more skilled or more good-natured typist than I had in Nancy Proctor.

1

Introduction to Labor Economics

INTRODUCTION

There are two basic ways to introduce the subject matter of an economics textbook. One way is to describe, usually in broad, abstract terms, the subset of economic problems on which the text focuses and how that subject matter is related to other parts of the discipline. This is the type of description that most economics instructors prefer. The other way is to outline some of the specific problems, issues, or policies that are part of the subject and which can be analyzed and understood using the ideas developed. That is the type of introduction that students usually prefer.

Fortunately, it is easy to describe the subject matter of labor economics in either way. Labor economics is a fundamental part of the body of economic theory and it is also readily and usefully applied to a wide range of interesting, important policy issues. Labor economics touches on some of the broadest issues considered by economics as well as providing insights into decisions and forces that may affect you in a very immediate and personal way.

Let's begin, then, with the broader view of labor economics. The title of this book, *Labor Market Economics*, is a good place to start. The key word there is the one to which you probably gave the least notice—*market*. If you have had a previous course in economics, you probably know that the study of markets is one of the fundamental topics in **microeconomics**, the branch of economics that studies the behavior of individuals and firms in the economy. Thus you might well suspect that labor economics is primarily microeconomic analysis applied to the special and distinctive characteristics of workers and labor markets. As the basic tool of microeconomics is supply and demand analysis, you might therefore expect to learn about labor demand curves, labor supply curves, and the factors that underlie them. Supply and demand analysis, of course, is especially useful for explaining the determination of price and quantity in a market. In the case of a labor market, the price is the wage rate of workers and the quantity is the amount of available employment—two economic indicators of great importance in any society.

Labor plays two related roles in an economy, roles that lead into the major themes of microeconomics. First, there is labor as a factor of production, used, together with land and capital, to help produce the goods and services that society consumes. Second, there is labor as an earner of income. When we consider labor from the standpoint of production, we focus on issues concerning the efficient use of scarce labor resources—what economists call the **allocation problem**. When viewed from the income side, the issues concern the division of the nation's output or income among individuals—in short, the **distribution problem**. The link between the production side and the income side, between the allocation of labor and the distribution of income, is the wage rate. It determines both the use of labor by firms and the income and living standards of workers and their families. The wage rate is certainly a price of special significance in the economy.

Labor economics is, then, one of the applied fields of microeconomics. Indeed, it is one of the oldest topics in economics, perhaps because its subject matter is ourselves. We, after all, are labor, and it is not surprising that economists might turn to the task of understanding what happens to us in our roles as worker, producer, and wage earner. Why are some persons or classes rich and others poor? Why are some countries rich and some countries poor? Or, as David Ricardo, one of the most famous of the early nineteenth-century British economists, expressed it: What are the *laws* that regulate the distribution of the produce of the earth among workers, landowners, and the owners of capital?

Although much of labor economics is firmly in the microeconomics camp, it does draw on other parts of economic theory as well. The analysis of employment and unemployment has traditionally been part of **macroeconomics**, the branch of economics that takes as its subject the performance of the economy as a whole. In recent years, however, some microeconomists have begun to invade the macroeconomic turf and have contributed significantly to an understanding of the causes of unemployment and the relationship between unemployment and inflation. Still, labor economics necessarily includes a healthy dose of macroeconomics.

Labor economics also draws on concepts developed in **capital theory**, a specialized part of microeconomics that analyzes the logic of investments in long-lived assets, such as machinery. With a little bit of footwork, we will show that something fairly similar occurs when individuals develop their own job skills and abilities in school and at work. The application of capital theory to individuals is, not too surprisingly, called **human capital theory**. It is now one of the most important parts of the theory of labor market economics.

So much, then, for the broad approach to labor economics. Labor economics is also a highly practical area of economics. It is instrumental in the informed analysis of many public policy issues and in intelligent individual decision making. Just listing some of the topics and questions that fall under the domain of labor economics should give you an idea of what lies ahead:

1. Why was the average income per person nearly $10,000 in the United States in 1978, but less than $1000 in seventy other countries?
2. Why do women earn, on average, only about three-fifths of what men earn in the United States? Why hasn't that figure risen in the past 25 years? Does the female–male gap in pay represent discrimination or are other factors at work? What exactly do economists mean by discrimination?
3. What accounts for the economic status of black workers in the United States? Why is the incidence of poverty so much higher for black families than for white families?
4. What is the effect of minimum wage legislation on the employment of less skilled workers? Is it a cause of teenage unemployment?
5. Why is the welfare problem in the United States so hard to solve? What are the problems of the current system? Does the welfare system affect the labor supply of individuals?

6. Why has the proportion of married women in the labor force risen so steadily over the past half-century?
7. Is a college education a good economic investment? Should a poorer, developing country expand its education system? How would you go about evaluating these investments in human capital?
8. Why do many athletes and entertainers earn so much more money than economics instructors? More generally, what influences the economic rewards that are received by persons with different skills? Are the income differences fair?
9. Why has unemployment become such a characteristic feature of industrialized economies? In the United States, why is unemployment so high for teenagers, especially minority teens? What policies might be effective in *permanently* reducing unemployment?
10. There have been large swings in fertility behavior in the United States over the past few decades. Some cohorts—persons born in the year—are unusually large (the "baby boom") and others (the "baby bust") are much smaller. What types of labor market problems will this cause?
11. What is the role of unions in the labor market? How do they affect wages and employment?

All these questions—and many more like them—can be addressed using the tools of labor economics. The answers are important, and in some cases, they may be surprising.

GETTING STARTED IN LABOR ECONOMICS: BASIC CONCEPTS

Like practitioners in almost every field of study, economists have developed a basic set of concepts and viewpoints that underlie most of their work. Some of this is a matter of specialized vocabulary, slightly complicated by the fact that economists have a habit of using ordinary terms in unorthodox ways. Others are perspectives and assumptions that help characterize the basic economics "way of thinking." Perhaps more than other social sciences, economics has developed a **paradigm**, that is, a set of ideas and perspectives which constitute the core of the discipline and which are accepted by most persons in the economics profession.[1] It is worth taking inventory of some of these ideas and concepts before heading into the heart of the subject matter in the next chapter.

The Labor Market

Since labor economics is primarily microeconomics and since microeconomics is the study of markets, the obvious place to begin is with the concept of a **labor market**. Introductory economics books usually define a

[1] The concept of a paradigm was developed by Thomas Kuhn in his book, *The Structure of Scientific Revolution* (Chicago: The University of Chicago Press, 1970).

market as an area in which buyers and sellers are in close enough contact so that a single price prevails for a homogeneous (identical) product. In what sense are we justified in applying this idea of a market to labor? What exactly is meant by the phrase "labor market"?

Admittedly, the idea of a market fits less comfortably on labor than it does, say, on oranges, steel, wheat, ball-point pens, and other relatively standardized products. It may seem to you that each worker is unique and that each job is different in its requirements and conditions. If so, then where is the homogeneity necessary for the existence of a market? In the extreme case, this view would suggest an almost infinite number of independent employment and wage arrangements, each individually negotiated between a single worker and a single firm for a specific job.

Whatever the merits of this view as an accurate description of real-world behavior—and frankly, most economists are inclined to doubt it even on those terms—it would mark the end of labor economics as a field of study. If each employment situation is unique, the laws of distribution are either nonexistent or are so variable as to be useless. After all, what could we conclude about the market for ball-point pens if we insisted on regarding each product in that market as distinct from every other?

One way out of this apparent dilemma is to think like an economist. Economists have an uncanny ability to find markets operating where, to the untrained eye, there is only chaos, let alone an organized interaction between suppliers and demanders. To do this yourself, you need to make what the nineteenth-century poet and critic Samuel Tayler Coleridge described as a "willing suspension of disbelief." He was actually referring to the act of reading fiction, an activity which is much improved by conveniently ignoring the fact—that is, suspending your disbelief—that all the characters and events are only the product of someone's imagination. The same mental device is needed in labor economics. You need to suspend temporarily the preoccupation with the differences among workers and jobs in order to see the similarities. You need to ignore selectively some features of workers and jobs in order to concentrate on others. Judicious abstraction is the key.

If you make that suspension of disbelief, you will find that in any geographic area, there are a relatively large number of workers, perhaps not identical in every respect, but similar enough to each other in their skills as to warrant linking them up in a single labor supply curve. On the opposite side are a large number of firms all requiring workers to do tasks which, however different they may be in actual content, require similar skills. These firms are, collectively, the demanders of labor. If all these workers can potentially perform adequately at each of the jobs and if each employer can potentially employ any of the workers, we would certainly expect their wage rates and other terms of employment to be related. We have now come a long way from the world of one-on-one bargaining between unique individuals and unique jobs. We have, in fact, created the concept of a labor market, whose characteristic feature is that terms of employment are determined not by a single individual or firm, but by the joint interaction of many participants.

This idea of a labor market does not require that all workers be identical in all respects, although we will in fact begin that way in the next chapter. There could be many groups of workers, perhaps differing by skill, as long as each group is large enough to avoid the small-numbers problem. It also does not require that *all* workers and *all* employers be in regular contact. "Potential mobility," wrote Sir John Hicks, a British Nobel prize–winning economist, "is the ultimate sanction for the interrelationship of wages."

One further point needs to be made about the notion of applying the logic of markets to labor. It is sometimes argued that in placing labor on the same analytical footing as oranges, steel, wheat, and ball-point pens, economists have transformed labor into a commodity and thereby stripped it of its humanity. Indeed, Section 6 of the Clayton Act, an antitrust law passed by the U.S. Congress in 1914, declared that the labor of a human being is not a commodity or an article of commerce. The Constitution of the International Labor Office, an agency of the United Nations, says much the same thing.

Perhaps you can anticipate the economist's response. There are, admittedly, many distinctive characteristics of labor that make it much more than a commodity and even different from other productive inputs, such as land or capital. For one thing, workers frequently care about their working environment—what economists call their **nonpecuniary job characteristics**. Workers also have the unique ability to take actions in their own behalf, principally by making investments in human capital. They also can control the quality of their work. Unlike land or capital, workers can be motivated and then perform well, or be angered and perform poorly. Finally, to repeat a point already made, the wage rate is a price of special significance in an economy. We cannot be blind to its effects on the welfare of families and children.

The recognition of the many human elements of labor markets should not, however, inhibit economic inquiry into the conditions of employment and the determination of wages. Thus, for some purposes, it is extremely useful to regard labor as a commodity whose equilibrium price and quantity are determined by supply and demand. Indeed, it is difficult to imagine how else wage rates and employment could be studied. To note that for some limited purposes, we may wish to regard both labor and capital as "inputs" or "commodities" certainly does not imply that people and machines are in all respects the same.

Opportunity Cost

It is difficult to escape from the first chapter of any economics book without coming across the concept of **opportunity cost**. This book is no exception in that respect. Opportunity cost is the economist's way of thinking about costs. Economists always measure the opportunity cost of some option not by its monetary cost directly, but rather as the most highly valued alternative which is forgone when that option is chosen.

Whenever a resource is scarce, it has an opportunity cost, and this is certainly true for labor. When labor is *used* in one place, it is *used up* as far as the rest of the economy is concerned. Labor employed in one industry is no longer available for use in another industry. In general, the opportunity cost of labor is the value of the goods and services inevitably forgone somewhere in the economy when labor is used in another place.

Frequently, the market wage rate is a good measure of the opportunity cost of labor. Suppose that firm *A* finds that it must pay $5 per hour to attract capable employees. Presumably, the $5 wage is equal to or just slightly above the wage that other firms are willing to pay. Otherwise, firm *A* would not need to pay as much. Go a step further. Why are other firms willing to pay workers a $5 wage? Because that must be approximately the value to their own customers of the output of an hour's worth of labor. That output is exactly what is forgone when firm *A* hires another worker. It is, therefore, the opportunity cost of increased employment by firm *A*. Thus the wage rate measures the opportunity cost of employing labor.

Application: Labor Costs, the Draft, and the Volunteer Army

Occasionally, wage rates are a grossly misleading indicator of true opportunity costs. A classic example of this is the analysis of the costs of a volunteer army versus a military draft as a means for satisfying military personnel requirements.

In June 1973, the peacetime military draft was abolished and was replaced by an all-volunteer system. Individuals were no longer required to serve in the armed forces, but were, instead, able to decide for themselves whether or not to enlist in the service. The all-volunteer system is still in effect, but there have been occasional criticisms of the excessive labor costs of the volunteer system compared to the draft.

Suppose that we want to determine which system of meeting military personnel needs is less costly. In terms of total monetary salary costs, there is no contest. With a volunteer army, recruits must be paid a wage that compares favorably with their available private-sector opportunities. Under the military draft, however, salaries could be—and were—extremely low since there was no need to offer a wage high enough to compete with private-sector opportunities. Thus salary costs are undeniably higher under the volunteer army.

But what about the opportunity costs of securing labor in these two systems? What is sacrificed by supporting the military is the value of goods and services forgone when people are removed from private-sector employment and "employed" in the military. If the military must rely on volunteers, it is in exactly the same position as was firm *A* discussed above. The wage it pays to volunteers is therefore a reasonable estimate of the private-sector opportunity cost of its volunteers. Thus total opportunity costs of obtaining military personnel in this way are approximately equal to the total salary costs. In contrast, the salary costs under a draft vastly underestimate the opportunity costs. If the draftees are about as competent as the volunteers, we can assume that no acceptable draftee would have had a lower private-sector salary than that of the volunteers. Thus it follows that the draft could never have a lower opportunity cost than that of a volunteer army. In fact, however, many draftees were more skilled in terms of their private-sector opportunities, although not necessarily in terms of their military skills. (Draftees were, for example, on average more educated than volunteers.) Their military salaries may have been low, but the opportunity cost was high because their services were highly valued in the private sector.

Thus it appears likely that to maintain a military force of given quality, the true labor cost to society will usually be higher under a draft system than under a volunteer system. The higher cost of the draft is disguised because much of the cost is borne by draftees as the difference between their market wage and the wage they receive in involuntary military employment. Indeed, one could argue that one of the virtues of the volunteer system is that all costs are explicit.

Cost may not be the only relevant criterion in evaluating the two systems. There may be other reasons for preferring a draft over a volunteer system. Perhaps the country feels that the burden of military service should be distributed more widely over all persons rather than concentrated among the less educated or among minority youth. The alleged lower budgetary cost of the draft is, however, not a valid reason. Properly evaluated, the costs are higher, not lower.

The Circular Flow of Income

We noted earlier that labor plays two related roles in an economy, first as a factor of production and a second as an earner of income. The famous way to represent this idea is by describing the **circular flow of income** in an economy.

The basic point is that there are two interactions between firms and consumers rather than one. Firms sell final products to consumers, and more or less simultaneously, the firms buy (actually rent) labor from workers in order to produce the goods which they will subsequently sell. In the first exchange, income flows from consumers to firms and finished commodities move in the other direction. In the second exchange, income goes from firms to workers, while raw materials, including labor, go the other way. But the consumers and the workers are not two distinct groups. They are the same group, observed at different points in the economy.

Most of the subject matter of labor economics focuses on the second half of the circular flow, that is, on the supply of and demand for labor and on the operation and outcomes of labor markets. But the circular flow emphasizes that the product market and the labor market are not independent spheres, but are actually closely linked parts of a whole system. For example, it should be obvious that the wage income of all workers is exactly equal to the labor costs of all firms. Moreover, a statement such as "an increase in interest rates will cost consumers so many million dollars" tells only half the story. The other half is the increase in the interest income of consumers whose savings are providing the money that banks are lending. But for an understanding of labor markets, the most important point made by the circular flow concept is why firms hire labor—namely, in order to sell the finished goods. Without the demand by consumers for the final product, there would be no demand by firms for workers to make the products. In formal terms, we can say that the demand for labor (or any factor of production) is ultimately derived from the demand for the final product it helps to produce. The demand for labor is termed a **derived demand**.

The Purpose of Employment

We have just seen that two things happen simultaneously in labor markets. Labor inputs are provided to firms and labor income is provided to workers. Is it possible to single out one of these as the principal function of labor markets?

Most people probably view the labor market from the perspective of an income earner. This is perfectly natural since most people *are* income earners. They implicitly assume that the function of a labor market is to provide income to workers and their families. In a sense, the goal of employment is realized by the receipt of income.

The link among employment, income, and family welfare is important and we will have much to say about it as we proceed. Nevertheless, most economists would not fully agree with the emphasis of the sentiments expressed above. Instead of thinking of employment as an end in and of itself, economists usually regard it as a means to the production of desired goods and services. This is simply the flip side of the derived-demand idea represented by the circular flow of income. In the words of another Noble prize–winning economist, James Meade: "The ultimate purpose is . . . not to give employment, but to obtain the largest possible output from the community's resources of land and capital and . . . labor."

In this view, the function of labor markets is to direct a valuable, scarce resource—labor—into its most productive use. The primary purpose of a wage rate is to guide this allocation. Providing income to workers is its auxiliary function.

This difference in perspective is greater than you may think. Consider, for example, the issue of technological change. On the one hand, technological change has obviously been a major factor in improving living standards, since it increases a country's capacity to produce desired goods and services. On the other hand, technological change is alleged to have a negative impact on employment and there is a long history of opposition to it on these grounds. The most famous historical example is that of the Luddites, a group of British textile workers who actually destroyed mechanized knitting machines in the late eighteenth and early nineteenth centuries in order to preserve their jobs. More recently, a legal suit was filed in California to prevent its state universities from carrying out research that might lead to increased automation of tomato harvesting. If technological change increases productivity and output, yet reduces employment for some workers, is it good or bad? Should it be encouraged or discouraged?

Most economists would come out strongly in favor of technological change rather than employment protection. The alleged conflict between output and employment is false in almost every case because it is posed too narrowly. Although technological change may reduce employment in a specific industry (and incidentally, it may not even do this), it does not cause unemployment in the sense of *permanently* reducing the number of job opportunities in an economy. Rather, it shifts the site of employment from one industry to another. If fewer workers are now required in the production of one product, more labor is available for the production of other products. Instead of thinking of the workers as unemployed, as if that were to be their permanent fate, think of them as being "released" into the economy to find productive employment elsewhere.

As a specific example of this process, let's look at agriculture in the United States. That sector of the economy now employs only about 3 percent of the labor force compared to nearly 40 percent at the beginning of the twentieth century. That decline is largely the result of technological change which greatly increased agricultural productivity and transformed agriculture from a labor-intensive industry to a capital-intensive industry. This change did not, however, lead to a permanent decrease in employment opportunities or a permanent increase in unemployment. Rather, the employment decline in agriculture created an enormous increase in the labor available for nonagricultural production, and most workers were eventually assimilated into that sector of the economy. The net effect of the technological change in agriculture has been an increase in our ability to produce both agricultural and nonagricultural goods.

Technological change may cause hardships for some workers in the economy. It may be difficult for workers to learn new job skills or to move from one industry to another or even from one geographic area to another.

(The agricultural example is a good example of this.) There may well be a need for public programs to aid in retraining and relocating workers displaced by technological change. But as serious as these problems may be for specific persons, they are essentially short run and transitional in nature rather than permanent. In the long run, technological change improves living standards without reducing employment opportunities.

Employment, Unemployment, Microeconomics, and Macroeconomics

This example also illustrates the way in which economists and noneconomists differ in their views about unemployment. The opposition to technological change reflects a belief that high unemployment is inevitable and that any means to reduce it is desirable. Most economists, however, are unwilling to accept that opinion about unemployment.[2] Unemployment, they would argue, is not something to be assumed but rather a phenomenon to be explained.

In studying labor economics, it is important not to allow a concern with unemployment to dominate every analysis of labor market issues. Unemployment is undeniably a serious economic problem and economists have analyzed it extensively. But unemployment is a different type of problem from the ones that will occupy us for the first part of the book. Many extremely important labor market issues remain even when unemployment exists.

In most of our study of labor economics, we will temporarily abstract from the existence of unemployment in order to focus on the type of microeconomic problems noted earlier in the chapter. Later, we return the favor, abstracting from some of the microeconomic aspects of labor economics in order to focus on macroeconomic forces and their effects on unemployment. Both sets of problems are important, but it is easier to study them one at a time. The "willing suspension of disbelief" is important once again.

THE METHODOLOGY OF LABOR ECONOMICS

When economists and researchers in other fields of study talk about **methodology**, they mean the set of methods and procedures that they regularly use in their work. The methodology of labor economics has undergone a tremendous change in the past twenty-five years or so. Before that time, labor economists primarily studied institutions in the labor market, particularly issues concerning unions, the collective bargaining process, the role of gov-

[2] This is actually a complex issue. Most economists would agree that some unemployment is inevitable and, in fact, the inevitable part is sometimes called the "natural unemployment rate." The implied disagreement in the text is about the "nonnatural" part of total unemployment. These issues are discussed fully in the last two chapters of this book.

ernment, and so on. The basic approach of these "institutional labor economists" was descriptive rather than analytical or predictive. They drew heavily on law, history, sociology, and political science and actually relied very little on economic theory of any kind. There was, for example, relatively little formal analysis of labor supply or labor demand.[3] Although the ideas to be presented in the next few chapters were known, they were not thought to be very important. Most of the ideas in the latter half of this book had not even been developed yet.

This kind of primarily descriptive institutional analysis still has a place in labor economics, but its role and influence are declining. Most of what was once institutional labor economics has been absorbed by the fields of labor and industrial relations, industrial sociology, and labor history. Today, labor economics has become more integrated into the mainstream of economic analysis. It has become a more theoretical subject, meaning not that it has become esoteric or irrelevant, but that the basic tools of economic theory are used to analyze labor market behavior and outcomes. The adoption of a more theoretical perspective doesn't mean that institutions and legal arrangements are neglected. If anything, the application of economic theory makes it easier to discover the effects of specific laws and institutions in the labor market.

Labor economics has also become a subject in which empirical, statistical research plays a larger role. Ideally, the theoretical and empirical approaches go hand in hand. Economic theory provides predictions about the *qualitative* nature of important relationships, whereas empirical analyses allow us to test those predictions and to determine the *quantitative* magnitude of those relationships.

Theory and Models in Labor Economics

Actual labor markets are very complex and so varied that they would seem, at first, to defy systematic analysis and the successful application of theory. To apply economic theory to labor markets, it is almost always necessary to make some set of simplifying assumptions. We have already seen that even the use of so basic a concept as that of a labor market requires a suspension of disbelief—in that case, involving a smoothing over of differences among individuals and jobs in order to construct market supply and demand curves.

As you will quickly see, economists rarely analyze real-world labor markets directly. Instead, the analysis is based on a simplified version of a labor market—in a word, a model of a labor market. When confronted with an interesting economic problem that is too messy to analyze—for example,

[3] One well-known economic theorist, Kenneth Boulding, described the field of labor economics in the late 1940s in this way: "One can hardly pick up a new book on labor nowadays without finding the author jumping gleefully on what he thinks is the corpse of supply or demand, or proclaiming with trumpets 'the labor market is dead, long live human relations.' "

what determines wage rates for different groups of workers or what are the effects of labor market discrimination—economists usually try first to analyze a simpler, less cluttered version of the problem. That is exactly what an **economic model** is. A model is a simplified, skeletal version of a real-world situation. If it is a good model, it captures the central features of the problem, yet excludes the details and fine shading which only complicate the problem without altering it in any fundamental way.

Bad models come in at least two forms. One form is too simple and too unrealistic. Actually, the problem is not that the model is unrealistic, but that it may yield few insights and poor predictions about the situation it was constructed to analyze. The other form of bad model is too detailed and too realistic, so that it no longer serves its function as a simplifying tool. The Argentine essayist Borges relates a parable about mapmakers who became dissatisfied with their work because they were acutely aware of the many omissions and distortions in their maps. They resolved to make their maps absolutely realistic, incorporating every real-world detail. In so doing, their maps expanded not only in complexity, but in size as well (to accommodate the detail), until they were exactly the same size as the real world! "The map of Spain," writes Borges, "was the same size as the country of Spain." Very realistic, to be sure, but not much of a model, which is exactly what a good map is. Which model was more useful to navigators and other potential users—the small-scale incomplete one or the life-size fully accurate one?

A good model, then, simplifies a problem without distorting it. Just like a good map, it is inevitably an incomplete or even unrealistic representation of the problem to be studied. But if its predictions are accurate and useful, the model passes the test. In the course of this book, we will develop and examine many different labor market models. Some, like the one in the next chapter, will be quite simple, while others will be more elaborate and complex. Even the fullest model will undoubtedly fail to do justice to all the details and richness of real-world labor markets. But no apologies are necessary. The simplifications are deliberate and the models have proved their usefulness over and over again.

One more brief comment is in order here regarding the use of models and theory in labor economics. A frequent and sometimes valid criticism of economic theorizing is this: Economists frequently exaggerate the role of economic factors at the expense of other factors. If economists cannot measure something, they assume that it is not important.

There is clearly an element of truth to this criticism, especially in labor economics. No single field of study can claim a monopoly on insights into a topic as broad as employment. Sociologists, psychologists, and other social scientists can and do provide valuable insights into the behavior of workers and firms. For example, although labor productivity does depend on some purely economic factors, such as the amount of physical and human capital, it also depends on broader sociological and psychological considerations.

Models from other disciplines also have explanatory power. But it is one thing to acknowledge that any single theoretical approach is incomplete, and something else—probably a mistake—to assert that it is therefore wrong. A good analysis of a portion of a complicated problem is almost certainly preferable to a weak analysis of all of it.

Application: The Use of Theory and Models

How do economists construct a model? How are models used? Here are two examples.

1. Economists usually attack a problem in stages, first studying a very simple version to derive the most basic principles and then adding more and more complexity. But details are added to a model only if they make a difference in the model's predictions.

   The analysis of labor demand presented in the next few chapters is an excellent example of this strategy. We begin in Chapter 2 with an analysis of the simplest possible situation, in which all workers are identical in their skills and firms are unable to alter the amount of capital they use. Next, we consider what happens to labor demand when firms *can* change their use of capital but all workers are still the same. Finally, we relax that assumption as well and see what happens when a firm can choose to employ workers of different skills. But even then, we only consider the case in which there are two groups of workers, such as skilled and unskilled. Two groups of workers, plus capital, is the minimum necessary to analyze a certain set of important relationships. More than two simply increases the difficulty of the model without providing any further insights. So that is where the model stops.
2. The economic analysis of labor market discrimination nicely illustrates both the limited nature of economic analysis and the potential role played by economic theory. Economists typically *begin* their analysis of discrimination where sociologists, anthropologists, and psychologists *stop* theirs. Researchers in these fields might investigate such topics as how and why feelings of discrimination develop, how those feelings persist or strengthen or erode, the forms that discrimination takes, the functions it serves, and its psychological and sociological effects on all parties. They do not, however, usually inquire into how these feelings are translated into the economic realm: how they influence economic behavior and economic outcomes. Is labor supply affected? Labor demand? Human capital investment? Economic efficiency? Those are the topics emphasized by economists in analyzing discrimination, precisely because those are the areas where economic theory can be usefully applied.

   Economists tend to ignore the development of discriminatory attitudes not because that topic is unimportant, but because economic theory has relatively little to contribute. Instead, as you will see in Chapter 9, the economic approach to discrimination is to pose the problem this way: Suppose that feelings of discrimination take the specific form that a firm prefers one type of worker over another, even if the workers were equally skilled and if their wages were the same. How will this affect labor market equilibrium?

The analysis of discrimination also shows the potential value of economic theory. Consider the following two assertions, both of which have supporters: (1) "Labor market discrimination is a natural outgrowth of the actions of profit-maximizing firms operating in an unregulated, competitive economy." (2) "Competitive markets tend to eliminate the effects of discrimination. Discrimination can thrive only when competition is weak." Clearly, only one of the two statements can be correct. The difference is not just academic. The design of effective government policy to eliminate discrimination in the labor market depends critically on which view is correct. Even worse, government policy, based on a mistaken hypothesis, could make discrimination more severe. Should we, then, restrict competitive behavior, as the first view suggests, or should we encourage competition and seek to strengthen it, following the second? How can we determine which of the two statements is correct?

That is exactly where economic theory comes in. We can save the details for later, but the basic idea is this. First, economists do not have to start from scratch in analyzing discrimination. There already exists a well-developed model—the *competitive model*—which has proved useful for analyzing the behavior of profit-maximizing competitive firms in the absence of discrimination. The analytical task, then, is to modify that model by incorporating discrimination and then seeing what difference it makes in the outcomes predicted by the model. How do the results with and without discrimination differ? For example, are discriminating firms more or less profitable than firms that do not practice discrimination? If the model suggested that discriminating firms were more profitable, this would lend support to the first assertion. But suppose that discrimination turned out to require a sacrificing of profits. That would certainly suggest that in competitive markets, where the profit motive is strong, discrimination might be weak. A good theoretical model of how discrimination affects the behavior of competitive firms should help us to find the answer.

Basic Assumptions in Economic Models

Underlying almost all models in microeconomics are some very basic assumptions about behavior. We cannot analyze economic behavior under a wide variety of circumstances unless we can identify the goals of firms and individuals. What motivates their behavior? Toward what ends are they striving? To know what they will *do*, we need to know what they *want*.

The economists' answer to these very profound questions is simple and almost evasive: Individuals and firms are seeking to **maximize their own self-interest**. As Adam Smith put it in *The Wealth of Nations* over two centuries ago: "It is not from the benevolence of the butcher, the brewer, or the baker that we expect our dinner, but from their regard to their self-interest. We address ourselves, not to their humanity, but to their self-love, and never talk to them of our necessities, but of their advantages."

To lend content and predictive power to this assumption of self-interest, we need to add two additional ideas. The first is that goals are relatively stable over time. The assertion of self-interested behavior would not tell us very much if interests changed each week. For the analysis of firms, the stability of goals poses no serious problem, since economists usually assume that firms seek to maximize their profits. But economists are much less precise about the corresponding goals of individuals. The preferences and tastes of different people are so diverse that economists assume only that each person's preferences are themselves well established and not constantly in flux. Then, given these preferences, whatever they may be, economists assume that individuals pursue the most favorable outcome that is attainable given their resources and opportunities.

The second additional assumption is that firms and individuals are generally aware of which actions will enable them to achieve their goals. They need not be omniscient, but neither are they thoroughly ignorant of the relationship between the goals they seek and the actions they take.

The hypothesis that individuals and firms pursue their self-interest in a reasonably effective and consistent way is a powerful tool of economic analysis. In particular, it enables us to interpret and give meaning to the economic behavior we observe. It suggests that the behavior of firms and individuals is purposeful and directed, rather than random. We can, then, expect both firms and individuals to pursue systematically those actions which are most in their interests and, more important, to modify their actions when conditions change if they conclude that their current behavior no longer increases their interests as much as would an alternative course of action. The previous two sentences actually summarize the basic approach of microeconomics: What is the best that can be done under the current conditions? How will those actions change when the conditions change but the goals and motivations do not? More formally, this is the study of **constrained maximization**, the science of doing the best you can in whatever situation you find yourself.

Economists frequently use the phrase "rationality" to describe this informed pursuit of self-interest, but the idea is easily misunderstood and frequently caricatured. Rationality does not imply perfection, nor does the pursuit of self-interest require anything as fanatical as Captain Ahab's quest for the white whale in *Moby Dick*. When economists speak of rational behavior, they mean only that to the best of their abilities, firms and individuals pursue those strategies that promise to advance their interests the most. They may be wrong and sorely disappointed, but they never deliberately choose inferior strategies when better alternatives exist.

The analytical value of these assumptions is that they simplify the problem and provide a consistent way of interpreting economic behavior. It is, frankly, difficult to predict with much success what poorly informed people will do. Analyzing the behavior under changing conditions of ill-informed persons who have constantly changing goals is hopeless. As for the assumption of self-interested behavior, it has the additional virtue of being, on the whole, correct.

Positive and Normative Analysis

The distinction between positive and normative analysis is especially important in labor economics. **Positive analysis** is always concerned with explaining what will happen in a certain situation, whereas **normative analysis** is concerned with evaluating the outcome. Is it fair? Is it just? Although economists undoubtedly have opinions about the desirability of any particular outcome, there are no scientific principles to guide us in normative analysis. The special contribution of economists *as economists* is confined largely to positive analysis, and most of this book will present that kind of analysis. Still, when the issues being studied are as central to economic well-being as are income and employment, normative analysis inevitably plays a role. Issues surrounding the distribution of income—the gap between the rich and the poor or between capitalists and workers—are among the most divisive and emotionally charged topics explored by economists. It is frequently difficult to remain scientific and dispassionate.

PLAN OF THE TEXT

Chapters 2 to 13 cover all of the traditional topics in labor economics and a few new, less conventional ones as well. Chapters 2 to 5 comprise a unit that covers the basic ideas of labor demand and labor supply. Chapter 2 focuses on the most fundamental "basics" of labor demand theory, analyzed within the context of an extremely simple model of the labor market. Chapter 3 treats more complex issues in labor demand: the role of market structure, the relationship between labor and capital, and the determinants of the elasticity of labor demand. It also presents an extended discussion of an important policy issue, minimum wage legislation.

Chapter 4 is concerned with individual decisions about desired hours of work—that is, labor supply. This is an especially interesting topic, full of theoretical twists and the subject of common misconception by noneconomists. It also figures centrally in the analysis of two major contemporary policy issues: reform of the welfare system and supply-side economics. Both of these are discussed in Chapter 4. Chapter 5 rounds out the labor supply discussion by examining the topic of labor force participation. It also presents an alternative way to analyze labor supply decisions by treating that choice as part of the broader issue of individual time use.

Chapters 6 to 11 form a second unified set of chapters that focus collectively on the analysis of wage differences. The topic of Chapters 6 and 7 is the human capital model, which is one of the truly important developments in all of economics in the past 25 years. It provides a unique and insightful way to think about common activities, such as attending school and working at a job. It also offers a basis for understanding the personal distribution of income. Chapter 6 concentrates on the basic topics in human capital theory. Chapter 7 examines some implications, some criticisms, and some related alternatives, including the credentialist and signaling models, the dual labor market model, and the idea of internal labor markets.

Chapter 8 covers three assorted topics in wage theory. The first of these is the idea of economic rent, used to explain the often high earnings received by people with skills that are unique and thus cannot be readily acquired by others. The second topic is the wage effects of differences in job characteristics. The third is an introduction to the economics of Karl Marx and others working in the Marxist tradition.

Chapter 9 is devoted to the discussion of labor market discrimination and the earnings differences that exist today between men and women and between black and white workers. This is one of the most highly charged issues in all of contemporary labor economics. The economic analysis of the issues involved is instructive but, unfortunately, inconclusive.

In Chapter 10 we look at the major institution in the labor market—the labor union. It has effects on both wages, employment, and productivity and we use economic theory to identify the probable effects. One of the rewarding aspects of this analysis is that it emphasizes the importance of the underlying economic theory. It is hard to know how one would assess the effects of labor unions without having that analytical framework as a point of reference.

Chapter 11 completes this set of chapters. Its focus is on the empirical dimensions of earnings differences and the distribution of income among persons and among factors of production.

Finally, the last two chapters examine the macroeconomic aspects of labor markets. The main topic is unemployment, especially what causes it. Chapter 12 looks at some conventional and unconventional explanations of unemployment, as well as describing some of what is known about the empirical aspects of unemployment. Chapter 13 looks at unemployment in relation to inflation and examines the role of government policy.

A FINAL NOTE OF INTRODUCTION

Labor economics is one of the most active fields in contemporary economics, both because the topics it considers are so important and because the theoretical issues it deals with are often quite difficult. The "core theory" of labor economics is well developed, but it is being modified and extended rapidly. It is also being applied with greater sophistication to improved data sources, yielding new empirical findings. Important research is ongoing in many areas and new findings are emerging regularly.[4] There are many topics about which we still have only incomplete information and tentative conclusions. As a result, perhaps more than in other areas of economics, labor economics must be studied more for its conceptual framework and its analytical perspective than for some set of fixed and final findings.

New Concepts

Allocation problem
Distribution problem
Capital theory
Human capital theory
Paradigm
Labor Market
Opportunity cost
Circular flow of income
Derived demand
Methodology
Economic model
Self-interested behavior
Constrained maximization
Positive versus normative analysis

[4] One indication of this is that a new journal, aptly called the *Journal of Labor Economics*, was started in 1983. An older economics journal, also emphasizing labor economics, is the *Journal of Human Resources*.

2

Fundamentals of Labor Market Economics

INTRODUCTION

In this chapter we begin our analysis of how labor markets work by considering a very simple model of a labor market. By keeping the model uncluttered at first, we can move quickly to derive basic principles and establish important results. We start by analyzing the nature of a firm's use of labor and conclude by showing how an equilibrium wage rate is determined. Along the way, we will gain an understanding of the link between productivity and living standards, whether athletes are paid more than they are worth, and whether the amount of employment in an economy is a fixed technological requirement.

A model in economics always begins with a set of assumptions that carefully define the situation to be analyzed. A model of the labor market requires assumptions about workers and firms which tell us something about them and how we expect them to behave. It also requires some assumptions about the economic environment in which both the workers and the firms operate. Once the assumptions are made, we can analyze the model to determine the expected outcomes. The simple model we consider in this chapter is based on the following assumptions.

First, we assume that all workers are equally skilled and are identical in all relevant respects. In more formal language, they are **homogeneous**.

Second, we assume that firms seek to maximize their profits. Each firm has a fixed amount of land or capital, which it cannot change. It can, however, hire as many workers as it wants. Thus the model focuses on the firm's profit-maximizing behavior in what economists call the **short run**. (The time period over which a firm can change its use of capital is called the **long run**. We consider that situation in Chapter 3.)

Third, both the labor market, where a firm hires workers, and the product market, where it sells its output, are assumed to be **competitive** markets. This means that each firm is small enough relative to the market that its own decisions about how many workers to hire and how much output to produce have no impact on the market as a whole. The result is that both the wage rate (w) and the product price (p) are treated as "givens" by a firm. Those prices are determined by the market and are not affected by the firm's own behavior.

The practical effect of the assumption of competitive markets is shown in Figure 2.1. The firm faces a horizontal demand curve for its output [panel (a)] and a horizontal supply curve of labor [panel (b)] at a price and a wage determined by the market. Whether the wage or the price is high or low is irrelevant. The important thing is that a competitive firm can sell as much as it wants at the prevailing price and can hire as many workers as it wants at the prevailing wage. At any price above p^*, it can sell no output at all, and at any wage below w^*, it can hire no workers.

One need not be an experienced observer of labor markets to recognize

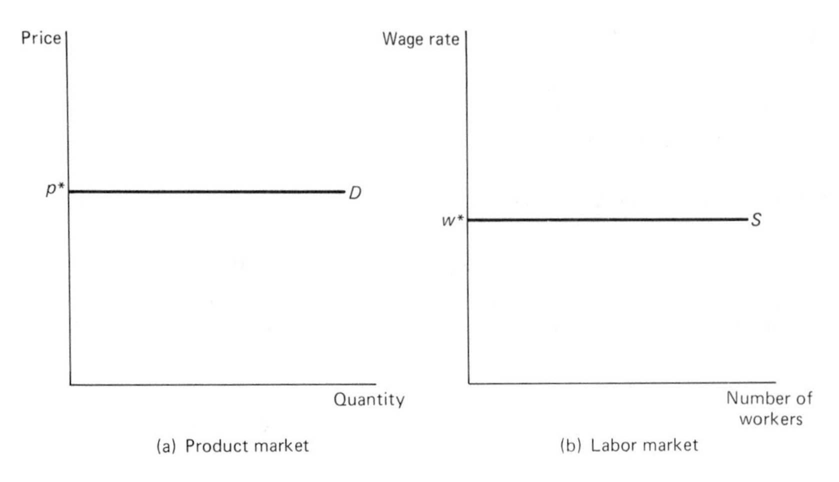

FIGURE 2.1 Product Demand and Labor Supply Curves for a Firm in a Competitive Product Market and a Competitive Labor Market

that no real-world economy conforms exactly—or even very closely—to the assumptions of the model. Conspicuously absent are many of the details and complications that make the analysis of labor markets both fascinating and difficult and which are the source of many labor market problems. There are no differences among individuals, no differences among firms, no laws or regulations, no unions, no discrimination, and no institutional arrangement of any kind. The labor market of this model is, admittedly, a pale imitation of the real thing.

Nonetheless, it is a useful starting place for the analysis of labor markets, especially for understanding the basic principles of labor demand. Just as the omissions on a road map make the primary routes easier to identify, so the simplicity of this model enables labor economists to identify and analyze some of the underlying principles that operate in labor markets. Moreover, the simple model is a useful, if not essential beginning for the analysis of more complex, more realistic, and more interesting labor market situations. If we want to understand what effect monopoly power or minimum wage legislation or trade unions or labor market discrimination has on labor market outcomes, we need to understand first how the labor market operates in their absence. The simple model provides a universal frame of reference—a point of comparison.

Do not let the abstractness and generality of this simple model put you off. The basic principles apply to any short-run employment decision, from the demand for accountants to the demand for farm workers to the demand for assembly-line workers in manufacturing. If the ideas applied only within the narrow confines of this model, it would not be worth our time to study it. The ultimate goal is not to understand this labor market model, but to understand the forces that operate in real labor markets. This model is simply a tool for doing that.

LABOR DEMAND IN THE SHORT RUN

Employment and the Law of Diminishing Marginal Returns

How does a profit-maximizing firm decide how many workers it wants to hire? Suppose that a firm is considering whether to add another worker to its work force. It is not hard to see that there are two effects to consider. On the one hand, the firm's cost will increase since it must pay wages to one more worker. At the same time, however, adding a worker usually increases the amount of output that the firm can produce and sell, so its revenues will rise as well. Whether it makes business sense to add another worker depends simply on whether the additional revenues are greater than the additional costs.

From the standpoint of a firm, the principal variable in this comparison is the amount of additional output that can be produced when an additional worker is employed. After all, neither the wage nor the price is subject to its own control. The firm must pay each worker the same wage and can sell each unit of output at the same price. Thus the only question is whether an additional worker increases output by enough so that given the wage and the price of the product, it will be profitable for the firm to increase its employment level. For example, if the wage rate is \$5 per hour and the market price of the firm's output is \$0.50 per unit, the firm would willingly employ any worker whose employment was expected to increase output by at least ten units. By the same logic, the firm would be unwilling to hire an additional worker if it determined that as a result, output would rise by fewer than ten units.

The increase in output when an additional unit worked is added is important enough to merit a special name—it is called the **marginal physical product of labor** or MP_L. More formally, it is defined this way:

$$MP_L \equiv \left.\frac{\Delta Q}{\Delta L}\right|_K \tag{2.1}$$

where the Δ (the Greek capital letter delta) stands for "change in" and the vertical-bar notation is a way of indicating the factors that are held constant in evaluating the concept. Note that the two sides of the equation are connected not by an equals sign but by three bars. That means that the equation is an **identity:** It is always true because it is a definition.

The marginal product of labor is *the* central concept in understanding the short-run demand curve for labor. It is also the subject of one of the oldest and most famous ideas in economics, the **Law of Diminishing Marginal Returns**. The basic idea is this: As more and more of one factor of production is added to a fixed amount of some other factor, the marginal product of the first factor will eventually fall. The law is perfectly general and applies no matter which factor of production is regarded as fixed and which is increased. Most often, though, labor is treated as the variable factor and capital (or land) as the fixed factor, so that the law predicts that MP_L will eventually decline. Additional workers will be less and less valuable, measured in terms of their contribution to output.

To see why eventually diminishing returns makes sense, think of a simple production process in which labor and capital are combined to produce output of some kind. Try to visualize that production process always operating with the same amount of capital but with different numbers of workers, beginning with just a few and then adding identically skilled workers one at a time.

Economists envision a sequence something like this. At first, there are simply too few workers relative to the amount of capital. Imagine, for example, one person trying to operate a large farm, a decent-sized restaurant, or a large warehouse alone. So much time would be spent moving from one task to another or one location to another that total output would be quite low. As additional workers are added, the amount of labor will be better suited to the amount of capital. Specialized tasks can be assigned to different workers and the time formerly spent in changing tasks and locations can now be spent in production. As a result, output rises quite rapidly—MP_L is increasing.

Eventually, though, the gains from further specialization will be smaller and smaller, because the capital stock cannot be increased. If labor and capital could be added together—with each additional worker, there is also an additional amount of farmland, or floor space in the restaurant or warehouse—then output might continue to rise at a constant rate. But that is not possible in this short-run situation. Instead, additional workers must share the use of the original capital; the larger the number of workers, the less capital there is per worker. The expected result is that output will now rise more slowly. Diminishing marginal returns have set in—MP_L is falling.

Finally, as employment is increased further, it is not hard to imagine that additional workers add nothing at all to output—there is nothing useful for them to do. Their marginal product is zero. It is even possible for overcrowding to become so severe that additional workers now impede production—the marginal product of labor is now negative.

Thus the Law of Diminishing Marginal Returns describes a complete short-run production sequence in which MP_L first rises and then falls, ultimately reaching zero (or even becoming negative) if the amount of labor used is grossly excessive. Its central prediction is that MP_L will eventually fall, not because additional workers are themselves less skilled, but because of the relative scarcity of capital as the amount of labor increases.

There is no way to *prove* that the Law of Diminishing Returns holds. It is not a law of economics in the sense that it can be derived logically from other ideas in economics. Rather, it is a feature of the technology underlying most production processes, so often observed in such a wide variety of settings that we can treat it as a general rule of production. There may be some exceptions to it, but its applicability appears to be quite broad. Think, for example, about your own previous work experience. Do you think that the marginal product of one more worker who is exactly like you would have been less than your own contribution to output? What about two more? Three more? How many more would it have taken for MP_L to be negative?

The exact shape of the MP_L curve will undoubtedly vary from one production situation to another. The Law of Diminishing Returns asserts only that MP_L will eventually fall—not when diminishing returns will set in nor how rapidly the returns will diminish nor whether the entire MP_L curve will be high or low. But we can generalize about those aspects of the MP_L curve. It is reasonable that the larger the amount of capital, the greater the number of workers that can be utilized before diminishing returns set in. A larger amount of capital also typically makes the entire MP_L curve higher, since workers who have access to more capital are able to produce more. The height of the curve will also depend on the underlying characteristics of the workers themselves: their strength, skill, health, motivation, and so on. Finally, whether returns diminish rapidly or gradually reflects, in part, the technological ease with which the available capital or land can be "shared" among additional workers. Where it is not difficult to give additional workers access to the fixed factor—agriculture is a good example of this—the MP_L curve may fall off gradually. Where, however, capital is very "person specific," the MP_L curve may decline quite steeply after some point.

A representative MP_L curve which reflects the Law of Diminishing Returns is shown in Figure 2.2. The horizontal axis shows the number of workers[1] and the vertical axis measures the amount of output, both measured over a common time period—a day, a month, a year, and so on. The height of the curve shows the increase in output due to each additional worker. Up to L_{max}, each additional worker adds more to output than did the previous ones, but beyond L_{max}, diminishing marginal returns set in. Do not confuse falling MP_L with falling total output. As long as MP_L is positive—as it is up to L^*—total output is rising. Diminishing returns simply indicate that output rises more slowly. Only when MP_L is negative does total output actually decrease.

[1] Technically, the amount of labor should be measured in hours, but it is much more convenient to speak of increases in the number of workers. For the moment, assume that each worker works a fixed number of hours, so adding another worker always means adding a specified number of hours of labor.

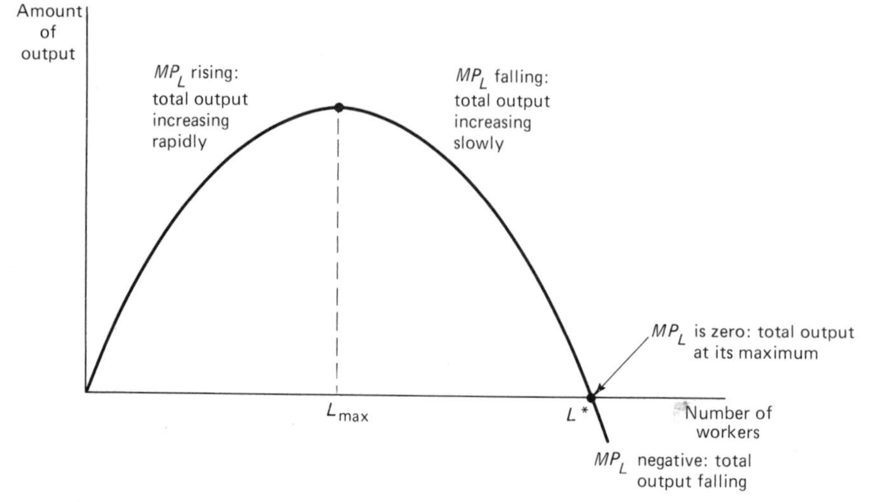

FIGURE 2.2 The Law of Diminishing Marginal Returns

If you are having difficulty grasping the relationship between marginal product and total product, look at Table 2.1. Column (1) shows the amount of labor used and column (2) the corresponding amount of output for some hypothetical production process. MP_L is presented in column (3); it is simply the difference in output from one level of employment to the next. You can verify for yourself that MP_L rises at first, reaches a peak at eighteen additional units for the fifth worker, and then declines. As for total output, it rises rapidly, then more slowly, finally peaking at 11 workers where $MP_L = 0$.

Finally, column (4) of Table 2.1 shows a second related measure of labor productivity—the **average physical product of labor**, or AP_L. AP_L is defined as total output divided by the number of workers:

$$AP_L \equiv \left.\frac{Q}{L}\right|_K \tag{2.2}$$

It measures the average amount of output produced by a group of workers and it is the concept of productivity most often used in popular discussions of productivity. For example, comparisons of the tons of steel produced per hour by American and Japanese steelworkers are measures of the average product. AP_L is easily calculated from the figures in columns (1) and (2).

If we graphed the MP_L and AP_L curves together, we would get something like Figure 2.3. The MP_L curve rises sharply and then falls. The AP_L curve has the same rising and falling pattern, but the changes are more gradual, as you can confirm by looking at columns (3) and (4) of Table 2.1. Note one more conspicuous feature: The MP_L curve and the AP_L curve

TABLE 2.1 A Numerical Example of the Law of Diminishing Returns

(1) AMOUNT OF LABOR	(2) AMOUNT OF OUTPUT	(3) MARGINAL PRODUCT OF LABOR	(4) AVERAGE PRODUCT OF LABOR
0	0	—	—
1	6	6	6.0
2	15	9	7.5
3	25	10	8.3
4	39	14	9.75
5	57	18	11.2
6	72	15	12.0
7	85	13	12.1
8	94	9	11.7
9	99	5	11.0
10	102	3	10.2
11	102	0	9.3
12	100	−2	8.3

intersect at precisely the maximum point of the AP_L curve. (This also works out approximately in Table 2.1.) In fact, this is always true and there is an arithmetic explanation for it that applies to any pair of averages and marginals. If the MP_L of, say, the fifth worker exceeds the AP_L of the first four, the AP_L will naturally increase as the fifth worker is added. A higher marginal score always pulls the average up, and a lower marginal score (MP_L less than AP_L) pulls the average down. So if $MP_L > AP_L$, AP_L will increase, and if $MP_L < AP_L$, AP_L will fall. As a result of this logic, when the MP_L and AP_L

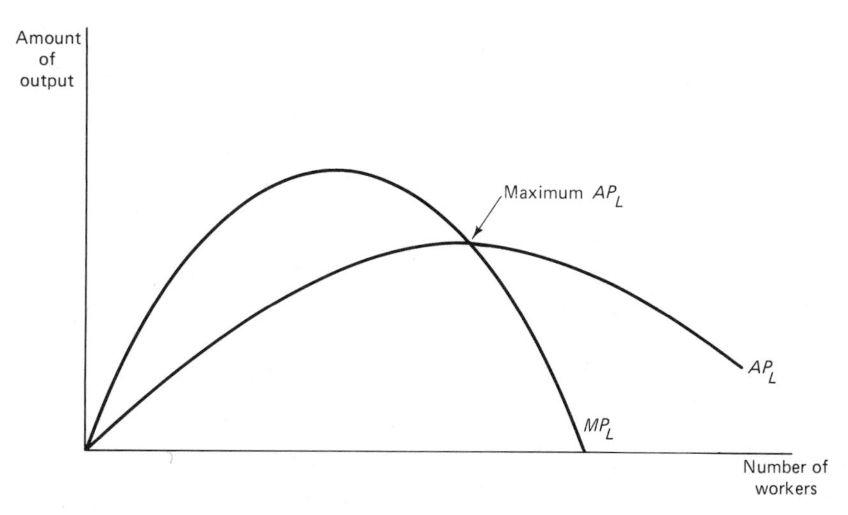

FIGURE 2.3 Fitting the MP_L and AP_L Curves Together

curves intersect (i.e., where $MP_L = AP_L$), the AP_L curve will be neither falling nor rising. It is, therefore, necessarily at its maximum.

Application: Living Standards and the Law of Diminishing Marginal Returns

From the Law of Diminishing Marginal Returns we know that both MP_L and AP_L will eventually fall in the short run as the amount of labor used increases. If the actual amount of labor used was very large relative to the amount of land or capital, it is possible that MP_L could fall to zero or become negative. Needless to say, production under those circumstances would be strikingly inefficient. Nevertheless, is it possible that situations like that do exist?

For reasons that will be obvious in a few pages, it is unlikely that a profit-maximizing firm would ever *knowingly* hire workers with a zero or negative MP_L. For possible real-world examples, we need to look outside the realm of profit-maximizing behavior. One possible setting, noted by anthropologists and sociologists as well as economists, is in a less developed country in which agricultural production is organized along traditional lines and where family size is large relative to the size of a family's plot of land.

Suppose that a family works on their own plot of land as a unit and shares the total output equally among themselves. Suppose also that most workers tend to be immobile—that is, they do not regularly move from one location to another to seek work. Perhaps the family places a high value on remaining together, or perhaps ties to the village or area are extremely strong. Alternatively, opportunities for work elsewhere may be limited or the costs of moving from one place to another may be prohibitive.

With land as the fixed factor, production will, of course, follow the general principles of the Law of Diminishing Marginal Returns, with both AP_L and MP_L rising and falling, just as in Figure 2.3. If family size is large relative to the amount of land, we can readily imagine that production occurs in the region in which the marginal and average product of labor are falling. A family in this situation might well choose to work and live together as a unit as long as they are able to maintain at least a minimally adequate standard of living. Now, any standard of living is defined simply by some level of output per capita—so many kilos of rice per person, for example. But output per capita is exactly equivalent to the average product of labor; both are total output shared (or divided) by the numbers of persons (or workers). Since production occurs where AP_L is falling, we know that MP_L will be less than AP_L. If the acceptable standard of living is fairly low—in a very poor country, it may be no more than a subsistence level—it follows that MP_L might be quite low. MP_L could, perhaps, even be equal to zero. The key is that because the family is sharing its total output among all family members, its focus is on the average product of labor which determines their standard of living, rather than on the corresponding marginal product of labor.

In looking for examples of this kind of behavior, economists have looked to poorer countries with an abundance of labor relative to land and with an emphasis on traditional economic organization. Indonesia, especially its heavily populated main island of Java, is a famous example. A 1980 census showed that 43 percent of all farm families in Java worked only six-tenths of an acre or less. Bangladesh and India are other possibilities. A general, nontechnical, theoretical discussion of this kind of situation was developed by W. Arthur Lewis, winner of a Nobel Prize in Economics, in his classic paper, "Economic Development with Unlimited Supplies of Labor."[2]

There is one important insight in this simple example. *Living standards ultimately depend on the average product of labor.* This is as true in the United States as in India. AP_L multiplied by the number of workers in the economy is the amount of output available for consumption. If everyone in an economy worked, the maximum consumption per person would be exactly equal to the average product of labor. If some persons do not work, the maximum standard of living is some fraction of the average product. This link between AP_L and the standard of living in an economy is the reason why productivity growth is such an important issue. Where productivity growth is rapid (the AP_L curve is shifting upward), the standard of living can also rise. But when productivity growth slows or even turns negative, as it has in the United States in the past decade, the material standard of living must inevitably fall.

Labor Demand by a Competitive Firm

To derive a firm's demand for labor, we need one more concept—the **marginal revenue product of labor** or MRP_L. MRP_L is defined analogously to MP_L except that it is measured in terms of revenue per additional worker rather than output. More formally,

$$MRP_L \equiv \left.\frac{\Delta \text{revenues}}{\Delta L}\right|_K \tag{2.3}$$

When the product market is competitive, so that the firm can sell as much output as it wants at a constant price, there is a very simple arithmetic relationship between a worker's *MP* and the corresponding *MRP*. In that case, *MRP* is just *MP* multiplied by the price of the product, or $MRP_L = P \cdot MP_L$. If a particular worker will add four units to output and the price of the product is \$2, the corresponding MRP_L is \$8. If the price had been \$3, MRP_L would have been \$12.

[2] See W. A. Lewis, "Development with Unlimited Supplies of Labor," *The Manchester School*, 22 (May 1954), 139–91.

Knowing the shape of the MP_L curve and the relationship between MP_L and MRP_L, it is easy to construct an MRP_L curve showing the revenues associated with each additional worker. The MRP_L curve will first rise and then fall, exactly corresponding to the rise and fall in the underlying MP_L curve. Diminishing returns in physical productivity necessarily causes diminishing returns on revenue productivity. A typical MRP_L curve is shown in Figure 2.4. Its shape, too, reflects the Law of Diminishing Returns. Its height depends on all the factors underlying the MP_L curve: the amount of capital, the skill and motivation of workers, and the price of the product. If the price were higher, the MRP_L curve would shift upward proportionately.

Now we are ready to return to our original question: How does a profit-maximizing firm decide how many workers it will hire? A firm need only compare a worker's MRP_L with the wage rate. Hiring a worker whose MRP_L exceeds the wage rate will always increase the firm's profits and, just as certainly, hiring a worker whose MRP_L is less than the wage will cause profits to decline. Thus, to maximize its profits a firm should expand its employment along its declining MRP_L schedule until for the last worker hired, the marginal revenue product just equals the wage rate. In symbols, the profit-maximizing rule for employment is that

$$MRP_L = w \tag{2.4}$$

where the equality holds for the last worker hired.

This idea is shown graphically in Figure 2.5, which shows only the declining portion of the MRP_L curve. (Where MRP_L equals the wage along the upward-sloping portion of the MRP_L curve, a firm can always increase its profits by increasing its employment level, because MRP_L for the next worker will exceed the wage rate.) If the wage is w_1, the employment level

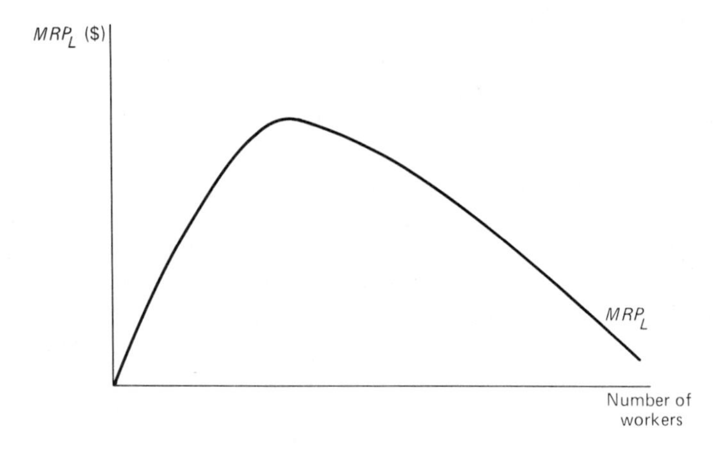

FIGURE 2.4 The Marginal Revenue Product of Labor Curve

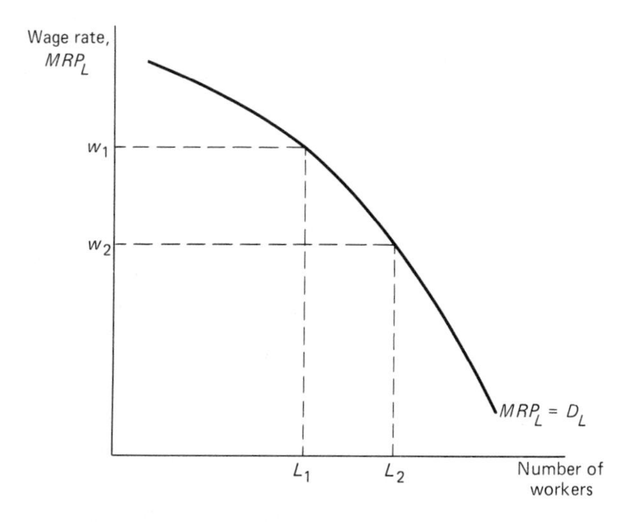

FIGURE 2.5 The Short-Run Demand Curve for Labor by a Competitive Firm

that maximizes the firm's profits will be L_1, where $MRP_L = w_1$. At wage w_1, all workers up to L_1 have an *MRP* greater than w_1 and thus hiring them increases the firm's profits. But for workers beyond L_1, their *MRP* is less than w_1—due to the Law of Diminishing Returns—and thus they are not employed by this firm at this wage. But what if the wage were lower? If the wage were, for example, w_2, some workers whose *MRP* did not merit employment at wage level w_1 will now be employed. The firm would choose to expand employment from L_1 to L_2. Higher or lower wages will produce the same kind of response: The firm will adjust its employment level until the marginal revenue product of the last worker hired just equals the now higher or lower wage.

Note that whatever the wage rate is, the profit-maximizing level of employment is shown by that point on the *MRP* curve at which the $MRP_L = w$. This tells us two very important things. First, in the short run, a firm's MRP_L curve is its demand curve for labor. That is, the MRP_L curve shows the amount of labor that a firm will employ at each possible wage rate. Second, a firm's demand curve for labor is, therefore, downward sloping; that is, there is an inverse or negative relationship between the wage rate and the amount of employment that will be offered.

Application: What Are Baseball Players Worth?

The simple rule of profit-maximizing employment—hire no worker whose *MRP* falls short of his or her wage—seems almost obvious, but its implications are actually quite strong. The rule is, in fact, applicable to more complex situations than the short-run homogeneous labor case just analyzed. As well as telling us what a firm *would* do if it knew an entire MRP_L schedule, it tells us what a firm is *not* doing if it is maximizing profits. For example, we can infer that no firm ever deliberately pays a worker more than that worker's MRP_L. That simple insight is enough to avoid some enormous errors of logic.

One application of this is to the highly publicized salaries currently being earned in professional sports. Major league baseball is a particularly interesting example, both because of the recent changes in the structure of the baseball player's labor market and the midseason labor strike in 1981, which focused attention on players' salaries. The structural change in the labor market occurred when the reserve clause was declared invalid by an arbitrator in 1976. That clause was a legal device which contractually bound a player to his current team year after year and thus prevented him from negotiating with several teams simultaneously. Now, any player with at least six years in major league baseball can declare himself a free agent and negotiate with a large number of teams.[3] Quite predictably, the increased competition caused salaries to rise. According to information provided by the Major League Players Association, the average salary has risen from $57,000 in 1976 to over $240,000 in 1982. The median annual salary in 1982 was $170,900 and thirteen players earned over $1 million.

One of the inevitable effects of the baseball strike was the frequent assertion in newspaper columns, letters to the editor, and sportscasts that baseball players were "overpaid," that their salaries were "excessive" or even "obscene." It seemed easy to cite other working groups in the economy who deserved more than that paid to ball players. After all, even the president of the United States barely earned more than the median major league salary. The self-evident conclusion always seemed to be that "no player is worth that kind of money."

That assertion begs for an economic analysis. Are baseball players paid more than they are worth? To anyone trained in the logic of profit-maximizing behavior, the analysis is clear. The players *must* be worth their salaries, since no profit-maximizing team would ever willingly and knowingly pay them more than that. With competition among owners, no owner will be able to pay a player less than he is worth. The answer, therefore, is no; baseball players are not deliberately paid more than they are worth.

You might object that this is a very narrow definition of worth. We are, it seems, measuring worth solely in economic terms by the ability to increase revenues. Shouldn't worth be measured by something other than cash register receipts?

Properly considered, this measure of worth is not as narrow as it seems. After all, what does the increase in revenues reflect? Ultimately, it must

[3] There are still some restrictions on the number of teams a player can negotiate with. As of 1983, a player could negotiate with at least 16 teams and as many as 26.

represent the increased willingness of people to pay to see baseball games either directly at the stadium or indirectly on radio or television. If we assume that people did so voluntarily and by consulting their own self-interest about the best way to spend their income, the increased revenues really just represent the additional value provided to consumers. The increased revenues are not themselves the source of the worth, just a convenient way to measure it.

The assertion that baseball players are not worth their salaries must rest on normative grounds. You must argue that people *should not* like baseball as much as they do and *should not* be willing to pay so much to watch skilled performers. As with most normative, arguments, there is something to this. Perhaps the world would be a better place if poets were more revered than athletes. But here we begin to tread on the shaky ground of normative economics. It is difficult to reach a scientific conclusion about the "true" worth of baseball players and poets.

To pin down the concept of worth and its relationship to a player's salary, consider the following more recent development in the world of baseball economics. In the summer of 1982, several baseball players filed suit in federal court asking that players be given a share of the income paid to the owners by the television networks for televising baseball games. A little bit of economic reasoning should convince you that in the long run, baseball players salaries would be essentially unchanged, no matter what the courts eventually decide. Here is why. The value of a player to a team consists of the revenues directly attributable to that player, including not only the revenues from ticket sales but also those from television and radio contracts. Subtract the television revenues and the value of a player will decline—and so, of course, will player salaries. Some players might end up better or worse off, depending on how the television revenues were distributed, but on the whole, total player compensations (salaries plus television revenues) should not change.

In the real world of business and baseball, things never work out quite as smoothly and simply as suggested above. It is not too difficult to cite examples of a player earning much more or much less than his "apparent worth." Is there any way to account for that? There are actually several possible explanations. First, things may not turn out as expected. There is a great deal of unpredictable variability in the year-to-year performance of a player. Good years may follow bad ones, and vice versa. Thus the assertion that players are paid what they are worth should be modified; perhaps we should say that "players are paid what knowledgeable people expected them to be worth." But nothing about profit-maximizing behavior assures that things will work out as predicted. In hindsight, it may be clear that a particular player was paid much more or much less than he turned out to be worth.

Second, the assumption of profit maximization may not always hold. Some baseball teams may be owned by wealthy (from nonbaseball sources) persons for whom owning a team is a pleasurable hobby rather than a profit-maximizing activity. They may derive satisfaction from "bringing a winner" to the long-suffering hometown fans, rubbing shoulders with famous athletes, or becoming a celebrity and being written about in newspapers or interviewed on television. (One or two baseball owners, noted for paying unusually high salaries, do seem to spring to mind.) This severs the direct link between *MRP* and salary. It is still true that no team will pay a player more than he is worth, but now worth includes both the revenue contribution and the approximate dollar value of all the intangibles. The existence of even a few owners like this is great for players and bad for an owner seeking to make a profit. Most knowledgeable observers, however, think that business objectives are important.

Finally, in some cases, salaries are now set by arbitrators who apparently base their decisions not on what a player is worth to his current team, but on what comparable players are earning elsewhere. With those guidelines, an arbitrator may well award a salary in excess even of a player's expected value. The profit-maximizing solution, though, is obvious—trade or sell the player to another team.

MARKET DEMAND, MARKET SUPPLY, AND THE EQUILIBRIUM WAGE RATE

We now know what a firm's demand curve for labor looks like. What we do not know is at what point on that demand curve a firm will actually operate, since that will depend on the wage rate that exists. To understand how a particular wage level comes to be established, we need to shift our analysis from the level of the firm to the labor market as a whole.

The total market demand for labor is simply the sum of the demands for labor for each industry at each possible wage. Thus for some wage w_1, the total labor demand is

$$L_1 = L_1^A + L_1^B + L_1^C + \ldots + L_1^Z \qquad (2.5)$$

where $L_1^A \ldots L_1^Z$ represent the amount of labor demanded in industries A to Z at wage w_1. Repeating this at each and every wage level traces out the total market demand for labor. As for the industry demands for labor, they are *based on* the underlying demands for labor by the firms in the industry, but they are not the sum of those demand curves. The reason for this is that if the wage rate were to change for all firms in a competitive industry, the market price of the product will change in the same direction, thus shifting the underlying *MRP* curves of the firms.[4] A more complete, graphical ex-

[4] Remember that a firm's MRP_L curve is drawn for a fixed price of its output.

position of the derivation of an industry demand curve is presented in Appendix 1 of this chapter. For our purposes it is sufficient to conclude that the industry demand curves, which incorporate the wage-induced price change, will be steeper than the underlying firm's *MRP* curves, but the industry demand curve will nevertheless always be downward sloping. From this we can draw another important conclusion: For an industry and for the economy as a whole, the short-run demand curve for labor will be downward sloping.

The demand for labor curve is, of course, not enough to determine what the equilibrium wage rate will be. As every economics student learns, it is the interaction of supply and demand—the two blades of the scissors—which sets the price in a competitive market. Thus we need to introduce labor supply to our model. In later chapters we examine an individual's labor supply decision in detail, but here it is sufficient to assert that, in general, at higher wage rates more labor hours will be supplied. Thus the economy-wide labor supply curve in our model will be upward sloping. Nothing important would be changed if the supply curve were vertical instead of being upward sloping.

Figure 2.6(a) represents the economy-wide labor supply and demand curves. The position of the demand curves reflects the amount of capital available in the economy, the equilibrium prices for all the products, and the homogeneous skill level of the workers. In this situation the equilibrium wage rate will be w^*, since only at that wage does the quantity of labor supplied just equal the quantity of labor demanded. At any wage above w^*, there is excess supply, since the higher wage both decreases the amount of employment that firms offer and increases the amount of employment that individuals want. In an unrestricted labor market, the wage would not stay permanently above w^*, since the existence of workers without jobs should put downward pressure on the wage rate. Could the wage fall below w^*? Not for long, since at any wage below w^* there would be excess demand—firms want to hire more workers at the prevailing wage than there are people willing to work. The expected result would be upward pressure on wages, increasing the amount of labor supplied and reducing the amount demanded until equilibrium is reestablished at w^*. Thus we conclude that with a particular labor supply and labor demand curve and a competitive market, there is a single real wage which will tend to be established. That wage is the *equilibrium wage rate* in the economy.

As for the firms in the economy, each will follow the profit-maximizing employment rule and employ workers until the *MRP* of the last worker just equals that wage rate. In a firm like the one shown in panel (b) of Figure 2.6, where the MRP_L schedule is relatively high, a high level of employment can be reached before MRP_L is reduced to w^*. In a different firm, however, where physical productivity and/or the product price is lower, the profit-maximizing level of employment would be smaller. This is shown in panel (c), where the desired employment level is L_B^*. This illustrates an important point: The equilibrium wage allocates scarce labor resources among alter-

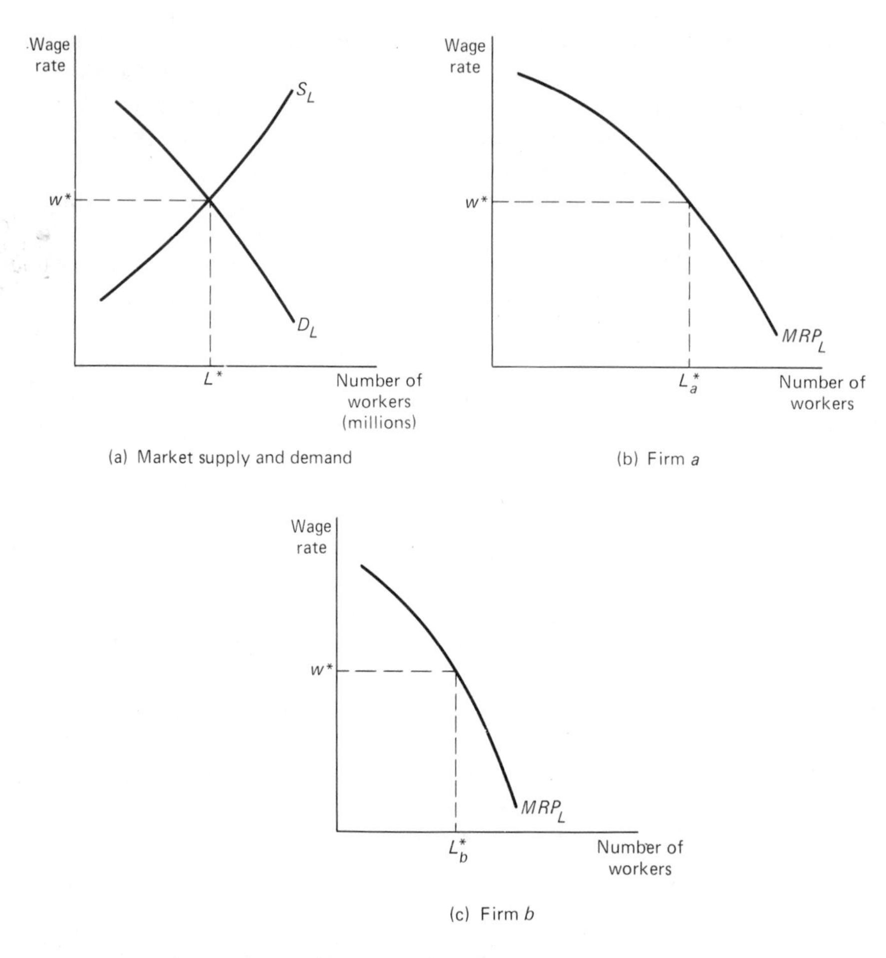

FIGURE 2.6 Labor Market Equilibrium and the Allocation of Labor

native uses. In this case it directs more labor resources to the firm in panel (b) and fewer to the firm represented in panel (c). (See Appendix 2 of this chapter for a theoretical evaluation of how well competitive labor markets allocate labor among alternative uses.)

Thus far we have considered the labor market from the perspective of the economy as a whole. Since all workers were assumed to be identical, there was only a single labor market to consider and only a single equilibrium wage rate. But the analysis and the results are perfectly general and apply even when all workers are not the same and many separate labor markets exist. Figure 2.6(a) could just as well represent the supply and demand conditions for accountants or computer programmers or secretaries or even for all unskilled workers in a particular area—indeed, for any group that constitutes a distinct labor market. In every case there is some equilibrium wage at which labor supply and labor demand just balance.

Application: The "Fixed-Employment" Fallacy

One of the most important implications of the concept of a labor market in equilibrium is that there is no such thing as a fixed number of jobs in an economy. As long as demand curves for labor are not vertical (and except in the very rarest of circumstances, to be discussed in Chapter 3, they are not) and as long as wages are not completely inflexible, the amount of available employment is determined by the equilibrium condition that quantity supplied equals quantity demanded. The number of jobs in an economy is *not* a piece of technological data to which the economy must adjust. The number of jobs is itself a variable, depending on the supply curve, the demand curve, and the equilibrium wage.

There would be no need to emphasize this point if it were not so frequently misunderstood, especially by policymakers. A few examples will illustrate the point. One of the oldest forms of this error is called the *lump of labor hypothesis*, according to which employment was regarded as a "lump" of fixed size. Employment thus becomes a *zero-sum game*, which means that providing employment for one more person requires creating unemployment for someone else. This became an almost accepted explanation of unemployment during the Great Depression. The problem, according to this theory, was simply too many people seeking a fixed number of jobs. In its contemporary form, the lump of labor hypothesis is invoked whenever someone argues that immigrants or illegal aliens "take away jobs" from Americans or that rising employment of women means certain, and perhaps offsetting unemployment for men. To be sure, increases in labor supply, whether it be men or women, immigrants or native-born workers, do affect the equilibrium wage in a labor market. It is, in fact, precisely those changes in wages that invalidate the lump of labor hypothesis.

Another version of the fixed number of jobs idea is the belief that it is possible to reduce unemployment by reducing the average workweek and spreading the extra work around. In 1981, the French government of Socialist Francois Mitterand adopted exactly this policy to solve their unemployment problems. The government ordered that the maximum workweek be reduced from 40 hours to 39 hours, with no reduction in weekly pay, and paid vacations were increased from four weeks to five weeks. The government apparently believed that a fixed number of labor hours were needed in France and that faced with a shorter workweek and longer vacations, firms would be compelled to hire more workers. Voilà—unemployment eliminated!

Will this policy work? One could certainly hope so, since it offers the same income and more leisure for currently employed workers and creates employment for unemployed workers. Everyone seems better off. There are, however, two fatal problems which you should already have noticed. First, there is, once again, no fixed number of labor hours to be distributed among French workers. Second, the reduction in hours and the increase in vacation time are both equivalent to wage increases. With a downward-sloping demand curve, firms will want fewer hours of labor, not more, at the now-higher wages. The probable result of the policy is the opposite of its intent—unemployment will rise, not fall.

Actually, you might have been suspicious of this scheme right from the start, even without using much economic analysis. If 39 hours of work for 40 hours of pay is good for everyone, wouldn't 38 hours be even better; and 37 better yet; and so on? Carrying this proposal to its logical conclusion suggests that unemployment could be banished forever by setting wages at high levels and reducing the average workweek to no more than a few hours per person. Unfortunately, downward-sloping demand curves are incompatible with the basic proposition.

As yet another example, consider the frequent reports that there are now too many new law school graduates or accountants or would-be teachers of history or English, so that unemployment is the inevitable result for an unfortunately large number. Again, the notion that there is a fixed number of available positions has crept into the analysis. Surely, as long as there are not so many entrants that the marginal product has reached zero, there must be some equilibrium wage at which all can be employed. What these reports really mean is that at current wage levels, there is an excess supply of qualified workers and that unemployment will result unless wage levels are adjusted.

In fact, in some cases wage levels may not be flexible enough to accommodate the larger supply, especially when the wage adjustment must be large. For example, few colleges and universities would consider offering a salary low enough that all new history Ph.D.'s could find employment. To do so would be "taking advantage" of the market situation and indeed, the equilibrium salary might be embarrassingly low. Instead, a respectable (above-equilibrium) salary is offered and the lucky few are employed. But the problem is not one of a technologically fixed number of job slots, but rather of an inflexible salary.

Wage Levels in a Competitive Economy

There is one more idea to discuss in this chapter and it is one of the most important. It is one thing to assert that there is an equilibrium wage rate in an economy or for a particular occupation. But what we often want to know is whether that wage will be high or low. More than any other price in the economy, the wage rate directly determines the standard of living of workers and their families. It is a price of unusual significance.

Think about the wage rate for the economy as a whole. The first thing to recognize is that nothing about an equilibrium wage rate guarantees that workers will have an adequate standard of living. Indeed, one of the oldest theory of wages, usually credited to Thomas Malthus, predicted that wages would always be reduced to the subsistence level by the pressures of population growth.[5] If matters are not quite as bleak as Malthus predicted, still the equilibrium wage for unskilled workers in much of the world is not far above subsistence. In 1978, annual income per person was less than $500 in fifty countries and under $300 in over thirty of them. The significance of an equilibrium wage is that it is the only wage at which the amount of labor demanded equals the amount supplied. If the labor market is left to operate freely, this is the wage likely to be established.

Like any price in the economy, the equilibrium wage depends on the relationship between the supply and demand curves. Where supply is large relative to demand, wages tend to be low. The equilibrium wage will be higher when demand is large relative to supply. A little bit of supply and demand curve manipulation should convince you of these propositions.

Saying that the wage depends on supply relative to demand is correct, but it begs the question of *why* the supply and demand curves have the particular positions that they do have. For labor supply, the answer is straightforward. The position of the labor supply curve is largely a function of population size. The larger the population, the greater the supply of labor.[6] As for the labor demand curve, its position depends both on the productivity and skills of the worker and usually also on the amount of capital or land that is available. Although there are exceptions, it is usually true that the greater the amount of capital or land which is used in production, the more productive are the workers.[7] Thus the labor demand curve will be positioned higher up when there is more capital or more land.

The relationship between demand and supply—between the amount of capital and the amount of labor—is crucial for understanding the equilibrium wage. In India, wages are low not just because the workers may be unskilled, but also because the amount of available capital is small relative to the amount of labor. In Java, the densely populated central island of Indonesia, it is land that is scarce relative to the population size. In both cases the productivity of all workers is consequently low, and thus the wage at which the last worker can profitably be employed is low.[8] In general, then, for a given supply curve of labor, the larger the amount of capital or land, the higher will be the

[5] This prediction has had a lasting impact on economics, even though it has turned out to be false. It was the original source of the designation of economics as the "dismal science."

[6] The proportion of the labor force that chooses to work—what economists call the *labor force participation rate*—also matters. We discuss that when we consider labor supply decisions in Chapters 4 and 5.

[7] When an increase in the amount of capital (or land) increases the MP_L curve, labor and capital are called *complements*.

[8] In 1978, average annual income was $180 per person in India and $360 per person in Indonesia.

equilibrium wage. By making workers more productive, a larger capital stock increases the wage at which the last worker can be profitably employed.

Exactly the same logic applies to the equilibrium wage in a specific occupation. Where supply is large relative to demand, the less productive will be the last worker hired and thus the lower the wage at which all can be employed.

SUMMARY

This chapter began with the demand for labor by a representative firm and concluded with an analysis of the determinants of the general level of wages in an economy. The demand for labor was analyzed under the simplest of conditions: All workers were identical, the labor market and the product market were competitive, and all inputs other than labor were fixed in amount. The key factor in deriving a firm's demand for labor was the inevitable decline in marginal productivity, a concept summarized in the Law of Diminishing Marginal Returns. Because of that decline, the marginal revenue product of an additional worker—the marginal product multiplied by the product price—will also decline. We concluded that the firm's short-run demand curve for labor will coincide with its marginal revenue product curve, since for any possible wage rate, it is most profitable for the firm to expand its employment until for the last worker, the marginal revenue product just equals the wage. The firm's demand curve for labor is, therefore, downward sloping—a conclusion of great importance.

The total demand for labor in an economy is related to each firm's demand for labor, although it is not simply the sum of all those demand curves. But the total market demand curve is, nevertheless, downward sloping. This demand curve, in conjunction with an upward-sloping supply curve, determines an equilibrium market wage at which the amount of labor supplied just equals the amount demanded. The same analysis can be used to understand how the equilibrium wage for any particular occupation is determined.

Finally, we noted that whether the equilibrium wage is high or low depends on whether the supply of labor is large relative to the demand for labor. Indirectly, it depends on whether the amount of capital or land that is available is large relative to the size of the population. Countries with a large amount of capital per worker tend to have higher wages than do countries that have less capital for each worker.

New Concepts

Homogeneous labor
Short run
Long run

Competitive labor market
Competitive product market
Marginal physical product of labor (MP_L)
Identity
Law of Diminishing Marginal Returns
Average physical product of labor (AP_L)
Marginal revenue product of labor (MRP_L)
Equilibrium wage rate
Lump of labor hypothesis

APPENDIX 2.1: Deriving the Industry Demand Curve for Labor

In constructing the industry demand curve for labor, it is necessary to allow for the possibility that changes in the wage rate will lead to changes in the product price. If, for example, the wage rate were lower, each firm's costs would fall and each would be willing to produce more output than before at any given price. For all firms taken together, these increases in output at the lower wage would shift the supply curve out and cause the market price to fall. Similarly, increases in the wage rate would cause decreases in supply and increases in the market price of the output.

This complicates the process of deriving the industry labor demand curve, since a firm's demand curve depends on the product price. Allowing for the subsequent effect of a wage change on the price of the product means that the firm will have a different demand curve for each wage rate. Rather than simply moving along a fixed *MRP* curve when the wage changes, the firm will now find the *MRP* curve shifting when the wage changes. The resulting employment levels at each wage, allowing for the price change, are the basis for the industry demand curve.

Figure A2.1 outlines the derivation of the industry demand curve. Panel (a) shows a typical firm, assumed to be one of many producing in the industry, while panel (b) shows the industry demand curve for labor. Suppose that initially the wage is w_1 and that given that wage and the market demand for the final product, the market price of output is P_1. This situation is represented by demand curve D_1. The firm's desired employment level is L_1 and the corresponding industry employment level is L_1^{IND} (a much larger amount), which is the sum of the employment of each firm at wage w_1 and the corresponding output price P_1. Thus point A' is one point on the industry demand curve.

Now consider what happens when the wage falls to w_2. If the output

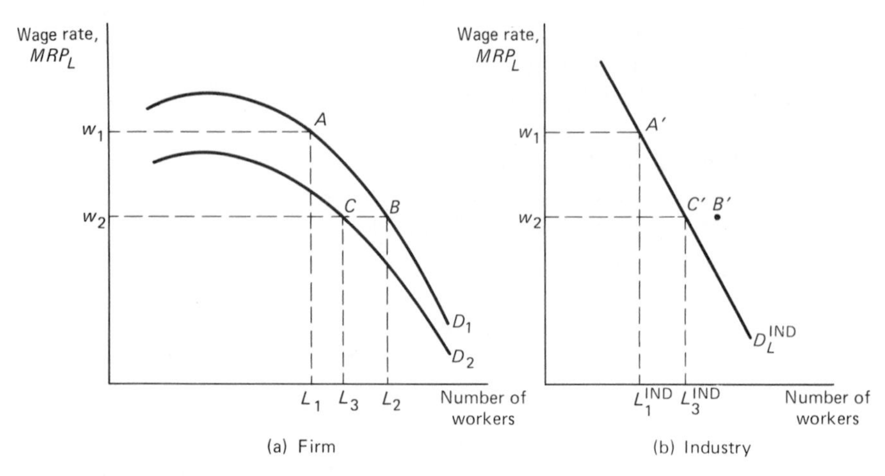

FIGURE A2.1 Deriving the Industry Demand Curve for Labor

price were still P_1, the firm would increase its employment to L_2, shown as point B in panel (a). This would, in turn, give industry employment shown by B' in panel (b). But because the price will fall when labor costs fall, the firm's demand curve for labor (the MRP curve) will fall too. D_2 is the new labor demand curve and the resulting employment level is now L_3 (point C)—an amount between L_1 and L_2. We can be certain that L_3 will be to the right of L_1. Output in the market has increased, and since the amount of capital is fixed, the firm must use more labor to produce the increased output level. The corresponding point on the industry demand curve is C', constructed in the same manner as A'.

The industry demand curve is thus not the sum of the underlying *MRP* or firm demand curves, but it is based on them. Each demand curve contributes exactly one point to the industry demand curve—point A for D_1 and point C for D_2. Note that the industry demand will always be steeper than the underlying firm demand curves, but that it will always be downward sloping.

APPENDIX 2.2: Economic Efficiency and the Allocation of Labor

In Chapter 2, we saw that the equilibrium wage rate determines the way in which total employment is allocated among different firms in the economy, as each expands employment until MRP_L equals the wage rate. Since "the allocation of scarce resources among alternative uses" is sometimes advanced as *the* definition of economics, it is worth examining the allocation of labor in competitive markets in greater detail.

First, recognize that the allocation of labor is a universal concern. Every economy, whether it relies on tradition or central planning or on markets and equilibrium prices to organize its economy, must consider how best to use the limited labor resources available to it. How many workers should be used in agriculture? How many in wheat production and how many in the production of tomatoes or carrots? What about the production of the vast numbers of consumer goods? The number of possible products and tasks is so large that some allocating mechanism is required.

To evaluate the allocation of labor in an economy, it is necessary to know what goals are being sought. Then we can ask whether the allocation is a good one in terms of advancing the goal. As a general rule, the best way to use limited labor resources will always involve making some goal or target as large as possible. But there is no single goal to which all countries subscribe. For example, China's goal during the decade of the Cultural Revolution (1966–1976) appears to have been the maximization of shared work experiences by the entire population and the minimization of any kind of "bourgeois" specialization of labor. To this end, workers were regularly rotated among jobs, from city to countryside, from skilled to unskilled, from industrial to agricultural work, and so on. The effects on output appear to have been disastrous and China has since renounced the practice. Another example of an unusual goal—and corresponding labor allocation—occurred in Cambodia in the late 1970s. There the Khmer Rouge leaders depopulated the urban areas to create an idealogically pure, preindustrial, egalitarian society. Again, the effects on output and living standards were apparently severe. Cambodia, now known as Kampuchea, is estimated to have the lowest per capita income of any country.

Although there is no scientific way to agree on the appropriate goal for all economies, there is a general consensus among economists in favor of **economic efficiency**. Economists usually assume that a society will seek to maximize the total value of the outputs it produces, given its endowments of labor, capital, and available technology as well as the tastes and preferences of its citizens. When this condition is achieved, economists term that allocation of resources *efficient*, which means that no changes—for example, reducing the amount of labor in one place in order to increase it somewhere else—could produce a more highly valued set of outputs.

If this criterion of efficiency is accepted, an extremely important conclusion emerges: The allocation of labor in a competitive market is efficient. Profit-maximizing employment decisions by firms result in exactly the "right" amount of labor being employed in each sector of the economy. This finding is intriguing, because it is completely inadvertent and uncalculating. Competitive firms employ workers not for the sake of economic efficiency, but in the interest of maximizing their own profits. Yet it works out perfectly.

It is easiest to understand this result by considering two firms (call them A and B) whose labor demand curves (MRP_L) are drawn in Figure A2.2. For the moment, ignore wage rates and the profit-maximizing employment rule and simply consider what allocation of labor between the two firms will satisfy the efficiency condition. Suppose that the initial allocation of labor is L_A^1 and L_B^1, so that the MRP_L in A exceeds that in B. Could that be an efficient allocation of labor? Consider what would happen if one worker transferred from firm B to firm A. As a first approximation, the value of output in B will fall by an amount equal to the MRP of the last (number L_B^1) worker in B, while in A, it will rise by the MRP of the last worker there (number L_A^1). Since the MRP_L in A is greater than that in B, the value of the increased output in A will exceed the value of the lost output in B. For example, if the MRP_L of the last worker in A were \$6 and that in B only \$3, then by transferring one worker from B to A, the value of output would rise by (\$6 − \$3) = \$3.

This means that the original allocation of labor, characterized by unequal MRP_L in A and B, must have been inefficient. In fact, only when for the last worker hired the MRP in A is equal to that in B is it impossible to increase the total value of output by reallocation. In that case the lost value in B (= MRP_L^B) is exactly balanced by the increased value in A (= MRP_L^A), so that no net improvement is achieved. Thus an efficient allocation of labor requires that MRP_L be the same in each firm. In Figure A2.2 the efficient allocation of labor would be L_A^* and L_B^*, where $MRP_L^A = MRP_L^B$ for the last worker hired in A and B.

We can readily show that profit-maximizing behavior by competitive firms leads to the desired equality of MRP_L. First, at the equilibrium wage rate, the maximum amount of labor is utilized. Lower wages would reduce the amount supplied, and higher wages would decrease the amount demanded. Second, since there is only a single wage rate for all firms; each firm

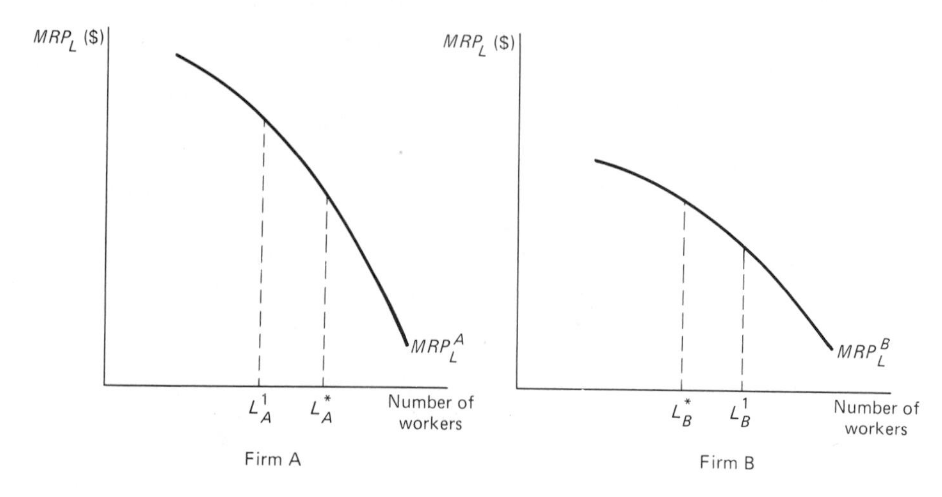

FIGURE A2.2 Economic Efficiency and the Allocation of Labor

hires workers until MRP_L equals the value of the common wage. This is true even if firm A and firm B have drastically different MRP_L schedules and it would hold not just for A and B, but for all firms in the economy. Thus we can conclude that profit-maximizing behavior in a competitive labor market with an equilibrium wage rate leads to an efficient allocation of labor among firms.

3

The Demand for Labor: Extensions and Applications

INTRODUCTION

In this chapter we look further at the demand side of the labor market. The first half of this chapter treats three theoretical extensions of the basic model. First, we examine the effects on labor demand, wages, and employment when the product market or the labor market are not perfectly competitive. Next, we consider a firm's demand for labor in the long run when it is free to change its use of capital as well as labor. Now the choice of how much labor to use also involves the related choice of how much capital to use. Finally, we turn to the quantitative measurement of the demand for labor. The important economic concept here is wage elasticity. This analysis summarizes much of the theory of the demand for labor developed thus far.

The second part of the chapter applies the theory of labor demand to two areas of public policy concern. One deals with the effects of direct wage setting by a government, usually in the form of a wage "floor" or legal minimum wage. The other topic, known as labor–labor substitution, is more general. These studies examine the production relationships among factors of production in order to determine how changes in the use of one factor of production will affect the labor market conditions of other groups in the labor market. As the degree of government intervention in the labor market has increased, studies like these have provided invaluable information about how a public policy, ostensibly directed at one group of workers, will also end up affecting other groups of workers.

IMPERFECT COMPETITION AND THE LABOR MARKET

Imperfect competition is a term used to denote any market structure that deviates from perfect competition. The various forms of imperfect competition all share one common feature—the prices that firms face for the goods they sell and/or the inputs they use depend on the level of their own activities. In contrast, in perfect competition each firm is such a small part of both the product and labor market that the product price and wage rate are unaffected by its own activities.

We could analyze the effects of imperfect competition by considering separately each of the conventional market structures of imperfect competition. On the product market side, these would include **monopoly** (a single seller), **oligopoly** (several sellers), and **monopolistic competition** (many small producers of related but differentiated products). The corresponding classifications on the labor market side are **monopsony** (a single buyer) and **oligopsony** (several buyers). Analyzing each of these cases in turn to identify their effects would be not only an extremely tedious process but a rather unproductive one as well. The best pedagogical strategy is to focus on the two polar cases of monopoly and monopsony, since they combine the salient features of imperfect competition with the important attraction of analytical simplicity. Remember, though, that the results we will establish would hold with only minor modification for the other market structures of imperfect competition.

Monopoly

Let's begin with the case of monopoly in the product market, but continue to assume that the labor market is competitive. The last assumption simplifies the analysis and allows us to focus exclusively on the effects of monopoly without introducing further complications. It is also a reasonable assumption, since even a monopolist could be a small demander of labor. In that case, the monopoly can hire as much labor as it wants at the prevailing wage, exactly like the situation analyzed in Chapter 2.

The important features of the demand curve for labor are not altered very much at all when there is monopoly in the product market. The Law of Diminishing Marginal Returns has no favorites, so the MP_L curve will be downward sloping in this case, too. The only difference here is that a monopoly cannot sell each unit of output at the same price. Instead, its demand curve is downward sloping, so it must lower its price in order to sell more output. The result is that its MRP_L curve will reflect not only the falling marginal product of each additional worker, but also the lower price that is necessary in order to sell the additional output. Both effects contribute to assuring that a monopoly's MRP_L curve will be downward sloping. Indeed, a monopoly's MRP_L curve would be downward sloping even if, for some reason, its MP_L curve were horizontal.

Just as in the case of a firm in a competitive market, a monopoly will always want to increase its employment level until the *MRP* of the last worker hired just equals the wage rate. Thus its labor demand curve will also be downward sloping. One final point is worth emphasizing: As long as the labor market is competitive, monopoly in the output market has no effect on wages. Workers are made neither better off nor worse off as a result of monopoly.

Monopsony

In a competitive labor market, neither firms nor workers are at a conspicuous disadvantage relative to one another. Because there are many firms demanding labor and many individuals supplying it, neither side of the market has the power to influence the outcome. The equilibrium wage is determined by the market as a whole rather than by any single firm or group of workers.

In pure monopsony, though, the situation is quite different. There are still many workers, but now there is only a single employer. The balance of power shifts toward the employer, and the outcomes, as you will see, are clearly less favorable to the workers. What is less clear is whether monopsony today is common enough to constitute a serious problem.

The distinguishing feature of monopsony is its supply curve of labor. Unlike a competitive firm which is small enough relative to the market that it can hire as many workers as it pleases at the *same* wage, a monopsony is large enough that it finds that the wage it must pay depends on how many workers it wants to hire. To increase its employment, it must draw workers away from somewhere else (another job, or another town) or something else (raising a family, or enjoying leisure), typically by offering a higher wage.

Who qualifies as a monopsonist? At a formal level, the answer is precise, if not very informative: A monopsonist is a firm that faces an upward-sloping supply curve for labor of a given quality. A university hiring economics instructors is most definitely *not* a monopsonist, because the relevant labor market is national and thus the number of other demanders is quite large. That same university may, however, be a monopsonistic employer of secretaries if it is quite large relative to the town in which it is located. A small-town hospital may be in the same position with respect to nurses, but not with respect to doctors (the market is national) or custodial help (the market is local, but many other employers exist). Sometimes, monopsony stems from monopoly. If a monopoly requires a specialized kind of labor that is used only for its product, it will find itself in a monopsony situation as well. A circus hiring clowns might fit that description. The small-town hospital also qualifies as far as nurses are concerned. If the airline industry became monopolized, pilots would probably find themselves in a monopsonistic market. A final instance of monopsony is the "company town," in which a single large firm dominates a small town. Although that situation is not as common now as it was at the beginning of the twentieth century, there may still be some company towns, especially in the South.

Do not make the mistake of confusing monopsony with bigness per se. The auto industry is a good example of this. It is certainly correct that the auto industry is a dominant employer in a number of cities. But it does not follow that the auto industry has monopsony power. In fact, it does not. Its labor supply curve is horizontal, at the wage agreed upon in negotiations between the auto industry and the United Auto Workers union. (Whether it might have monopsony power without the union is a different issue.) At that contract wage the auto industry has no difficulty in hiring as many workers as it wants. Analytically, then, its employment situation corresponds more closely to the case of a competitive firm than to that of a monopsony.

The analysis of employment and wages under monopsony conditions is a bit more complicated than in the case of a competitive firm, with all the complications arising from the difference in the supply curves. Consider a monopsonist's decision about whether or not to add one more worker. On the revenue side, it would, as always, consider the worker's expected *MRP*—there is nothing about monopsony that affects the properties of the *MRP* curve. Its additional employment costs, though, are different than in the competitive case. Precisely because its labor supply curve is upward sloping, it will now have to offer a wage slightly higher than the wage that was necessary to attract a slightly smaller work force. Exactly how much more will depend on the particular supply curve it faces.

It is possible that the monopsonist could pay the higher wage just to the extra worker it is trying to attract, keeping all the others at the lower wage. But that is not very likely—at the very least, worker morale might be a problem with that type of wage policy. If, instead, the monopsonist always pays all its workers the same wage, it must recognize that the cost of adding one more worker has two separate components. There is, first, the wage that must be paid to that worker, and second, the now-higher wage that will be paid to the workers who would otherwise have received a slightly lower wage. Put differently, under monopsony, the cost of hiring another worker exceeds the direct wage payment to that worker. With competitive conditions, the direct wage payment is all that must be considered.

A bit of arithmetic may help here. Suppose that for its particular labor supply curve, a monopsonistic employer finds that it can employ six workers at a wage of \$25 per day, but it must offer \$27 to attract a seventh worker. What is the cost of the seventh worker? It is not just the wage (\$27), but must also include an additional \$12 of wages paid to the first six workers, each of whom will now receive \$27 instead of \$25. If we call the additional wage costs of hiring a worker the **marginal labor cost** or *MLC* and if w is the wage paid to a worker, then for a monopsony it follows that $MLC > w$. For the example above, the *MLC* is \$39 even though the wage is \$27.

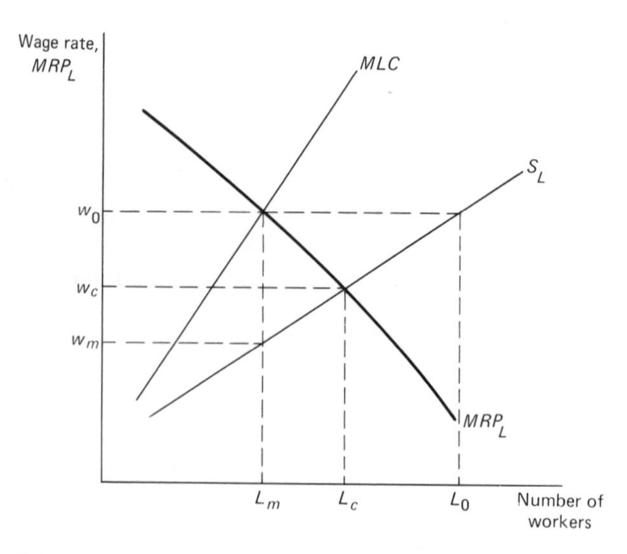

FIGURE 3.1 Employment and Wages under Monopsony

The relationship between a monopsonist's labor supply curve and its *MLC* curve is shown in Figure 3.1. Where the supply curve shows the wage necessary to attract any specified amount of *total* labor supply, the *MLC* curve shows the cost of attracting the *last* worker. Because $MLC > w$, the MLC curve always lies above the supply curve. The vertical distance between the two curves represents the additional wage payments made to the workers who were otherwise willing to work at a lower wage. Note that the two curves are not parallel; the *MLC* curve is always steeper than the supply curve.

How does this affect the firm's choice about the level of employment that will maximize its profits? The basic profit-maximizing logic is unchanged except that the relevant labor cost is not a worker's wage rate, but rather, the *MLC* of that worker. Thus a monopsonistic firm would choose to expand its employment until for the last worker hired, the marginal revenue product just equals the marginal labor cost. In symbols, the employment rule for monopsony is

$$MRP_L = MLC \tag{3.1}$$

where the equality holds for the last worker hired. Figure 3.1 illustrates the effects of monopsony on wages and employment. The most profitable level of employment is L_m, where $MRP_L = MLC$. The monopsony wage, though, is *not* found by moving horizontally across to the wage axis, to w_0. Indeed, at a wage of w_0 there would be an excess supply of labor, equal to $L_0 - L_m$. Instead, the monopsony wage is found by moving down to the labor supply curve and identifying the wage necessary to attract L_m workers. In the figure, this turns out to be w_m.

To see how monopsony affects employment and wages, suppose that Figure 3.1 represented a competitive labor market instead of a monopsony. Each firm, being small, would perceive its own labor supply curve as horizontal, even though the market labor supply curve was upward sloping. Each firm's MRP_L curve would be its demand curve and the curve that represented the monopsonist's MRP_L curve in the figure would instead be the market labor demand curve. Equilibrium would occur where the labor supply and labor demand were in balance, at a wage of w_c and a corresponding level of employment of L_c. Thus the effect of monopsony is to reduce both the wage rate and the amount of employment compared to a competitive labor market. Clearly, as far as the workers are concerned, labor market structure makes a difference.

The monopsony result differs from that of a competitive market in a second way as well. Under competitive conditions, all workers receive a wage equal to the value of output contributed by the last worker hired (i.e., $w = MRP_L$). The firm gives to all workers exactly what it received from the last one. Since all workers are homogeneous and any one could equally well be considered the last worker, there is something "fair" about this compensation scheme. But under monopsony, all workers receive a wage that is less than the *MRP* of even the last worker hired. This follows from the equality of the MRP_L and the *MLC* under monopsony and the fact that the wage rate is always less than the *MLC*. In Figure 3.1, this is the difference between w_0, which is the MRP_L of the last worker hired, and w_m, the monopsony wage. This gap between additional value produced and wage received is called **monopsonistic exploitation.**

The effects of monopsony become more severe the steeper the labor supply curve—that is, the farther the supply curve is from the horizontal supply curve of a competitive firm. An extreme example would be a vertical labor supply curve, which depicts a situation in which the same amount of labor is offered an *any* wage. This is not particularly likely, because it implies that workers have absolutely no other employment opportunities and thus find themselves in a "take it or leave it" situation. In any event, a situation like that is shown in Figure 3.2. The equilibrium wage *looks* like it would be w^*, where the quantity demanded equals the fixed supply. But the monopsonist need not pay a wage as high as that. If the workers really have no alternatives, any wage above zero will do. The wage might turn out to be w_m, perhaps just high enough for workers to maintain some minimum standard of living. If the market had been competitive, w^* would be the equilibrium wage.

Pure monopsony is almost certainly less common today that it was 75 to 100 years ago. Labor markets today cover a geographic area that was unthinkable early in the twentieth century, thanks to the development of the automobile, an extensive road system, and a general increase in the geographic

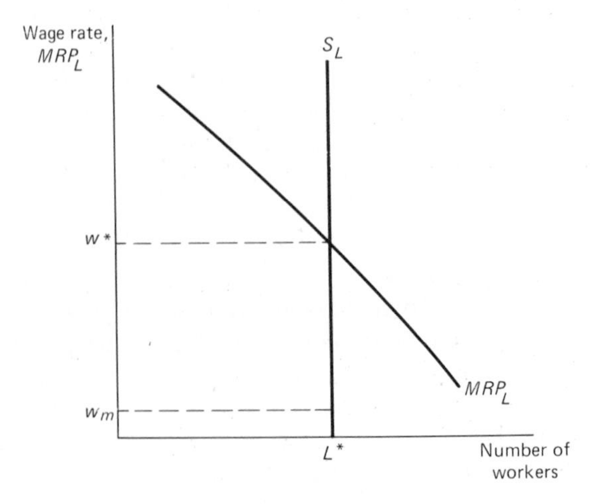

FIGURE 3.2 A Monopsonistic Labor Market with a Perfectly Inelastic Labor Supply Curve

mobility of workers. As a result, it is now unusual to find a situation where workers must deal with only a single employer or, equivalently, where an employer has very much monopsony power. Other potentially monopsonist markets have been converted to competitive markets (at least as far as the labor supply curve is concerned) through unionization.

Application: Monopsony, Nurses' Salaries, and the Nurse Shortage

One of the most widely studied examples of labor market monopsony is the labor market for nurses. The monopsony element here is especially interesting because of its possible relationship to the long-running, highly publicized policy debate about whether nurses are underpaid and whether a national nursing shortage exists.

The nurse labor market provides many of the necessary ingredients for monopsony. First, nursing is a specialized skill, not readily transferable to other employment opportunities. Second, most nurses work in hospitals and, except for larger cities, there may be only a few hospital-employers in any geographic area. In 1970, for example, 70 percent of hospitals were located in a one-hospital community. Third, nurses have often been geographically immobile, especially in the case of married nurses with a working spouse.

A simple hypothesis about monopsony and nurses wages could be formulated as follows: Other things equal, nurses working in more monopsonistic labor markets would have lower wage rates. (Notice that "monopsonistic" is used here in a general sense, referring not just to pure monopsony but to oligopsony or just "concentration.") This prediction can be tested by examining nurse salaries in cities that differ in the degree of monopsony. A number of studies have done that and the results confirm the monopsony wage effect. One study found that nursing salaries in one-hospital towns were 10 to 11 percent below those earned by similar nurses in competitive markets. Another study concluded that a doubling of the degree of monopsony in the nurse labor market reduced 1973 annual starting salaries by $400.[1]

How does monopsony relate to the nursing shortage? In economics, a shortage always refers to a case of excess demand at the prevailing wage (i.e., a wage below the equilibrium level). It is certainly possible to imagine a wage temporarily below its equilibrium level, perhaps following a sharp rise in demand. Something like this may well have occurred in the nurse labor market following the introduction of Medicaid and Medicare in the 1960s. But it is

[1] These findings are from Charles R. Link and John H. Landon, "Monopsony and Union Power in the Market for Nurses," *Southern Economic Journal*, 1975, and Charles R. Link and Russell F. Settle, "Labor Market Concentration and Nurses' Earnings," *Research in Nursing and Health*, 1979.

hard to explain why the nurse wage should have been *continually* below its equilibrium level for the two decades since the nurse shortage was first identified. Long-term labor market shortages are not easily explained.

Monopsony does provide a possible explanation for this result. In a monopsonistic labor market, there could be shortages in the sense that employers would like to hire more workers at the *current* market wage, but are unable to. The problem is that as a consequence of the upward-sloping labor supply curve of monopsony, additional workers are not, in fact, available at that wage. To see this, look at Figure 3.3, which presents a basic monopsony diagram. The monopsony wage rate would be W_m and employment would be L_m. If more nurses could be hired at wage W_m, the hospital would want to increase its employment to L^*. The difference between L^* and L_m could be regarded as an equilibrium monopsony-induced shortage—unfilled positions at the current market wage. The problem is the upward-sloping labor supply curve. Only at a wage of W^* would L^* workers be available.

There are two other explanations of the nurse shortage, not related to monopsony, which are worth considering. One views the shortage as affecting only certain nursing positions; the shortage is specific rather than widespread. The shortage may, for example, be confined largely to certain locations (rural or inner-city urban), work shifts (midnight), or specialties (emergency, intensive care, psychiatric) which are considered exceptionally arduous, stressful, or otherwise undesirable.

The other possible explanation is that the shortage is not the type recognized by economists, but instead has a *normative* basis. For example, it may be argued that we *need* more nurses if we are to meet certain health care goals. A shortage defined in this way could exist even when there is an equilibrium wage in the labor market.

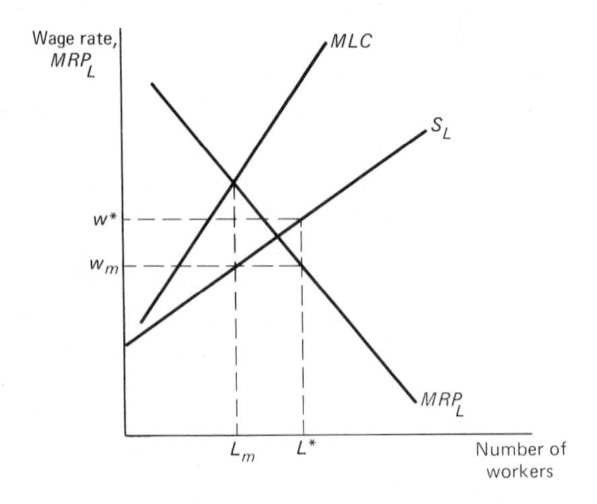

FIGURE 3.3 Monopsony and the Nurse Shortage

LABOR DEMAND IN THE LONG RUN

In Chapter 2, when we first analyzed labor demand, we assumed that a firm had a certain amount of capital and that it could not change that amount when there was a change in the wage rate. That simplification was useful for the purpose at hand—deriving the short-run demand curve for labor—but it is weak in at least two respects. First, a firm does not just happen to *have* a certain amount of capital. Rather, it *chooses* a desired amount of capital and we need to understand something about how that is done. Second, the short run does not last forever. Sooner or later, a firm can respond to a change in the wage rate by adjusting not only the amount of labor it uses, but also its use of capital. What will a firm's demand curve for labor be like in that circumstance?

Isoquants and Input Choice

To understand a firm's demand curve for labor in the long run, we need to examine two aspects of a firm's behavior. The first involves *cost minimization*, that is, the task of producing output at lowest possible cost. The other involves *profit maximization*—choosing how much output to produce. As you will see, the wage rate affects both decisions, which, in turn, determine the amount of labor a firm will use.

The first point to make is that a firm's choice of *how* to produce its output is *not* simply a technological matter—something for the engineers to decide. Noneconomists often think of there being a single technologically determined way to produce output, typically involving the best technology available. Economists, however, argue that that conception is fundamentally wrong and that, instead, it is virtually always the case that there are a number of ways for a firm to produce its output. Some ways may use a lot of labor and relatively little capital, a situation that economists call **labor intensive**. Others may involve using more capital, but less labor—that is, they are more **capital intensive**. In general, it is useful to think of a firm as having a set of alternative production techniques to choose from, where each technique is characterized by the amount of labor and amount of capital it requires. There are probably few production situations where only a single technique is feasible.

To represent the different production techniques available to a firm, economists use the idea of an **isoquant**. An isoquant is a graphical representation of all the combinations of labor and capital that can be used to produce the *same* amount of output. For each available production technique, there is one point on an isoquant, indicating the amount of labor and capital that would be required to produce that amount of output using that technique. For each possible output level that a firm could produce there is a separate isoquant showing the labor–capital combinations that are feasible.

The exact shape of an isoquant will vary from one firm to the next depending on the nature of the alternative technologies that exist for that firm's particular product. There are, however, some features common enough that they are deemed typical, in much the same way that the Law of Diminishing Marginal Returns describes the typical relationship among labor, capital, and output in the short run. A typical set of isoquants is shown in Figure 3.4. The amount of labor is measured along the horizontal axis and the corresponding amount of capital is shown along the vertical axis. The numbers attached to the isoquant—in this case, 25, 35, and 50—denote the amount of output available from the various designated input combinations. Each point on an isoquant actually represents three quantities: the amount of labor, the amount of capital, and the corresponding amount of output.

There are four important features of this set of isoquants. First, isoquants are negatively sloped. Alternative production techniques involve more of one input and less of another, not more of both. Second, isoquants for higher outputs lie to the northeast, since producing a larger output will require more of at least one input and often more of both. Third, the isoquants are continuous (a smooth curve with no gaps) rather than consisting of just a few points. The economic meaning of this is that a firm has not just three or five or ten ways to produce any amount of output but an infinite number of ways. You may regard this either as a realistic description of an enormous number of production alternatives or as a bit of artistic license, useful to avoid having to specify exactly where the actual alternatives for each firm are.

Finally, notice that the isoquants in the figure do not have a constant slope, but are instead steeper at the top end (capital-intensive techniques)

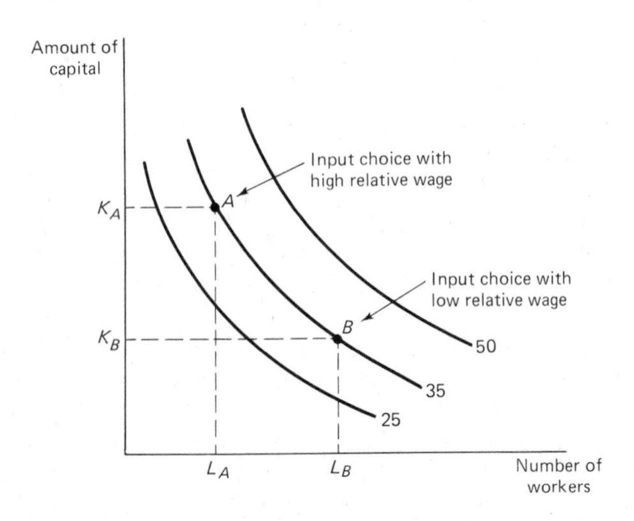

FIGURE 3.4 Isoquants and Input Choice

and flatter at the bottom (labor-intensive techniques). An intuitive, nontechnical explanation draws on the conflicting tendencies of specialization and overcrowding which we used to derive the short-run MP_L curve. Look at point A in Figure 3.4 which represents a capital-intensive way to produce 35 units of output. To be specific, think of it as a large warehouse with very few workers. If *more* workers were added without reducing the amount of capital, output would probably rise rapidly, owing to the productivity gains of specialization. Alternatively, the *same* output could be produced by reducing the size of the warehouse sharply and adding a modest number of workers. Thus the isoquant will be steep in the vicinity of A. At B, though, the situation is reversed. There are now so many workers relative to the size of the warehouse that for output to remain constant, any *further* reduction in warehouse size must be offset by a large increase in the amount of labor used. Graphically, the curve flattens out in the vicinity of B.

On technical grounds alone, none of the points on an isoquant are superior to the rest. Rather, which production technique is best depends on economic considerations—namely, which is cheapest for whatever output level the firm wants to produce. But no single combination along an isoquant is always least costly. When the wage rate is relatively low, labor-intensive techniques will be cheaper than more capital-intensive methods. If the wage rate were higher, all the techniques would be more costly then before, but the techniques that were more capital intensive would now be *relatively* cheaper. Thus a firm seeking to minimize its production costs will select a capital-intensive input combination such as point A when the wage rate is relatively high, while a lower relative wage rate would lead it to choose a combination such as point B. For each production technique represented on an isoquant, there is *some* combination of the wage rate and the price of capital at which it would be cheapest.[2]

The wage rate also affects how much output a profit-maximizing firm will produce. To maximize its profits, a firm should always expand its production up to the point where the marginal revenue for the last unit produced just equals the marginal cost of producing it. When wages are high, a firm's marginal costs will be high, and thus the point where marginal revenue equals marginal cost will be reached at a relatively small level of output. Conversely, when the wage is lower, and all else is the same, the profit-maximizing level of output will be larger. Figure 3.5 shows this for a competitive firm. The profit-maximizing output is Q_1 when the wage rate is relatively high and Q_2 when it is lower. Thus wage rates affect employment in two analytically distinct ways: by influencing *how much* it is profitable to produce and by influencing *how* that output is produced.

[2] This entire discussion can be presented with more precision by introducing the concept of the isocost line. See the Appendix to this chapter for that analysis.

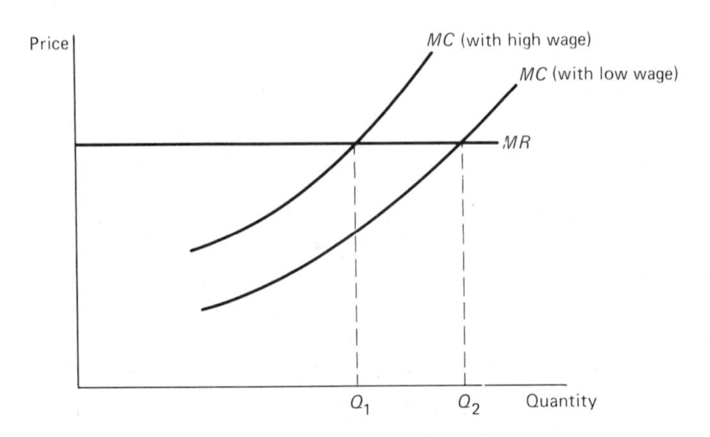

FIGURE 3.5 The Effect of Wages on the Profit-Maximizing Level of Output

Deriving the Long-Run Labor Demand Curve

With those ideas in hand, it is not hard to show how a firm adjusts to a change in the wage rate in the long run and to derive the corresponding long-run demand curve for labor. Suppose that for the current values of the wage rate, the price of capital, and the price of the product, a firm's profit-maximizing and cost-minimizing choices are represented by point A in Figure 3.6(a). Its output is Q_1, and it is producing the output with L_A units of labor and K_A units of capital. Now suppose that the wage changes from its current value (w_0) to some higher wage (w_1). Exactly as described above, the firm will make two separate adjustments. Even if the firm were to continue producing at its current level, it would shift to a more capital-intensive means of production—something like point B. This movement, with labor use falling from L_A to L_B, is called the **substitution effect**, since one input is substituted for another. In addition, though, now that the wage is higher, the firm will produce less output, and thus the amount of labor it uses will usually fall for that reason as well. This effect is called the **output** or **scale effect**, and it is shown in the diagram as the movement from point B to point C.[3] The amount of labor used falls to L_C. The total effect—from L_A to L_C—is the sum of the change due to the substitution effect and the change due to the output effect.

The long-run demand curve for labor consists of points like A and C, where a firm is both minimizing its costs of production and maximizing its profits. The combination (w_0, L_A) is one point on the long-run demand curve and (w_1, L_C) is another. The result, as shown in Figure 3.6(b), is a downward-

[3] Exactly how much less the firm will produce will depend on the details of how its costs are affected by an increase in the wage rate.

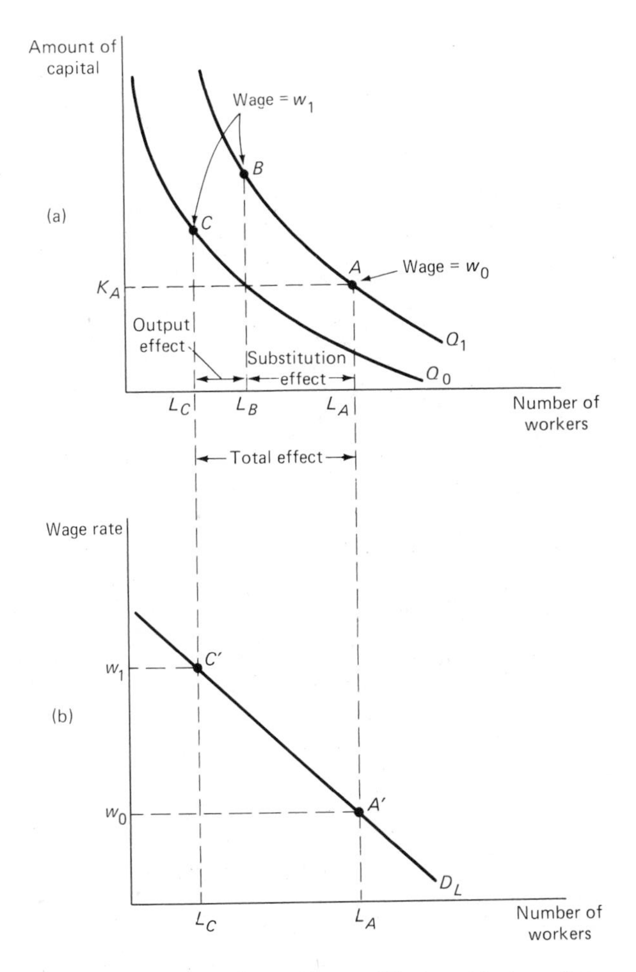

FIGURE 3.6 Substitution and Output Effects and the Long-Run Demand Curve for Labor

sloping demand curve for labor. In that graph, point A' corresponds exactly to point A in the graph just above it, and points C' and C also match up.

We have now seen that a firm's demand curve for labor is downward sloping, both in the short-run when the amount of capital is fixed and in the long run when it is not. One final point remains to be considered. How do the two demand curves fit together? When the wage changes, does the firm change its use of labor more in the long run or in the short run?

The answer to this is important, but it is, unfortunately, quite complicated and depends on some highly technical features of production. The basic result, though, is shown in Figure 3.7. Suppose that the wage is w_0 and given the price of the product and the price of capital, a firm chooses to use L_0 labor and K_0 capital. That choice is represented by point A, which is simultaneously a point on the long-run demand curve, D_{LR}, and on a specific short-run demand curve, D^0_{SR}. In the short run, wage changes lead to movements along D^0_{SR}. Thus if the wage increased to w_1, the firm would move to point B, and if the wage were to fall to w_2, it would move to C. In the long-run, the firm's response is greater. In this case the firm would move to point D when the wage rose to w_1 and it had sufficient time to adjust its use of capital. Similarly, it would move to point E if the wage fell to w_2. Once the firm has made its capital adjustment, we again have a short-run situation. This time the relevant short-run curves are D^1_{SR} (for point D) and D^2_{SR} (for point E).

The important result is this: The long-run adjustment in employment following a change in the wage rate exceeds the short-run adjustment. Put differently, a firm's long-run demand curve for labor is always flatter than the underlying set of short-run curves.

Application: Factor Prices, Production Choices, and the Distribution of Income

In Chapter 1 we noted that the wage rate was a price of special significance in an economy, performing two economic functions simultaneously. We asserted there that the wage rate served as the link between the allocation of labor among alternative uses and the distribution of income among the various factors of production. Now let's look at that idea more carefully.

Consider an economy with a large labor supply relative to the available

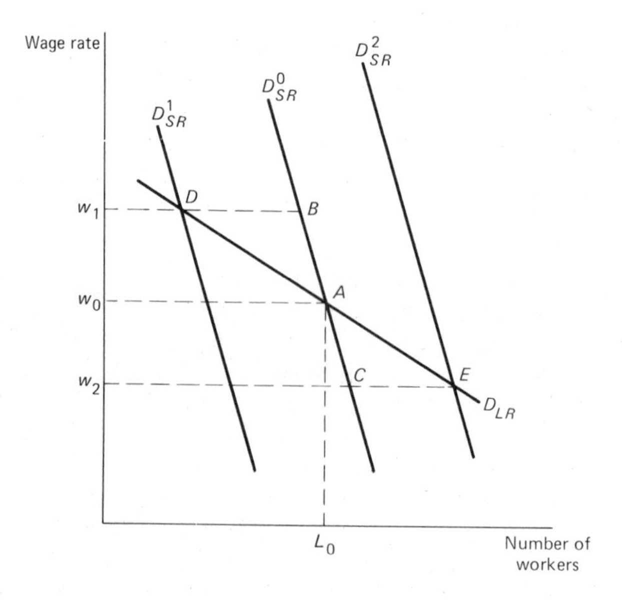

FIGURE 3.7 Comparing the Short-Run and Long-Run Demand Curves for Labor

stock of capital. We already know that in such an economy the equilibrium wage rate will be low. The low wage provides firms with an incentive to adopt labor-intensive production techniques, thereby making extensive use of the more abundant resource and economizing on the scarce one. In the opposite circumstance in which capital is more abundant relative to labor, the wage rate would be higher and firms would choose production techniques that were less labor intensive.

Thus a firm's cost-minimizing choice of inputs and the distribution of income in an economy are closely related. Indeed, they are linked by the equilibrium prices of the factors of production. The use of labor-intensive production techniques and the existence of a low standard of living for workers go hand in hand, both reflecting the underlying factor prices and factor supplies. You need only think of agriculture in much of the Third World to recognize the logic of this—extremely labor intensive and producing very low incomes for agricultural workers. In contrast, consider the far more capital-intensive production techniques and higher farm incomes in the United States.

THE ELASTICITY OF DERIVED DEMAND

Every labor demand curve we have encountered thus far has been downward sloping with respect to the wage rate. This holds for a firm, an industry, and an entire economy, the short run and the long run, competition and monopoly. But it clearly makes an enormous difference whether a 10 percent increase in the wage rate will cause a decline in employment of 2 percent, 10 percent, or 20 percent—even though all satisfy the rule of downward-sloping derived demand. When wages rise or fall, economists would like to be able to say more than "employment will always change in the opposite direction." We would like to be able to understand how large a change will occur.

Measuring Elasticity

When economists want to measure the relationship between price and quantity, they usually use the concept of elasticity. The **wage elasticity** of demand is calculated as the percentage change in employment divided by the percentage change in the wage rate, moving along a demand curve. In symbols, the elasticity expression is

$$\eta = \frac{\%\Delta L^D}{\%\Delta W} \tag{3.2}$$

where L^D represents the amount of labor demanded and η is the symbol for wage elasticity. Elasticities always involve percentage changes, so that the resulting number is independent of the units in which the price or quantity term is measured. Since wages and employment are inversely related along a downward-sloping demand curve, η will always be negative.

It is conventional to classify labor demand curves according to whether the percentage change in employment is greater than, equal to, or less than the percentage change in the wage rate. When the employment change is greater, the demand curve is **elastic** and η will have a value between -1 and $-\infty$. The demand curve is said to be **inelastic** when the employment change is less than the wage rate change; in this case, η falls between 0 and -1. In between is the situation where the percentage change in employment just equals the percentage change in the wage rate. Economists call this **unitary elastic**, and you can easily verify that $\eta = -1$. In the earlier example of a wage increase of 10 percent, the labor demand curve would be elastic if employment fell by 20 percent ($\eta = -2$), inelastic if it fell by 2 percent ($\eta = -0.2$), and unitary elastic if it fell by 10 percent ($\eta = -1$).

The concept of elasticity is related to the slope of the labor demand curve, but it is not exactly the same thing. The general rule of thumb is that a steep demand curve is inelastic and a flat one is elastic. Unfortunately, that rule is only approximate, since the slope of a labor demand curve shows the relationship between wages and employment measured in absolute units (hours and dollars), not in percentages as required by the elasticity formula.[4] Frequently, however, the rule is good enough. If we are interested only in comparing demand curves—which one is more elastic, for example—the steep versus flat rule of thumb works well. If two demand curves intersect, the steeper curve is always less elastic than the flatter one if they are compared in the vicinity of the intersection point. For example, in Figure 3.7 the long-run labor demand curve is more elastic than the short-run curve at point A, where they intersect. For more precise elasticity calculations, however, it is necessary to know not only the slope of the demand curve but also the point on the demand curve at which the elasticity is to be calculated. Frequently, reported elasticities refer to the average wage and employment being studied or to the current wage and employment.

[4] In fact, the elasticity is different at every point along a labor demand curve which is linear. To see this, rewrite equation (3.2) this way:

$$\eta = \frac{\%\Delta L^D}{\%\Delta w} = \frac{\Delta L^D/L^D}{\Delta w/w} = \frac{\Delta L^D}{\Delta w}\frac{w}{L^D}$$

The first term on the right-hand side of the equation, $\Delta L^D/\Delta w$, is related to the slope of the labor demand curve—in fact, it is the reciprocal of that slope. Along a linear demand curve, this term always has the same value at every point. But the second term, w/L^D, takes on a different value at every point along the demand curve. Moving down the demand curve, w falls and L^D rises, so the fraction w/L^D falls continuously. But this means that the elasticity of labor demand along a linear demand falls steadily. Linear labor demand curves are always more elastic at high prices than at low prices. As a result, a steep demand curve may, nevertheless, be elastic at a high wage, and a flat one may be inelastic when the wage rate is low.

Sometimes it is not the wage that changes initially, but the quantity. Suppose, for example, that the labor supply curve shifted out; recent examples could include the increased numbers of women, teens, or college graduates entering the labor market. In this case we might ask: What reduction in the wage rate will be sufficient to provide employment for the now large numbers? Again, the answer depends on the demand elasticity. Rearranging equation (3.2), we have $\%\Delta W = \%\Delta L^D/\eta$, which shows that the more elastic the demand curve (η is large in absolute value), the smaller the necessary wage adjustment. Women, teens, and young college graduates will certainly be better off with a more elastic labor demand curve.

The Laws of Derived Demand

Economists can do more than simply measure the elasticity of a labor demand curve. It is possible to generalize about the circumstances that will be likely to make a labor demand curve more or less elastic. There are, in fact, four famous rules that lay down the general principles. They are known as the **Hicks–Marshall laws of derived demand**, after two very famous British economists, Alfred Marshall and Sir John Hicks, who developed the ideas. The rules are easy to understand if you keep in mind that changes in the wage affect both *how* a firm produces and *how much* it produces.

First, consider the firm's choice of *how* to produce. Certainly, the firm would want to substitute capital for labor if the wage rate increased, to minimize its costs of production. But how much substitution will occur? In some rare cases there may be only a single capital-to-labor ratio available to a firm for the production of a specified amount of output, so no substitution will occur at all. But even where input substitution is technologically possible, it may sometimes be economically unwise to carry it very far. Why? Suppose the wage rate does increase but that it takes increasingly larger amounts of capital to replace each additional unit of labor. If so, the new cost-minimizing input choice might well be arrived at before very much labor is replaced. The magnitude of the firm's response will depend on how *easy* it is to make *further* substitution of capital for labor, where "easy" means that relatively small amounts of capital are sufficient to replace labor. *The easier additional substitution is, the more elastic the demand curve for labor will be.* That is the first of the Hicks–Marshall rules.

One thing that might limit this substitution of capital for labor along an isoquant is an increase in the price of capital, since it is the *relative* price of labor and capital that matters as far as cost minimization is concerned. Suppose that the wage did increase and the supply curve of capital were perfectly elastic[5]—that is, horizontal. In that event the firm could increase its use of

[5] The elasticity of supply is defined as the change in the quantity supplied divided by the change in the price, both measured in percentage units.

capital without increasing the price of capital, and thus the amount of substitution of capital for labor would depend only on the ease of substitution (rule 1). If, instead, the supply curve of capital is upward sloping, the attempt to substitute capital for labor will cause the price of capital to rise somewhat, which, in turn, will reduce the amount of substitution that is economically sensible. The more elastic (less elastic) the supply curve of capital, the smaller (larger) will be the increase in the price of capital. Thus, holding constant the technological ease of substitution, the extent to which capital is substituted for labor when the wage increases will be greater when the supply curve of capital is elastic than when it is inelastic. This is the second Hicks–Marshall rule: *The demand for labor is more elastic the more elastic the supply curve of capital is*. Although we derived this rule in terms of capital, it is perfectly general and applies to any input that could be substituted for workers whose wage has increased.

Now consider how a wage change will affect the firm's choice of *how much* output to produce. Other things equal, the greater the change in output, the greater will be the change in employment and the labor demand curve will be more elastic. The final two rules concern the magnitude of that effect.

The first of these involves the elasticity of the demand curve for the product that the firm produces. When wages increase, production costs rise, and eventually the price of the firm's product will also rise. Unless the demand for the firm's product is completely inelastic, the increase in price will reduce the quantity demanded, and that, in turn, will reduce the amount of labor needed. When the product demand curve is elastic, the decline in quantity demanded for a given increase in the price will be larger than when the product demand curve is inelastic. It follows that the reduction in employment will be greater when the product demand curve is more elastic. Thus *the elasticity of the demand curve for labor is greater the more elastic the demand for the final product is*. That is the third Hicks–Marshall rule.

The final Hicks–Marshall rule concerns the share of total cost accounted for by labor. To see this, suppose first, that wages increased by 25 percent, and second, that it is technologically impossible to substitute capital for labor along an isoquant. If labor costs were only 10 percent of total costs (i.e., the process was capital intensive), total production costs would rise by only 2.5 percent (10 percent times 25 percent). If, however, wages amounted to 50 percent of the total (a more labor-intensive production process), the increase in costs would be five times as large—12.5 percent (i.e., 25 percent times 50 percent). The increase in costs will, in turn, lead to an increase in price, which, as we noted just above, leads to a reduction in the quantity demanded of output and consequently, of labor. The idea here is that this effect will be strongest when labor accounts for a larger share of production costs. Can you follow through with this logic? The greater labor's share of costs, the greater the increase in costs for any wage increase, and thus if we were to compare product demand curves of equal elasticity, the greater would be the decrease in output and employment. Thus the fourth Hicks–Marshall elasticity rule is that *the demand for labor is more elastic the larger labor's share of total cost.*

Pulling together all the ideas developed in this section, we now know that the demand for labor will be more elastic:

1. The easier is additional substitution between inputs in production
2. The more elastic the supply of other inputs
3. The more elastic the demand for the final product
4. The larger the share of total production cost accounted for by labor

The demand for labor will, of course, be more inelastic in the opposite situations.

Using the Laws of Derived Demand

There are a number of dividends to this analysis of the elasticity of derived demand. One is a better understanding of the central proposition developed thus far—that the demand curve for labor is downward sloping. Although this assertion is not controversial among economists, many labor market policies seem to be developed on the assumption that labor demand curves are vertical or perfectly inelastic. (Recall, for example, our earlier analysis of wage policy in France and the lump of labor hypothesis.) Yet the logical requirement for labor demand curves to be perfectly inelastic is that there be not only no substitution for labor in production but also no change in quantity demanded by consumers. Neither of these is a very likely occurrence except in the very, very short run. The probability that both necessary conditions might hold simultaneously over any kind of extended time period would be about as low as your odds of winning the Irish Sweepstakes.

It is also easier to understand why long-run labor demand curves are more elastic than short-run curves. Frequently, the supply curves of other factors are relatively inelastic at first and then become more elastic over time as the producers of capital goods increase their production. By rule 2, this would cause the labor demand curve to become more elastic over time. It usually takes time for consumers to adjust to price changes—by adjusting their habits or, in the case of durable goods, waiting for their current model to wear out. By rule 3, this gives us another reason to expect labor demand curves to become more elastic in the long run.

We can also use the Hicks–Marshall rules to make some predictions about the elasticity of labor demand for specific groups of workers. For example, it seems reasonable to expect that it would be easier to substitute capital for less skilled workers than for more skilled workers, because of the nature of the tasks typically performed. If so, then by the first elasticity rule, we would expect the demand curve for less skilled workers to be more elastic. Similarly, labor demand curves might be relatively inelastic in certain service occupations, such as nursing, airline pilots, and police and fire work, since it is relatively difficult to subsitute either capital or less skilled workers in the performance of their duties. Of these, we might further expect pilots to have the least elastic labor demand curve since, in addition to the limited substitution, labor costs account for a relatively small share of total production costs in the airline industry.

Workers in firms facing competition from imported goods of comparable quality and lower price are likely candidates for elastic labor demand curves, by the third Hicks–Marshall rule. In this case the availability of imports provides the substitute goods which tend to make the product demand curve more elastic. In the United States, workers in the textile, clothing, and footwear industries probably fall into this category. More recently, it is likely that the increased availability of imported steel and automobiles has increased the elasticity of labor demand for workers in those industries.

Finally, many empirical studies have attempted to estimate the elasticity of labor demand, using information for the economy as a whole or for specific industries or groups of workers. Measuring the actual importance of each of the four Hicks–Marshall rules is beyond the capability of the data available to economists.[6] Instead, most studies settle for estimating the overall elasticity of labor demand or the separate contributions of the substitution and output effects. Even that is a fairly formidable task, partly because it is difficult to measure the price of capital accurately and also because other things (e.g., the level of technology) may be changing at the same time that the wage rate changes. If those changes affected employment, they might "blur" the relationship between wage rates and employment.

With these qualifications in mind, we can examine some of the findings. As of the mid-1970s, the consensus estimate of the elasticity of labor demand was about -0.32, approximately equally divided between the substitution and output effects.[7] In a more recent study, which took a slightly different approach, the elasticity due only to the substitution effect was estimated to be close to -0.5.[8] Although this estimate is about three times as large as the substitution elasticity previously estimated, it still leaves the total elasticity in the inelastic region. Computed elasticities for specific groups of workers confirm the hypothesis that less skilled workers do have more elastic demand curves than those of skilled workers. For blue-collar, production workers, estimated long-run elasticities range from about -0.5 to -1.20, while for

[6] It is almost impossible to estimate a supply curve of capital, as is required by the second Hicks–Marshall rule. Most studies implicitly assume that the supply curve of capital is infinitely elastic.

[7] These findings are summarized in Daniel S. Hamermesh, "Econometric Studies of Labor Demand and Their Application to Policy Analysis," *Journal of Human Resources*, (November 1980).

[8] See Kim B. Clark and Richard B. Freeman, "How Elastic Is the Demand for Labor?" *The Review of Economics and Statistics*, (November 1980).

white-collar, nonproduction workers, they are about half as large.[9] A similar relationship emerges in the pattern of elasticities for workers according to their education level. Here the estimated elasticities appear to decrease as the amount of education increases. Finally, one group that is consistently found to have a highly elastic demand curve is teenagers. Reported elasticities for this group range from -1.3 to a striking -7.1. Since teenagers comprise a relatively inexperienced, unskilled group of workers, their highly elastic demand curve is consistent with the findings for the other less skilled groups.

APPLICATIONS OF LABOR DEMAND ANALYSIS

In this section we illustrate the usefulness of labor demand theory by showing its application to two important public policy areas. The first is an old topic in labor economics, the analysis of the labor market effects of legislation that establishes a legal minimum wage. The United States has had legislation like that since 1938 and so now do many other countries, among them France, Mexico, Costa Rica, Chile, and Puerto Rico. Although minimum wage legislation has been with us for over forty-five years, it has recently become a controversial and widely studied topic because of its possible link to the very low rates of employment and high rates of unemployment among teenagers. Labor demand theory provides a useful framework for examining the probable consequences of that kind of policy.

The second application is not a specific public policy, but is, instead, a new approach in applied labor economics which has proved useful for analyzing a variety of issues. It is sometimes referred to as labor–labor substitution and it is especially important for discovering how changes in the labor market conditions for one group of workers, perhaps due to a change in a government program, will affect the conditions for other groups of workers in the labor market.

The Economics of Minimum Wage Legislation

In the United States, a minimum wage was first established in 1938 at $0.25 per hour, which was about 40 percent of the average wage in manufacturing at that time. The legislation originally applied to a limited number of workers; approximately half of all workers were covered and two traditionally low-wage industries, retail trade and services, were largely exempt from its provisions. Since then, the level of the minimum wage has been updated periodically to adjust for inflation and for the general growth of

[9] The rest of the findings reported in this paragraph appear in Daniel S. Hamermesh and James Grant, "Econometric Studies of Labor–Labor Substitution and Their Implications for Policy," *Journal of Human Resources*, (Fall 1979).

TABLE 3.1 Minimum Wage Legislation in the United States, 1938–1981

EFFECTIVE DATE OF MINIMUM WAGE CHANGE	NOMINAL MINIMUM WAGE	MINIMUM WAGE RELATIVE TO AVERAGE HOURLY WAGE IN MANUFACTURING	
		Before	*After*
10/24/38	$0.25	—	0.403
10/24/39	0.30	0.398	0.478
10/24/45	0.40	0.295	0.394
1/25/50	0.75	0.278	0.521
3/1/56	1.00	0.385	0.512
9/3/61	1.15	0.431	0.495
9/3/63	1.25	0.467	0.508
2/1/67	1.40	0.441	0.494
2/1/68	1.60	0.465	0.531
5/1/74	2.00	0.363	0.454
1/1/75	2.10	0.423	0.445
1/1/76	2.30	0.410	0.449
1/1/78	2.65	0.430	0.480
1/1/79	2.90	0.402	0.440
1/1/80	3.10	0.417	0.445
1/1/81	3.35	0.403	0.435

wages in the economy. Table 3.1 summarizes the history of the changes in the minimum wage. Typically, the minimum wage is set at about 50 percent of the average hourly wage in manufacturing, falls over time to about 40 percent, and then is revised upward. As of 1984, the legal minimum wage was $3.35 per hour and no immediate increases were contemplated.

There have also been major extensions in the coverage of the legislation. Major changes in 1961, 1967, and 1969 greatly increased coverage in the trade and service sectors. In 1982, over 90 percent of all nonsupervisory, nonfarm wage earners were covered, including over two-thirds of all workers in the service sector and about 60 percent in retail trade. Still exempt from minimum wage provisions are businesses with annual sales below a specified dollar amount ($362,500 in 1982), workers on tips, some agricultural and transportation workers, and a limited number of students in part-time jobs.

Thanks to many recent studies,[10] we now know a great deal about who the minimum wage workers are and where they work. Table 3.2 summarizes some of that information, as of 1980. The numbers in column (1) are the proportion of all minimum wage workers who were in each designated cat-

[10] In 1977, Congress established the Minimum Wage Study Commission to examine some of the more controversial issues concerning minimum wage legislation. An extensive research effort was undertaken and was published in 1981 in twelve volumes. Volume I provides a very readable and interesting summary of the issues and the findings of the Commission.

egory, and those in column (2) are the proportion of workers in each category who worked at or below the minimum wage. If we want to know who the minimum wage workers are, the numbers in column (1) are the relevant ones. If, however, we want to know which groups are most affected by the minimum wage, column (2) gives the appropriate information.

As shown in the first line of column (2), 12.4 percent of all workers in 1980—10.6 million people—earned less than or equal to the minimum wage. Column (1) shows that almost a third were teenagers and just over 60 percent were between the ages of 20 and 64. More than half were either the head of household or spouse and almost 80 percent of them worked in just six occupations—sales, clerical work, household domestic service, other service employment, and both farm and nonfarm laborers. Over three-fourths of minimum wage workers were white.

The numbers in column (2) give a very different impression of the minimum wage population. Minimum wage employment is relatively rare for household heads and spouses and for persons between the ages of 25 and 64—about 8 percent of both groups earn the minimum wage. The incidence is much higher among groups that include large numbers of less skilled work-

TABLE 3.2 Selected Characteristics of Minimum Wage Workers, Second Quarter, 1980

GROUP	(1) PERCENT OF ALL MINIMUM WAGE WORKERS	(2) PERCENT OF GROUP WHO WERE MINIMUM WAGE WORKERS
All workers	100.0	12.4
Age		
16–19	30.8	44.2
20–24	17.4	14.2
25–64	45.4	7.7
65+	6.4	38.0
Race		
White	76.0	11.3
Black	15.0	18.1
Household status		
Head or spouse	52.4	8.3
Occupation		
Sales	9.1	19.8
Clerical	15.6	9.4
Household domestic service	7.1	74.8
Other service	35.0	33.3
Nonfarm laborer	7.5	18.6
Farm laborer	4.3	47.4

Source: Report of the Minimum Wage Study Commission, Vol. I, Tables 1-1, 1-4, 1-5, 1-11, Figure 1-1, U.S. Government Printing Office, Washington, D.C., 1981.

ers. For instance, 44 percent of all employed teens (ages 16 to 19) in 1980 were minimum wage workers; a finer breakdown indicates that 62 percent of 16 and 17-year-olds were. Among employed workers, blacks were about one-and-a-half times as likely as whites to be minimum wage workers. By far the highest occupational concentration of minimum wage workers was among household service workers, where almost 75 percent earned no more than the minimum wage. A high proportion of workers in other service jobs and of farm laborers also earned the minimum wage.

Theoretical Analysis of Minimum Wage Legislation

The basic analysis of the effects of minimum wage legislation on the labor market is fairly straightforward. To begin, we need to relax our assumption of homogeneous workers. Instead, suppose that there are many different groups of workers in the economy, ranging from unskilled to highly skilled and that for each group there is an equilibrium wage that would exist in the absence of any legislation. Presumably, the established minimum wage exceeds the equilibrium wage for at least some of the low-wage unskilled groups—otherwise, it would have no effect at all. As we saw in Table 3.2, this is clearly the case. The fact that a large number of persons were employed at or below the minimum wage indicates that their equilibrium wage must have been no higher than that.

The situation for one such group is shown in Figure 3.8. The equilibrium wage is w^* and the legislated minimum is w^M. As long as the demand curve is downward sloping, minimum wage legislation accomplishes two things—it raises the wage rate and it reduces the amount of employment, in this case from L^* to L^M. That result, however simple, is fundamental: *Minimum wage*

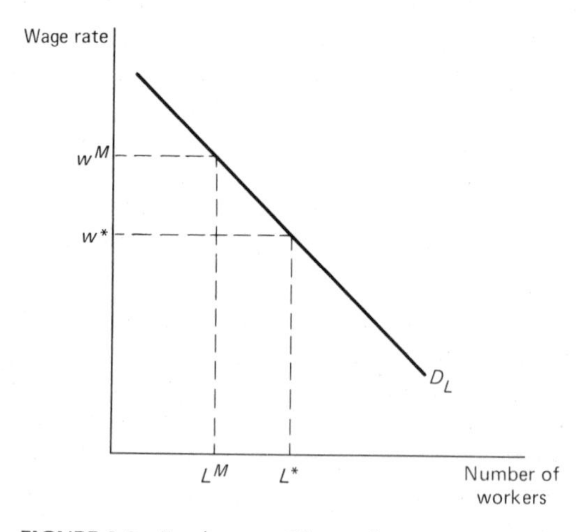

FIGURE 3.8 Employment Effects of a Minimum Wage

legislation that is effective reduces employment opportunities. The size of the employment loss depends on both the difference between w^M and w^* and on the elasticity of the labor demand curve. The more elastic (flatter) the demand curve and the greater the wage difference, the larger will be the resulting loss in employment. From this we can draw a second important conclusion: The employment effects of minimum wage legislation is greatest for precisely those workers who would otherwise have had the lowest wages. For them, minimum wage legislation is a double-edged sword, reducing the probability of employment, but increasing the wage rate for those who do secure employment.

You might think that minimum wage legislation also causes unemployment to increase, since less employment is offered and more labor is supplied at the higher wage. Although there is an excess supply of labor, that is not the same thing as measured unemployment. To be considered unemployed in the United States, a person must not only be without a job, but also have made a specific effort to seek employment. Since there is no way to predict whether workers without jobs will actively look for other employment, the effect on unemployment is ambiguous. That is why economists emphasize the effects of minimum wage legislation on employment.

The results so far pertain to the situation where all jobs are **covered** by the minimum wage provisions. In fact, we know that some jobs are exempt, and in still other cases there apparently is noncompliance with the law. The existence of an **uncovered** sector where the minimum wage is not in force changes the analysis somewhat. These effects are shown in panels (a) and (b) of Figure 3.9, which refer respectively to the covered and uncovered sectors. Originally, wage rates are identical in the two sectors, since there is no distinction between the sectors until the minimum wage is introduced. Wages then rise to w^M in the covered sector, with employment there falling to L^M, just as in Figure 3.8. The next step depends on what workers unable to find minimum wage employment choose to do. If they are willing to work at w^* or below, they may seek employment in the uncovered sector, especially if it is geographically adjacent. But in so doing, they increase the labor supply curve there and thereby reduce the wage rate in the uncovered sector. As shown in panel (b), the supply curve shifts out to S_1, wages fall to W_1, and employment rises to L_1. In this case it is not clear whether the average wage rate for this group of workers rises nor whether total employment falls. With complete coverage, the entire adjustment to minimum wages is in terms of employment. With an uncovered sector, there may be one wage that is flexible, so a reduction in employment is not inevitable.

There are a few standard rebuttal arguments to these conclusions. One is based on the possibility that the labor market is monopsonistic rather than competitive, in which case the results are, admittedly, quite different.[11] But since the likelihood that low-skilled workers face only a single employer is

[11] In the monopsony case, a wage increase due to minimum wage legislation can actually cause employment to rise.

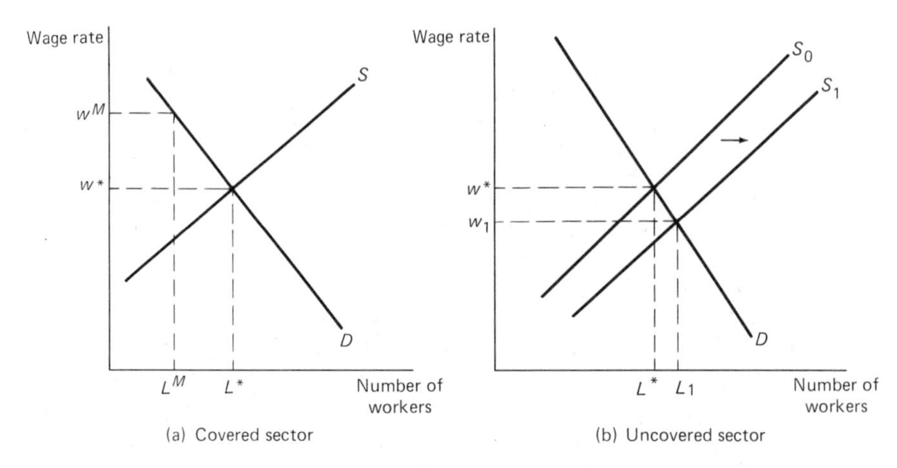

FIGURE 3.9 Employment and Wage Effects of a Minimum Wage with an Uncovered Sector

quite low, we can skip that argument here and examine it later in the analytically similar but more plausible case of collective bargaining. A second argument, usually referred to as the **shock effect**, goes like this. If a minimum wage is established and wage rates rise, affected firms will be compelled to become more efficient to compensate for the higher labor costs. They will, it is said, do things they should have done anyway, with the net result being higher productivity and no reduction in employment. Minimum wage legislation is thus represented as an unambiguously good thing. The problem with this kind of argument is that it assumes that firms are fundamentally inefficient without demonstrating why that is so. In fact, most economists conclude just the opposite—that the presence of competition compels firms to be efficient. If so, the shock effect argument loses virtually all its power.

Finally, it is sometimes argued that minimum wage legislation offers protection from "unfair," low wages. That may well be so—it is a normative issue—but it is important to remember that equilibrium wages are not just random numbers, but actually derive from genuine supply and demand forces. Attempts to change wage rates legislatively, without altering the conditions that cause those wages in the first place, will necessarily affect the employment of some workers.

Empirical Studies of the Effects of Minimum Wage Legislation

The theoretical analysis thus far makes clear predictions about the probable effects of minimum wage legislation, but it does not tell us how large those effects will be. But the size of those effects is extremely important for evaluating minimum wage policy. If, for example, the result of the minimum wage is that wages rise for many workers and employment is reduced relatively little, society might then decide that it makes good sense. The few without employment could, perhaps, be given economic assistance in some other way. If, however, the relevant labor demand curves were very elastic, so that employment fell sharply as a result of minimum wage legislation, we might reach a very different conclusion.

Determining the quantitative impact of minimum wage legislation has not been a simple task. There is, by now, a large body of empirical research about the effects of the minimum wage, and although the findings are quite consistent, they are not as strong as many economists would expect. The problem is a familiar one in economics—the available data simply are not very good. Ideally, economists would like to measure the impact of the minimum wage on the employment of workers who would otherwise have earned less than that. Unfortunately, there is no way to identify that group. Instead, researchers have focused on the effect of minimum wages on the employment of teenagers, since, as we saw above, a large proportion of them do work at about the minimum wage and might therefore have earned less than that otherwise. The usual empirical procedure is to relate changes in the minimum wage over time to corresponding changes in the proportion of teenagers who are employed.

Before turning to the findings, let's note some further complications and problems:

1. Not all teenagers are affected by the minimum wage. In 1980, over half of employed teens earned more than the minimum wage. Even those who do earn the minimum are not a homogeneous group.
2. The impact of the minimum wage on employment should depend on the gap between the minimum wage and the equilibrium wage that would have prevailed. But once the minimum wage is imposed, it is no longer possible to observe the equilibrium wage. Instead, economists measure how high the minimum wage is by expressing it as a fraction of the average hourly wage of nonsupervisory employees in the economy. When the minimum wage is relatively high compared to the average wage, the employment effects are expected to be large.

   There are two problems with using this measure. First, it may not always be a good proxy.[12] Second, there has not been very much variation in this measure over the last 20 years. It is frequently difficult to identify the effects of something when the changes are relatively small.
3. Many other things that may affect teenage employment also change over time, and these changes complicate the task of determining the impact of the minimum wage. For example, employment could increase from one year to the next, even though the minimum wage increased, if the increase coincides with rapid economic growth and very favorable economic con-

[12] For one thing, it is necessarily assumed that the true, unobserved wage for low-wage workers would have increased at the same rate as the observed average wage in the manufacturing sector. Considering among other things the sharp changes in the size of the teenage population in the 1970s and the increase in the labor supply of women, there is no reason to expect this to be true.

ditions. Alternatively, the increase in the size of the teenage population in the early 1970s—the result of the baby boom of the mid-1950s—could cause the proportion of employed teenagers to fall even when the minimum wage as a fraction of the average hourly wage was falling. (In both of these cases, what we want to know is how much higher employment would have been had it not been for the minimum wage.) It is necessary to control for these other influences, lest the effect of minimum wages be confounded.

Keeping all these problems in mind, let's look at the empirical findings. Most studies examine the period since 1954, when data on teenage employment first became available. Although each study differs slightly, the estimated effects on teenage employment are quite similar, ranging from a decline in teenage employment of from 1 to 3 percent due to a 10 percent increase in the minimum wage. In the most recent study,[13] the authors concluded that 1 percent was the most reasonable single estimate and that the effects were similar by both race and sex. Since there were about 8 million employed teenagers in 1982, this means that a 10 percent increase in the minimum wage would eliminate about 80,000 jobs. Taken at face value, these results suggest that the employment impact of the minimum wage is not severe. Alternatively, it is possible that the effect is greater than this but that the ability to measure it is severely limited.[14]

One final effect of minimum wage legislation is its impact on the income of workers and their families. Improving the standard of living for even the poorest segments of society was, after all, the original intent of the legislation. How effective is the minimum wage in this respect?

On this virtually all studies are in agreement: The minimum wage has very little impact on reducing poverty or on making the distribution of family income more equal. There are two major reasons. First, if the minimum wage is intended to alleviate poverty by providing an adequate wage to the primary income earner in a family, it is too low. Even full-time work at the minimum wage (which is rare) leaves a family under the official poverty threshhold.[15] Second, to the extent that the minimum wage enables some workers to receive higher wages than they would otherwise, this helps not only some adults in low-income households, but also many teenagers who still reside in households with substantial income. In one study[16] households were ranked according to

[13] For a summary of previous studies, see Charles Brown, Curtis Gilroy, and Andrew Kohn, "The Effect of the Minimum Wage on Employment and Unemployment," *Journal of Economic Literature*, (June 1982). Their own study, "Time-Series Evidence of the Minimum Wage on Youth Employment and Unemployment," appeared in the *Journal of Human Resources*, (Winter 1983).

[14] A few studies, using a very different research methodology, have found much larger effects. One such study is Peter Linneman, "The Economic Impact of Minimum Wage Laws: A New Look at an Old Question," *Journal of Political Economy*, (June 1982).

[15] For example, the poverty standard in 1978 for a family of four was $6,662. Full-time work at the minimum wage, then $2.65, earned a worker $5,512.

[16] William R. Johnson and Edgar K. Browning, "The Distributional and Efficiency Effects of Increasing the Minimum Wage: A Simulation," *American Economic Review*, (March 1983).

their total income in 1975 and were then placed into ten deciles, each containing exactly 10 percent of the population, in order of increasing income. Thus the first decile contained the poorest 10 percent of all families, the second decile the next poorest 10 percent, an so on, up to the tenth decile, which included the richest 10 percent of all families. The authors then looked at the corresponding distribution of minimum wage workers and found that minimum wage workers were distributed in almost equal percentages in every decile. For example, 11.5 percent of all minimum wage workers were in the lowest decile, but 11.1 percent were in the highest decile. In low-income households there were usually adults who were the only income earner, whereas in higher-income families, the minimum wage workers were almost always teenagers. As a result, increases in the minimum wage are unlikely to do very much to reduce the income gap between rich and poor families.

Substitutes, Complements, and Labor Market Analysis

How will changes in the number of skilled workers in the economy affect the wages of less skilled and semiskilled workers? How will increases in the number of working women affect the wages of working men or of younger workers? Will subsidies for capital investment help skilled workers more or unskilled workers more? These are the types of questions that the area of labor economics called **labor–labor substitution** is designed to answer.

To analyze these issues, we need to extend our analysis of labor demand from just two factors—labor and capital—to three or more. The simplest case is one in which there is still a single kind of capital, but there are now two or more distinct kinds of labor—perhaps skilled, semiskilled, and unskilled workers; young and old; male and female; college educated and high school educated. This may seem like an innocent extension, but it is sufficient to allow us to analyze a wide range of interesting labor market problems and public policy issues.

To analyze this more complicated production situation, we need to introduce a new set of terms. Different factors of production are said to be **complements** or **substitutes** depending on whether having more of one factor makes a second factor more productive or less productive. If, for instance, increasing the amount of capital increases the MP_L curve of workers by making them more productive, then labor and capital are complements in the production process. If the same change reduced the MP_L curve—think of a machine making a worker unnecessary—they are substitutes. If there is no effect at all, the two factors are called **independent** factors.

You might expect that factors that are relatively close to each other in terms of their skill level will be substitutes. In this case, both groups could perform essentially the same job, but the more skilled group could do it somewhat better or faster than the other group. Similarly, the more different the two groups are in skill level, the more likely they are to be either complements or independent factors. In that case they might either work together, doing different tasks, or work completely independent of each other.

When factors of production are interrelated, as in the case of substitutes or complements, a change in the price of one factor will eventually affect the prices of the other factors as well. Consider, for example, a fall in the wage of one group of workers, perhaps as a result of an increase in their supply curve or the advent of a government program.[17] Normally, if the wage changes, a firm will adjust its use of that factor. But it will not stop there. It will now also want to adjust its use of all factors which are substitutes for and complements of that factor. These second-order effects are *shifts* in the factor demand curves rather than movements along them. Moreover, if the initial change is one that is common to most firms, as is likely for broad demographic changes or for government policies, the total market demand curves for these factors will be affected as well. (Recall from Chapter 2 that the total demand curve is derived from the labor demand curves of the firms.) Finally, the demand curve changes lead to a change in the equilibrium wage or price for those factors of production.

We can be quite specific about the changes in wages that are likely to occur. If the two groups are complements, the changes will be in opposite directions; for example, a fall in the wage for group A would increase the use of A, which would increase the demand curve for its complement, group B, which would increase B's wage. For substitutes, the changes are in the same direction: If the wage of one group falls, the wage of its substitute will also fall, owing to a decline in the demand for its (the substitute's) services. Figure 3.10 shows these effects for the case in which there is a fall in the wage rate for a group of workers. In panel (a), the two factors are complements, so the demand and wage rate rises; in panel (b), they are substitutes, and both the factor demand and wage fall. If the initial effect had, instead, been an increase in the wage rate, panel (a) would represent the case for a substitute and (b) would be that of a complement.

Now we can look at the effects of the types of policy changes that we posed originally. Consider first changes in the number of working women and the possible effects on male wage rates. If there were complete occupational segregation by sex, so that men and women worked in separated sectors of the economy, male labor and female labor would be independent factors. The wage effects of the increased female supply would be confined to their own wages and men would be unaffected. Suppose, instead, that men and women did work together, but in a strict hierarchical fashion in which men held supervising positions and women performed production tasks. In that event the two factors would probably be complements. The increased

[17] Relevant government programs include wage subsidy programs such as the Targeted Jobs Credit for low-skilled workers. There have also been increases in the supply curve of working women and in the teenage population.

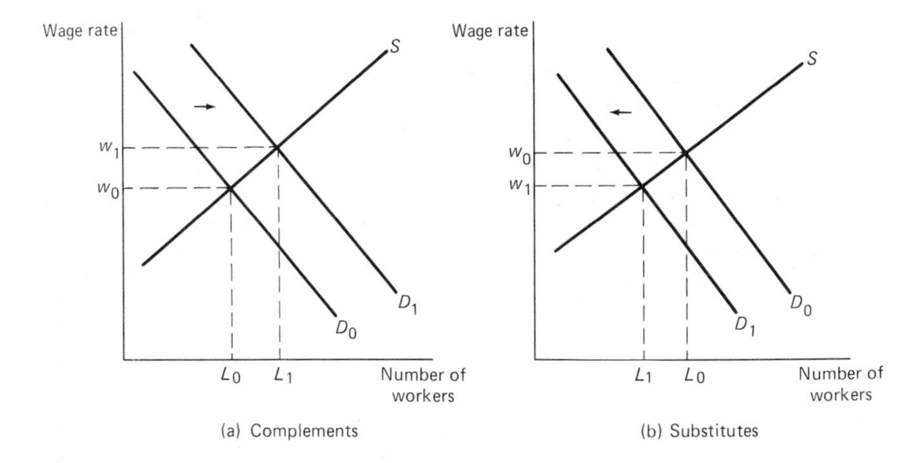

FIGURE 3.10 The Effects of a Wage Decrease for One Input on the Demand for Complements and Substitutes

number of women production workers would increase the demand for male supervisors and thus actually increase male wages. Finally, in a nondiscriminatory society in which men and women of equal skill were treated equally, the two groups would be substitutes. Both men's and women's wages would fall when female labor supply rose.

The effects of wage rates of government programs to increase capital investment can be analyzed similarly. If the least skilled workers were substitutes with capital and the most skilled were complements, increased capital investment would tend to reduce the wages of less-skilled workers and increase those of more skilled workers. Since the wages of the less skilled workers were lower initially, the result is that the distribution of income would become more unequal. The wage gap between skilled and unskilled would rise. So might the gap between the incomes of black and white workers if blacks are more concentrated in the less skilled categories.

The empirical task of determining the relevant production relationships is a very complicated one. As in much empirical work in economics, the available information does not correspond exactly to the underlying economic theory. (Sometimes the correspondence is distressingly inexact.) Thus the results are still somewhat tentative and need to be interpreted cautiously. The following findings stand out thus far:[18]

1. Capital and skilled labor are complements, but capital and unskilled workers tend to be substitutes. Thus our discussion about the possible effects of

[18] These findings are summarized in Daniel S. Hamermesh and James Grant, "Econometric Studies of Labor–Labor Substitution and Their Implications for Policy," *The Journal of Human Resources*, (Fall, 1979), and in Grant and Hamermesh, "Labor Market Competition among Youths, White Women and Others," *The Review of Economics and Statistics*, (August 1981). A simpler treatment of these issues is contained in Hamermesh's article, "Substitution and Labor Market Policy," *Challenge*, (January–February 1980).

increased capital investment on the relative wages of unskilled and skilled workers has some validity.

2. Youth (ages 14-24) and adult white women (ages 25-64) appear to be strong substitutes, based on information as of 1970. If so, the recent increase in the labor supply of women would reduce the demand for younger workers. Typically, this would lead to a reduction in youth wage rates, but in this case there is the complication of minimum wage legislation, which prevents downward adjustment in wage rates. If wage rates are not flexible, the induced decline in the demand for youth labor would reduce employment opportunities rather than wage rates. Although this evidence is not conclusive, it suggests that there may be a link between the employment problems of teenagers in the 1970s and 1980s and the increased labor force activity of women.

   One more caveat is in order concerning this result. The statistical study tells us how youths and adult white women were treated by employers in 1970, a result that could reflect prevailing discrimination as well as worker's skills. Studies of a more recent period in which employment opportunities for women were better might give a different result.

3. All demographic groups for which information is available—youth, adult blacks, adult white men, and adult white women—appear to be complements with capital. This is not too surprising because each demographic group includes a large number of skilled workers for whom the complementarity with capital is expected. The result does allay the concern that increased capital investment could increase the wage gap between white and black workers.

The theory of complementarity and substitutability relationships among factors of production does not itself provide an exact answer to public policy issues. But like the most useful portions of economic theory, it does provide an analytical framework for addressing the issues. It helps a researcher pose the relevant questions and helps avoid the obvious errors of ignoring the interrelationships among factor prices.

SUMMARY

In this chapter we considered several extensions of the basic theory of labor demand. In the first section we investigated the effects of different market structures on the demand for labor. We found that monopoly in the product market did not affect wage rates as long as the labor market was competitive. But when there was only a single demander of labor—what we called monopsony—both wages and employment would be reduced compared to a competitive market. We also noted that except for some specialized labor markets, monopsony power is unlikely to be an important real-world factor.

We then considered how the demand for labor would be affected when a firm could adjust its capital stock as well as its employment when there was a change in the wage rate. We noted that the wage rate affected employment both via a firm's cost-minimizing decision about *how* to produce and its profit-maximizing decision about *how much* to produce. Changes in how to produce when the wage changed gave rise to a substitution effect, and changes in how much to produce resulted in an output effect. Together, those two responses constitute a firm's long-run adjustment to a change in the wage rate, and the long-run labor demand curve reflects those changes. We concluded that the long-run labor demand curve was more elastic than the underlying short-run labor demand curves.

We also introduced the oft-used economic concept of elasticity, in this case the relationship between the percentage change in employment and the percentage change in the wage rate. We defined the various categories of elasticity and noted its rough correspondence to the slope of a labor demand curve. In the last part of the section, the four Hicks–Marshall rules concerning the elasticity of derived demand were presented. These rules summarize the factors that influence the elasticity of a labor demand curve.

In the last part of the chapter, we considered two applications of labor demand theory. With downward-sloping demand curves for labor, the imposition of a minimum wage that is above the equilibrium wage rate will either reduce employment or reduce wages elsewhere. The extensive empirical literature on the effects of minimum wage legislation in the United States has not documented a large negative effect on teenage employment, but neither does the legislation do much to improve the distribution of income among families. Finally, we briefly examined the area of labor–labor substitution. If the substitutability–complementarity relationships among factors of production are known, it is possible to predict how changes in the wage or employment of one factor will affect all the other groups.

New Concepts

Imperfect competition
Monopoly
Oligopoly
Monopolistic competition
Monopsony
Oligopsony
Marginal labor cost
Monopsonistic exploitation
Labor intensive
Capital intensive
Isoquant
Substitution effect
Output (scale) effect

Wage elasticity
Laws of derived demand
Covered sector
Uncovered sector
Shock effect
Labor–labor substitution
Substitutes and complements

APPENDIX: The Isoquant–Isocost Line Approach to Input Choice

It is possible to be much more precise about a firm's choice of an input combination along an isoquant by introducing the idea of an **isocost line**. Just as an isoquant shows all input combinations that give the same output, an isocost line shows all input combinations that *cost* the same amount. Since the total input cost is just the amount paid for capital plus the amount paid for labor, the general algebraic expression of an isocost line is

$$wL + rK = C \tag{A3.1}$$

where C is a designated level of total cost and r is the price of a unit of capital. If C, w, and r are known, we can find the set of K,L combinations that satisfy equation (A3.1)—that is, their combined cost is exactly \$C.

To graph an isocost line, it is convenient to express equation (A3.1) in a form in which K depends on all the other terms:

$$K = \frac{C}{r} - \frac{w}{r}L \tag{A3.2}$$

This is the equation of a straight line whose Y-intercept is C/r—the maximum amount of K that can be bought if no L at all is used—and whose slope is $-(w/r)$—the negative of the ratio of the input prices.

A representative isocost line is drawn in Figure A3.1. The axes of an isocost line graph are exactly the same as the graph of an isoquant. Just as we represented the amount of output implicitly in the isoquant graph, here we do the same for total cost. All the K,L combinations along the line cost exactly \$$C$ at the current values of w and r. The two extreme points, A and B, represent the maximum amounts of K and L, respectively, which could be bought for that expenditure at those input prices. To be concrete, suppose that C = \$1000, w = \$4 per hour, and r, interpreted as the rental price of an hour of capital's services, is \$5 per hour. Then the maximum amount of

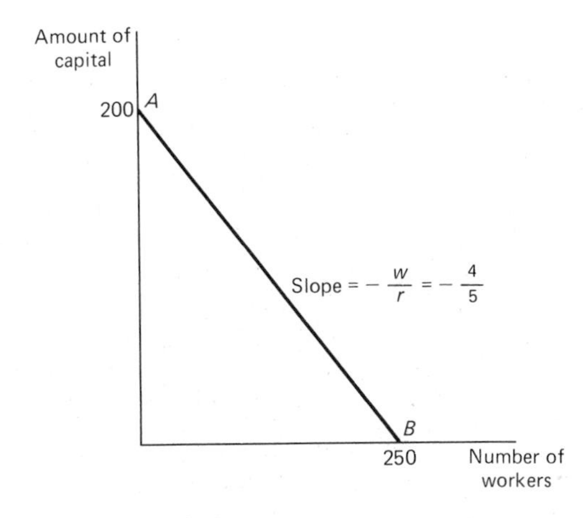

FIGURE A3.1 Isocost Line for w = \$4, r = \$5, c = \$1000

K that could be obtained for \$1000 is C/r = \$1000/\$5 = 200 units and the maximum amount of labor is 250 (= \$1000/\$4). The slope of this isocost line is $-w/r = -\frac{4}{5}$.

An isocost line is drawn for specific values of w, r, and C, so whenever they change, the line changes its position or slope. Changes in C are easiest: The slope is unchanged, so the line shifts in a parallel fashion, moving in for lower cost levels and out for higher ones. Continuing our previous arithmetic example, if C were doubled to \$2000, the maximum K would double to 400 (= \$2000/\$5) and the maximum L would be 500 (= \$2000/\$4).

Changes in w or r affect the slope of the isocost line. The important point to remember here is that the slope depends on the ratio of w to r, so that an increase in the wage rate has the same effect on the slope as does a decline in the rental price of capital. If the wage rises, the isocost line becomes steeper, pivoting around point A; the maximum K is unchanged, but the maximum L would now be smaller. Similarly, if r fell, the maximum L would be unchanged, but the maximum K would rise, also making the line steeper. You should be able to convince yourself that a rise in r or a fall in w would both make the line flatter. Finally, what would happen to the slope if w and r both rose proportionately? Answer: nothing. Each input combination would cost more than before, but the slope would not be changed because the original ratio of w to r was preserved.

Linking isoquants with isocost lines allows us to characterize cost-minimizing input choice more formally. Identifying the least expensive way to produce a given level of output is equivalent to finding the point on an isoquant that lies on the lowest feasible isocost line. Graphically, this has a special representation: The cost-minimizing input combination occurs where an isoquant is tangent to an isocost line. Figure A3.2 shows this. Suppose that we

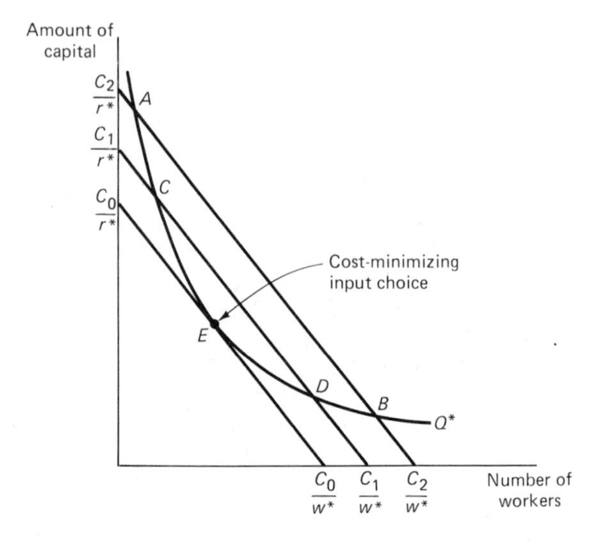

FIGURE A3.2 Determination of the Cost-Minimizing Input Choice

are trying to determine the cost-minimizing input combination for output level Q^*, given input prices w^* and r^*. Three parallel isocost lines with slopes equal to $-w^*/r^*$ are drawn, for cost levels C_0, C_1, and C_2. Output Q^* could be produced with the input combinations represented by points A and B at cost C_2 or as at points C and D, with a lower cost level, C_1. But the least-cost input combination is point E, where the isoquant has the same slope as the isocost line. No lower isocost line provides a large enough expenditure to produce Q^*, and all higher ones are more costly. Thus the cost-minimizing input choice is characterized graphically by a tangency between an isocost line, representing the input prices, and an isoquant, representing the required amounts of inputs.

In the main body of the text, we concluded that when the wage rate was relatively high, a firm would choose an input combination that was relatively capital intensive and it would do exactly the opposite when the wage was low compared to the price of capital. That idea is shown in Figure A3.3, which shows a typical isoquant together with two different isocost lines for different w and r combinations. When the wage rate is relatively low, the isocost line is relatively flat like MM' and the cost-minimizing input choice for output Q_o will be far down the isoquant. Point A in the figure shows this. But if the wage were higher—or the price of capital lower—the isocost line would be steeper (NN'). If the firm were to continue to produce Q_o, it would now choose a point like B where the capital-to-labor ratio was higher.

Finally, we can now show the substitution and output effects of a change in the wage rate. Consider the case of an increase in the wage rate. Figure

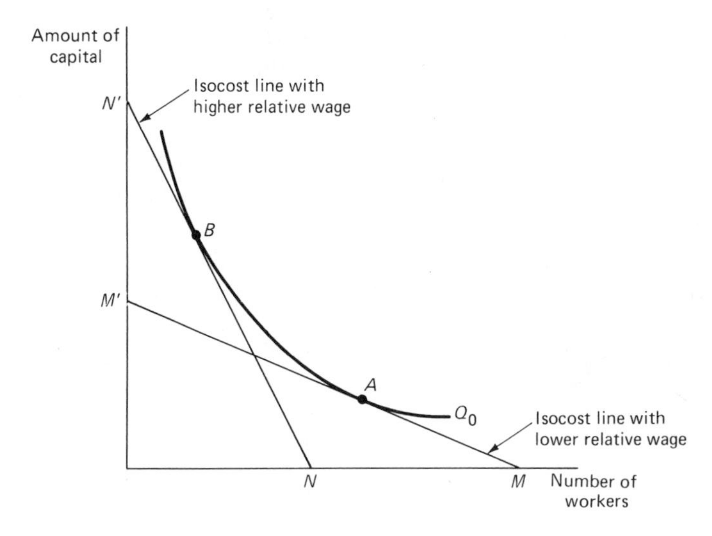

FIGURE A3.3 Input Choices with Different Relative Factor Prices

A3.4 represents the situation. Initially, the firm is producing Q_1 units of output using the input combination represented by point A. When the wage rises, the isocost line becomes steeper, and if the firm were to continue production at Q_1, it would now move along the isoquant to point B. This movement is

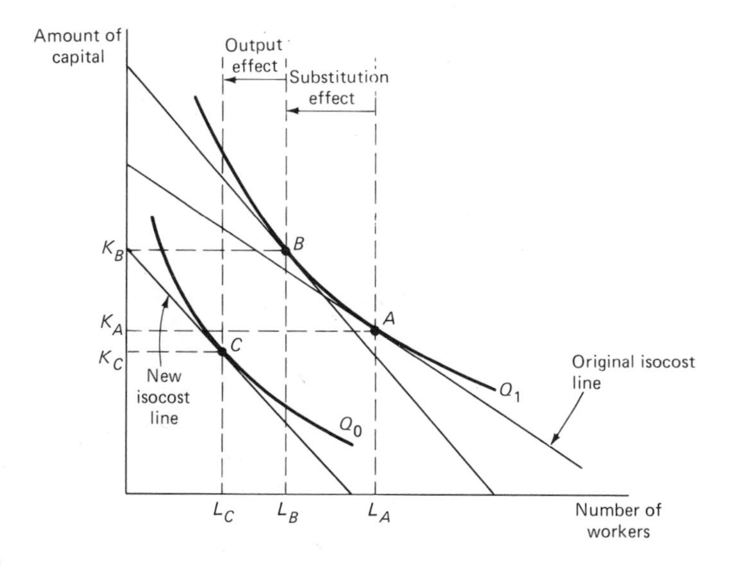

FIGURE A3.4 Substitution and Output Effects of a Wage Increase

the substitution effect; the use of labor falls from L_A to L_B while capital rises from K_A to K_B. The output effect represents the input adjustments that occur when output is reduced, at the new set of input prices. Graphically, we draw in a lower isocost line, parallel to the steeper isocost line which is tangent to isoquant Q_1 at B. It is not possible to identify exactly how large the output reduction will be nor exactly how the capital-to-labor ratio will be affected. One possibility is an input combination such as point C. The output effect, as shown, is L_A-L_C and the total effect is L_A-L_C, the sum of the substitution and output effects. The corresponding long-run labor demand curve is composed of points such as A and C.

4

Labor Supply

INTRODUCTION

In this chapter and the next, we shift our attention from the demand side of the labor market to the supply side, from the behavior of firms to the behavior of individuals. In Chapter 2 we drew a labor supply curve for the economy as a whole that was upward sloping, but we did not explain why that might be true, nor did we pay any attention to the underlying behavior of individuals. Now it is time to examine the labor supply curve with more care. Theoretical completeness will not be the only reward. Many aspects of labor supply have attracted an enormous amount of public policy attention in recent years. Many government programs and policies—from Social Security to welfare to the tax system—affect a person's wage rate or wealth and thus have potential effects on labor supply decisions.

Labor supply can be measured and analyzed in a number of different ways and from several perspectives. One way is to focus on how many hours a person would choose to work at different wage rates—in other words, construct a person's supply curve of labor. For other purposes it is useful to note simply whether or not a person chooses to work. Economists refer to that as **labor force participation**. For still other purposes, we may be interested in considering not whether a person works, or how much he or she works, but in what occupation or with what set of skills. That topic involves understanding the qualitative aspects of individual labor supply rather than its quantitative measure.

In this chapter and the following one, we focus on the quantitative features of individual labor supply. We begin by considering, using a very simple model, how people decide how many hours to work. From that we will derive a labor supply curve, first for an individual and then for the market as a whole. This chapter concludes by taking an in-depth look at two important current policy issues which involve labor supply analysis: the effect of the welfare system on the labor suppply of low-income persons and the effect of the income tax system on the labor supply of high-income persons.

Chapter 5 continues the analysis of quantitative labor supply. The first part of the chapter discusses a different, broader, and more complex model of individual labor supply. The latter part turns to the second quantitative measure of labor supply: the rate of labor force participation.

The analysis of labor quality deserves a separate chapter, not only because it is such an important topic, but also because it is quite different from the material to be presented in this chapter and the next. It moves the analysis of labor markets away from a world of homogeneous workers and into a more complicated one in which workers are heterogeneous, largely as a result of their own endeavors. An entire branch of labor economics, called the human capital model, has been developed in the past two decades to address labor quality issues. The human capital model is the subject of Chapters 6 and 7.

THE ECONOMIC ANALYSIS OF INDIVIDUAL LABOR SUPPLY

A Simple Model of Labor Supply

Before we turn to the details of the analysis, one issue is worth addressing. Students often think that there is relatively little to decide about labor supply. After all, relatively few of us will ever negotiate directly with our employer about exactly how many hours we want to work. It often appears that workers face "take it or leave it" labor supply situations, in which the employer unilaterally sets the terms. Is there really any reason to analyze labor supply as if it were a matter of individual choice?

The answer is "yes" and it is important to understand why. First, there is much more choice than you may think. There is certainly variation among different occupations in the number of hours normally worked and in the amount of flexibility allowed, so job choice is one way to exercise a labor supply choice. If self-employment is treated as an option, the range of labor supply possibilities increases further. Moreover, there are a number of dimensions to labor supply, including hours per day, days per week, weeks per year, and even years per career. There is almost always some margin at which labor supply can be adjusted. (Even absenteeism can be a way of adjusting labor supply.) In most of this chapter we discuss labor supply in terms of hours per week, but that is primarily a matter of expositional convenience. The analysis and results apply more generally.

Second, and more important, even if work hours are fixed, it does not follow that the level at which they are fixed is independent of the labor supply preferences of individuals. Economists point out that it is in the economic interest of a firm to offer a fixed-length work week which is roughly consistent with their employees' preferences. In a competitive labor market, any firm that requires people to work more hours than they would freely choose to will have difficulty in attracting workers. The firm may find it necessary to pay a wage premium to induce workers to accept the otherwise undesirable labor supply terms. Thus, to avoid paying that wage premium, firms have an incentive to accommodate workers' preferences. This does not mean that every person will be able to find employment which exactly suits his or her labor supply preferences, but for preferences near the average, this should be roughly true. The important point, though, is that there is no reason to assume the absence of a choice process concerning a person's supply of labor.

Like any model, the simple model of labor supply includes a number of simplifying assumptions. Here are the major ones, together with an explanation of what they accomplish and what they entail.

First, it is assumed that a person spends his or her time doing one of two things: working or enjoying leisure. In this usage, work means time spent in paid employment, and leisure refers to all unpaid uses of time which provide utility. (Recall that utility means satisfaction or pleasure.) Given this assumption, it follows that hours of work and hours of leisure are automatically inversely related to each other. If leisure hours rise, work hours must fall, and vice versa. It is impossible to change one without changing the other equivalently in the opposite direction.

By virtue of this simplification, we can analyze labor supply *directly*, or if we prefer, we can approach it *indirectly* by focusing on a person's demand for leisure and recognizing the link between the two. In fact, that is the way in which economists usually analyze labor supply. That may seem like a peculiar thing to do, but it is actually a clever transformation of the problem which greatly facilitates the analysis. In particular, it enables economists to draw on the well-established ideas of consumer demand theory to analyze individual choices about labor supply.

Although this assumption is extremely useful, it is, admittedly, not very accurate. Very few of us find ourselves doing nothing but enjoying leisure in our nonworking time. Rather, we actually spend much of our leisure time doing things for which we receive no pay, but which are not in and of themselves enjoyable—such activities as shopping, cleaning, caring for a sick child, painting a house, and so on. The reason we do those things is that we derive utility from the final product—a clean house or a healthy child. Still, in terms of the definitions above, activities such as these qualify as neither work nor leisure. As far as this simple model is concerned, it is as if those activities did not exist.

This may sound like a glaring omission, but it turns out not to matter very much for analyzing labor supply choices. Both leisure and nonmarket work time share a crucial feature—they are time spent not earning income. Moreover, both do create utility, the difference being that one does so directly and the other indirectly. Analytically, there is not really much difference between the two. For the moment, then, we can informally include nonmarket work time in the leisure category.[1]

Second, it is common to assume that a person has a constant hourly wage rate and can work as many hours as he or she wants at that wage. This enables the analysis of labor supply to focus exclusively on how many hours a person wants to work without worrying about whether there might be limitations on that choice. If limitations do exist, we can think of them later as constraints on a person's choices.

The final assumptions concern the general nature of a person's behavior and preferences. There are three principal ideas here. First, we assume that people seek to maximize their **utility**, an assumption that parallels the idea of profit maximization on the part of a firm. Second, for analyzing labor supply choices, it is useful to think of people as drawing utility from just two

[1] Alternatively, think of the time spent on those nonleisure, nonwork activities as taking up a fixed amount of time. The model then concerns the time not spent in those activities.

broad categories—leisure time (l) on the one hand and all goods and services (G) on the other. Note that work is not itself usually regarded as a source of either utility of disutility—something that common experience suggests is probably untrue. For better or worse, work is often an integral part of a person's sense of well-being. Nevertheless, in this simple model, time at work serves simply as the link between the consumption of leisure and the consumption of goods. Working more hours means simultaneously enjoying less leisure but consuming more goods. With fewer hours of work, there would be more leisure but fewer goods.

Finally, economists assume that both the consumption of leisure and the consumption of goods are subject to **diminishing marginal utility**, which means that the *additional* utility derived from each *additional* hour of leisure or quantity of goods is declining. In other words, the more leisure you already have, the less valuable yet another hour is likely to be. Exactly the same idea applies to the consumption of goods and services.

The idea of diminishing marginal utility is illustrated in Figure 4.1, which shows marginal utility (MU) schedules for goods and leisure. The height of the curves shows the marginal utility associated with each additonal hour of leisure and unit of goods. As you can see, marginal utility is falling—the curves are downward sloping.

Do not confuse falling marginal utility with falling total utility. The same relationship holds here as in the case of marginal product and total output. As long as marginal utility is positive, total utility is still increasing. Diminishing marginal utility simply means that total utility rises more slowly.

There is no reason to think that everyone has the same preferences—and no need to. People who get great satisfaction from leisure will have higher MU curves for leisure, whereas those who crave material pleasures will have

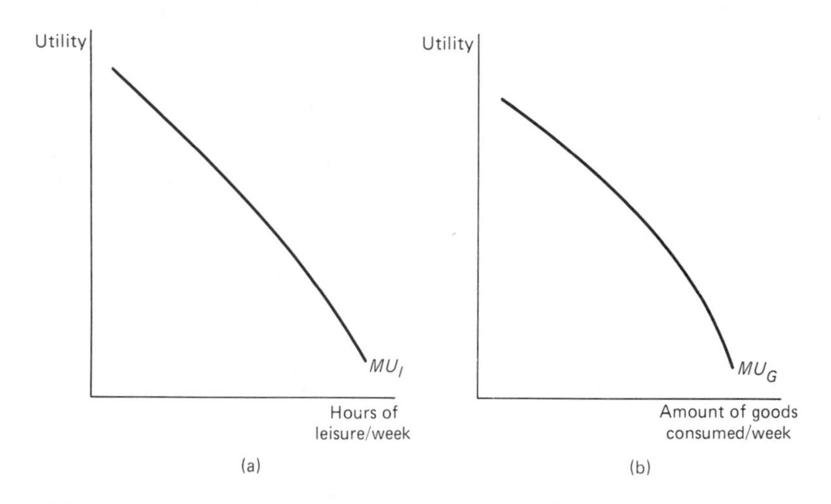

FIGURE 4.1 Marginal Utility Schedules for Leisure and Goods

higher MU curves for goods. But the important point is that the MU curve will always be downward sloping.

Utility Maximization and Labor Supply[2]

In many ways, the analysis of labor supply parallels the analysis of labor demand. In that analysis, we posed the following question: Given a firm's technology, the wage rate, and the price of its product, how much labor should it employ to maximize its profits? Here we ask: Given preferences for leisure and goods, a wage rate, and the prices of all goods and services, how many hours should a person work to maximize his or her utility? A firm's labor demand curve describes how that choice changes when the wage changes. A person's labor supply curve does exactly the same for hours of work.

We noted above that economists usually analyze labor supply indirectly by focusing on a person's **utility-maximizing** choice of leisure and goods and then using the link between labor and leisure to derive the corresponding amount of labor supplied to the market. Viewed this way, a person is engaged in a process of buying goods and leisure in order to maximize utility. The idea of buying goods is familiar, but what does it mean to "buy leisure?" Obviously, there is no store at which leisure is bought, nor is there any explicit cash transaction involved in purchasing it. Rather, you buy it from yourself, and its price is the income you forgo by taking one more hour of leisure and thus working one hour less. Since, by the second assumption of the model, you can work as many hours as you like at a constant wage rate, that wage rate is the income forgone. Thus the price of leisure is the wage rate—it measures the opportunity cost of enjoying an hour of leisure.

Now the problem can be posed in the familiar terms of consumer choice theory. Let the price of all goods and services be denoted by p (think of p as a price index that measures the average price of all goods together) and let w be the wage rate. Then the utility-maximizing choice of leisure and goods must always satisfy the following equality:

$$\frac{MU_l}{w} = \frac{MU_G}{p} \tag{4.1}$$

where the equality holds for the last hour of leisure and the last unit of goods bought.

This idea may be familiar to you from a previous course in microeconomics. It is a universal rule for utility maximization, whether the choice is between leisure and goods or among a vast array of consumer goods. To see the logic of the rule, consider what happens when the equality does not

[2] For a more formal exposition of the ideas in this section, using the graphical technique of indifference curves and budget lines, see the Appendix to this chapter.

hold. To simplify, suppose that $w = p$ and that at the currently chosen consumption levels of leisure and goods, $MU_l > MU_G$. Could that be a utility-maximizing choice? Since goods have low marginal utility and leisure a high marginal utility, it is both sensible and feasible (since $w = p$) to work one hour less, consume fewer goods, and take one more hour of leisure. In doing so, you would give up utility equal to MU_G, but gain the larger amount, MU_l. Clearly, utility rises. If $MU_l < MU_G$ and ($w = p$), it would be sensible to give up leisure, work more, and enjoy more goods. In this example, only when $MU_l = MU_G$ is it *impossible* to alter your current decision and increase your utility.

Exactly the same logic applies even where $w \neq p$. Then, if $MU_l/w > MU_G/p$, utility can be increased by working less, consuming fewer goods, and taking more leisure, while the opposite adjustment would be appropriate if the inequality was reversed. Only when the equality of equation (4.1) holds is no improvement in utility possible.

Indirectly, this utility-maximizing choice of leisure and goods determines the number of hours a person will want to work. The time not spent in leisure is the time spent at work, and that amount is one point on a person's labor supply curve. It is the number of hours it is utility maximizing to work given the wage rate, the price of goods and services, and the person's preferences for leisure and goods.

This analysis framework readily accommodates differences among individuals in their preferences for goods or leisure. For "goods preferrers" the entire MU_G schedule is high, so the necessary equality of equation (4.1) will involve many goods (to make their MU_G low) and relatively less leisure. Similarly, "leisure preferrers" will find the equality satisfied only when the amount of leisure is large, thus driving down the value of the last hour. In labor supply terms, the goods preferrer will choose to work a large number of hours, whereas the leisure preferrer will work less, assuming that the wage rate is the same for both.

The Supply Curve of Labor

A labor supply curve shows the amount of labor that a person will choose to supply at various wage rates, holding everything else (prices, nonlabor income, preferences) constant. In economics we are accustomed to thinking of supply curves as being upward sloping, but a labor supply curve is quite unlike the supply curves used to describe a firm's production choices. This supply curve is actually a leisure demand curve in disguise. To understand how an increase in the wage will affect a person's labor supply, we need to examine how an increase in the price of leisure will affect a person's demand for leisure.

It is useful to begin by considering not the demand for leisure, but the demand for an ordinary consumer good—oranges, gasoline, television sets, and the like. When the price of a commodity goes up, there are always two separate effects on how much of that product a person will buy. First, there is an incentive to substitute other similar products for this one, because the other products are now *relatively* cheaper. Second, the price increase affects the amount demanded by reducing a person's *real* income. This effect is subtler and also usually less important. It is not that a person's *actual* income is any lower, but the purchasing power of that income is reduced by virtue of the price increase. A person's original income now buys a smaller amount of goods and services than before, exactly as if his or her income had been suddenly cut. Consequently, there must be some reduction in total consumption in order to bring expenditures in line with income. Often this is accomplished by making small reductions in the amount bought of many goods, including the one whose price went up in the first place. Thus there is a further reduction in quantity demanded.

Economists refer to these two effects as the **substitution effect** and the **income effect**, respectively. Both occur simultaneously when the price of a good changes and a person's change in quantity demanded incorporates both effects. Solely for analytical purposes, economists pretend that the two changes occur in sequence, first one and then the other. The substitution effect then refers to the change that would occur if the price changed but there was no simultaneous change in real income. (Since there is, in fact, a change in income, economists imagine that at the same time that the price changes, there is a compensating change in the person's income that just eliminates the real income change of the price change.) A person's subsequent response to the actual change in real income is then used to isolate the income effect.

It is usually the case that substitution and income effects reinforce each other. When the price of some good rises, a person will buy less of it both because it is now relatively more expensive (even if his or her income were not reduced) and also because he or she is now in reality a bit poorer. Conversely, if the price fell, both effects would cause the quantity demanded to rise. The result is the familiar **Law of Demand**—price and quantity are inversely related.

The chain of events described above actually applies only for **normal goods**—goods whose consumption increases when a person's income rises and falls when that income falls. There are some goods, however, whose consumption falls as income rises and rises as income falls. Economists call them **inferior goods**[3] and if you try to trace through the logic of income and substitution effects, you will discover that something peculiar occurs. Income and substitution effects always conflict for an inferior good, because the

[3] Exactly which goods are inferior goods varies from one person to the next. Cheap cuts of meat, rice, potatoes, cheap wine and beer, artificially flavored ice cream, and long-distance bus travel are common examples. To identify your own, try to imagine what your consumption pattern will be like in the future when your income is higher. Any good whose consumption you hope to reduce from its current level is an inferior good.

income effect is reversed. An increase in price still makes a person poorer, but that reduction in income now causes consumption to rise, not fall. If the income effect is stronger than the substitution effect (which is not changed), it is possible, although unlikely, that the Law of Demand may not hold. Demand curves could be upward sloping for strongly inferior goods.[4]

Whether a good is normal or inferior, it is usually true that the income effect on quantity demanded is small. First, the actual amount by which a person is made richer or poorer when a price increases or decreases is often relatively small. If you are currently buying a gallon of milk a week and if its price goes up by $0.25 per gallon, you are poorer by only about $1 per month. Unless the quantity demand and/or the price increase is very large, the actual income change is not likely to be large. Even then, the reduced income affects the consumption not just of the good whose price increased, but of all goods. Thus the total change in quantity demanded due to the income effect of a price change is frequently of secondary significance.

Suppose that we apply this analysis to the effects of a change in the wage rate on the amount of leisure demanded. When we know what the leisure demand curve looks like, we can easily derive the corresponding labor supply curve. Common sense suggests that leisure is probably a normal good, something that most people want more of when their income rises. Thus you might reason that a wage *increase* would necessarily *reduce* the amount of leisure demanded. Just as in the case of an ordinary product, the income and substitution effects would work together to cause a person to buy less leisure. Viewed in terms of labor supply, a wage increase would therefore always lead to an increase in hours of work. The labor supply curve would be upward sloping.

There is, however, a flaw in that reasoning. In the case of leisure demand, the income effect of a price change is peculiar in yet a different way. In the analysis of price changes for ordinary consumer goods, a person was always made poorer when the price of a product went up. But when the price of leisure—the wage rate—rises, a person certainly is not made poorer. Quite the opposite. A wage increase always makes you richer, since any number of hours worked now produces a larger income than before. The reason the income change is reversed is simple. In the usual case, a person is exclusively a buyer of the product in question, but in this case the person is both a buyer of leisure and a seller of labor. Thus, when the wage increases, he or she faces a higher price as a buyer, but simultaneously enjoys a higher income as a seller.

The result of this is that *the income and substitution effects of a wage change will conflict even though leisure is a normal good.* A wage increase

[4] Goods with upward-sloping demand curves are called *Giffen goods* after Sir Robert Giffen, who claimed to have observed the phenomenon following a sharp rise in the price of potatoes in Ireland during the nineteenth century.

does raise the price of leisure, and if a person were made neither richer nor poorer, he or she would find it advantageous to substitute goods for leisure as a source of utility. Thus the substitution effect of a wage increase causes the amount of labor supplied to increase. But the person is simultaneously richer and better able to afford leisure, even at its now-higher price. Moreover, the resulting change in income is often large, precisely because the amount of labor supplied just before the wage increase is often large. For a person working forty hours per week, an increase of $0.25 per hour results in an income increase of $10 per week. Thus the income effect causes the person to choose more goods and more leisure, thereby reducing the number of hours worked. The income and substitution effects necessarily conflict.

To make sure that you understand the logic here, think about the effects of a fall in wages. On the one hand, leisure is now relatively cheaper and thus, through the substitution effect, there is an economic incentive to increase the amount of leisure and decrease both the amount of labor supplied and the amount of goods consumed. On the other hand, the person is now poorer. The original combination of leisure and goods is no longer feasible. Both the amount of goods and the amount of leisure will be reduced, which means that the amount of time spent working will increase. Again, the income and substitution effects conflict.

What, then, can economists conclude about the probable shape of a person's demand curve for leisure and supply curve of labor? Do desired hours of work rise or fall when the wage rate rises? The answer is that we really cannot know, on the basis of theoretical inquiry alone, because economic theory cannot tell us whether the income or substitution effect is stronger. The logical possibilities are summarized in Table 4.1. If the substitution effect is stronger than the income effect, a wage increase causes hours of work to increase and a wage decrease causes hours of work to fall. If, however, the income effect is stronger, the results are exactly the opposite. A person's labor supply curve will, therefore, be positively sloped if the substitution effect outweighs the income effect and negatively sloped when the income effect is stronger.

You may find this "nonresult" about the effects of wage increases on individual labor supply frustrating. What, you may ask, is the point of studying something only to conclude that there is no firm answer? To that, there are at least two answers. First, one function of intellectual inquiry is to determine what can be known with certainty and confidence. Knowing correctly that wage changes have an indeterminate effect on labor supply is absolutely preferable to assuming incorrectly that only a single response is sensible. Second, the analysis of income and substitution effects has applications both to policy issues of major importance and to features of everyday life. Do income taxes reduce labor supply, as the supply-side advocates argue? Does the welfare system reduce work incentives? Why do firms pay higher wage rates for overtime hours? How has the labor force activity of married women

TABLE 4.1 The Effects of a Wage Change on Hours of Work

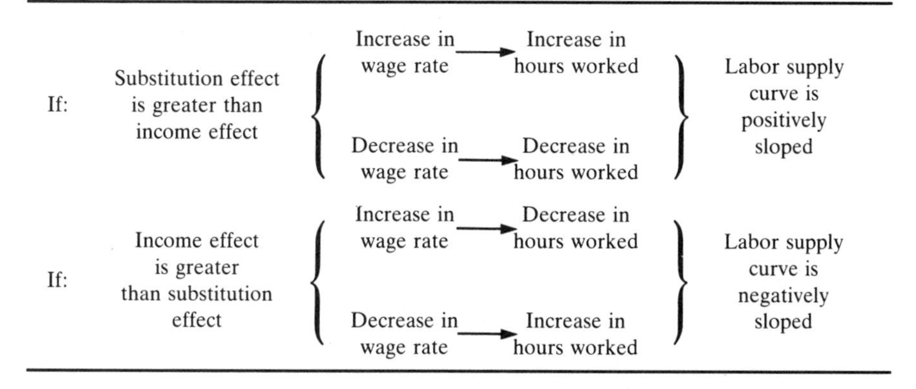

If:	Substitution effect is greater than income effect	Increase in wage rate → Increase in hours worked Decrease in wage rate → Decrease in hours worked		Labor supply curve is positively sloped
If:	Income effect is greater than substitution effect	Increase in wage rate → Decrease in hours worked Decrease in wage rate → Increase in hours worked		Labor supply curve is negatively sloped

been affected by changes in their potential wages and by technological changes that have made their work time at home more productive? The proper use of income and substitution effects is indispensable in answering such questions.

There is, in any event, a famous generalization about the shape of individual labor supply curves, known as the **backward-bending labor supply curve**. The underlying logic is this. Starting at a low wage, wage increases will, at first, often increase desired hours of work. People treat a higher wage primarily as an opportunity to increase their material standard of living, perhaps substantially. The income effect is "spent" mostly on additional goods and much less on leisure. But as both wages and hours worked increase, still further increases in the wage will eventually cause hours of work to fall. For one thing, the income change resulting from a given increase in the wage is larger the more hours a person is working.[5] This, by itself, would tend to strengthen the income effect relative to the substitution effect. In addition, though, additional goods may not be very highly desired if the standard of living already achieved is quite high. This would tend to weaken the substitution effect and also sway the income effect toward additional leisure rather than additional goods.

A typical backward-bending labor supply curve is shown in Figure 4.2. As the wage rate rises from w_0 to w_1, hours of work increase, but thereafter further increases in the wage cause labor supply to fall. Nothing in economic theory tells us at what point the labor supply curve shifts from a positive slope to a negative one. That depends on the preferences of individuals. But it is almost inevitable that a person's labor supply curve will eventually exhibit a

[5] The change in income created by a change in the wage is $L^*\triangle W$, where L is the number of hours currently worked. Obviously, the larger L is, the larger is the income change of a constant increase in the wage rate.

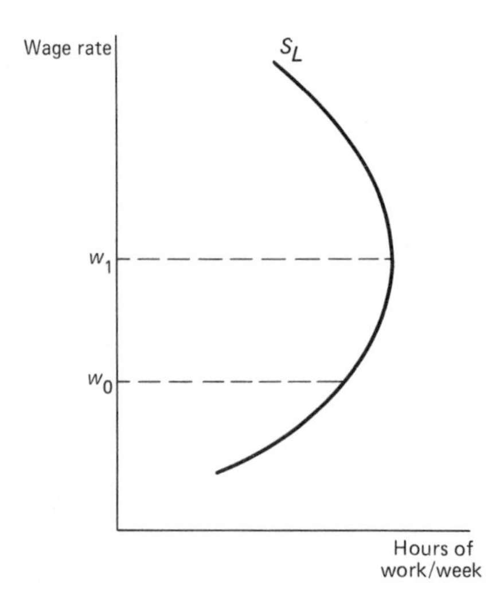

FIGURE 4.2 The Backward-Bending Supply Curve of Labor

negative slope. No matter how materialistic you are, there must be *some* higher wage rate ($20 per hour, $100 per hour, $1000 per hour) at which you could work less than now and still consume in lavish style. The important question, then, is at what level that might set in. Economists would ask: Is the labor supply curve backward bending in the relevant range of wage rates?

Application: *Overtime Pay and Labor Supply*

By federal law, most employees are paid time-and-a-half whenever they work more than eight hours a day or more than forty hours a week. Whether required or not, that practice often makes sense from the standpoint of a firm trying to increase the labor supply of its employees. The ideas of income and substitution effects are crucial for understanding the situation.

What could a firm do to increase the labor supply of its employees? One possibility is to offer higher wages, but whether this will be effective depends on whether the substitution effect of the higher price for leisure outweighs the income effect of being richer. An alternative strategy is to raise wages only for the additional hours in question—in other words, offer premium pay for overtime hours. Since this policy makes a person no richer at the original labor supply point, there is no income effect at all. But because the price of leisure increases, there is a substitution effect, causing a worker to supply additional labor hours.[6] The key is that the wage changes only "on the margin."

[6] There is actually one possible complication even here. Overtime pay makes a person richer at the end of a week than he or she would otherwise be. From the standpoint of future labor supply, this is a pure increase in income, and thus we might expect a worker to try to reduce future labor supply, if possible.

The analysis of overtime pay illustrates an important principle of general applicability in studying labor supply choices. To the extent that wage changes are effective only on the margin, as in the case of overtime pay, there is a substitution effect, but no potentially offsetting income effect. Similarly, anything that changes a person's income without changing the wage on the margin induces only an income effect. These conclusions will be invaluable later when we consider the labor supply effects of alternative tax systems.

The Market Supply Curve of Labor

Now that we have analyzed individual labor supply behavior, it is time to shift our attention from the supply curve of labor to the market as a whole. The basic idea is the same as in the construction of the market labor demand curve in Chapter 2: At each wage rate, we simply add up each person's desired hours. At a wage of w_1, this is $L_1^a + L_1^b + \cdots L_1^z$ for workers a to z, and similarly at wages w_2, w_3, and so on. Some of the L's may be zero at some wages, representing the case of a person who chooses not to work at that wage.

What does the market labor supply curve look like? When we first drew a labor supply curve in Chapter 2, we assumed that it was upward sloping. Now, however, we know that individual labor supply curves may well be backward bending. What does that imply about the shape of the labor supply curve? Will it be backward bending or even negatively sloped, like a demand curve?

In principle, it could be, but it is a bit less likely—at least in the "vicinity" of the equilibrium wage. There are two reasons. First, although some workers may reduce their work hours, others may do just the opposite. The result is uncertain, as long as preferences differ. Second, there are some people for whom wage increases cause only a substitution effect. They are persons who choose not to work at lower wages, but do find it worthwhile to seek work as the wage rate increases.[7] (Economists say that these persons have a high **reservation wage**, defined as the lowest wage at which they choose to work.) The income effect is measured in terms of the increase in income at the *original* hours of work, so it must be zero for nonworkers. There is only a substitution effect for these people, so wage increases will definitely increase their desired hours of work. On the whole, it is probably reasonable to assume that over most of its range, the market labor supply curve will be upward sloping.

This idea is shown in Figure 4.3, which includes a set of individual labor supply curves in part (a) and the corresponding market supply curve in part (b). Note that the scales of the diagrams are different—the individual supply curves measure hours of work per week, whereas the market supply would

[7] That is, they choose not to work in the labor market. In many cases, they may be actively involved in nonmarket work, an idea that we explore in the next chapter.

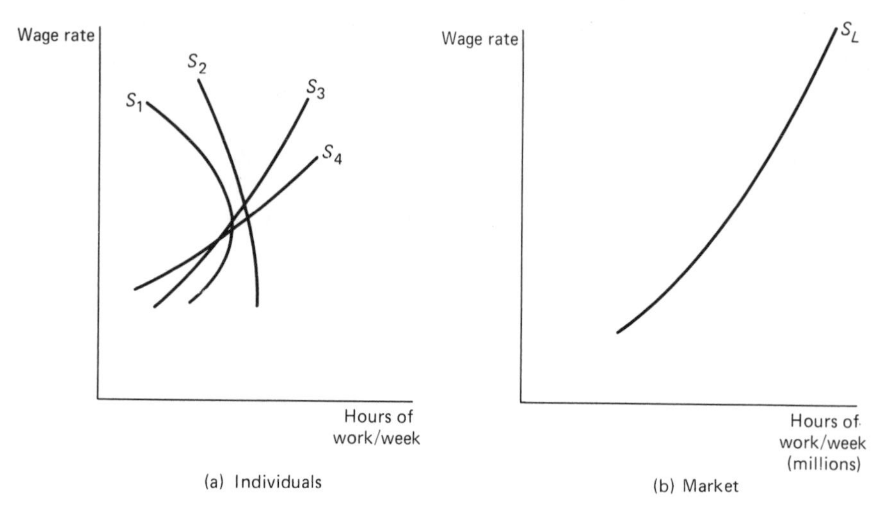

FIGURE 4.3 Deriving the Market Supply Curve of Labor

be measured in millions of hours of work per week. The market supply curve in part (b) is the horizontal summation of the individual curves and it is represented here as being upward sloping throughout most of its range.

Application: *A Potpourri of Labor Supply Curves: Textile Workers in the Industrial Revolution, African Villagers, and Pigeons*

The idea that people might choose to work fewer hours at higher wages often strikes noneconomists as evidence of "noneconomic," irrational behavior. Consider the following account of the labor supply problems of the British textile industry in the nineteenth century, drawn from a famous book on the Industrial Revolution, *The Unbound Prometheus*, by the historian David Landes.

The textile industry was probably the leading industry in the early stages of the Industrial Revolution. By about 1830 it was the largest industry in Great Britain and dominated the world trade in textiles. One problem that faced the industry as it grew was assuring itself an adequate supply of labor. At first, the industry expanded into new geographical areas throughout England, but these possibilities were largely exhausted by the end of the eighteenth century. "In the short run" according to Landes, "the manufacturer who wanted to increase output had to get more work out of the labour already engaged."[8] The problem, though, was the labor supply curve of textile workers. Production at this time was still carried out not in a centralized factory,

[8] Landes, *The Unbound Prometheus*, p. 57.

but under what was called the "putting-out" system. Workers did the actual spinning and weaving in their own homes without direct supervision from an entrepreneur. Pay was on a piecework basis (so much per square inch of cloth, etc.) rather than an hourly basis, and in the absence of supervision, workers were free to work whatever hours they chose. This situation corresponds quite closely to the simple textbook model used to analyze individual labor supply choices.

What could the textile industry do to increase the labor supply of their workers? They could raise the piecework rate, which is equivalent to raising wage rates in a conventional payment scheme. This, however, turned out to be a self-defeating measure. According to Landes:

> While the employer could raise the piece rates with a view to encouraging diligence, he usually found that this actually reduced output. The worker, who had a fairly rigid conception of what he felt to be a decent standard of living, preferred leisure to income after a certain point; and the higher his wages, the less he had to do to reach that point. . . . Thus precisely at those times when profit opportunities were greatest, the manufacturer found himself frustrated by this unreasonable inversion of the laws of sensible economic behavior: the supply of labor decreased as the price rose.[9]

This is, of course, a description of a backward-bending labor supply curve, a result that is certainly not an "unreasonable inversion of the laws of sensible economic behaviour." It is simply a case where the income effect outweighs the substitution effect.

If higher wages only reduced work effort, you might wonder why the textile industry did not respond by lowering piece rates to increase work effort. The answer is that they could not, because rising wage rates elsewhere in the economy effectively placed a floor on wage levels in the textile industry. The textile industry was in the position of being a wage taker in a competitive labor market.

What, then, was to be done? A growing labor supply was required if the textile industry was to grow and prosper. Some historians have suggested that faced with this labor supply dilemma, the textile industry moved to replace the traditional putting-out system with a centralized, supervised workplace—in short, a factory system. According to the historians, this both facilitated the mechanization of the textile mills and removed control of labor supply from the individual workers.

A second famous historical case was described by Elliot Berg in his article, "Backward-Sloping Labor Supply Functions in Dual Economics—The African Case."[10] Berg's analysis focuses on a time period when much of sub-Saharan Africa was characterized by a "dual"economy. There was both

[9] Landes, p. 59.

[10] Berg's article was published in the *Quarterly Journal of Economics*, 1961, pp. 468–492.

a modern, wage-labor economy, usually in urban areas, as well as a rural, traditional, agricultural sector in which there were no wage payments. Unskilled workers in the modern sector were usually temporary emigrants from the subsistence sector. It was the labor supply curve of these people in which Berg was interested.

Remember that labor supply depends on both wages and preferences for goods and leisure time. Berg suggested that for most villagers preferences had two special characteristics. First, they had a strong desire to remain in the village. Second, a villager had, in Berg's words, "a relatively low, clearly-defined and rigid income goal; he wants money to pay head and hut taxes, to make marriage payments . . . or to purchase some specific consumer durable."[11] Given those preferences, an *individual's* labor supply curve will inevitably be backward bending. A villager would spend just enough time in the exchange sector to earn the "target income" and then return to the village. Thus higher wages would reduce total work time in the modern sector. If the income goals are absolutely rigid, a 10 percent increase in wage rates would reduce work time by exactly 10 percent.

It does not follow, however, that the aggregate labor supply curve to the modern sector was necessarily backward bending. Although a higher wage might cause each person to spend less time at work, it might well induce others to seek employment in that sector. In our terms, there are people with higher reservation wages—they might be from villages which were further from the modern sector or which had a higher village standard of living. The net effect is indeterminate.

Over time, however, the individual and aggregate labor supply curve changed, according to Berg. The key factor was the effect of increased contact with the modern sector on increasing the material wants of villagers. There was no longer a rigidly defined target income, and thus time in the modern sector did not necessarily fall as wages rose. Instead, many emigrants took advantage of higher wages to increase their standard of living. Berg concluded that by about 1950, the labor supply curve to the modern sector was upward sloping.

Berg's analysis serves to emphasize two important ideas. First, backward-bending individual labor supply curves are compatible with upward-sloping aggregate labor supply curves, as long as reservation wages differ. Second, target earners, whether they be African villagers or teenagers earning money for a specific item, always have backward-bending labor supply curves. But the less rigidly consumption wants are specified, the more likely it is that a person's labor supply curve is upward sloping.

Finally, there has been substantial research in recent years, carried out jointly by economists and experimental psychologists, to determine whether basic principles of rational economic behavior also apply to animals in lab-

[11] Berg, p. 474.

oratory experiments. One example is an attempt to examine the labor supply behavior of laboratory animals.[12]

Here is how the experiment worked. The subjects were pigeons that were given the opportunity to gain access to a food hopper for three seconds whenever they pecked a response key some specified number of times. If the required number of pecks is large, that is exactly like giving the pigeon a low wage rate, since the pigeon must work longer or harder to obtain the food. The fewer the number of required pecks, the higher the wage. In the experiment, the required number of pecks varied from as little as 12.5 pecks to as much as 400 pecks—a wage differential of 32 times. There was also a source of nonlabor income in the form of access to the food hopper unrelated to a pigeon's work effort. Finally, to measure the substitution effect of a wage change exactly, the researchers adjusted a pigeon's wage rate and nonlabor income simultaneously so that at the original level of work effort, the pigeon's total food would be unchanged. They could also change only the level of nonlabor income, thus causing a pure income effect. Obviously, these are opportunities that labor economists do not get in their studies of the labor supply of human beings.

What kind of income–leisure trade-offs did the pigeons exhibit? Believe it or not, they regularly behaved in accordance with the standard economic analysis of labor supply choices. In 19 out of 22 experimental cases, the substitution effect was exactly as expected on the basis of economic theory. A reduction in the wage decreased work effort and an increase in the wage led to more work. In the words of the authors, "compensated wage decreases resulted in reduced labor supply as hungry birds gave up food to spend more time in nonwork activities."[13] As for the income effect, it was consistent with leisure being a normal good in every single case. With increased nonlabor income and constant wages, pigeons worked less. The authors concluded that "to the extent we can rely on the available data, the income–leisure tradeoffs of pigeons are in many respects similar to those of humans."[14]

EMPIRICAL EVIDENCE ON INDIVIDUAL LABOR SUPPLY

There are two basic ways to study the labor supply behavior of individuals. One involves looking at changes in the average hours of work over a long period of time. The other approach focuses on different workers at a

[12] See Raymond C. Battalio, Leonard Green, and John H. Kagel, "Income–Leisure Tradeoffs of Animal Workers," *American Economic Review*, (September 1981), and the many references there.

[13] Battalio et al., p. 626.

[14] Battalio et al., p. 631.

single point in time and attempts to relate the different wages of these persons and their hours of work. The latter approach is called *cross-sectional*, whereas the former is a *time-series* analysis. Neither approach is ideal; it is, for example, difficult to measure many of the things besides the wage rate that affect labor supply decisions. A person's preferences for leisure and goods and his or her nonlabor income are two of the more important factors for which good information is usually either completely unavailable or imperfectly measured. Moreover, there are a set of serious statistical problems involved in obtaining accurate estimates of labor supply relationships. Some recent studies have attempted to correct many of these problems, but as a result, they are quite complicated and often difficult to interpret.

With these caveats in mind, let's look at some of the information available. From time-series information, it is clear that average weekly hours of work have fallen. Today the average workweek is a bit under 36 hours, higher than that in manufacturing and mining, lower in wholesale and retail trade and in the service sector. One hundred years ago, the average workweek was 53 hours, almost 50 percent larger. The change occurred in several stages. There was a gradual decline in the first part of the twentieth century to about 48 hours in the mid-1920s and then a sharper drop when the time-and-a-half overtime pay provisions were instituted, effective at 40 hours per week, in 1938. Since then average weekly hours have declined gradually—about an hour each decade.

How can we explain the downward trend in hours worked? There are at least two possibilities. Real wages have risen steadily throughout this time period. In manufacturing, for example, hourly earnings in 1980 were about four times as high as in 1914. Thus falling hours in conjunction with rising wages could be evidence that individual labor supply curves are backward bending. The income effect of increased wealth outweighs the substitution effect of rising wages. Figure 4.4(a) shows this—as wages rise over time, due to rising labor demand, average hours worked fall from L_1 to L_2 to L_3.

Together with the increase in wages there has been an increase in the nonlabor income of individuals—income from property, stocks, and bonds. Since we expect leisure to be a normal good, this increase in wealth would lead individuals to "buy" more leisure, thereby causing individual labor supply curves to shift to the left. In that case, the observed fall in the average workweek could be the result of a movement across a set of positively sloped labor supply curves, each corresponding to a higher level of nonlabor income. This is shown in Figure 4.4(b); the fall in average hours is depicted in the movement from A to B to C.

The possibility that individual labor supply curves are backward bending also appears in cross-sectional studies of the labor supply of men. Many studies of this kind have been done in the past decade, and although the range of estimates is fairly wide, most researchers have concluded that the labor supply curve for adult males is negatively sloped. The net effect of wages on hours

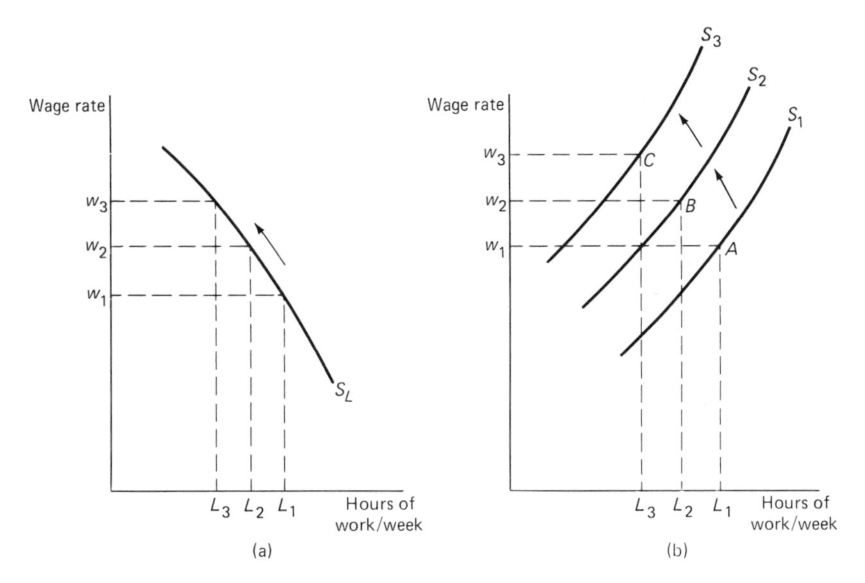

FIGURE 4.4 Explaining the Decline in the Average Work Week

is fairly small, however—a 10 percent higher wage rate is associated with about a 1 percent reduction in hours worked per week. Interestingly, the findings are quite different for married women, whose labor supply decisions have been the subject of much analysis. It appears that their labor supply curve is positively sloped and quite responsive to changes in the wage rate. A consensus estimate is that a 10 percent increase in wages leads to a 10 to 11 percent increase in average work hours. More detailed analysis shows that the difference between the results for men and for married women is due primarily to a much larger substitution effect for women (the income effects are apparently quite similar). This finding is quite plausible once it is recognized that married women frequently choose not just between hours of leisure and hours of market work, but among leisure, market work, and work in the home. As a result, the substitution effect of a higher wage may cause married women to reduce not only their leisure time but also their work time at home. We look more closely at this three-way allocation of labor in Chapter 5.

LABOR SUPPLY ANALYSIS AND PUBLIC POLICY

The derivation of labor supply curves and the analysis of income and substitution effects is not just a dry academic exercise. To the contrary, these ideas have figured prominently in a series of important public policy issues over the last decade or two. By far the most studied is the welfare system, which affects the labor supply of low-income persons. This case is an especially interesting and important one, not only because it was one of the first major applications of labor economics to a public policy issue, but also because it involved an unusual form of economic research. A second famous public policy application concerns the effects of income taxes on labor supply. In fact, the controversial "supply-side" income tax reductions, which were enacted in 1981, were, in part, a response to concerns about the negative work incentives of high tax rates. Let's look at these issues in some detail.

Labor Supply and the Welfare System

One of the most basic premises of labor supply analysis is this: Anything that changes a person's wage rate and/or nonlabor income is likely to have labor supply consequences. An especially clear and important example of this concerns the effect of welfare programs on the labor supply of low-income persons. As you will see, it is very difficult to design a welfare program that simultaneously provides income to persons living in poverty while maintaining reasonable work incentives, all at acceptable budgetary cost.

To appreciate the labor supply effects, some familiarity with the mechanics of the welfare system is necessary. Welfare programs in the United States fall into two general categories. Some provide direct cash payments to eligible poor families, whereas others provide goods and services directly either at no cost or at a highly subsidized price. The best known cash program is *AFDC*, Aid to Families with Dependent Children. In 1983, about 3.3 million families received AFDC benefits, and total state and federal government expenditures were $13.4 billion. Medicaid, public housing, and food stamps are prominent examples of the other assistance strategy.

The labor supply effects stem from the characteristic way in which welfare benefits vary with a family's income. The AFDC program is typical in this respect. It provides a specified level of benefits to a family with no income of its own and proportionately less to families with some income. At some point, called the **break-even income level**, a family's income becomes sufficiently high that it no longer qualifies for any benefits. The reduction in benefits as income rises is essential if welfare benefits are to be limited primarily to those with very low incomes, but it also has the effect of sharply reducing the net wage rate of a person on welfare. Suppose that benefits were reduced at a 50 percent rate, meaning that for every dollar earned, welfare benefits are cut by $0.50. As a result, a wage of, say, $4 per hour actually increases total income by only $2 per hour after taking account of the reduction in welfare benefits. The higher the benefit reduction rate, the greater the decrease in the wage rate. Analytically, the benefit reduction rate acts exactly like an income tax, creating a sizable wedge between the apparent wage and the actual after-tax wage. Economists refer to the benefit reduction rate as the **implicit tax rate** of the AFDC program.

In practice, benefit reduction rates have historically been set at a very high level to avoid providing benefits to nonpoor families. Prior to 1969, the benefit reduction rate in AFDC was set by law at 100 percent—benefits were reduced on a dollar-for-dollar basis as a family's earned income rose. This had two effects. First, the welfare population was limited almost entirely to persons whose potential earned income was less than the maximum welfare benefit level.[15] Second, almost no one receiving welfare worked, since the 100 percent benefit reduction rate had the effect of reducing a person's wage rate to zero. (Including work-related expenses, the true wage rate was probably negative.) It is not difficult to see that that might provide a considerable disincentive to work, unless a person was able to earn considerably more than the welfare allowance.

In response to this adverse labor supply incentive, the AFDC tax rate was reduced in 1969 to 67 percent—benefits were now reduced by $2 for every $3 earned. This actually had two distinct labor supply effects, one for persons currently on welfare and another for persons made eligible by the lower tax rate. For persons on welfare, most of whom were not working, the lower marginal tax rate increased their wage rate, thus potentially increasing their labor supply via a substitution effect. There was no offsetting income effect since they were not working in the first place and thus were not any richer at the original hours of work. As their labor supply increased, their welfare benefits fell, thereby having the further desirable effect of reducing the budgetary costs of the welfare system.

Unfortunately, there is a second effect which tends to decrease labor supply and increase program costs. A decrease in the tax rate increases the size of the population eligible for welfare, by increasing the break-even income level. It is easiest to show this with arithmetic. If the basic grant is $4000 per year, and the tax rate is 100 percent, the break-even income is exactly $4000. Anyone with an income above $4000 is ineligible for welfare. If, however, the tax rate was 50 percent, the break-even income rises to $8000, and it would be $16,000 if the rate were reduced to 25 percent. More generally, the break-even income level can be calculated by dividing the basic income grant by the tax rate.[16]

For these "newly eligibles," the labor supply effects are more complex. Compared to the situation of no welfare, they now find themselves with a source of nonlabor income—the basic welfare grant—and a "new" wage rate that is sharply lower, courtesy of the 67 percent AFDC tax rate. The combined effect is that a person is simultaneously richer at his or her original hours of

[15] It is possible that some people who could earn a bit more than the welfare grant might choose to stop working, accepting lower income but much more leisure.

[16] The basic AFDC benefit formula is $P = G - tY$, where P is the actual payment, G the payment to a family with no earned income, Y a family's earned income, and t the benefit reduction rate. The break-even income level (Y^*) is the value of Y for which $P = 0$. Setting $G - tY = 0$ and solving for Y^* gives $Y^* = G/t$.

work and has a lower wage rate. The lower wage causes a substitution effect, reducing labor supply, and the higher income level generates an income effect which further reduces labor supply. Thus here the income and substitution effects work together—not in opposition—to decrease work incentives.

At this point you should be able to appreciate the basic labor supply dilemma inherent in the design of a welfare program. A high tax rate limits the number of people whose labor supply may be affected, but causes sharply reduced work incentives for those who do qualify. A lower rate will improve work incentives for this group, but it increases the size of the population eligible for welfare and provides reduced work incentives for these newly eligibles. It also greatly increases the budgetary cost of the program, simply by increasing the number of welfare recipients. The policy response has been to set the implicit tax rate at high levels, limiting the scope of the program but impairing the labor supply of recipients. Recent changes to the AFDC program reinstituted a 100 percent tax rate, effective after a welfare recipient worked for four months.

Welfare Reform and the Negative Income Tax Experiments

There is one final part to the story of welfare and labor supply. In addition to the labor supply problems of any welfare system, the U.S. welfare system has several other features which have been matters of concern for nearly two decades. Since its inception, the AFDC program has limited eligibility to families with children that are headed by a single parent. Two-parent families or persons without children are categorically ineligible for AFDC benefits, regardless of their income.[17] This creates two problems. First, a substantial number of two-parent families, usually referred to as the "working poor," remain in poverty. In many cases, their standard of living falls short of that available to single-headed families receiving welfare benefits. For example, in 1966, one-third of all poor persons were members of two-parent families in which the husband worked; in 1982, half of all families in poverty were two-parent families. Second, because welfare eligibility is dependent on marital and family status, it is possible that people may adjust their behavior to qualify for AFDC. In particular, economists and other policymakers have been concerned that AFDC provides economic incentives that encourage the breakup of families, discourage marriage or remarriage, and promote illegitimate births. Clearly, these are undesirable side effects.

When these problems were first identified in the mid-1960s, they gave rise to serious efforts at welfare reform. A reform proposal known as the **negative income tax** (NIT) was first suggested by the economist Milton Fried-

[17] In some states these people are eligible for a version of AFDC called AFDC-UP. "UP" stands for unemployed parent. The impact of this program is relatively minor.

man, and since then, virtually all welfare reform proposals have adopted the basic structure of his proposal.[18] The basic design of an NIT is similar to AFDC, with some basic income grant given to a family with no income of its own and an implicit tax rate determining the rate at which benefits fall as income rises. The important difference, however, is that under most NIT plans, only a family's income, not its marital status, would be relevant in determining eligibility. Two-parent families would no longer be categorically ineligible. These changes would, it was thought, both eliminate the undesirable family incentives of the current system and reduce the incidence of poverty.

Welfare reform along these lines actually received a great deal of legislative attention in the early 1970s. A version of the NIT, called the Family Assistance Plan, was nearly enacted into law in 1970.[19] Another version, called the Program for Better Jobs and Income, was developed during the Carter administration, but was never seriously considered by Congress. Since that time, welfare reform along these lines has not been a high priority.

Even at the time when it was under consideration, it was recognized that an expansion of the welfare system to include the working poor could have potentially serious labor supply consequences. The situation is, in fact, exactly the same as the one we discussed above concerning a reduction in the AFDC tax rate and the effect on newly-eligibles. The income of the working poor would be increased by the income grant of the NIT and their wage rate would be sharply cut by its high implicit tax rate. Both a substitution and income effect would cause a reduction in labor supply.

Although the direction of the expected impact is clear, economic theory does not suggest how large the labor supply adjustments might be. For policy purposes, it is the magnitude that is crucial. If, for instance, the labor supply response was small, a more adequate welfare support system could be established without disrupting low-wage labor markets and requiring enormous increases in government expenditures. But if the labor supply effects were large, the feasibility of the program would be in jeopardy.

The concern with possible labor supply effects ultimately led to an unprecedented form of economics research—real-world experimentation with human subjects.[20] Between 1968 and 1978, the federal government sponsored

[18] Friedman called it the negative income tax plan to emphasize its relationship to the more conventional positive income tax system. In Friedman's system, people with incomes above some threshold would pay positive taxes, whereas people below that threshold would pay "negative income taxes"—that is, receive income from the government.

[19] The Family Assistance Plan would have provided assistance to all poor families with children. The basic grant was $1600 for a family of four. The benefit reduction rate was 50 percent, but the first $120 of earned income did not result in any loss of welfare benefits.

[20] There was nonexperimental information on how differences in wages and nonlabor income affected labor supply, but the range of estimates was too large to be used for a major policy reform like this. Also, previous studies were for the population as a whole, rather than for the working poor.

a series of large-scale NIT experiments to provide direct evidence of the probable labor supply effects. In each experiment, one group of low-wage workers was given the opportunity to receive welfare payments according to an NIT formula, while a second group of otherwise similar workers remained ineligible for welfare. These experiments are not perfect, since not everything can be controlled in the real world, but they are as close to laboratory conditions as labor economists are likely to get. They have provided useful information not only about the feasibility of welfare reform, but also about the underlying economic model of labor supply behavior.

In all, four separate experiments were performed. The first NIT experiments were carried out in New Jersey and Pennsylvania between 1968 and 1972. Similar experiments took place in Gary, Indiana, from 1970 to 1974 and in two rural areas of North Carolina and Iowa from 1969 to 1973. The largest and most ambitious experiment was conducted in Seattle, Washington, and Denver, Colorado. It covered eight years (1970–1978), 4800 families, and eleven combinations of a basic income grant and tax rate. Known as **SIME/DIME** (for Seattle–Denver Income Maintenance Experiment), this last experiment has provided the best information yet about the probable labor supply effects of a negative income tax.

What are the results of SIME/DIME, and what do they tell us about the labor supply behavior of low-wage workers under an NIT plan?[21] There are several ways to summarize the findings. First, there is the *change* in labor supply for all persons involved in the SIME/DIME experiment. Usually, this is computed as the difference between their labor supply the year before the experiment and then during the experiment. On average, husbands receiving NIT payments reduced their annual labor supply from 7 to 13 percent and wives from 15 to 27 percent (the range of estimates covers the different payment plans that were tested). The larger effects for the women are not surprising, since in many cases, they have valuable nonmarket uses of their time in child care and/or housework.

Second, it is possible to derive direct estimates of the income and substitution effects themselves. These numbers are potentially more useful than the simple averages above, because they can be used to predict the effects of any proposed NIT plan, not just the ones tested in the SIME/DIME experiment.[22] They also provide a direct test of the economic theory of labor supply. For each person, the researchers could calculate how much the NIT tax rate had changed the wage rate and also how much richer he or she was

[21] The results discussed in the text are from the *Final Report of the Seattle–Denver Income Maintenance Experiment*, Vol. I, published by SRI International. Other articles summarizing the SIME/DIME findings include Michael Keeley et al., "The Labor Supply Effects and Costs of Alternative Negative Income Tax Programs," *Journal of Human Resources*, (Winter 1978), and the entire Fall 1980 issue of that journal.

[22] The 11 plans tested in SIME/DIME were very generous compared to NIT plans, usually considered politically feasible.

TABLE 4.2 Income and Substitution Effects from the SIME/DIME Experiment

GROUP	CHANGE IN ANNUAL HOURS WORKED DUE TO: *Substitution Effect (per $1 decrease in wage)*	*Income Effect (per $1000 increase in annual income)*
Husbands	−71	−95
Wives	−152	−197

Source: Final Report of the Seattle–Denver Income Maintenance Experiment, Vol. I, *Design and Results*, Table 3.11, SRI International, 1983.

made (measured at the original number of hours of work) by the program. Since these are the changes needed to measure the substitution and income effects, they can be related to the corresponding change in labor supply to isolate the two effects.

The results of this "structural analysis" for husbands and wives are presented in Table 4.2. As you can see, the substitution effect of a lower wage rate caused both groups to reduce their annual labor supply, exactly as the economic model of labor supply predicts. The best estimate is that a $1 decrease in the wage would cause annual work hours to fall by 71 hours for husbands, and 152 hours for wives. The second column shows the effect of a $1000 increase in annual income; as predicted, the effects are negative. The total effect is the sum of the two effects, multiplied by the actual changes in the wage and in nonlabor income for each person. If, for example, an NIT plan reduced a husband's wage rate by $1 per hour and also increased his annual income (measured at the original labor supply point) by $1000, it would, on average, lead to an annual reduction in labor supply of 71 + 95 = 166 hours. For wives, the same changes would reduce labor supply by 152 + 197 = 349 hours.

Using these estimates of income and substitution effects, the researchers could then predict the expected impact on labor supply of any proposed NIT plan. For most plans considered feasible, the effects are not too large, because the actual wage and income changes are not large for most persons. The predicted impact of two plans is shown in Table 4.3. With an income grant equal to 75 percent of the official poverty standard[23] and a tax rate of 50 percent, the labor supply of husbands who received NIT income would fall by 4.8 percent; for wives, the corresponding figure is 13.2 percent. With both a higher income grant (100 percent of the poverty standard) and a higher tax rate (70 percent), both labor supply responses are greater. The labor supply of husbands now falls by 8.0 percent and wives by 21.1 percent.

What has been learned from the NIT experiments? It seems clear now

[23] The poverty standard is the official government estimate of the cost of a minimum standard of living. In 1982, the poverty standard for a family of four was $9862.

TABLE 4.3 Predicted Labor Supply Effects of Two NIT Plans

NIT PLAN	CHANGE (%) IN ANNUAL HOURS OF WORK OF:	
	Husbands	*Wives*
Income grant = 75% of poverty standard; tax rate = 50%	−4.8	−13.2
Income grant = 100% of poverty standard; tax rate = 70%	−8.0	−21.1

Source: Final Report of the Seattle–Denver Income Maintenance Experiment, Vol. I, *Design and Results*, Table 3.31, SRI International, 1983.

that low-income persons do respond to changes in their wages and in their nonlabor income much as the economic model of labor supply predicts. It is therefore unlikely that welfare benefits can be extended to married couples without affecting their incentives to work. It is probably fair to say that the labor supply results fall somewhere in between the fears of the NIT critics that the effects would be enormous and the hopes of its supporters that they would be very small. The finding that wives, rather than husbands, responded more sharply is important since this is unlikely to represent a shift into pure leisure. As for the desirability of implementing a negative income tax plan, that is a normative question and not one that can be decided on the basis of the experimental findings alone. Future reconsideration of welfare reform along the lines of a NIT will depend on whether, as a society, we conclude that the interest in providing more adequate relief from poverty and in eliminating the other undesirable effects of the current program is worth the additional costs involved.

We close this discussion with some facts that may be surprising to you. Thanks to several recent studies, it is now becoming clear that welfare status is typically *not* a long-term condition. Rather, most persons who are ever on welfare leave the welfare rolls relatively quickly. One major study[24] examined women who were ever on welfare between 1968 and 1980. Thirty percent of them spent less than a year on welfare, 50 percent less than two years, and about two-thirds less than four years. Long-term welfare recipients—defined to be women who spent at least eight consecutive years on welfare—amounted to less than 15 percent of the welfare population over that time period. Thus, although AFDC does reduce the labor supply of persons receiving welfare, it does not typically lead to long-run welfare dependency.

[24] Mary Jo Bane and David Ellwood, "The Dynamics of Dependence: The Routes to Self-Sufficiency," Final Report to U.S. Department of Health and Human Services, 1983.

Income Taxes and Labor Supply

The possible negative effects of income taxes on work incentives is one of the oldest topics in labor supply analysis. Until the late-1970s, it was a matter of concern only to economists, but with the development of supply-side economics, the effect of taxes on labor supply became an issue of much greater note. Supply-side economics, which came to play a major role in the Reagan administration, greatly emphasized the role of supply-side incentives and disincentives, especially the tax system. In a major reform, income tax rates were cut by 25 percent over three years, with an unusually large share of the tax reductions concentrated on those with a high income. In this section we consider the way in which taxes might be expected to affect labor supply.

Economists typically distinguish among three different kinds of income taxation systems. One is called **proportional**, and in such a system, all income is taxed at the same rate. The rate might be 5 percent, and that rate would then apply to the income of poor people and rich ones equally. Richer persons would end up paying more in taxes, but only because their income is higher. In progressive and regressive tax systems there is a sequence of tax rates rather than a single rate. In a **progressive** system, the tax rate rises with income. A rate of 5 percent might apply to the first $10,000 of income, a slightly higher rate to the next $10,000 of income, and so on through the entire range of income. Thus a person with $20,000 of income and one with $40,000 of income both pay the same tax on income up to $20,000, but the richer person would then face a higher tax rate on the next $20,000 of income. With a **regressive** system, the rate structure is reversed—higher tax rates apply to the first (lower) income levels and steadily lower rates to higher income levels. In most industrialized countries, including the United States, the income tax is progressive.

The way in which income taxes may affect labor supply is not difficult to understand if you keep in mind the distinction between the marginal tax rate and the average tax rate. The **marginal tax rate** is the tax rate that applies to the last (or next) dollar of income that a person earns, while the **average tax rate** is simply the ratio of total taxes to total income. In a proportional system, the marginal and average rates are exactly the same, because each dollar of income is taxed at the same rate.[25] In a progressive system, though, the marginal tax rate always exceeds the average rate because, as we saw, the tax rate rises with income. A person in the United States who complains about being in the 50 percent tax bracket almost always means that his or her marginal rate is 50 percent; the corresponding average rate will be considerably lower.[26] Table 4.4 shows the average and marginal federal income tax rates in the United States in 1983.

[25] This is strictly correct only if no income is exempt from taxes.

[26] You may recognize this as another application of the marginal–average relationship which we considered in Chapter 2. It follows that in a regressive tax system, the average rate exceeds the marginal rate.

TABLE 4.4 Average and Marginal Federal Income Tax Rates for Married Couples, 1983

TAXABLE INCOME	AVERAGE TAX RATE (%)*	MARGINAL TAX RATE (%)
$ 0 –$ 3,400	0	0
$ 3,400–$ 5,500	0	11
$ 5,500–$ 7,600	4.2	13
$ 7,600–$ 11,900	6.6	15
$ 11,900–$ 16,000	9.7	17
$ 16,000–$ 20,200	11.5	19
$ 20,200–$ 24,600	13.1	23
$ 24,600–$ 29,900	14.9	26
$ 29,900–$ 35,200	16.8	30
$ 35,200–$ 45,800	18.8	35
$ 45,800–$ 60,000	22.6	40
$ 60,000–$ 85,600	26.7	44
$ 85,600–$109,400	31.9	48
$109,400–	35.4	50

*The average tax rate is computed at the lower end of the income range.

With two tax rates to consider, which is relevant for labor supply decisions? It turns out that both of them are, but in different ways. A change in the marginal tax rate is relevant for evaluating the substitution effect, because it determines the price of leisure at the margin at which labor supply decisions might be changed. But for the income effect, we need to determine how much richer or poorer a person is at the original hours of work. Since the average tax rate reflects the total taxes paid, it is a change in the average rate which is relevant for evaluating the income effect. The distinction is important. Some tax changes affect primarily the average rate but not the marginal rate, whereas others change primarily the marginal rate.

To see how this works out, consider two extreme cases. First, suppose that the tax system was progressive, a person earned $30,000, and that suddenly all taxes on income up to $30,000 were lowered but all higher rates were left unchanged. For this person there is no substitution effect, since the relevant marginal tax rate is unchanged. There is, however, an income effect, since the person's total tax bill is reduced. Thus there is only an income effect, which will reduce the desired labor supply. Now, consider the opposite situation, in which tax rates below $30,000 are unchanged but those above it are lowered. Here there is no income effect—total taxes at the original point are eventually unchanged—but there is a substitution effect. The price of additional leisure is now higher and the person, being no richer, will choose to take less leisure and increase labor supply.

These two examples are, admittedly, highly artificial—most tax changes affect both marginal and average tax rates and thus induce both substitution and income effects. If taxes increase, the substitution effect reduces labor supply (leisure is cheaper), whereas the income effect increases it (the person is poorer). When taxes are reduced, the two effects just reverse. Although it may seem that we are once again in the region of uncertain conclusions, we can derive the following important result: *Tax cuts (increases) are more likely to increase (decrease) labor supply the greater their impact on marginal tax rates than on average tax rates.*

That insight is the basis for the classic labor supply argument against a steeply progressive income tax system. Changes in marginal tax rates for high incomes will typically have large substitution effects and smaller income effects, because only a relatively small portion of a person's income is affected by the tax change. (The change in the average tax rate is small). As a result, it is plausible—not certain—that increases in marginal tax rates would decrease labor supply, whereas decreases in the marginal rate might increase hours of work. In contrast, tax changes in a proportional tax system necessarily have stronger income effects, because the tax change affects *all* of a person's income. In fact, in a proportional tax system, a tax change is exactly equivalent to a wage change—a tax increase reduces your wage rate and a tax decrease increases it.

Evidence on the labor supply effects of taxes, especially progressive taxes, is not easy to come by. We do read occasionally of "tax refugees"—persons who change their place of residence to avoid taxes. Bjorn Borg left Sweden for Monte Carlo and Ringo Starr abandoned England for the United States, both apparently to avoid marginal tax rates in excess of 90 percent. Those changes, however, involve primarily *where* labor is officially supplied, not how much. For many years, economists tended to believe that the effects were small, on the basis of two kinds of evidence. First, direct surveys of high-income professional workers—doctors, lawyers, and accountants—found little or no self-reported labor supply effects. Second, independent studies of individual labor supply curves suggest that hours worked are not very responsive to changes in wage rates, especially for men. In both cases, however, the evidence is far from perfect. Inferences from an individual labor supply curve are appropriate only for assessing the effects of changes in proportional taxes, not for progressive ones. Also, self-reported explanations of behavior are notoriously unreliable; economists place much more faith in what people actually do than in what they claim to do.

More recent economic studies of tax effects have used modern statistical techniques and have paid special attention to the progressivity of the tax code. One recent study by Hausman concluded that the labor supply effects were substantial—an 8 percent reduction for husbands and above 30 percent for wives.[27] (Hausman assumed that wives were "second earners" in the household, so, in effect, their income was taxed at higher marginal tax rates than

[27] See Jerry Hausman, "Labor Supply," in Henry J. Aaron and Joseph A. Pechman, eds., *How Taxes Affect Economic Behavior* (Washington, D.C.: Brookings Institution, 1981).

those of their husbands. That helps explain the much larger effect for women than for men.) These findings are quite new and it is prudent to treat them cautiously until further studies confirm them. Even so, they certainly do indicate that progressive income taxes may have a greater impact on labor supply than was previously thought.

What does all of this tell us about taxes and public policy? Certainly, it would be unwise to design tax policy without recognizing the possible labor supply effects. This is equally true for increases and decreases in tax rates. Reductions in labor supply are not just a matter of hours worked. Ultimately, the income of the country is affected, since labor is the primary input into production. It does not, however, necessarily follow that we should abandon a progressive structure in favor of one that has more desirable labor supply effects. Equity considerations concerning the distribution of the nation's tax burden across individuals is also important. Indeed, it has traditionally been regarded as equitable that richer persons should pay a higher percentage of their income in taxes. What is really involved in the design of a tax system is a trade-off between equity and efficiency. Understanding the possible efficiency effects is an essential part of making wise decisions about tax policy.

SUMMARY

This chapter tackled the analysis of individual labor supply decisions concerning the number of hours of work. The key insight was in treating this decision as an aspect of individual utility maximization. People receive utility from goods and leisure. Labor supply is the link between the two, providing the income to purchase goods, but only at the sacrifice of leisure. By recognizing that the price of leisure—its opportunity cost—is the wage rate, it is possible to apply the formal economic logic of utility maximization to the choice of leisure, goods, and work.

Deriving a person's labor supply curve involved the analysis of income and substitution effects, applied in a nonstandard way. Because a person is simultaneously a buyer of leisure and a seller of labor, the income and substitution effects conflict even if leisure is a normal good. The substitution effect of a higher wage leads to a reduction in the consumption of leisure and thus an increase in hours of work. But the income effect of the higher wage increases a person's income and thus typically leads to an increase in leisure time and a reduction in hours worked. Economic theory tells us only that the net effect is uncertain. Working fewer hours at higher wages is certainly not an indication of irrational behavior. Indeed, an eventually backward-bending individual labor supply curve is a well-established idea. (It even appears to apply to pigeons.) It does not, however, follow that the market supply curve will also be backward bending, since higher wages may attract additional workers into the labor market.

The analysis of labor supply decisions in terms of income and substitution effects is extremely valuable. It is, for example, useful for analyzing the potential labor supply effects of any government program that alters either a person's nonlabor income or wage rate. Two policy issues were considered in detail. The first was the labor supply effects of the welfare system and of the negative income tax system. Efforts to target income to poor families inevitably entail income and substitution effects, which in this case both reduce labor supply. The results of the NIT experiments support these predictions, although the labor supply response is not as large as critics had feared. The experiments themselves were an unprecedented development in economics research.

The other policy issue involved the potential adverse effect of income taxes on labor supply decisions, an idea much emphasized by the proponents of supply-side economics. Here the key insight is that in a progressive tax system, two tax rates are relevant to labor supply decisions. The marginal tax rate determines the strength of the substitution effect, while the average tax rate determines the income effect. An adverse labor supply effect is plausible, although by no means certain, in a progressive tax system if the marginal tax rate is sufficiently high. Conversely, reducing the progressivity of the tax system could possibly increase the labor supply of some high-income persons. Equity considerations about how the tax burden should be distributed are also relevant, however, in the design of a tax system.

New Concepts

Labor force participation
Utility
Diminishing marginal utility
Utility maximization
Income effect
Substitution effect
Law of Demand
Normal good
Inferior good
Backward-bending labor supply curve
Reservation wage
AFDC
Break-even income level
Implicit tax rate
Negative income tax (NIT)
SIME/DIME
Proportional, progressive, and regressive taxes

Marginal tax rate
Average tax rate

APPENDIX: Indifference Curves and Labor Supply Analysis

The analysis of individual labor supply behavior can be presented much more precisely by using the basic graphical tools of consumer theory. The conclusions, of course, are exactly the same as the ones drawn in the text. Only the form of presentation differs.

The graphical tools are very similar to those used in the discussion of long-run demand in Chapter 3, especially in the Appendix to that chapter. The basic graphical device is an **indifference curve**, which represents all combinations of goods (G) and leisure (l) that provide the same level of utility or satisfaction to a person. (A person is said to be indifferent among the various combinations represented by such a curve, which accounts for its name.) Typical indifference curves are shown in Figure A4.1. The vertical axis measures the amount of goods consumed, and the horizontal axis shows both the amount of leisure and the amount of work time, measured here on a weekly basis. Leisure hours (l) are measured in the usual direction from 0 to 168 (the number of hours in a week), while labor hours (L) are measured in the opposite direction. Labor supply is zero when leisure time equals 168 hours, and it would be 168 hours in the improbable case in which leisure was zero. The reason we can measure leisure and work time simultaneously is that, by assumption, they are the only two possible uses of time.

You may have noticed that the indifference curves in the figure have the same shape as an isoquant. They are negatively sloped and they are convex to the origin—steeper at the top and flatter toward the bottom. We do not actually observe an indifference curve, but its properties can be deduced. Its slope will be negative as long as both goods and leisure provide utility to a person. If the amount of goods increased, but the amount of leisure time remained constant (or vice versa), the person would certainly be better off—that is, total utility would rise. Those combinations would therefore lie on a higher indifference curve. In Figure A4.1, then, indifference curve U_2 represents a higher utility level than U_1 because the combination of goods and leisure at D and E is definitely preferred to that at B. If, however, the amount of goods decreased and the amount of leisure increased, the level of utility could be constant. Combinations like that—A, B, and C on U_1, D and E on U_2—lie on a single indifference curve. Thus an indifference curve has a negative slope, just like an isoquant.

The changing slope of an indifference curve reflects a property that economists call **diminishing marginal rate of substitution**. The marginal rate

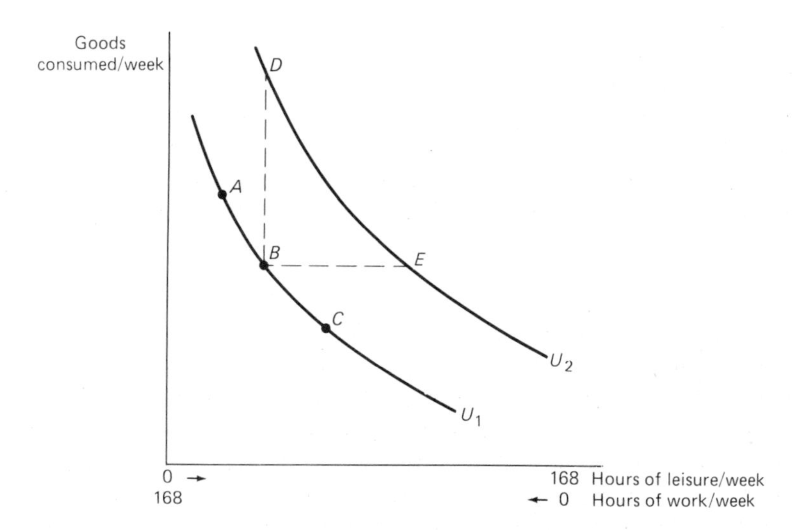

FIGURE A4.1 Indifference Curves for Leisure and Goods

of substitution (*MRS*) is defined this way: It is the maximum amount of one good that a person is willing to give up to obtain an additional amount of a second good, such that the person's utility level remains unchanged. For instance, in the case of the choice between goods and leisure, the *MRS* would measure the amount of goods that a person is willing to give up to obtain an additional hour of leisure. In symbols, $MRS_{lG} = \left.\frac{\Delta G}{\Delta l}\right|_u$, which is exactly equivalent to the slope of an indifference curve. By *diminishing* marginal rate of substitution, economists mean that the amount of goods that a person is willing to give up to obtain an additional hour of leisure will be greater when the amount of leisure consumed is small and much less when the amount of leisure is large. This makes perfect sense: When leisure is scarce, an additional hour is highly valued and when it is more abundant, an additional hour is less highly valued. Thus, the amount of goods willingly given up to obtain more leisure falls as the amount of leisure already consumed increases.

The indifference curves in Figure A4.1 exhibit a diminishing marginal rate of substitution of goods for leisure. At point *A* on indifference curve U_1, the amount of leisure consumed is relatively low. Thus, the MRS_{lG} at that point will be high and the indifference curve will have a steep slope there. Moving down the curve to points *B* and *C*, the amount of leisure increases and, consequently, the MRS_{lG} diminishes. Thus, the indifference curve becomes flatter at its lower end.

Finally, the shape of an indifference curve may vary from person to person, depending on a person's preference for goods compared to leisure. Consider a person who receives tremendous utility from leisure and relatively less from goods. (We might call that person a leisure preferrer.) Because this person values leisure so highly, he or she would be willing to give up a large amount of goods in return for an additional hour of leisure. Thus, the MRS_{lG} is large and the corresponding indifference curve will be steep, like U_l in Figure A4.2. In the opposite case of a goods preferrer, the indifference curve would be flatter throughout, since the person is willing to give up fewer goods to obtain more leisure. The indifference curve for a goods preferrer is shown as U_G in Figure A4.2.

To analyze a person's choices, we need to know not only his or her preferences, as represented by a set of indifference curves, but also the opportunities that are possible. For that, we construct a **budget line** or **budget constraint** which shows all the combinations of leisure and goods which are feasible. What is feasible depends partly on natural laws—you cannot consume more than 168 hours of leisure per week under any circumstances. More important, it depends on a person's wage rate, nonlabor income, and the average price of goods and services. For example, if your wage is fairly low and you have no nonlabor income, it is not possible to consume both goods and leisure in abundance. Of course, if your wage were higher, perhaps that would be feasible.

What does a typical budget line look like? We assume that a person can work as many hours as he or she wants at a constant wage rate and also, just for the moment, that there is no nonlabor income. Let p stand for the average price of goods. One feasible point on the budget line is obvious, if somewhat foolhardy. It is always possible to consume 168 hours of leisure per week together with no goods at all. The other feasible points, though, depend on the relationship between w and p. For each hour of leisure forgone (by working), a person can earn $\$w$ and, in turn, can purchase w/p more units of goods. For example, if the wage is \$4 and the price of goods is \$1, then for each hour of work, 4 units of goods can be acquired. The entire set of

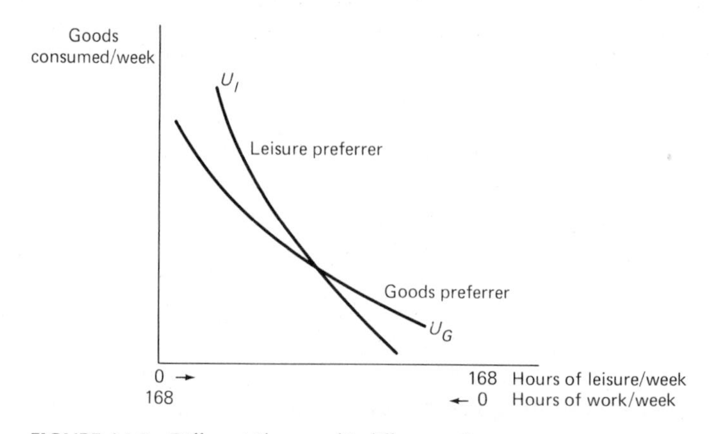

FIGURE A4.2 Different Shapes of Indifference Curves

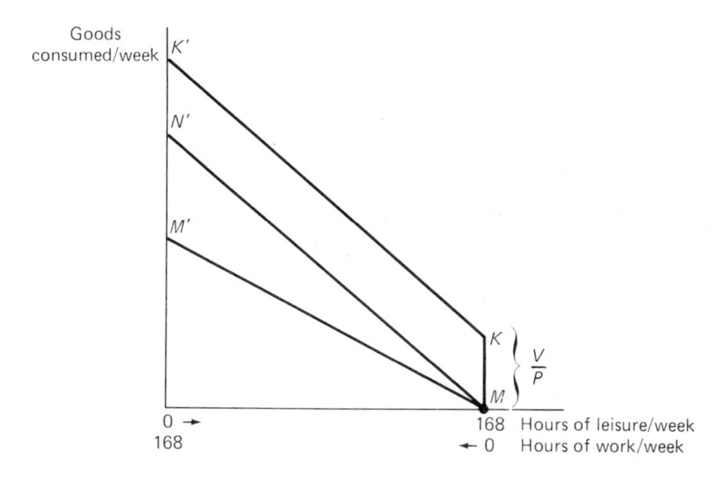

FIGURE A4.3 The Budget Constraint for the Choice between Leisure and Goods

feasible leisure–goods combinations for this person can be derived by successively reducing leisure consumption by one hour and increasing the amount of goods by w/p units. The result is a budget line which is a straight line and whose slope is w/p—the rate at which it is possible to forgo leisure and obtain goods.[28] The budget line begins at the point of maximum leisure on the horizontal axis and stretches to a corresponding point of maximum goods and no leisure time on the vertical axis.

Three different budget lines are drawn in Figure A4.3. Budget line MM' shows the set of feasible leisure–goods combinations for a person who has a relatively low wage and no nonlabor income. The line is relatively flat, which tells us that for this person reductions in leisure do not yield a large increase in the amount of goods that can be consumed. If this person's wage rate were higher, the budget line would be like MN'. Its slope is steeper and the maximum amount of goods on the vertical axis is greater. Both budget lines, though, start from the same point on the horizontal axis. Finally, suppose that this person had the higher wage rate, but now had a source of nonlabor income equal to $\$V$. The new budget line would be parallel to the MN', but it would be shifted up, like MKK' in the figure. The vertical distance between the two parallel budget lines is equal to V/p, the amount of additional goods the person can consume with the nonlabor income. For each of the budget lines, all the combinations above and to the right are not feasible. They require either more nonlabor income or a higher wage than the person has.

Maximizing utility involves choosing the most preferred combination of goods and leisure from among the possibilities along the budget line. Indirectly, that determines the person's labor supply. Figure A4.4 illustrates the

[28] Actually, the slope is $-w/p$, since the budget line has a negative slope.

utility-maximizing choice for a person with a fixed wage (W_1), no nonlabor income, and preferences represented by this set of indifference curves. The leisure–goods combinations represented by points A, B, C, D, and E are all feasible, but you can easily see that, of these, C provides the highest level of utility. In fact, no higher indifference curve contains any feasible points, so point C represents the utility-maximizing choice. The amount of leisure would be l_C and labor supply would be L_C. This gives one point on a labor supply curve: At a wage of W_1 and with no nonlabor income, this person would choose to work L_C hours per week.

The actual labor supply choice in Figure A4.4 depends not only on the wage rate and the level of nonlabor income, but also on the person's preferences as reflected in the shape of the indifference curves. For a leisure preferrer whose indifference curves are steeper, the utility-maximizing point would involve less work and more leisure, while for a goods preferrer, the preferred combination would be just the opposite.

Deriving the Labor Supply Curve

If we assume that a person's preferences are stable, we can analyze how the utility-maximizing labor supply choices change in response to changes in nonlabor income or in the wage rate. The effect of a change in nonlabor income is shown in Figure A4.5. The initial budget line is MM' and utility maximization is at A. With an increase in nonlabor income, the budget line shifts out to MNN' and if leisure is a normal good, the person will choose to take more leisure and work fewer hours. The new utility-maximizing point will lie somewhere to the right of point A; in the figure it is shown as point B, with labor supply falling from L_A to L_B. Thus, exactly as in the text, the income effect on labor supply is negative.

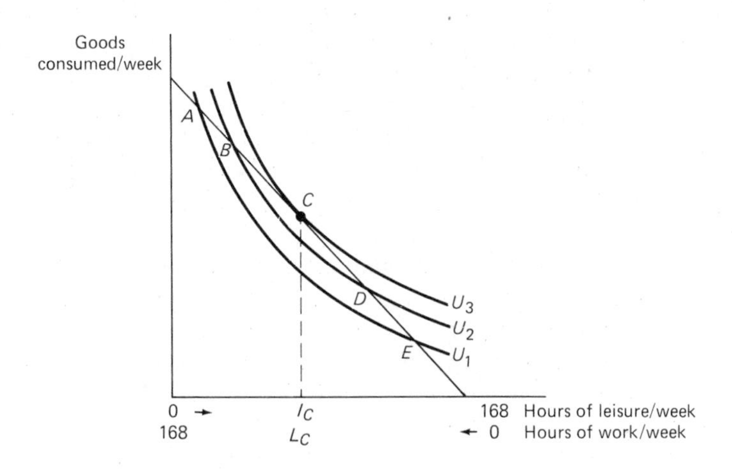

FIGURE A4.4 Utility Maximization and Labor Supply

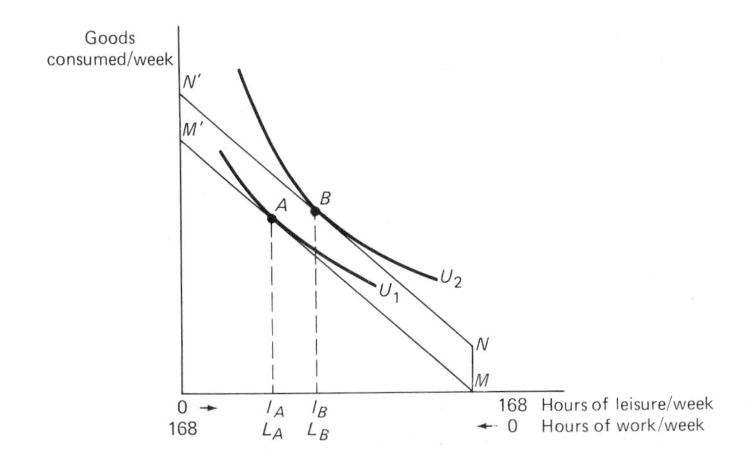

FIGURE A4.5 The Income Effect and Labor Supply

When the wage rate changes, the budget line pivots around the point on the leisure axis. Figure A4.6 illustrates the case of an increase in the wage rate from budget line *MM'* to *MN'*. The original utility-maximizing point is shown as *A* on indifference curve U_l. The wage rate change affects labor supply in two distinct ways: It alters the relative price of goods and leisure and it changes the person's real income. The **substitution effect** is designed to measure the first of these, by temporarily removing the effect of increased income. It is measured as the change in labor hours that would occur if when the wage rate changes, a person's income were adjusted so that the maximum utility that could be attained was unchanged. Graphically, the substitution effect is represented by a movement along the original indifference curve, U_l, from point *A* to a tangency with a new, hypothetical budget line, *KK'*, which is parallel to *MN'* but has a lower level of nonlabor income. The new utility-maximizing point is shown as *B*, with labor supply increasing to L_B, leisure time falling, and the amount of goods consumed rising. The substitution effect on labor supply is, therefore, positive. Changes in wages and changes in hours of work go in the same direction.

The **income effect** measures the change in labor supply due only to the change in the person's income which is caused by the change in the wage rate. Conceptually, it is exactly like the income effect shown by itself in Figure A4.5. In this figure it is shown as a movement from point *B* on the hypothetical budget line *KK'* to a utility-maximizing point on the new budget line *MN'*. Assuming again that leisure is a normal good, we know that point will lie somewhere to the right of *B*—leisure will increase and labor hours will fall, relative to *B*, as a result of the income effect. Notice that this effect conflicts with the substitution effect. So the net effect on labor supply will depend on which is stronger—a result we also saw in the text. In Figure A4.6 the new utility-maximizing choice is point *C*, but this is only one of several equally

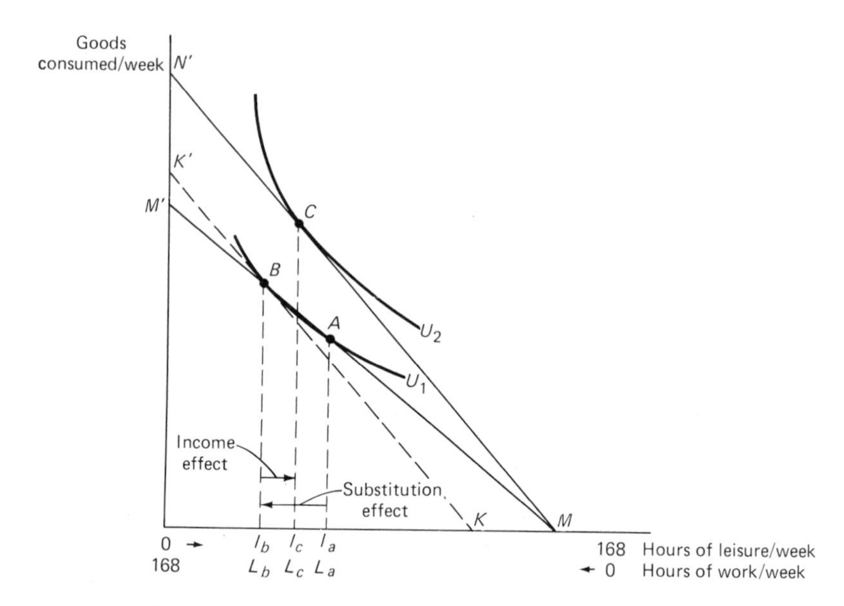

FIGURE A4.6 Income and Substitution Effects of a Wage Increase

plausible results. In this case the income effect decreases labor supply from L_B to L_C, but the net effect is an increase in labor supply from L_A to L_C. This is therefore the case in which the substitution effect outweighs the income effect, and it results in an upward-sloping labor supply curve. Wage rates and hours of work supplied go up and down together.

The opposite case is not shown here, but you can derive it yourself. If the substitution effect had been smaller and/or the income effect larger, the new utility-maximizing choice could well have ended up to the right of the original point. That result occurs when the income effect is larger than the substitution effect, so that labor hours supplied fall when the wage rate increases. In this event the labor supply curve would be negatively sloped. The famous backward-bending labor supply curve corresponds to the situation in which the substitution effect dominates at low wage levels, while the income effect dominates at higher wage levels.

This graphical form of analysis is extremely valuable in trying to assess the effects of government programs such as welfare and Social Security, and common employment practices such as overtime pay. The common feature of all of these is that they change the person's budget constraint. If you can depict the new budget constraint and the original one, you can often determine the income and substitution effects and deduce the probable changes in labor supply.

5

Extensions of Labor Supply Theory

INTRODUCTION

This chapter continues and extends the discussion of individual labor supply decisions. The first part presents an alternative, broader, and more sophisticated way to analyze the labor supply behavior of individuals. This alternative view is an application of a new theoretical approach in economics, based primarily on the influential work of Gary Becker.[1] Now known as the **new home economics**, it involves a major reorientation of the way in which economists analyze the consumption activities of individuals. In the process, labor supply decisions become just one aspect of a broader economic problem—the allocation of time among its alternative uses.

This broader approach to labor supply actually does not alter any of the basic labor supply results which we derived from the simpler approach used in Chapter 4. The new home economics approach changes principally the way we think about the problem of labor supply rather than the conclusions we draw. The basic ideas are interesting, though, and perhaps you will experience the intellectual pleasure of recognizing a clever application of economic thinking.

The second part of the chapter turns to the topic of labor force participation—the decision about whether to seek employment at all. No new theoretical concepts are needed here. The analysis of labor force participation decisions is exactly the same as the analysis of desired hours of work, except that differences in hours among working persons are ignored and only factors affecting the decision as to whether to work are considered. The insights of the new home economics approach to labor supply are especially valuable in this analysis.

There is also a considerable amount of empirical material about labor force participation to consider, especially concerning changes over time or differences among groups. Why has the proportion of women working in the labor market increased throughout this century? Why has it fallen for men? What about teenagers? What is the significance of differences between blacks and whites in the labor force activity of prime-age males? We look at the answers to these questions in the last part of the chapter.

HOUSEHOLD PRODUCTION, TIME ALLOCATION, AND INDIVIDUAL LABOR SUPPLY[2]

The Economics of Household Production

The new home economics begins by reinterpreting the economic role of a household.[3] It had been traditional in economics to regard production

[1] The basic work in this area is Becker's "A Theory of the Allocation of Time," *Economic Journal*, 1965. A more accessible (but still difficult) version is Robert T. Michael and Gary Becker, "On the New Theory of Consumer Behavior," *Swedish Journal of Economics*, 75 (1973), 378–396. It is reprinted in Gary Becker, *The Economic Approach to Human Behavior* (Chicago: The University of Chicago Press, 1976).

[2] This section can be omitted without loss of continuity.

[3] The terms "household" and "persons" will be used interchangeably. A household could, for example, be composed of a single person.

activities as occurring exclusively in firms and consumption activities exclusively in households. But in this new view, households play a dual role, as both producer and consumer. Instead of regarding individuals as if they received utility directly from goods and leisure, the new home economics approach argues that households actually engage in a vast array of production activities in which they combine their own time with various purchased inputs in order to produce "household commodities" for their own use. It is these **household-produced commodities** that are the ultimate source of utility to the household. A household becomes rather like a small firm specializing in the production of its own utility.

The idea of household production is especially useful as a way to describe those uses of a person's time which cannot readily be classified as either leisure or work. Time spent in shopping, cleaning, ironing, repairing, or caring for a child, for example, usually does not directly provide utility, so it is not leisure. But no wage is received, so it is not labor either. It makes perfect sense, though, to describe time uses such as these as time spent in household production. In activities of this type, people use their own time and usually also some purchased inputs in order to produce something—clean clothes, a well-stocked refrigerator, a healthy child—which does provide utility.

The new home economics approach actually goes a step further and extends this production analogy to *everything* that households consume. Leisure and goods disappear as direct sources of utility; the consumption of household-produced commodities using time and goods takes their place. This is a very abstract idea, so some examples may help to make the point. Producing a good dinner takes food, wine, kitchen equipment, and preparation and eating time. They are all inputs into the production of the household commodity "dinner." Producing physical fitness requires time but also an array of equipment (clothing, a tennis racket, a Nautilus machine) and an occasional doctor's visit. Producing a happy, healthy, well-educated child takes a set of time and goods inputs too diverse to list here. What would normally be called leisure now appears as a commodity with a very time intensive production technology. (Think, for instance, about the relative amounts of time and goods used in getting a suntan or watching television.) If you think cleverly enough, you can probably take almost any household activity and identify the purchased inputs and labor time used to produce it.

Just as in the case of production by a firm, here, too, it is natural to assume that there are alternative ways to produce household commodities by varying the amount of time and goods. To be specific, think about the production of the household commodity "spaghetti dinner." The technological production possibilities include making the pasta and sauce from scratch; using a pasta machine; or opening up a jar of sauce and a package of pasta, both bought at the local supermarket. (Assume, perhaps a bit unrealistically, that the same quality of spaghetti dinner could be achieved with each technology.) The first technique is highly time intensive, the second less so, and the third least of all.

This idea of alternative production techniques is, in fact, general and not confined to the production of spaghetti dinners. To represent the idea of alternative production techniques, we turn once again to production isoquants. Having done the hard work of developing the properties of isoquants in Chapter 3, there is no need to repeat it here. A set of household production isoquants is illustrated in Figure 5.1. In this case the isoquants show the different combinations of a person's time and various purchased goods (which can include someone else's time) that can be used to produce the same amount of some household commodity. Note along the horizontal axis that time used in household production is measured from right to left and hours of work are measured beneath that from left to right. (They are the only two uses of time.) Isoquants representing greater output lie, as always, farther to the northeast.

Utility Maximization, Household Production, and Labor Supply

In the labor–leisure model, the person's objective was to select a combination of goods and leisure—and thus also hours of work—which gave maximum utility. The problem here is essentially the same, the only difference being that the effect of goods and time in utility is indirect by means of the production of household commodities. The notation of utility maximization changes, but not its logic.

Suppose, for simplicity, that there is only a single household commodity (Z) and that it can be produced with goods (G) and time (T) in varying

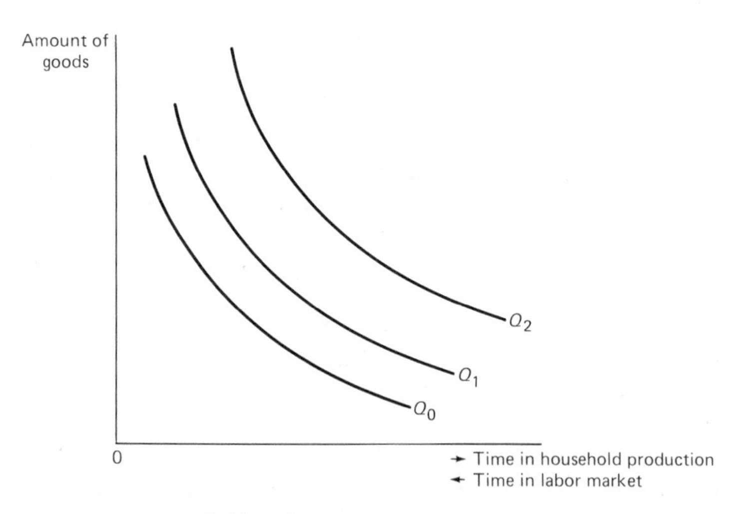

FIGURE 5.1 Household Production Isoquants

amounts.[4] The price of goods is p and the price of time is a person's wage rate, w. (We continue to assume that a person has a known wage and can work as many hours as he or she wants at that wage.) Working more hours now means spending less time on household production and simultaneously adopting a more goods-intensive production technique.

Consider the effect on utility of spending an additional hour in household production. There would be, first, an increase in the amount of Z produced and thus, second, an increase in total utility due to the increased consumption of Z. In symbols this can be expressed as

$$\frac{\Delta U}{\Delta T} = \frac{\Delta Z}{\Delta T}\frac{\Delta U}{\Delta Z}$$

The two terms on the right-hand side of this expression have familiar interpretations—$\Delta Z/\Delta T$ is the **marginal product of time** in the production of Z (MP_T) and $\Delta U/\Delta Z$ is the marginal utility of Z (MU_Z). Their product is the increase in utility from using one more hour of time in household production, a term that it is convenient to label the **marginal value of time** or MV_T.[5] Using the ideas and notation above, it follows that

$$MV_T = MP_T \cdot MU_Z \tag{5.1}$$

Considering, in exactly the same way, the effect of an additional unit of goods used in household production, we should get

$$MV_G = MP_G \cdot MU_Z \tag{5.2}$$

which is the utility value of an additional unit of goods (MV_G is the marginal value of goods and MP_G is the marginal product of goods).

Since spending more time in household production means working less in the labor market and thus using fewer goods in household production, the utility-maximizing condition involves a comparison of MV_T and MV_G. If $w = p$, it would always make sense to choose T and G so that $MV_G = MV_T$. In any other circumstance, utility could be increased by reducing by one unit or hour the lower-valued input and substituting one hour or unit of the other

[4] One commodity is sufficient to analyze the choice between time and goods used in household production. With more than one, there is the additional complication—which adds nothing to the analysis of labor supply—of how much time and goods to use in the production of each one.

[5] MV_T is very similar to MRP_L, which was discussed in Chapter 2. Both represent the value of an input to a "firm," one in terms of additional utility, the other in terms of additional revenues.

one. More generally, when $w \neq p$, the utility-maximizing condition will be

$$\frac{MV_T}{w} = \frac{MV_G}{p} \tag{5.3}$$

where the equality holds for the last hour of time and unit of goods used in household production. Time not spent in household production is supplied to the labor market. Except for the change in notation to accommodate the production aspect of the problem, this condition is identical to the one derived for the labor–leisure model. In both models, time and goods should be chosen so that their utility values are proportional to their prices.

Equation (5.3) includes the net effect of both *how* time and goods are combined to produce Z and *how much* Z is produced. A very specific and interesting prediction of this approach concerns differences in how different households will choose to produce household commodities. A necessary condition for utility maximization is that household commodities be produced in the least costly way. Just as firms choose among various combinations of labor and capital on the basis of the relative prices of the two inputs, so individuals must make the same kind of choice in light of the relative prices of goods and time. As a first approximation, the price of goods is the same for everyone, but that is not true for the price of time, simply because wage rates differ among individuals. Thus, high-wage individuals will usually choose more goods-intensive ways to produce household commodities (the relative price of goods is lower for them), while individuals with lower wage rates will use more time-intensive techniques.

This prediction is shown in Figure 5.2. People with high wage rates would choose points like A, which use relatively little time and correspondingly more goods. For persons with lower wages, points farther down the isoquant, like B, are preferred. Although people with higher wages will produce any given amount of a household commodity with less time and more goods than people with lower wages, it does not follow that they will spend less total time in household production. Their higher wage enables them to afford more time and/or more goods. They would, therefore, typically end up on a higher isoquant, but still using a more goods-intensive production technique. In Figure 5.2 this is represented by point C. There is no certainty about whether C lies to the left or right of B.

The Supply Curve of Labor

To derive the supply curve of labor, we need to consider how time spent in household production will change when the price of time changes. It is common to think of a firm using less of any factor of production whose price increases, but again, this situation is peculiar because an increase in price increases the wealth of this "firm."

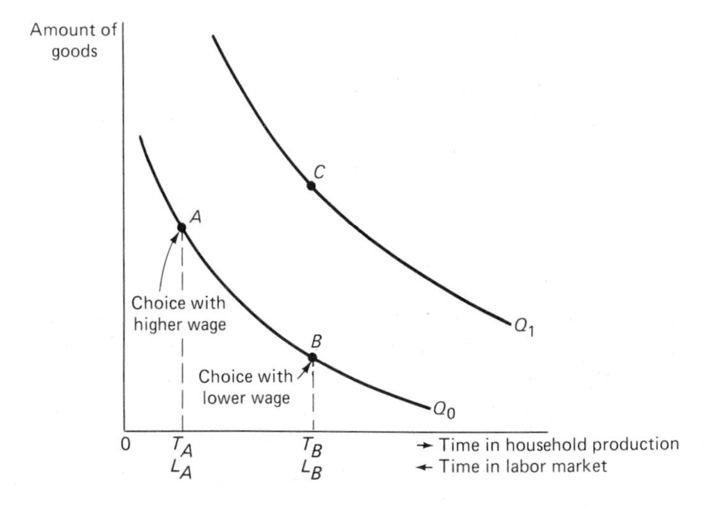

FIGURE 5.2 The Effect of Wages on the Use of Time and Goods in Household Production

The effects can be explained with the help of Figure 5.3. Suppose that a person's initial position was described by point A. An increase in the wage would have two effects. First, with the now higher price of time, the person would, even if the same amount of output were to be produced, move to a point like B, substituting some now relatively less expensive goods for time. This is exactly like the substitution effect in a firm's choice of inputs, and the effect on labor supply is exactly like the substitution effect in the labor–leisure analysis. It causes a person to work more hours in response to a wage increase.

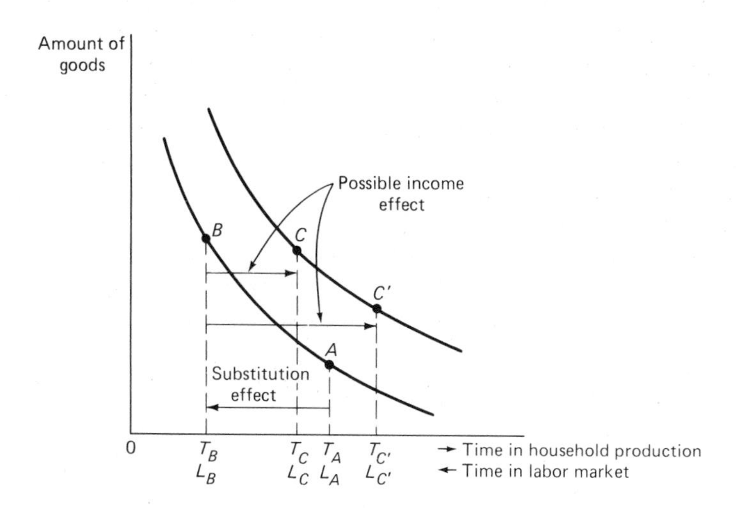

FIGURE 5.3 Household Production and the Supply Curve of Labor

In addition, there is an income effect to contend with. The higher wage rate increases a person's income, making it possible to purchase more goods and more time and thus increase the production and consumption of household commodities. How will this affect labor supply? In the labor–leisure case, the higher income led to increased consumption of leisure under the reasonable assumption that leisure was a normal good. Here the effect is not quite so straightforward. It is usually true that it is more efficient (less costly) to increase production of a commodity by adding more of all factors of production, rather than just one. If so, in this case, the income effect would cause a person to increase the amount of both goods and time, thereby reducing hours of work in the labor market. The final result could be a point like C or C', depending on the strength of the income effect. Just as in the labor–leisure model, the income and substitution effects conflict. Economic theory does not predict whether labor hours will rise or fall when the wage rate increases.

When all is said and done, the results of this novel approach to labor supply are exactly the same as in the less complex version, which is a strong argument in favor of the simpler, if less realistic labor–leisure model.[6] This version does, however, suggest one important idea that cannot be derived from the simpler model. Recognizing the role of time as a productive input raises the possibility that its productivity might change over time or that technological change might affect the household production process. Changes like that, which are not suggested by the labor–leisure model, will be an important part of understanding changes in the labor force activity of married women in the twentieth century.

LABOR FORCE PARTICIPATION

Thus far we have looked at only a single dimension of labor supply—a person's decision about how many hours to work. It is natural to emphasize that aspect, because it leads directly to a labor supply curve. It is, however, often useful to examine labor supply from a slightly different perspective, by looking at the number of *individuals* who are willing to work rather than the number of *labor hours* supplied to the market. Here the focus is on the issue of *labor force participation*, which involves an analysis of whether or not a person's desired hours of work are greater than zero.

The standard measure of labor force participation is the **labor force**

[6] The real power of this approach has been in opening up entirely new areas of human behavior to economic analysis, primarily those involving nonmarket uses of time. A long list of traditionally noneconomic activities—from marriage and divorce to fertility behavior and "parenting" to choice of travel mode—have been analyzed within the theoretical framework of the new home economics. The verdict is not yet in on this work, but the ideas are intriguing and the potential is great.

participation rate, or LFPR. The LFPR measures the proportion of the population (age 16 or older) who are either employed or officially classified as unemployed.[7] Unemployed persons are considered as labor force participants because their *desired* labor supply is greater than zero, even though their *actual* hours of work are not. It is a simple matter to calculate LFPRs, either for the economy as a whole or for any specific group in the economy. If E is the number of employed persons, U the number of unemployed persons, and P the size of the relevant population, the LFPR $= (E + U)/P$. In 1983, for instance, the civilian population over age 16 included about 172 million persons, of whom 99.5 million were employed and 10.7 million unemployed. The LFPR, then, was $(99.5 + 10.7)/172$ or about 64 percent. Data on LFPRs are collected and published monthly by the Bureau of Labor Statistics on the basis of information provided by a regular monthly survey, the Current Population Survey.

Labor force participation rates are studied by economists for several reasons. The LFPR tells us something we do not learn directly from a labor supply curve, namely the extent of attachment or "connectedness" to the labor market. There is no numerical standard by which to evaluate LFPRs—high rates are not necessarily better than low ones, nor is the reverse true. But changes in LFPRs over time or large differences between relatively similar groups often indicate that something significant is happening. Second, the LFPR is one labor supply statistic that does exhibit a great deal of variation, both across demographic groups at a point in time and for the same group over time. Trying to explain the historical patterns and the current differences is an interesting but difficult task.

An Economic Analysis of Labor Force Participation[8]

The economic analysis of labor force participation draws directly on the basic principles that we have already developed to analyze decisions about hours of work. The similarity of the analysis is actually not surprising, since the decision not to participate in the labor market is the same thing as the decision to supply zero hours of work. The important point is that nonparticipation is a utility-maximizing choice under particular circumstances.

Before we turn to that analysis, we need to clear up one matter. Labor supply decisions have been analyzed from two different perspectives: first, as the choice between labor and leisure, and second, as the choice between

[7] To be officially considered as unemployed, a person must have taken a specific action to find employment within the previous four weeks. Otherwise, he or she is classified as "not in the labor force." We look further at these definitions in Chapter 12 when we discuss unemployment.

[8] See the Appendix to this chapter for a graphical analysis of labor force participation using indifference curves and budget constraints.

time spent in the labor market and time spent in household production.[9] The basic logic of utility maximization is similar, but its precise form and the resulting notation differs. Which approach should we use to analyze labor force participation? Simplicity favors the labor–leisure model, but the idea of household production is indispensable for understanding nonparticipation. A compromise is definitely in order.

The discussion of labor force participation that follows will be greatly simplified if we first refer to time not spent in the labor market by the generic title **nonmarket time**, and second, use the neutral term **marginal utility of time** (MU_T) to refer to the value of an additional hour of nonmarket time. In this use, nonmarket time could be either leisure or time spent in household production. Similarly, the marginal utility of time could represent either the direct effect on leisure on utility, as in the labor–leisure model, or its indirect effect, as in the household production model.

Using this notation, the condition for utility maximization requires that time and goods be chosen so that

$$\frac{MU_T}{w} = \frac{MU_G}{p} \tag{5.4}$$

where, as always, the equality holds for the last hour of time and last unit of goods used. It is especially useful to note that if $MU_T/w > MU_G/p$, utility can be increased by substituting time for goods, thereby reducing hours of work in the labor market, and if $MU_T/w < MU_G/p$, utility could be increased by increasing labor hours and goods while cutting back on nonmarket time.

The easiest way to understand the issue of labor force participation is to think about whether or not it might ever be utility maximizing for a person to work zero hours in the labor market and instead, spend all of his or her time in nonmarket uses. The key is whether the equality of equation (5.4), necessary for utility maximization, holds when MU_T and MU_G are evaluated at that point of zero labor supply.

One common possibility is that a person finds that at zero hours of work, $MU_T/w < MU_G/p$. In that event, utility can be increased by increasing hours of work and decreasing nonmarket time (thereby raising MU_T) and increasing the amount of goods consumed (which lowers MU_G). A person like that will choose to participate in the labor market, supplying labor until the necessary equality of equation (5.4) holds.

In contrast, some people may find instead that at zero hours of work, $MU_T/w \geq MU_G/p$. If the equality holds, exactly zero hours of work would

[9] If you skipped the section on the household production approach to labor supply, a brief summary will help. The basic idea is that households produce their own utility by combining some purchased inputs with their own "leisure time." In this view, leisure and goods disappear as direct sources of utility and the consumption of household-produced commodities takes their place.

be utility maximizing. When the inequality holds, the person would actually choose to supply negative hours of work if that were possible. (Since it is not, zero hours of work is the utility-maximizing choice.)

Posing the labor force participation decision in this way suggests something about the circumstances in which nonparticipation is likely to occur. In a formal sense, anything that raises the value of MU_T/w relative to MU_G/p, both evaluated at the point of all nonmarket time and no work, is a likely candidate. If we examine the terms one at a time, we can identify the possibility.[10]

Start with the marginal utility of goods. If a person has no source of income other than his or her potential labor market earnings, the MU_G at zero hours of work will be extraordinarily high, since no goods at all can be consumed. In that case, labor force participation is virtually certain. Put simply, persons who must work in order to eat invariably do work. The opposite case is one in which a person does have a source of nonlabor income, so that the MU_G, even at zero hours of work, is much lower. The greater the nonlabor income, then, other things the same, the lower is the MU_G at zero hours, and the greater the possibility that nonparticipation will be utility maximizing.

Nonlabor income can come from many sources. Various government programs, including AFDC, Social Security, and even unemployment compensation are examples. Inherited wealth and private pensions are other possibilities. Finally, the labor income of one spouse—the primary earner—can be treated as nonlabor income from the standpoint of the other, since it is income not dependent on his or her own labor supply.

A second possible effect concerns the MU_G curve itself. People with strong preferences for goods and material possessions will have MU_G curves which are positioned very high, whereas people with much more modest desires will have MU_G curves that are everywhere lower. The weaker are preferences for goods, the lower will be the MU_G at zero hours of work.

On the other side of the equation, nonparticipation is more likely when MU_T is high and/or the wage rate is low. The most common cause of a high MU_T is a high value of time in household activities—especially caring for young children or a large family. A strong preference for leisure is a second possibility. In either case, the entire MU_T curve would be shifted upward, so that its value even at the point of maximum nonmarket time is still quite high. It takes only a little imagination to visualize the upward shift in the MU_T curve of one or both parents which occurs with the birth of a child. (Think about the shift in the MU_T curve with twins or triplets.) As for a low wage, it lowers the price of time, thus increasing the amount of nonmarket time consumed.

[10] As a first approximation, all persons face the same prices for goods and services, so there is no need to discuss the effects of differences in p.

TABLE 5.1 Likely Conditions for Nonparticipation in the Labor Market

CONDITION	REASON
MU_T high	High productivity of time in household production Strong preference for leisure
MU_G low	Nonlabor income allows consumption without working Weak preference for goods
Wage low	Low price of nonmarket time

Table 5.1 summarizes the discussion above, showing the circumstances under which nonparticipation might be more probable. When several conditions hold at once, nonparticipation becomes more likely. Examples are not difficult to construct. As we saw in Chapter 4, the welfare system both provides income not dependent on work (lowering MU_G at zero hours of work) and sharply reduces a person's wage rate, which in many cases is quite low to begin with. Nonparticipation is a likely outcome. The same is true of Social Security. Another common case involves the nonparticipation of married women. Not surprisingly, participation is less frequent among women with young children (the entire MU_T schedule is higher) and also for women whose husband's income is high (the MU_G at zero hours of work is lower).

Finally, we should briefly consider several factors which often complicate real-world labor force participation decisions without altering the basic logic. People do not, for instance, always have the opportunity to work exactly the amount they want, especially if that amount is relatively small. For practical reasons, employers may often require some minimum number of hours per week. If the minimum is high enough, even a person who satisfies the logical requirement for labor force participation of equation (5.4) might choose not to work. The decision here involves an "all-or-nothing" comparison rather than one involving small adjustments at the margin.

A similar choice may develop as a result of the costs associated with working, expenditures for such items as clothing and transportation. If these costs are at least partially fixed—that is, they are about the same no matter how many hours a person works—it may not make sense to work only a few hours. Again, a person is confronted by an all-or-nothing choice.

Trends in Labor Force Participation

From 1948, when regular data on LFPRs first became available, until the late-1960s, there was virtually no trend at all in the LFPR for the U.S. economy as a whole. The civilian LFPR never fell more than a few tenths of a point below 59 percent and never climbed above 60 percent. That apparent stability, though, was misleading. During that period there were substantial changes in the extent of labor force participation for different groups in the economy, but the changes offset each other. Since the late 1960s, however, and continuing into the 1980s, the aggregate LFPR has moved steadily upward at an unusually rapid pace by historical standards. In 1984 the civilian labor force participation rate was over 64 percent, the highest annual rate ever recorded.

Labor force participation rates are more interesting and more revealing when they are disaggregated on the basis of race, sex, or age. There the patterns are very different and some of the historical changes are quite significant. Below, we look separately at each of the major demographic groups in the economy.

Adult Women. The demographic group that has attracted the most attention from economists interested in labor force participation is women, especially married women. This is not very surprising: the labor force activity of women has increased dramatically in the twentieth century, especially in the period since World War II. That increase has not only had a major impact on the labor market, but it has transformed the traditional structure of family life. The old stereotype of a family with a working husband and a full-time "nonworking" housewife is now far from the norm. In March 1980, for example, less than one-fourth of all married households in the United States fit this pattern. In that year, for the first time, over half of all married women with husband present were in the labor force.

Before trying to explain these far-reaching changes, let's first note the basic facts and trends which are summarized in Table 5.2 At the turn of the century, the labor force participation of women was confined largely to unmarried women. Nearly 40 percent of single women worked, but less than 5 percent of married women did. World War II, with its image of "Rosie the Riveter," is often regarded as marking a sharp change in women's labor force participation. Participation rates for married women did rise sharply, from 14 percent in 1940 to 23 percent during the peak war-production year of 1944. Since then the rates have risen steadily for virtually all groups of women. For all women (age 16 and older) the participation rate increased by nearly 20 percentage points between 1950 and 1983. Even more rapid were the increases for married women—nearly 30 percentage points—and for married women with preschool-age children, whose participation rate increased fourfold. Note that for married women the increase in participation rate is not just a phenomenon of the 1970s, something that occurred only due to the emergence of the women's movement and the often difficult economic environment of that decade. Rather, participation rates rose steadily throughout the 1950s, the 1960s, and the 1970s. Only for married women with young children do the 1970s show an acceleration in the rate of growth of the participation rate.

Finally, there had historically been a very substantial difference in the labor force participation rates of black women and white women. In 1954, the difference was about 13 percentage points—46 percent versus 33 per-

TABLE 5.2 Female Labor Force Participation Rates (%) by Marital Status, Race, and Year

	1950	1954	1965	1974	1983
All	33.9	34.6	39.3	45.6	52.9
Married, spouse present	23.8	26.6	34.7	43.1	52.2
Married, spouse present, with children below age 6	11.9	14.9	23.2	34.4	49.9
White	—	33.3	38.1	45.2	52.7
Black	—	46.1	48.6	49.3	54.4

cent—but the gap has steadily narrowed since then, due to the more rapid increase in the rate for white women. By 1983, there was only a 2 percentage point difference by race for all women. Interestingly, black women who are married with spouse present are still considerably more likely to work than are similar white women, but the reverse is true for never-married women.

Any change whose effects are as far-reaching as the rise in women's labor force participation is bound to attract a great deal of study, from non-economists as well as economists. There is room here for many different explanations. Sociological explanations have emphasized the effects of changes in the attitudes of both men and women regarding the role of women in both family life and in the workplace. Attitudinal survey data show a growing acceptance of women working outside the home and of the idea that work activities for a woman do not necessarily interfere with family life. Sociologists have also pointed to changing life-style patterns—for example, later age of marriage, increased incidence of divorce, and smaller family size—all of which are associated with greater labor force activity. It is, however, not clear that these changing life-style patterns are the *cause* of the changing labor force participation rates. They could just as easily be the result of it or, as many economists would be inclined to argue, the joint result of other underlying changes. Some demographers have stressed the development and widespread use of modern contraceptives, which have made it possible to control the number and timing of pregnancies.

The economic approach to this phenomenon is a bit different from these. As is usually the case, most economists emphasize the roles of prices, income, and individual choice and tend to avoid relying on changes in individuals' preferences or social institutions. Recall that participation is utility maximization when $MU_T/w < MU_G/p$ and nonparticipation when $MU_T/w \geq MU_G/p$, both evaluated at a point of no work. Since labor force participation has risen, it follows logically that MU_T/w must have fallen over time relative to MU_G/p. Both sides may have risen or both may have fallen, but there must have been a relative change in the values. This is a logical inference from the assumption of utility maximization. The burden of explanation, then, is to show how or why that change might have occurred.

One factor which economists think has had a major effect is the increase in the average wage rate of women throughout most of the postwar period. With the exception of the last decade, the postwar period was one in which economic growth was substantial and both labor productivity and wages rose steadily and substantially. Even after adjusting for the effects of inflation, average gross hourly earnings for all workers in the economy nearly doubled between 1947 and the mid-1970s.[11] As wage rates rose, this increased the price of nonmarket time and thus provided an incentive for a nonworking woman to substitute market goods (prepared foods, day care, etc.) for her own time. In labor supply terms, there is a substitution effect, increasing the probability of labor force participation. Because there is no offsetting income effect of a wage increase for women not already working in the labor market, the net effect of this definitely is to increase the LFPR.

Occurring at about the same time, there have also been enormous changes in the technology of household production. Think for a moment about the "capital equipment" now readily available for household production which was either completely unavailable or very expensive previously. The list would include such things as refrigerators, freezers, stoves, microwave ovens, food processors, washers and dryers, vacuum cleaners, prepared foods, permanent-press fabrics, and so on. The introduction and spread of these greatly increased the possible substitution for a person's time in household production. In conjunction with the general rise in wage rates for women, this provided a second force leading to increased labor force participation.

There are at least two other economic explanations of the rising trend in LFPRs for married women. It is possible that families have become more consumption-oriented than in the past (their MU_G schedule has shifted up) and thus have chosen to have the wife forgo some leisure, work more, and together enjoy a higher material standard of living. That is certainly possible, but there are some problems with this explanation. For one thing, it depends on an unobservable change in preferences, which is the kind of argument that economists are reluctant to accept. Second, the postwar period was, as noted just above, one in which wage rates for men rose quite consistently. For most families, income increased substantially, so it would have been possible to enjoy a higher material standard of living even without the labor force participation of the wife.

A subtler argument along these lines is the **relative income hypothesis**, also known as the **Easterlin hypothesis** after the economist, Richard Easterlin, who advanced it.[12] There are three principal parts to his argument. First, Easterlin assumes that people acquire from their parental home an expectation of what their own adult standard of living should be. For example, children

[11] Because the ratio of women's earnings to men's earnings has been quite stable during this period, it is safe to assume that women experienced increasing wage levels.

[12] See Richard Easterlin, *Birth and Fortune* (New York: Basic Books, Inc., 1980).

in the Great Depression era developed modest income expectations, while those in the early postwar period typically had higher expectations since family incomes were higher and had grown steadily. Second, Easterlin noted that there had been a cyclical pattern in average family size in the United States—very low during the Great Depression, peaking during the baby-boom years of the early-to-mid 1950s, and then falling through the 1960s and 1970s. Ultimately, these fertility swings will affect the labor market via the supply curve of labor. If other things are about equal, we would expect adults who were born during low-fertility periods to have greater labor market success (they are part of a smaller supply of labor) than the adults of baby-boom periods.

Taken together, these two factors have caused individuals' income expectations to be frequently frustrated. Consider, for example, children who were born during the 1950s baby boom. According to Easterlin, they acquired high income expectations because of their parent's economic success. Their own adult incomes, however, were lower than they expected, precisely because of the unusually large supply of labor caused by the baby boom.

Finally, Easterlin links these events to the changes in the LFPR of married women. He argues that the primary cause of the increase is the failure of husband's incomes to be as high as expected. Their income is low not in any absolute sense, but only *relative* to their expectations—hence the name, "relative income hypothesis." Women, then, enter the labor market primarily to compensate for the gap between actual income and expectations.

Easterlin's hypothesis is a broad, sweeping one, attempting to account not only for trends in labor force activity, but also in fertility behavior and in income. You should note that it is somewhat unorthodox—at least, for economics—since it relies so heavily on unobservable changes in the preferences of individuals. Although the model captures some of the broad secular changes, tests with data on individuals have not been very supportive of its predictions.

Thus far, we have tried only to explain the changes in female labor force participation which have occurred over time. But even in 1985, only about half of all women were in the labor force. What types of factors explain the differences among women in the labor force participation at a point in time?[13]

To almost no one's great surprise, the presence of very young children has a strong negative impact on labor force participation. In 1983, the participation rate was nearly 65 percent for married women with no children under age six and 50 percent for women who did have children under age six. One need not be an economist to recognize the importance of that, although probably only an economist would describe the care of young children as an especially time-intensive household production activity. Actually, it is not obvious that this parental time need be the wife's, although that is

[13] You may recall that this kind of analysis is called cross-sectional analysis.

still the most common arrangement. But why? If a wife's wages were lower than her husband's for any reason whatsoever (even including labor market discrimination against women), it might be sensible for a husband and wife to specialize in market and nonmarket work, respectively, when there are young children. Similar specialization might also be indicated if women were somehow more productive in household activities than men were. (Of course, exactly the opposite results would make sense if women were better paid and/or men the more productive at home.) In truth, the evidence here is not as clear as economists sometimes suggest. On average, women are paid less than men, but what matters are the relative wages of wives and their husbands. The number of men who are out of the labor force to care for children while their higher-paid wives work is still small enough to be regarded as newsworthy. The productivity of household time is very difficult to measure, so the task of determining whether sex-based differences exist is not promising. Economic forces such as these may be important in determining whose time is devoted to child care, but they are unlikely to be the whole story. Noneconomic factors are almost certainly relevant as well.

Two other factors affecting female labor force participation are frequently noted. One is the income of the husband, which has been found to have a negative effect on a wife's labor force activity. That is, among women who are otherwise in similar circumstances, those whose husbands have higher incomes are less likely to participate. A good example of this is the higher participation rate of married black women, which is due partly to the fact that black men, on average, earn less than white men. A second factor is a married woman's education, which usually increases the likelihood that she is in the labor force. This suggests that education increases the wage rate more than the value of time at home. There is, however, one interesting exception to this. Studies of time diaries show that more educated women spend *more* time than do less educated women in child-care activities for preschool children, but spend less time in other household production activities. As a result, labor force participation rates for women with different levels of education are similar when there are preschool children, but different at other points in the life cycle. This could reflect either very limited substitution possibilities in the case of young children or, perhaps, a beneficial effect of education in the value of time in child care.

Adult Men. In our society, most men are now and have always been regular participants in the labor market. The work decision is almost automatic for most men, and it is the exceptions that attract the attention of economists. For all males over age 20, the LFPR was 78.5 percent in 1983, but for prime-age males between the ages of 25 and 54, the rate was between 93 and 94 percent and for married men it was higher yet. Since 1948, the overall rate for men has fallen nearly 10 percentage points, owing largely to a sharp, but not surprising, decline in the LFPR of older males. In 1948, over 70 percent of all men age 55 and over were still in the labor force, whereas in 1983 only 46 percent were. The explanation is straightforward. There has been a substantial income effect reducing labor supply due to greater personal wealth, substantially increased Social Security benefits, and the increased availability of private pensions. LFPRs for prime-age males have also fallen since 1948 but by just a few percentage points.

The other notable development in adult male LFPRs has been the decline in the relative LFPR of black males. Table 5.3 presents the basic information for selected years beginning in 1954, when separate data by race first became available. Black and white LFPRs were virtually identical through 1968 (although both declined between 1954 and 1968), but since then a 5 to 10 percentage point differential has emerged. As the 1982 data show, the LFPR differential exists throughout the prime-age categories.

These race differences in LFPRs are both important and puzzling. They are important because they tell us that between 10 and 20 percent of prime-age black males have no connection at all to the labor market, surely not an encouraging statistic as far as the economic status of black families is concerned. It is puzzling, moreover, because the LFPR difference has developed during the period of the 1970s, in which labor market conditions for black workers actually improved substantially. With that more favorable economic climate, increased labor force participation might more reasonably have been expected.

Although there are, as yet, no definitive explanations, some tentative ideas follow:

1. Many blacks still have less education and fewer skills than whites, so their labor market opportunities may be much worse. This is negatively related to labor force participation for both blacks and whites.
2. Health also appears to be a factor—a much larger fraction of blacks who

TABLE 5.3 Male Labor Force Participation Rates (%) by Race

YEAR	GROUP	WHITE	BLACK
1954	Age 20 and older	87.8	87.1
1960	Age 20 and older	86.0	86.2
1968	Age 20 and older	83.2	82.2
1975	Age 20 and older	80.7	76.8
1980	Age 20 and older	79.8	75.9
1983	Age 20 and older	78.9	75.2
	Age 20–24	85.4	76.2
	Age 25–34	95.1	88.7
	Age 35–44	96.2	90.4
	Age 45–54	92.3	84.3
	Age 55–64	69.6	64.2

are nonparticipants report they are disabled. These reports are subjective, so we cannot be certain what it means, but clear differences exist.

3. Marital status also appears to matter, although the causal relationship is unclear. There is, for example, virtually no LFPR difference between black and white males who are married with spouse present. But a much smaller percentage of black males than white males—half compared to two-thirds—fall into that category. A large fraction of black males are "never married" and have LFPRs that are quite low. Does marital status affect labor force participation, or is it just the opposite? Or do underlying factors affect both similarly? We really do not know.
4. Finally, several economists have attributed the falling LFPR to the growing attractiveness of government welfare programs.[14] One program in particular which is thought to have had an adverse effect is the Social Security disability program, which began in 1957 and grew rapidly through the 1970s. The AFDC-UP program is also cited, although no quantitative estimates of its effects are available.

Teenagers. The LFPR of teenagers has been the most difficult to understand in the past 30 to 35 years. For both sexes and races together, the teenage LFPR first fell steadily from 53 percent in 1948 to a low of 43.6 percent in early 1965 and then began to rise just as steadily to nearly 60 percent in the late 1970s and early 1980s. That pattern accurately depicts the experience of white teenagers, but the trend for blacks is quite different. For black male teens, the LFPR continued to fall steadily even after 1965, and in 1983 the rate was under 41 percent—its lowest mark ever and nearly 20 percentage points lower than for white males. (This low figure is all the more astonishing when you recognize that a large proportion of black teens classified as labor force participants are, in fact, unemployed.) The LFPR for black female teens is also lower than for whites, but it has moved erratically between 30 and 40 percent without any obvious trend. In 1983 the rate stood at 33.4%, also 20 percentage points below the corresponding rate for whites.

Here, too, it must be admitted that the causes of the changes in the participation rates for both white and black teenagers are not well understood. It has not been easy to identify factors that abruptly changed in 1965—for whites only. There have been large changes in school enrollment rates and in military conscription, as well as a large movement of blacks from the rural South to urban areas in both the North and the South. Each of these may have had some impact. But as a recent BLS report concluded: "No simple explanation seems to conform with the observed patterns."[15]

[14] See Donald O. Parsons, "Racial Trends in Male Labor Force Participation," *American Economic Review*, 1980, and Richard Butler and James Heckman, "The Government's Impact on the Labor Market Status of Black Americans: A Critical Review," Industrial Relations Research Association Series, 1977.

[15] *Recent Trends in Labor Force Participation: A Chartbook*, U.S. Department of Labor, Bureau of Labor Statistics, 1980, Report 609, p. 2.

SUMMARY

In this chapter we first considered a second approach to labor supply analysis and then looked at a second dimension of labor supply. The household production approach developed by Becker offers new insights into the broader issue of time allocation, of which time supplied to the market is now but one aspect. The transformation of households into producing-and-consuming units is both ingenious and undeniably correct. It is also undeniable that labor supply decisions are much more difficult to analyze. For the purpose of analyzing individual labor supply decisions, the simpler labor/leisure model of Chapter 4 is actually preferable. The simpler model, though, is useless when it comes to analyzing the different nonmarket uses of time, and it also falls short in trying to assess how developments in household technology would affect labor supply. The strengths and weaknesses of the two approaches to labor supply illustrate a basic idea about the use of models in economics—the amount of useful detail in a model depends on the purposes for which it is used. There is no single best model. Sometimes, a more unrealistic model is better than one that is more realistic. For other purposes, it may be inferior.

The analysis of labor force participation provides a second labor supply statistic. It is easily measured and it provides useful information on the extent of labor market attachment for different groups in the economy. The economic analysis of the labor force participation decision is exactly the same as the analysis of the hours-of-work decision. The decision not to participate is, after all, also an hours-of-work decision—namely, the decision to work zero hours. Economic theory suggests that nonparticipation will be more common when nonmarket time is highly valued, when nonlabor income is relatively high, and when the wage rate is low.

The most important trend in labor force participation is the rising rate of participation for married women. Economists attribute much of the increase to rising wage rates coupled with the introduction of laborsaving technology in the household. A puzzling and worrisome development is the fall in the LFPR of adult black men (compared to whites) in the period since the mid-1960s. Between 10 and 20 percent of prime-age black men are not classified as being in the labor force. Also not well understood is the enormous current differential in the LFPRs of white and black teenagers. This, too, is a matter of concern and one that needs further study.

New Concepts

New home economics
Household production
Marginal product of time (MP_T)
Marginal value of time (MV_T)

Marginal product of goods (MP_G)
Marginal value of goods (MV_G)
Labor force participation rate (LFPR)
Nonmarket time
Marginal utility of time (MU_T)
Relative income hypothesis

APPENDIX: A Graphical Analysis of Labor Force Participation

The indifference curve–budget constraint approach can be readily applied to the analysis of labor force participation. Nonparticipation is simply the special case in which the tangency between an indifference curve and the budget line occurs at zero hours of work. Economists often call that a **corner solution**—the solution is in the corner of the diagram—compared to the usual case which is called, for obvious reasons, an **interior solution**.

In analyses of nonparticipation, it is common to assume that the person in question has a strong preference for nonmarket time, regarded either as leisure or time in household production. For expositional and graphical ease, let's treat nonmarket time as leisure, which enables us to draw indifference curves without also considering the production aspect of the problem. The corresponding indifference curves would be relatively steep, indicating that a person is willing to give up a large amount of goods in return for additional hours of leisure.

As always, utility maximization involves choosing a point on the highest attainable indifference curve. A series of budget constraints are shown in Figure A5.1, each for the same, relatively low wage rate, but with differing amounts of nonlabor income. If AA' were the budget constraint—that is, there is no nonlabor income—the person would choose point M, working L_M hours. An increase in nonlabor income (budget line ABB') reduces labor hours to L_N, and a further increase, to ACC', results in nonparticipation. The tangency between that budget line and the highest attainable indifference curve occurs at point C, where hours of work are zero. Intuitively, the amount of consumption available at point C is large enough that relative to this person's preferences and wage rate, it is not sensible to sacrifice leisure to obtain more goods.

The decision not to participate in the labor force depends on the particular configuration of preferences, prices (including the wage rate), and the nonlabor income. Thus Figure A5.1 showed that for a given set of preferences and a fixed wage, nonparticipation depends on the level of nonlabor income. Similarly, for given preferences and nonlabor income, the wage rate is decisive. Figure A5.2 repeats budget line ACC' from Figure A5.1, but also includes a second budget line representing the same nonlabor income, but a

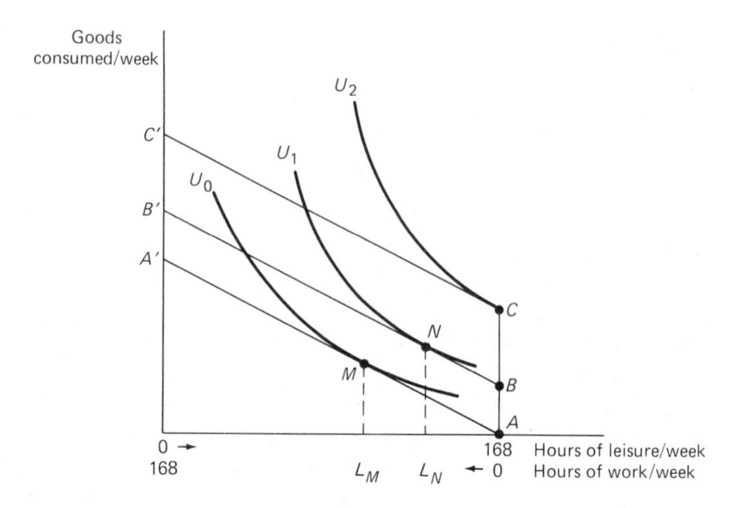

FIGURE A5.1 The Effect of Nonlabor Income on Labor Force Participation

higher wage. This is shown as ACD. With that budget line, utility is maximized at P on indifference curve U_3. It is now utility maximizing to participate in the labor force. The lowest wage at which a person is willing to work is the reservation wage. As you can readily see, it is a function of a person's preferences and nonlabor income.

Finally, for a given wage and nonlabor income, nonparticipation depends on preferences. The flatter the relevant indifference curves, the more likely the participation. This is shown in Figure A5.3. With preferences as

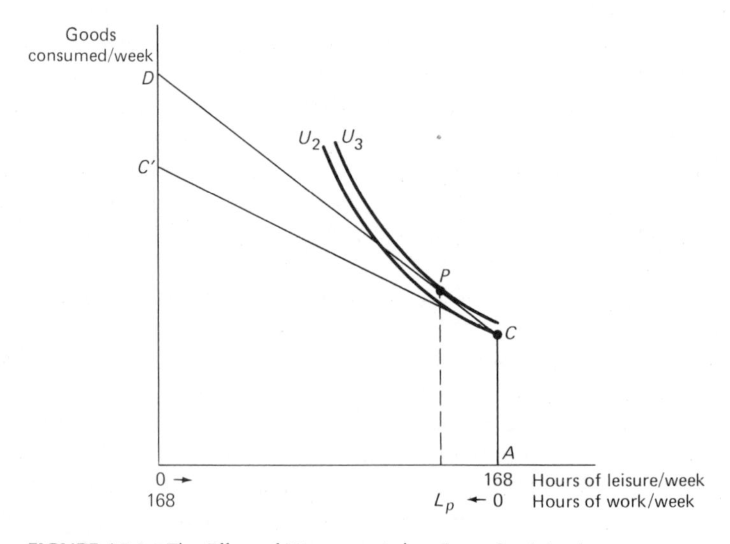

FIGURE A5.2 The Effect of Wages on Labor Force Participation

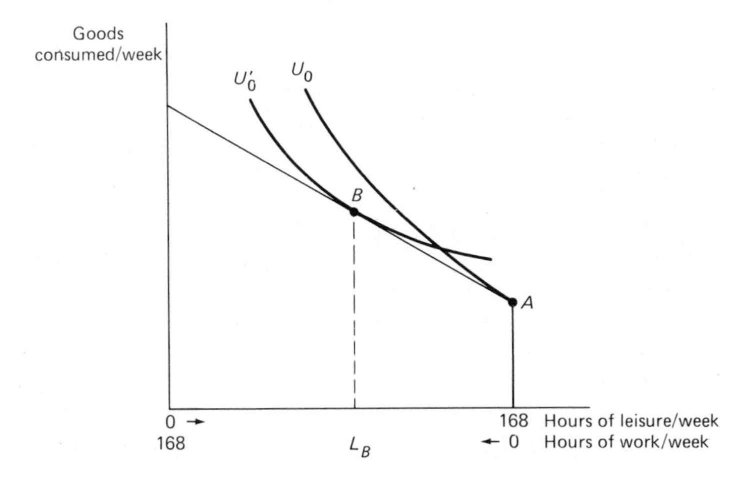

FIGURE A5.3 The Effect of Preferences on Labor Force Participation

represented by U_0, utility maximization occurs at point A and labor supply is zero. But if preferences are as represented by curve U_0', the same wage and nonlabor income would lead to participation in the labor force.

6

Human Capital

INTRODUCTION

In this chapter we take a major step forward in our analysis of the labor market by dropping the least realistic of the basic assumptions with which we began in Chapter 2. That is the assumption that all workers are identical, an assumption which, although extremely useful for isolating the basic principles of supply and demand, clearly lacks the ring of truth. In reality, labor is heterogeneous and not homogeneous, and we now turn to the analysis of these differences. Indeed, the differences among individuals and the labor market effects of those differences will occupy us for much of the rest of this book.

Needless to say, workers differ from one another in an almost endless number of ways. We focus in this chapter on one important kind of difference among individuals—differences in the labor market skills and abilities that they acquire. The key word here is *acquire*. In later chapters we look at two other kinds of differences, those due to skills which are essentially inborn and hence unlearnable, and those arising from an individual's race, sex, or other personal characteristics. The first of these leads to the concept of economic rent, which concerns the pricing of unique or highly specialized resources, while the other involves the analysis of labor market discrimination. We look briefly at the concept of economic rent in Chapter 8 and much more extensively at labor market discrimination in Chapter 9.

The set of ideas we present in this chapter is called the human capital model and its development in the early 1960s ushered in a new era of research by labor economists.[1] With skill differences among workers recognized and made a central feature of the analysis, labor economists could—and did—tackle a new set of topics, many of which turned out to be among the most important and controversial economic issues of the day. For example, economists began to examine the causes of differences in income among individuals, something they could do in only a limited way using the ideas presented thus far (Chapters 2 to 5). The analysis of poverty and of wealth—of the personal distribution of income and inequality of opportunity—became an integral part of labor economics. Economists also began to analyze the process by which individuals acquired valuable labor market skills in the first place. In more formal economics language, workers' skills were now treated as **endogenous**, meaning that they were themselves the focus of analysis. (In contrast, in Chapters 2 to 5 workers' skills were treated as **exogenous**, something that was simply taken as given and neither analyzed nor explained.) In doing that, economists using the human capital approach greatly altered the simple conception of the labor market and also provided a novel way to look at some common individual activities, such as going to college, learning skills

[1] The concept of human capital is actually an old idea in economics, first discussed by Adam Smith in *The Wealth of Nations*. But between 1776 and the early 1960s, the concept fell into disuse as labor economists focused primarily on the ideas presented in Chapters 2 to 5.

at work, and even the time parents spend with their children.

To appreciate the significance of the human capital model, consider first the phrase itself—**human capital**. It is really a very strange but revealing amalgam of ideas. Traditionally, labor and capital had been treated by economists as two distinct factors of production. Labor was a homogeneous human input and capital was machinery. An even more basic distinction was that capital was itself a "produced means of production." That is, it did not fall from the skies or grow in abundance from the trees. Rather, capital had to be produced, meaning that some scarce resources which could have been used to raise *current* living standards were used instead for capital investment.

The essential truth, suggested by the name "human capital," is that these ideas apply to labor as well. Think for a moment about yourself and the skills you now possess. You can read, write, and think analytically (we hope); some of you may know accounting, others calculus or computer programming. Still others know carpentry, plumbing, or welding. You are, to say the least, quite different than you were on the day of your birth. Virtually no one will dispute that your labor market productivity has increased tremendously. How did these changes occur? The important point is that they did not occur automatically or costlessly, all by themselves. Rather, they were *produced* as the result of a great deal of deliberate effort, by your parents, by your teachers, by yourself, and by many others. That is the sense in which you are not raw labor, but rather are human capital, a produced means of production embodied in a human being.

There is little doubt that the human capital model is one of the major intellectual developments in economics in recent decades. Its modern founder, Theodore W. Schultz, was honored in 1980 with the Nobel Prize in Economics for his work in this area. It has had a major impact on work in other areas of economics, including economic development, international trade, and public finance. The phrase "human capital" has itself joined the ranks of economic concepts that have moved into common parlance, regularly used not only by economists, but also by other social scientists, government officials, and even journalists.

At the same time, however, many of the ideas of the human capital model are highly controversial and widely criticized. As you will see later, many of the conclusions of human capital research concerning poverty and discrimination are decidedly conservative, especially in terms of the kinds of government action they suggest. This has generated some criticism and inspired alternative labor market models. (We consider those criticisms and some of the alternatives in Chapter 7.) But even the basic approach is sometimes regarded as misguided and inappropriate. The issue is whether treating human beings as conceptually similar to capital goods is a demeaning one. We touched on an argument something like that in Chapter 1, but here the criticism struck a raw nerve. Schultz himself summarized those objections in a now-famous address he presented at the 1960 meeting of the American

Economics Association, a speech usually regarded as marking the modern origin of the model:

> The mere thought of investment in human beings is offensive to some among us. Our values and beliefs inhibit us from looking upon human beings as capital goods, except in slavery, and this we abhor. . . . Hence, to treat human beings as wealth that can be augmented by investment runs counter to deeply held values. It seems to reduce man once again to a mere material component, something akin to property.[2]

There is no definitive answer in matters of this type; opinions and feelings rather than scientific fact are at issue. Schultz, however, sharply disagreed with those views and it is worth considering his ideas. He argued that the human capital approach was valuable as an analytical perspective and was, moreover, not antagonistic to human values. In that same speech, he said: "By investing in themselves, people can enlarge the range of choice available to them. It is one way that free men can enhance their welfare." He concluded that "the most distinctive feature of our economic system is the growth in human capital. Without it, there would be only hard, manual work and poverty except for those who have income from property."

In this chapter we look closely at the idea of human capital and the related idea of investment in human capital. In the first part, we identify the major forms in which human capital investment occurs and then develop the technical tools necessary to evaluate human capital investments. Having done that, we turn to the two most conspicuous forms of investment in human capital: education and on-the-job training. We also consider the important idea of an equilibrium rate of return to human capital investment and the implication of that for explaining wage differences among workers with different amounts of human capital.

INVESTMENT IN HUMAN CAPITAL

To begin, we need to be specific about the kind of activities and behaviors we will consider as an investment in human capital. Gary Becker, whose work on household production theory we discussed in Chapter 5, characterized it this way in his influential book, *Human Capital*:[3] "This study is concerned with activities that influence *future* monetary and psychic income by increasing the resources in people. These activities are called investments in human capital."

[2] The quoted passages are from Theodore W. Schultz, "Investment in Human Capital," *American Economic Review*, March 1961, pp. 1–17.

[3] Gary S. Becker, *Human Capital* (New York: National Bureau of Economic Research, 1975), chap. 1.

The important point here is the future orientation: Like any investment, the benefits of human capital investment occur in the future, usually over an extended period, while their costs are incurred currently. In contrast, the benefits and costs of **consumption** activities both occur at the time that consumption takes place. There are an almost unlimited set of activities that could qualify as human capital **investments**, but economists have usually stressed the following:

1. Formal education at all levels
2. Training activities on the job
3. Improved health care
4. Parental time devoted to the care of their children
5. Job search activities by workers
6. Migration of workers from one area to another

There are certainly many differences among these forms of investment in human capital. For example, the first four are investments that increase the amount of human capital possessed by a person, while the last two concern the most productive and profitable utilization of a person's human capital. There are also differences in who finances the investment. Education at the primary and secondary levels and health care are paid for in large part by society at large through direct government provisions, whereas migration, job search, child care, and most training are usually the result of individual actions. Nevertheless, they all clearly fall into the category of human capital investments. In the words of one economist: "What knits these phenomena together is not the question of who undertakes what, but rather the fact that the decision-maker, whoever he is, looks forward to the future for the justification of his actions."[4]

Although the distinction between present-oriented and future-oriented activities—between consumption and investment—is an important one, the dividing line is not always clear. For some students, education may provide immediate intellectual or social enjoyment completely unconnected to its effects on productivity; for others, the process of studying and being tested may be a thoroughly unpleasant way to spend time. For better or worse, then, education involves consumption as well as investment. The same is certainly true of improved health. Good health is of value in and of itself, independent of the fact that healthier people are also usually more productive in the labor market. The frequent link between consumption and investment is an inevitable result of the fact that human capital is embodied in a human being. Because you can not have someone acquire human capital on your behalf, your feelings, positive or negative, about the consumption aspects of a human capital investment may well be important.

[4] Mark Blaug, "Human Capital Theory: A Slightly Jaundiced Survey," *Journal of Economic Literature*, (September 1976), p. 829.

In what follows, however, we will tend to ignore the consumption aspects, both because they are likely to be less important and also because there is no easy way to measure them. You can think of the consumption aspect as an additional factor to be considered when the pure economic analysis of a human capital investment is concluded.

A natural question to ask about investments in human capital is why they are undertaken in the first place. The answer, of course, must have something to do with the relationship between its costs and benefits. But how should we properly assess those costs and benefits to determine whether, by economic criteria, a particular investment in human capital made sense? For example, a college student considering going on to graduate or professional school might want to know whether the higher salary will compensate for the costs that he or she will incur. Similarly, a less developed country might want to compare the value of a public-sector investment in increasing literacy or improving sanitary conditions in villages with the value of making an investment in physical capital, such as improving its transportation system. To do that, we need a general technique for evaluating investments, whether they be in human or physical capital. Doing that correctly involves taking an excursion into investment theory and, in particular, accounting for the complication created by the fact that the costs and benefits of an investment accrue at different times.

ACCOUNTING FOR TIME: DISCOUNTING, PRESENT VALUE, AND RATE OF RETURN CALCULATIONS

Suppose that you are faced with the following human capital investment opportunity. For an expenditure of $\$C$ today, you will be able to increase your earnings by $\$B$ for each of the next ten years. The investment activity in question could be a speed-reading course, attending graduate school to earn an M.B.A. degree, or moving to Alaska. Should you do it? How profitable an investment opportunity is it? How would you analyze your opportunity from an economic standpoint?

The first thing to do is to resist the temptation simply to add up the total benefits over all years and compare it to the costs you will incur. That is incorrect—and can lead to some very poor decisions—precisely because the costs are incurred now and the benefits accrue in the future. Here is why. If you placed money in a bank or a money-market fund and left it there for a year, you would end up with a larger sum than you started with because your money will have earned interest. For instance, if you began with $100 and the interest rate was 10 percent, you would have exactly $110 at the end of the year. Now, although the $110 certainly appears to be greater than the $100, they are actually *equivalent* sums which appear different only because they are received in different time periods. \$100 today and \$110 in one year are, at a 10 percent interest rate, equally valuable because with \$100 today you can readily have \$110 next year by putting your money in the bank and watching it grow at the market rate of interest. You might prefer to have your money now rather than later—in that case, economists would say that you exhibit **positive time preference**—but the dollar sums themselves are equal. Technically, we would say that \$110 is the **future value** in one year of \$100 today or that \$100 is the **present value** of \$110 available in one year's time. Finding future values of current sums is called **compounding**; finding the present value of future sums is called **discounting** or, more fully, **discounting to present value**. The important point is that any amount of money received in the future is equivalent to a smaller amount as of the current time period, because there is a positive rate of interest. It is impossible to assess human capital investments correctly without making some adjustment for that fact.

The exact relationship between present and future values can be derived with a bit of algebraic manipulation which is well worth understanding. Let r be the interest rate and assume, for simplicity, that it is constant in each year. Let Y_t stand for the amount of money in any year t, and let FV_t and PV_t represent the future and present values in year t, respectively. Thus, with this notation, $FV_1(Y_0)$ stands for the future value in year 1 of income received in year zero and $PV_0(Y_5)$ would be the present value of income available five years from now.

Although we are primarily interested in the process of discounting, it is easier to begin with the more familiar, related process of compounding. With an interest rate of r, any current sum, Y_0, will in a year's time, earn interest equal to rY_0. \$100 invested at 10 percent interest earns \$10 (= 0.10 × \$100) interest in one year. Thus the value after one year of Y_0 is the original sum itself (Y_0) plus its accrued interest (rY_0). Using the notation above, we have

$$FV_1(Y_0) = Y_0 + rY_0 = Y_0(1 + r) \tag{6.1}$$

As long as the interest rate is constant, income continues to grow from one year to the next at rate $(1 + r)$, always representing the principal carried forward plus the additional interest earned during that period. Thus for year 2 we have

$$FV_2(Y_0) = [FV_1(Y_0)](1 + r) = [Y_0(1 + r)](1 + r) = Y_0(1 + r)^2 \tag{6.2}$$

Equation (6.2) says that the value in year 2 of Y_0 is its value in year 1 multiplied by the compounding factor $(1 + r)$. Substituting and simplifying gives the more compact expression, $FV_2(Y_0) = Y_0(1 + r)^2$. Proceeding in exactly the same way, the future value of Y_0 in any year t is

$$FV_t(Y_0) = Y_0(1 + r)^t \tag{6.3}$$

Equation (6.3) is the general formula for finding the future value of a current sum.

Discounting to present value is based on the same algebraic relationship, but in reverse. The present value of some future amount of money, Y_t, is the amount of money which, if available today, would by virtue of compounding, equal exactly Y in year t. Since current sums grow at rate $(1 + r)$ each year, future sums must be discounted by that same rate. Thus $PV_0(Y_1) = Y_1/(1 + r)$, which gives the current sum which when multiplied by the compounding factor $(1 + r)$ just equals Y_1. The present value of money in future years follows the same pattern:

$$PV_0(Y_2) = \frac{Y_2}{(1 + r)^2} \tag{6.4}$$

and, more generally,

$$PV_0(Y_t) = \frac{Y_t}{(1 + r)^t} \tag{6.5}$$

This last expression corresponds exactly to the general compounding formula in equation (6.3). Just as the future value of a current sum is that sum multiplied by $(1 + r)^t$, so the present value of a future sum is that sum divided by $(1 + r)^t$.

In this age of pocket calculators, computing future and present values is an easy matter. You should have no difficulty in proving to yourself that with an interest of 5 percent, the future value in year 5 of \$100 today is $\$100(1.05)^5 = \$127.62$ and that the present value of \$100 available in year 12 is $\$100/(1.05)^{12}$ or \$55.68.

There is one final technical point about discounting which is important. We have all become accustomed to the presence of inflation and it is natural to inquire how that will affect present-value calculations. In most cases, the answer is, fortunately, that it has essentially no effect. The reason is that inflation simultaneously increases both the nominal dollar values of future benefits and the interest rate used to discount those benefits, so that the two effects cancel each other out.

Now back to the original problem. For an expenditure of $\$C$ in year 0, $\$B$ will be gained in years 1 through 10. Although any common year could be used for comparison, most often the present year is used since that is when the investment decision is made. Thus we need to find the present value of the entire stream of future benefits, which is simply the sum of the present values of each year's benefits:

$$PV_0(B_1 \cdots B_{10}) = \frac{B_1}{1 + r} + \frac{B_2}{(1 + r)^2} + \frac{B_3}{(1 + r)^3} + \cdots \frac{B_{10}}{(1 + r)^{10}} \quad (6.6)$$

More compactly, this can be written as

$$PV_0 (B_1 \cdots B_{10}) = \sum_{t=1}^{10} \frac{B_t}{(1 + r)^t}$$

where Σ is the summation operator. Finally, that sum can be compared to the costs. If $PV_0(B_1 \cdots B_{10}) < C$, the investment is simply not a good one, unless there are also large consumption benefits. You could do better by investing $\$C$ in year 0 and allowing it to earn the market rate of interest each year. But when the appropriately discounted stream of future benefits exceeds the costs, the investment is a sound one on economic grounds.

Exactly the same technique and logic can be used to evaluate the worth of a public-sector human capital investment project, although we interpret the result more broadly. If the present value of benefits exceeds costs, the resources devoted to the human capital investment are being used more productively than they could be used elsewhere in the economy. But if the costs are greater, then on economic grounds alone the investment cannot be justified. The resources might in that event be better used for some other purpose, unless the consumption benefits of better health or increased literacy are so large that the program has merit anyway.

Equation (6.6) reveals several important features of present-value calculations. First, the further in the future that benefits accrue, the less valuable they are in present-value terms. Arithmetically, that is because the **discount factor**, $(1 + r)^t$, increases exponentially as t increases. In the example above, the benefits in years 1 to 10 were equal, but their present values are quite different. Winners of million-dollar state lottery prizes inevitably find, to their disappointment, that their payments are staggered over many years, thereby reducing the present value well below the stated jackpot.

Second, the greater the discount rate, r, that is used, the smaller will be the present value of any stream of future benefits. Benefits to be received fairly far into the future are especially strongly affected, again because of the use of exponents in the formula. Thus, with a high discount rate, investments whose benefits develop only after a substantial period of time are rarely desirable by present-value calculations. That means that the choice of the appropriate discount factor is crucial. For simple individual calculations, the prevailing interest rate, for example, on money-market funds, could be used, but for larger-scale government projects, where other factors may affect the discount rate, the choice is not so simple.

To avoid choosing a discount factor, economists frequently evaluate human capital investments using a closely related, alternative method. This involves finding the **internal rate of return** to an investment, defined as that discount rate at which the present value of future benefits just equals the costs. In symbols, the internal rate of return, designated as r^*, is the solution to the equation

$$C = \frac{B_1}{1 + r^*} + \frac{B_2}{(1 + r^*)^2} + \cdots + \frac{B_t}{(1 + r^*)^t} \qquad (6.7)$$

The larger are the undiscounted benefits relative to the costs, the larger, in general, will be the value of r^* that satisfies equation (6.7).[5] By virtue of the correspondence between compounding and discounting, you can interpret r^* as the rate of interest earned by a human capital investment of $\$C$. That is, with an interest rate of r^*, an investment of $\$C$ would grow over a period of t years to a sum equal in value to the actual stream of benefits, B_1 to B_t.

The internal rate of return is thus a simple measure of the net profitability of an investment, and it can be used to evaluate those investments. The general rule is that the larger r^* is, the better is the investment. To determine whether the investment is actually worthwhile, you would want to compare r^* to the rate at which you can borrow money. If the internal rate of return is greater, the investment in question makes sense.

If you know C and $B_1 \cdots B_t$, you can calculate r^* on a hand-held calculator with a bit of effort using a trial-and-error procedure. Simply choose a discount rate and find the present value of the benefits using equation (6.6). If the present value is greater than C, repeat the process with a higher discount rate, and so on, until equation (6.7) is approximately satisfied.

Table 6.1 shows how this is done for a hypothetical investment which involved costs of \$200 in year 0 and which provided benefits of \$50 or \$60 per year for five years. The numbers in the table are the present value of the two benefit streams at the various interest rates, computed according to equation (6.6). Thus, with benefits of \$50 per year and costs of \$200, the internal rate of return is a shade under 8 percent. If the benefits had been, instead, \$60 per year, the internal rate of return would have been just above 15 percent.

We will use these techniques of discounting and finding the internal rate of return regularly throughout this chapter. It is an idea and a technique with which you should become familiar for your own decision making as both a consumer and investor. Whenever you need to compare a current expenditure with expected future benefits, these are the right tools for the job.

[5] There is one general exception to this. If benefits are received well into the future, the internal rate of return may be small even if the undiscounted benefits are quite large relative to costs.

TABLE 6.1 Calculating the Internal Rate of Return for a Hypothetical Investment with Costs of $200 in Year 0

INTEREST RATE (%)	BENEFITS = $50/YEAR FOR FIVE YEARS	BENEFITS = $60/YEAR FOR FIVE YEARS
5	$216.47	$259.77
6	210.62	252.74
7	205.01	246.01
8	**199.60**	239.52
10	189.54	227.45
12	180.24	216.29
15	167.61	**201.13**
16	163.72	196.46

Note: Figures in the table are the present value of benefits at the interest rate indicated.

EDUCATION AS AN INVESTMENT IN HUMAN CAPITAL

Education is the most conspicuous example of an investment in human capital. As we begin kindergarten, few of us can read or write, think critically, do mathematics, work with computers, speak French, or know where Brazil is. Twelve or sixteen or more years later, most can do those things and many others besides. Both in the United States and in other countries, it seems clear that schooling does increase people's skills and thereby makes them more productive in the labor market. It is equally clear that schooling is a costly activity, both for individuals and for society as a whole.

Initially, the idea of evaluating education, especially college education, as an investment in human capital seemed foreign and indeed offensive to many educators. Education, it was argued, was an intellectual pursuit, not an activity to be evaluated in crude economic terms. Admittedly, the consumption aspects of education are important. But the investment aspect is also substantial. The provision of education involves a major use of scarce resources (teachers, students, and many forms of capital goods) which could otherwise be utilized elsewhere in the economy. It is therefore certainly worth inquiring whether or not the benefits it produces are large relative to its costs.

The Costs and Benefits of Education

In thinking about the costs and benefits of education, it makes a difference whether we adopt the perspective of an individual or of society as a whole. The costs and benefits for these two groups are by no means identical, although they do share some common ground. Since both individuals and society as a whole share the costs of education, it makes sense to consider the issue from both perspectives.

Consider things first from the standpoint of a person contemplating an investment in his or her education. The costs include direct schooling costs for tuition, books, and so on, and any living expense over and above what would be incurred if he or she were not in school. For public education through grade twelve, these costs may be essentially zero, but for higher education, they certainly are not. We might also want to recognize the existence of "psychic costs"; not everyone enjoys school.

A noneconomist might stop there, but an economist, always aware of the existence of **opportunity costs**, must go on. The true costs of education also include the earnings that a person forgoes by virtue of being in school. In the United States today, the opportunity costs of primary and secondary education are probably quite low, but it was not always so. In the nineteenth century, before the advent of a universal-free public education, it was noted that reductions in school fees had relatively little impact on the enrollment of children from working-class families. One educator, who clearly appreciated the idea of opportunity cost, wrote: "It is not for the sake of saving a penny per week but for the sake of gaining a shilling or eighteen pences per week that a child is transferred from the school to the factory or the fields."[6] In other words, the factor reducing school enrollments was not the direct costs but the opportunity costs. This is often still an important influence on school enrollments in less developed countries. In the United States today, the opportunity costs of education become important primarily for postsecondary education. Even with the rapid increases in college tuition, it is still common that the opportunity costs of attending college exceed the direct and out-of-pocket costs. For graduate or professional school especially, the opportunity costs can easily be quite substantial.

On the benefit side of the ledger, there is also a substantial list. First, and probably foremost, education typically leads to higher earnings. For private rate-of-return calculations, the appropriate income figure to use is the after-tax increase in lifetime earnings due to education. Table 6.2, which shows recent estimates of the expected lifetime earnings (before taxes and with no discounting) for men with different amounts of education, provides a rough idea of the magnitude of these benefits. The actual figures depend on assumptions about the rate of productivity growth in the future, since that determines the rate at which earnings can be expected to increase. With either productivity assumption, the income gains to further education are substantial. (The income gains reported in the table include both the direct impact of education on earnings and its role in protecting against unemployment.) High school graduates are predicted to earn over 40 percent more over their careers than workers without a high school degree—an income differential of from $260,000 to $430,000. For college graduates compared to high school graduates, the lifetime earnings difference is also about 40 percent, repre-

[6] This quote comes from Horace Mann.

senting an income difference of from $330,000 to $630,000. These figures do not prove that education is the source of the higher earnings, but they are suggestive.

In addition to these monetary gains, increased education often leads to increased fringe benefits and to improved working conditions. There are also many nonmarket benefits, including significant effects on health, on the quality of leisure time, on the health and educational development of one's children, and on the ability to make better choices as a consumer. We should also recognize the "psychic benefits" of education, the pure enjoyment of learning for learning's sake.

Viewing the same educational investment from a public or social standpoint, both the costs and benefits are larger and are interpreted slightly differently. Now, the relevant costs include all educational costs, not just the ones paid for by students. Public education through grade twelve is usually costless—ignoring opportunity costs—to individuals, but not to society. Nor do university tuition charges cover typically more than half of college expenses. The full costs represent the value of goods and services currently forgone to provide education. To that should be added the individual opportunity costs, also representing the value of goods and services forgone.

In calculating the public benefits of education, all the individual benefits are, with minor modification, appropriately included. The increase in a person's income is now interpreted as a measure of the increase in the economy's ability to produce goods and services. Thus it is the **pretax** income gain that is relevant here. There are also some benefits of education that accrue not to the people who acquire the education, but rather to others. For example, more education is associated with lower crime rates and with lower rates of welfare dependency, which helps both potential victims and taxpayers. Education is also alleged to improve the functioning of the political system and of product markets that would benefit all of us. These are examples of **positive externalities** and they should be counted among its social benefits, even though people will typically ignore them in their own private decisionmaking. Ex-

TABLE 6.2 Expected Lifetime Earnings for Men by Amount of Education

	ASSUMED RATE OF FUTURE PRODUCTIVITY GROWTH	
AMOUNT OF EDUCATION	*0%*	*2%*
Less than 12 years	$ 601,000	$1,001,000
High school graduate	861,000	1,430,000
College graduate	1,190,000	2,062,000

Note: Earnings are not discounted and are before taxes.
Source: U.S. Bureau of the Census, Current Population Reports, Series P-60, No. 139, *Lifetime Earnings Estimates for Men and Women in the United States: 1979*, (Table 1), U.S. Government Printing Office, Washington, D.C., 1983.

ternalities are, however, notoriously difficult to quantify and assign a monetary value. Often, they are left as a "fudge factor" in making final decisions.

The Rate of Return to College Education: Theory

There have been many studies of the rate of return to a college degree in the United States and elsewhere and we will look at those presently. But before we do that, it is instructive to consider what economic theory suggests about the value that the internal rate of return might be expected to take if individuals adopted an investment perspective in making college attendance decisions. In posing the issue this way, we are really asking whether there might be, in equilibrium, some likely figure for the internal rate of return to a college education. More generally, though, the logic here applies to any investment as human capital, not just higher education.

The basic idea is a straightforward application of the idea of equilibrium, which in this context refers to a situation in which all persons are content with their choices about investment in human capital and the wages of workers with and without a college education are therefore stable. Acquiring a college education involves bearing costs in anticipation of future benefits. Rational individuals will choose to bear those costs only if they expect the benefits to be sufficiently large—that is, large enough to provide a reasonable rate of return on the investment costs. There is no obvious definition of exactly what constitutes a reasonable rate of return. But economists usually think of it as being defined in relation to the rate of return available on alternative investment opportunities, such as stocks and bonds, which represent investment in physical capital. Thus, we would make the following prediction: In an equilibrium situation, the wage premium attached to a college education will be just large enough so that, given its costs, the rate of return is comparable to the rate of return to investments in physical capital. If the benefits were larger, more people would choose to attend college, thereby increasing the supply and ultimately reducing the wage for college-educated workers. Exactly the opposite would occur if the benefits were too small. In between is a wage premium consistent with an equilibrium rate of return to a college education.

This basic equilibrium condition should have a familiar ring to it. It is, in fact, analogous to the prediction that all firms (usually assumed to be identical) will earn zero economic profits in long-run competitive equilibrium. Zero economic profits means that firms are doing at least as well as in their next best alternative; that is, they are earning a reasonable or normal return on their investment. That must also be true in equilibrium for people making an investment in a college education or, for that matter, any investment in human capital.

A statement about an income in equilibrium is exactly that and no more. It does not mean that the result will hold exactly at each and every point in time. In a world that is complex and often subject to unanticipated changes, equilibrium is *not* the usual state of affairs. In this case, departures from equilibrium are probably to be expected. Future income can never be known with certainty; disappointment and surprise about actual outcomes is virtually certain. Moreover, college-age "investors" are not perfectly adept at rate-of-return calculations. Some, indeed, may make no economic calculations at all, whereas for others, the noneconomic aspects of education may be more important. Thus it would not be too surprising if the rate of return to a college education was a bit "out of line" with the rate of return on other investments.

Thus far, the discussion of the benefits of a college education has steered clear of the demand side of the market. Indeed, we came close to suggesting that the higher income received by college graduates was the result of nothing more than their having borne the investment costs of acquiring the education in the first place. In fact, the demand side is important and higher costs alone are not in and of themselves sufficient grounds for receiving higher income. Two simple points about the demand for educated workers need to be made. First, the existence of an equilibrium wage premium for college-educated workers strongly suggests that acquiring a college education does increase the labor market skills of students.[7] If that were not true, profit-maximizing firms would not be willing to hire them and pay them the wage premium necessary to induce college attendance. Second, the demand for college-educated workers depends, as does every labor demand curve, on the wage rate. In this case, it is useful to think of the demand as depending on the *relative* wage of college-educated workers, that is, w_C/w_{HS}, where C and HS stand for college educated and high school educated, respectively. At a high relative wage, firms will use relatively few college-educated workers, reserving them only for the most crucial uses, and will substitute less educated, less costly workers for many tasks. At lower and lower relative wages, though, firms will want to employ more college-educated workers. Thus, in the usual way, the demand curve for college-educated workers will be downward sloping. This is shown in Figure 6.1.

If all persons were exactly the same, the supply curve of college-educated workers would be horizontal, positioned at the point where the benefits of college attendance are just large enough, relative to its costs, to provide a reasonable rate of return. In Figure 6.1, this is shown as $(w_C/w_{HS})^*$, which is interpreted here as a measure of expected lifetime benefits. At any larger wage differential, everyone would choose to attend college, while with a smaller difference no one would.

In fact, however, people are not all identical and, as a result, a college education is not an equally good investment for everyone. Anything that causes the benefits or costs of a human capital investment such as college to

[7] The issue is slightly more complicated than suggested here. We look at some other possibilities in Chapter 7.

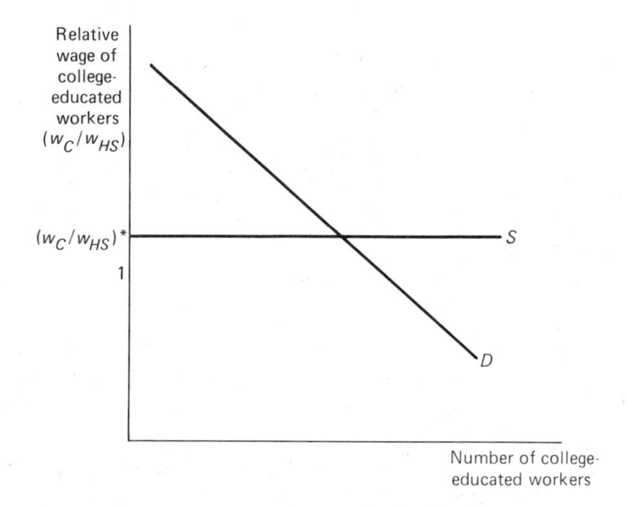

FIGURE 6.1 The Supply of and Demand for College-Educated Workers When Individuals Are Identical

differ among individuals will cause the rate of return to that investment to differ as well. That, in turn, will often result in differences among individuals in their human capital investments.

In the case of college education, there are a number of factors that could affect the benefits and costs facing a person. Because human capital is embodied in a human being, its market value is lost during periods of nonparticipation in the labor market, at retirement, and finally at death. (That is not true of the ownership of physical capital). As a result, the benefits of a college education will usually be higher for a younger student than for an older one. Benefits may also be greater, on average, for men than for women, if, as is often the case, women work less continuously after college than men do. An individual's academic ability may also affect the amount of benefits. Casual observation suggests that not every student learns the same amount in a college education—and it is the amount of human capital acquired rather than mere years of schooling that *should* have market value. It is a mistake to think of college graduates as homogeneous.

There are also likely to be differences in the costs of acquiring a college education. The direct costs depend on the availability of scholarships or loans and also on whether your parents, rather than you, are paying the bills. (This distinction matters only for assessing the private, not the social, rate of return.) Opportunity costs may also differ among individuals, since that depends on the specific employment alternatives available to a person. To cite an extreme example, Ralph Sampson, a seven-foot four-inch basketball player for the University of Virginia, chose to play a fourth season of college basketball in 1982 rather than accept a professional basketball contract. Judging from his subsequent contract, it appears that his opportunity costs were nearly $1 million. (His direct costs were essentially zero since he received an athletic scholarship.) Less dramatically, older people will typically have higher opportunity costs, because their earnings are usually greater. This provides a second reason why it is economically sensible to go to college directly after high school.[8] Ability may also play a role in determining costs. Better students may be able to complete their education more quickly than poorer students, thus reducing the costs and extending the period of benefits. There may also be differences in the psychic costs and benefits of education. Some students find the "educational routine" a pleasurable way to spend four years, whereas others can barely tolerate it.

A final possible influence is labor market discrimination. If the effect of discrimination is to reduce equally the pay of a high school graduate and a college graduate, it lowers both the costs and the benefits of acquiring more education. The rate of return could, as a result, be unaffected. But if discrimination is more severe for workers with more human capital, benefits will fall by more than costs and the rate of return will be affected.[9] That, in turn, may reduce the incentive to acquire education, a result with serious long-term consequences.

Differences such as these help explain why not everyone chooses to go to college. For some, the benefits relative to costs provide a more than adequate rate of return, whereas others find that considering their own situation, the rate of return is too low. They would choose to attend college only if the benefits were larger or the costs smaller. Graphically, the supply curve of college-educated workers will now be upward sloping, as shown in Figure 6.2. As shown, at a relative wage of 1 ($w_C = w_{HS}$), no one chooses to attend college, but at successively higher relative wages more and more persons choose to do so. Those persons who would acquire a college education even if the wage advantage were small must have lower-than-average costs or higher-than-average benefits or else must place a very strong value on the pure consumption features of education. As the wage advantage rises, more persons will find that their own personal rate of return rises to an acceptable level and thus they, too, will choose to attend college. The *position* of the curve depends on the direct costs of a college education. If the costs were higher—universities doubled their tuition rates—any wage premium would translate into a lower rate of return. Fewer persons would, therefore, choose to attend college; graphically, the supply curve would shift to the left to something like S_2. Exactly the opposite would occur if costs were reduced,

[8] It is possible that previous labor market experience increases a student's ability to benefit from a college education. If so, this would provide a reason to delay college attendance.

[9] If more educated workers experienced *less* discrimination, there would be an incentive to acquire *more* education. Until fairly recently, though, this was probably not the case in the United States for blacks or women.

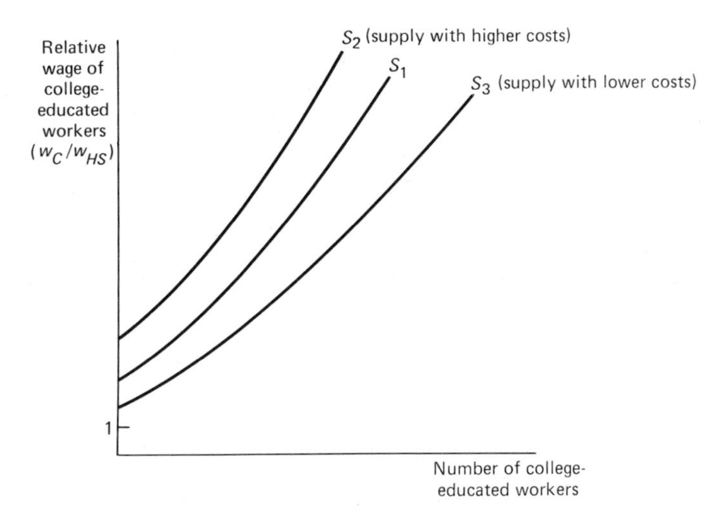

FIGURE 6.2 The Supply of College-Educated Workers When Individuals Are Not Identical and Costs Differ

say as a result of an increase in public subsidies to higher education. Supply curve S_3 shows that situation.

Figure 6.3 shows the market equilibrium in this kind of situation. The three potential equilibriums—points A, B, and C—all represent a situation in which the wage advantage is, on the margin, just large enough to provide a reasonable return on the costs involved. Note that, at least in equilibrium, the larger wage premium at A than at C does not mean that the rate of return is higher. Rather, the larger wage premium simply adjusts for the larger costs so as to equalize the rate of return.

The Rate of Return to Education: Evidence

Since the mid-1960s, there have been many studies by economists of the rate of return to education. In the United States, these studies have usually focused on the return to a college degree, but studies of education in less developed countries have often examined the return to primary and secondary education. Since education is financed both by individuals and by society as a whole through the public sector, both private and social rates of return are of interest.

Although conceptually, it is straightforward to compute the internal rate of return to a college education, in practice there are some complications. Information is needed on the average after-tax earnings for each year of their career for workers who completed college and also on what their earnings

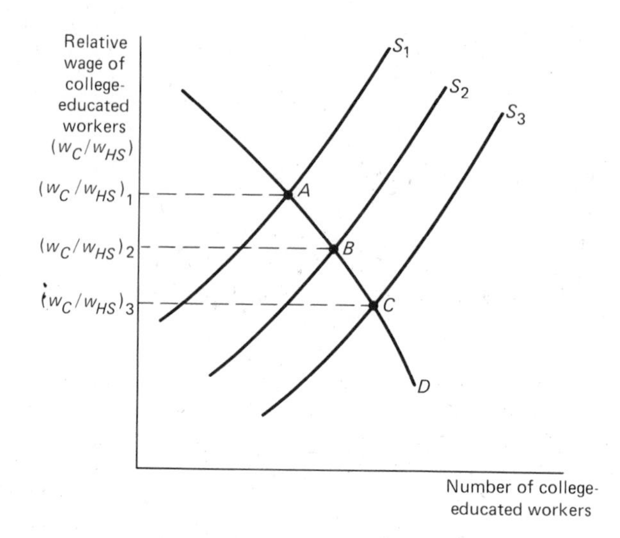

FIGURE 6.3 Market Equilibriums with Different Costs of a College Education

would have been had they not gone to college. Obviously, though, only one set of numbers exists for each person—we do not get the chance to observe the lifetime earnings without college for persons who do attend college. What economists typically do, therefore, is to assume that the college-educated workers would otherwise have earned about the same amount as people who did not go to college actually did earn. In effect, economists assume that the college and noncollege workers are alike except for the difference in education. With that assumption, the opportunity cost of college can be measured by the earnings of the noncollege workers during the years corresponding to college attendance and the earnings differences in subsequent years are the benefits. Earnings information like that is now available in census data every ten years and also annually in data from the Current Population Survey, a national survey of households in the United States conducted by the Bureau of Labor Statistics (BLS).

The assumption that people are alike but for their education is understandable, but it is also questionable. After all, one reason that some persons go to college and others do not is that they are more able to benefit from it. If so, their labor market opportunities are probably better as well, regardless of their college education. In that case, the observed earnings difference attributed to college would overstate the real effect, since part of the difference is really due to skill or ability differences that existed prior to college. By the same logic, the opportunity cost of college, inferred from the earnings of noncollege workers, understates the true costs. The net result of these biases would be to *overstate* the true internal rate of return, whether it is calculated on a private or a social basis.[10]

Balancing this problem somewhat is the omission of some relevant benefits. For instance, increased fringe benefits and improved working conditions are frequent results of acquiring a college education, but they are not readily measured, and thus they are invariably omitted from rate-of-return calculations. Also omitted are the many noneconomic benefits of education—its effects on the quality of leisure time and on health, for instance—as well as its many alleged positive externalities. (The latter category would be relevant only for assessing the social rate of return.) The omission of these factors would, taken by itself, lead to an *underestimate* of the true rate of return to education. There is some comfort in recognizing that the measurement problems are potentially offsetting.

In interpreting the results of rate-of-return studies, you should bear in mind two final points. First, the rate of return is an average and does not apply to each and every person who graduates from college. There is, in fact, substantial variation in the earnings of college graduates. Some students may learn more than others, whereas others may learn skills that are more valuable. Second, although the thrust of rate-of-return calculations is forward looking, the empirical computations are necessarily based on the past labor market experience of workers with different levels of education. Virtually all studies use cross-sectional data, which provide information as of some date on the income of different persons of different ages and education. Information on the earnings of the same person throughout his or her lifetime is extremely rare. Thus the many empirical studies actually tell us the rate of return that, on average, a college student might expect to earn if the future resembles the past.

As a result of many studies, the following findings have emerged:

1. The private internal rate of return to a college education in the United States has been quite respectable. Most estimates covering the periods since 1959 fall in the 10 to 15 percent range, which is in line with—actually slightly above—the average rate of return to investments in physical capital. These figures indicate that a college degree has been a good investment for students over the past few decades. They also suggest that students may make college-attendance decisions by assessing its costs and benefits, since, as we saw earlier, that would make the rate of return to education approximately equal to the rate of return on alternative investment opportunities.
2. The social rate of return and the private rate of return are roughly similar. The social costs are larger, but so are the benefits. Higher education has, on the whole, been a good public investment.
3. The private rate of return to college education was extremely low for blacks

[10] This kind of problem is called *selection bias*, since individuals select themselves into college on the basis of their perceived benefits. Sophisticated statistical techniques have been developed to deal with the problem.

through the 1960s. One indication of this was the fact that black income as a function of white income was lower for college graduates than for less educated workers. A well-known study by Giora Hanoch[11] of 1960 census data found that returns for whites ranged from 11 to 13 percent, whereas those for blacks were 7 to 8 percent. Not surprisingly, relatively few blacks acquired a college education. There is considerable evidence that this situation no longer exists, and black college enrollment rates have risen substantially.

4. In less developed countries the rate of return to primary and secondary education has been very high. In studies of thirty low-income countries, the average social rate of return to primary education was over 24 percent and it was more than 15 percent for education at the secondary level.[12] There is also substantial evidence that primary and secondary education of parents causes reductions in infant mortality rates and in fertility rates—two important non-labor market effects.

5. There is now substantial evidence, primarily from the work of Richard Freeman,[13] that the rate of return to a college education began to fall in the early 1970s. To some extent the surprise is that the return to a college degree remained relatively constant from 1949 to 1969 in the face of a 91 percent increase in the number of B.A. graduates. In the early 1970s, however, there was, according to Freeman, a slowdown in the rate of growth of professional and managerial jobs. Compounding that problem was an unusually large increase in supply, due to the size of the baby-boom cohort then graduating from college. The result was a reduction in employment opportunities and in salaries for young college graduates. By Freeman's calculations, the private internal rate of return to a college degree fell from 11.5 percent in 1969 to 10.5 percent in 1972 and then to a worrisome 8.5 percent in 1974. The social rate of return was, by his computations, about a point lower. On the basis of his findings, Freeman questioned whether there was not **overinvestment in education** in the sense that the private and social rate of return was now below the return on alternative investment opportunities.

   Through at least the late 1970s, the income benefits of college remained at a depressed level, according to Freeman. For example, for workers age 25 to 34, the average earnings of college graduates in 1977 were only 16 percent above that of high school graduates. In 1969, the corresponding figure had been 38 percent. Although Freeman did not present rate-of-return calculations for 1977, the low earnings differential for the younger workers suggests that it would be near the 1974 figure.

   Freeman's work has generated a great deal of controversy, both among economists and among the academic community. Most economists agree that the return to a college degree has fallen, but some have questioned whether the fall was as large as Freeman indicated and whether or not it

[11] Giora Hanoch, "An Economic Analysis of Schooling and Earnings," *Journal of Human Resources*, (Fall 1967).

[12] These findings are reported in *Poverty and Human Development*, published for the World Bank by Oxford University Press (New York: 1980).

[13] Freeman's research includes "Overinvestment in College Training?" *Journal of Human Resources*, (Summer 1975); "The Facts about the Declining Value of College," *Journal of Human Resources*, (Winter 1980); and *The Overeducated American* (New York: Academic Press, Inc., 1976).

represented a long-term phenomenon. Some have argued that the findings reflected primarily the rather turbulent economic times of the mid-to-late 1970s, although why college graduates should be adversely affected by that is not clear.

It is also worth noting that the observed economic benefits of a college education depend partly on who attends college. As the proportion of college-age persons who attend college rises, it is conceivable that the average ability level of college students might fall. If so, that could account for at least part of the decline in the economic benefits of higher education.

In any event, there may already be some small improvement in the economic benefits of college. The comparable data for 1982 show a more optimistic picture. For men who were full-time year-round workers—the group analyzed by Freeman—the income difference was 28 percent.

Application: "Ph.D. Phoolery": The Economic Benefits of a Ph.D. in History

When the *Wall Street Journal* received a solicitation from Columbia University to contribute funds to help recruit graduate students in history, they decided to compute the economic value of a Ph.D. in history. After all, history is an area where job prospects have been usually poor, even for graduates of the finest graduate schools, and the *Journal* printed an editorial, entitled "Ph.D. Phoolery," to show what a poor use of funds this was.[14] In the process, they also showed something else—evaluating an investment in human capital is not as easy as it looks.

Here is what they did. First, they estimated the costs of obtaining a Ph.D. in history at $21,000 per year, representing $6,000 per year in direct costs and $15,000 in forgone earnings. (The $6000 figure is probably too high, since most graduate students either receive financial aid or teach. But the results would not change much even if the costs were lower.) Since the costs are not incurred all at once, they should be discounted back to the first year. The *Journal* used 3 percent as the discount factor[15] and found that the present value of the costs was about $114,000.

Next, they calculated the benefits of the Ph.D. degree. To do that, they needed to estimate a history professor's expected salary over his or her career. Obviously, that can not be known perfectly in advance, so the *Journal* made some assumptions. They assumed a starting salary of $17,500, and since they were using 3 percent as a discount factor, they correctly ignored future salary increases due to inflation. Perhaps for simplicity, they ignored salary increases due to all other factors as well, and thus assumed a constant $17,500 salary for 34 years. (Again, that may not be strictly correct, but it does not matter very much.) The total lifetime salary is $595,000 ($17,500 × 34), but at 3 percent the present value is only $310,000.

[14] The editorial appeared August 18, 1981.

[15] Three percent is frequently regarded as the "real" rate of interest, that is, the interest rate that would exist if there were no current or expected inflation.

In fact not all graduates will actually get such a job. Columbia University had noted that about 65 percent of its graduates obtained teaching positions, so the *Journal* multiplied the benefits by 0.65 to get the expected, "risk-adjusted" benefits of an average student. That came out to about $201,000, which, according to the *Journal*, represents the economic benefits of earning a history Ph.D.

Finally, back to the costs again. To the direct costs of $114,000, the *Journal* added in a $109,000 risk premium, for a total of $223,000 of costs. The $109,000 is the difference between the riskless present value of $310,000 and the risk-adjusted present value of $201,000. With total benefits of $201,000 and costs of $223,000, a Ph.D in history looks like an investment of rather poor quality. Presumably, the *Wall Street Journal* decided, in the interest of resource allocation, not to contribute money to the history department.

How well did the *Journal* carry out this exercise? To be blunt, they did everything wrong except for their initial calculation of the schooling costs of earning a Ph.D. Here are some of the errors, which you may already have spotted:

1. The benefits should include only the *increment* in salary due to the Ph.D. rather than the whole salary. Using their own figures, this is $2500 per year, the difference between the salary with and without the degree. The present value of the benefits, still using 3 percent and assuming no salary increase, is $44,286, not $310,000.
2. The risk adjustment may be too severe, but the basic idea is fine. The *Journal's* calculations assume that the unlucky ones who do not obtain a teaching position earn no more than they would have without the degree. On the contrary, they might obtain employment in a related line of work and there might still be economic benefits to the degree. In any event, following the *Journal's* approach, if we multiply $44,286 by 0.65, we arrive at a risk-adjusted present value of $28,786 after subtracting a risk premium of $15,500.
3. Should this $15,500 then be added to the costs, as the *Journal* did? Of course not. It has already been subtracted from the benefits. Adding it to costs gives it double weight.
4. The correct comparison, then, is of $114,000 of costs with $28,786 of benefits. The difference is a negative $87,214, which still makes the history Ph.D. a poor economic investment.

That is not quite the end of the story. The *Journal's* editorial called forth an unusually large number of interesting letters to the editor. One pointed out many of the errors noted above. Two of the others, one by a professor of economic history, the other by a professor of history, challenged the basic approach. One essentially argued that there were important externalities benefiting society as a whole and that on that basis support was warranted, no matter what rate-of-return calculations showed. In colorful language, he wrote: "Unless there is some human purpose which looks beyond the immediate technical and economic application, the day will come when the hand will lose its cunning and life will be found to be devoid of purpose." The other letter echoed some of this: "No one with any sense would rest the case for the graduate study of the liberal arts on the narrow and naive standard of economic good you have used. By that standard, Plato's Academy would have been turned into a weight-loss salon." But it also pointed out that some people would choose to become historians even with knowledge of the bleak economic calculations. Apparently, they value the study of history as a consumption good, enjoyable in and of itself, independent of its effects on their income. That observation should remind us of one of the limitations of the investment approach to education: its exclusive emphasis on the monetary aspects of education.

Application: Financing Investments in Higher Education

Although we have thus far emphasized the similarity between investments in human capital and investments in physical capital, there is one crucial difference which has important implications for financing the two kinds of investments. Physical capital can be freely bought and sold; its title (i.e., ownership rights) can be transferred from one person to another. But in a nonslave society, that is not true for human capital, precisely because human capital is always embodied in a human being.

The reason this distinction matters is that it can bias investment away from human capital and toward physical capital. To see why, consider trying to borrow money from a bank to finance two investment opportunities which, for the sake of argument, we will assume have exactly the same expected rate of return. One is an investment in physical capital—a pizza parlor or something of that sort. The other is a college education or perhaps a graduate program of some kind. We further assume that both investments contain an element of risk, again assumed to be similar for both investments. Since future outcomes can never be guaranteed, virtually all investments contain risk. Tastes for pizza may change or the investor may turn out to be inept at running a pizzeria. Similarly, a student-borrower may not have the necessary abilities to benefit from a college education, something which, in many cases, may not be readily apparent to either an 18-year-old student or a banker. Even if college is completed successfully, the skills obtained may not turn out to be as useful as expected, if demand conditions shift.

By itself, the existence of risk is rarely sufficient to prevent a loan from being made, as long as there is some way to reduce the lender's risk. In the case of an investment in physical capital, a common practice is for the capital good actually financed to serve as collateral for the loan. That means that if the investment turns out poorly and the borrower cannot repay the loan, the lender gains title to the asset. The lender can then sell the asset and hope to recoup the loss.

If a banker tries to apply the same procedure to an investment in human capital, trouble immediately arises. Pledging the acquired human capital as collateral is not very useful, since the bank could not acquire title to the human capital it financed without getting the rest of you as well. Can you imagine the bank auctioning you off to the highest bidder if you were unable to repay the loan? The important point is that in a nonslave society, human beings cannot be used as collateral for a loan in the same manner that physical capital can be. Thus, with the existence of risk, lenders would understandably favor investments in physical capital over investments in human capital.

There is, however, a solution to this problem. What is needed is an alternative way to reduce the lender's risks of making human capital investments. One way might be for the federal government to assume the bank's risk by agreeing to pay off the loan should the borrower default. That, in fact, is exactly what happens in the Guaranteed Student Loan (GSL) program, and that explains why your local banker was probably quite willing to lend you money. From the bank's standpoint, the loan is now riskless.

In practice, the GSL program also includes two other provisions. Interest payments are deferred while the student remains in school and the interest rate itself is subsidized. As late as 1981, the interest rate was 8 percent, far below the rate banks were then charging to even their best corporate borrowers. The budgetary costs of the interest rate subsidy were very large and in the wake of the Reagan administration's attempt to reduce the federal budget, a number of proposals to pare back the program were advanced. The key insight from the analysis above is that while the guaranteed aspect is crucial and the interest payment deferral is a very useful practical device, the interest rate subsidy is not essential.

ON-THE-JOB TRAINING AS AN INVESTMENT IN HUMAN CAPITAL

A second important form of human capital investment, much emphasized by economists, is **on-the-job training**, which refers to the learning and skill development that takes place in the labor market. Again, the idea makes sense intuitively. Very few of us find that our learning abruptly ends when we finish our formal education; rather, learning on the job, improving one's skills, is probably the norm. An apprenticeship program in which an untrained worker labors under the direction of a skilled one is a formal example of that. But even in less structured learning situations, economists believe that workers learn skills that make them more productive and more valuable to their employers. Sometimes this is "learning by doing" or "learning from experi-

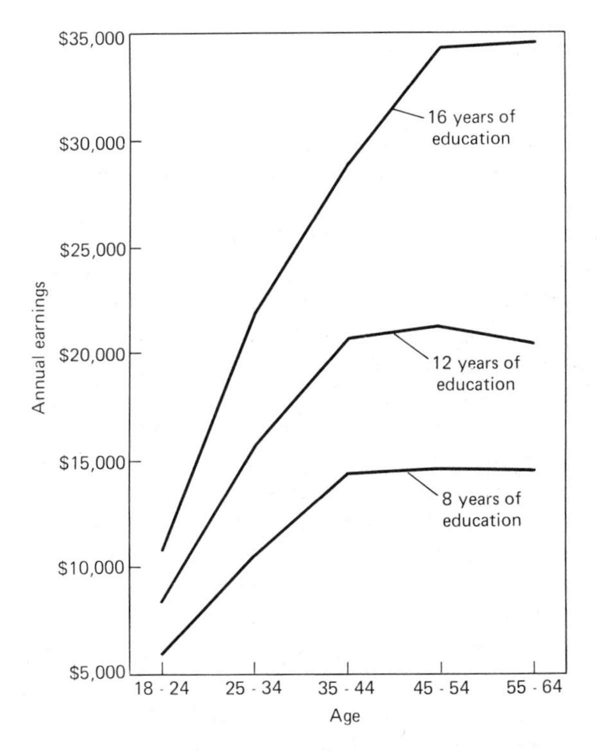

FIGURE 6.4 Average Male Earnings by Age and Years of Education, 1982

ence"; sometimes it may be "learning by observation" or even learning by the casual transmission of information and skills from trained workers to untrained ones. In any case, surveys of workers about where they learned their job skills usually find that training on-the-job is the most common source.

There is another reason to suspect that the learning process continues on the job. It is regularly observed that a person's earnings tend to increase over most of his or her career. A pattern like that is evident in Figure 6.4, which shows average earnings by age and education as of 1982.[16] If, as economists believe, earnings reflect skills, this fact certainly suggests that a worker's skills continue to develop on the job.[17]

[16] The earnings patterns in the figure are based on cross-sectional data. Such data show the earnings of different people at different ages, rather than the same person at different ages, which is what we are interested in. The cross-sectional data are not perfect, but they do give a rough idea of what a person can expect as he or she ages.

[17] Again, the issue is slightly more complicated than suggested. We look at an alternative explanation in Chapter 7.

General and Specific Training

The idea that workers might learn things on the job is by itself not novel. The important insight is that this process of learning has both costs and benefits and thus can be considered as an investment in human capital, much like formal education. To identify those costs and benefits, we need to consider the concept of on-the-job training more closely.

The particular job skills that workers on different jobs learn vary in an almost unlimited number of ways. In each job, there may be special skills that contribute to doing a job better or doing it faster. There is no value, however, in enumerating the exact job skills of each job separately. Rather, the many different types of skills that are learned on the job are, for analytical purposes, placed into two broad categories called **general training** and **specific training**. The difference between training that is general and training that is specific lies in how useful any learned job skill is in firms other than the firm in which a worker received the training. If the training is equally valuable in other firms, then no matter what the exact nature of the skill is, it is general training. If, however, it increases a worker's productivity by more in the firm that provides the training than in other firms, it is regarded as specific training; that is, its value is, in some respects, specific to employment with that firm. The extreme case in which a skill has no effect at all on a worker's productivity in other firms is called **completely specific training**.

A few examples may help illustrate the difference between general and specific training. Sales work usually includes both general and specific training. Learning general sales techniques is an example of general training since they would be valuable in any sales job. Learning about the details of the product line you are selling, though, is specific training. Selling real estate is another apt example: many of the skills involved in selling real estate in Wilmington, Delaware, would be of little or no value in, say, Omaha, Nebraska, and vice versa. A worker in a stationery store warehouse might need to learn the number and location of several thousand stock items, knowledge that undoubtedly makes him or her extremely valuable to the current employer but much less so to employers in other fields. Supreme Court clerks probably receive a great deal of general training in the law, useful in almost any law firm, and interns in hospitals receive a great deal of general medical training. Indeed, education itself is regarded as a classic example of general training in the sense that it prepares students equally well for a wide assortment of potential employments. The development of appropriate work habits and attitudes is another example. On the specific training side is knowledge that is so specialized that it pertains only to the current site of employment—how to get a machine to work properly, how to work with your superior, and other peculiarities or idiosyncracies of the job.

Probably, most jobs provide some training that is general and some that is specific. It is not easy to think of many jobs on which nothing at all is ever learned. But the total amount of training undoubtedly does vary from one job to another, as does the proportion of training that is general versus specific.

The Costs and Benefits of Training

The reason the distinction between general and specific training is made is that the costs and benefits are somewhat different in the two cases. First, consider general training. Suppose that prior to receiving any on-the-job training a person has skills that would bring a wage rate of w_0. After a period of training, however, the person's skills will have increased, and, corresponding to that new skill level, there is a higher wage rate, w_G. The benefits, then, will be the higher wage rate after training, either at the firm at which the training is received or at some other firm.

What about the costs? What are they and, more important, who pays them? Training typically involves the use of resources that could otherwise be used by a firm to produce more output instead. At the least, there is the time spent by already trained workers and by trainees in the training process. For example, if a supervisor must closely monitor the work of new employees, that would be a cost of providing training. In addition, there may be costs of equipment and/or materials if they are required to facilitate training.

You might think that, of course, the firm bears these costs; it is certainly not the rule that employees make regular payments to their employers for any training received. But it is, in fact, more plausible that workers and not firms should pay for general training. Here is why. The benefits will definitely go to workers since as their skills increase, their wage will rise as well. As long as other employers value the skills, we can be certain about that. A situation in which the benefits were received by workers and the costs were borne by firms would be one-sided indeed. As an individual investment in human capital, it would offer an infinite rate of return—there would be benefits but no associated costs. For the firm providing the training, however, there would be costs but no benefits. In that situation, the supply of labor to a job with general training would be extremely large, since nearly everyone would want to take advantage of this costless way to increase income. That would, therefore, be an unstable wage structure. The only plausible equilibrium situation is one in which workers not only receive the benefits but also bear the costs of general training. They do this not through direct payments, but rather by accepting a lower initial starting salary than they could otherwise have earned. Their cost is implicit, not explicit.

This idea is shown in Figure 6.5. The vertical axis in the diagram shows the worker's wage or, equivalently, the equilibrium level of the MRP_L for workers of that skill level. The horizontal axis measures time. Consider a very simple situation in which training occurs through some time denoted as T^* and that the workers change from untrained to trained instantaneously at

T^*. (Obviously that is unrealistic, but it makes for a simpler diagram; we will relax that assumption momentarily.) w_0 and w_G still represent the worker's original alternative wage level and the expected wage level after general training. In addition, let w_U be the wage rate during the training period for untrained workers. In this example, then, the individual would earn w_U during the training period and w_G thereafter. Considered as a human capital investment, the costs are the forgone earnings, $w_0 - w_U$, through T^* and the benefits are $w_G - w_0$ subsequently.

Now consider the situation in which the training is completely specific. Because a worker's increased skills are not valuable to other employers, there is no necessary reason for a worker with specific training to receive a higher wage than a worker without specific training. If a worker's initial alternative wage is w_0, the wage might easily be constant at w_0 during and after specific training. In that case, both the costs and benefits of specific training go to the firm.

This possibility is shown in Figure 6.6. Now the horizontal line at w_0 represents the worker's wage path over time and the stair-step line is the worker's *MRP*. During training, the firm pays workers more than their MRP_L, thus incurring the costs of specific training. But it then recoups those costs after T^* by paying workers less than their *MRP*.

This makes perfect sense except for one thing. In a nonslave society, workers are free to change jobs whenever they like. What is there to prevent a worker from receiving training until T^* and then suddenly quitting to take employment elsewhere at the standard, alternative wage, w_0? The worker would be no worse off by such a maneuver, but not so the firm. It would have incurred the costs of specific training and received none of the benefits—not a very profitable investment.

There are at least two solutions to this predicament. One is a return to

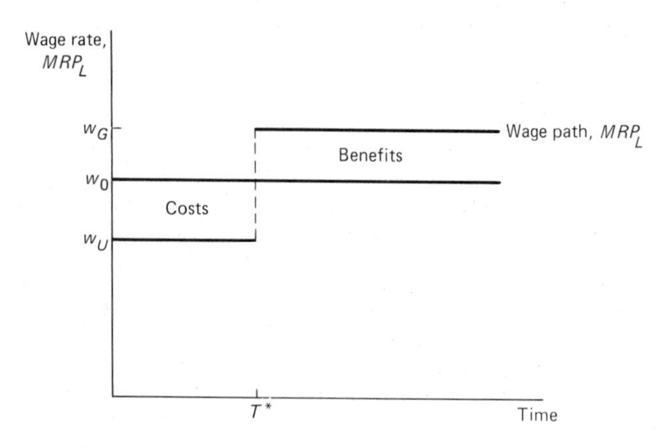

FIGURE 6.5 The Wage Effects of General Training

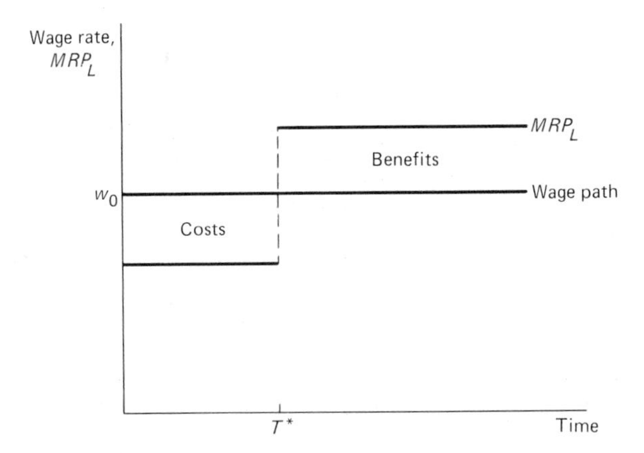

FIGURE 6.6 Possible Wage Effects of Specific Training

slavery or at least to enforceable long-term labor contracts, like the indentured servants of the past. Neither society at large nor the courts, however, look fondly on that. Moreover, it is virtually impossible to compel an employee to perform a job satisfactorily if he or she no longer cares about continued employment. Alternatively, firms could provide fully trained workers with an incentive not to quit by raising their wage after T^*. That might well alleviate the quitting problem, but it is not the end of the story. If the worker's wage in a job with specific training was equal to w_0 during training and was higher than that afterward, the acquisition of specific training becomes a costless human capital investment for a person. Presumably, the number of people seeking employment under these conditions would be extremely large. In response, it is likely that the wage during training might fall below w_0.

All of this is illustrated in Figure 6.7. w_0 is the alternative wage, w_S the wage after specific training, and w_U the wage during training. The worker's time path of productivity is again depicted by the solid stair-step line, denoted as MRP_L, while the wage path follows the dashed line. Both during and after training, workers and the firm share the costs and benefits. During training, the worker's costs are the difference between w_0 and w_U, while the gap between w_U and the MRP_L line is the firm's costs. After training, the firm's benefits are the difference each time period between MRP and w_S; the gap between w_S and w_0 represents the benefits of specific training to the workers. Exactly how the costs and benefits are shared is indeterminate, except that the division of costs and benefits has to be acceptable to both the firm and the individual. Both must expect to earn a reasonable rate of return on the investment in specific training.

In both of these examples, we assumed that workers shifted instantaneously from untrained to fully trained. It is more likely, however, that a worker's productivity rises gradually as training occurs. In that case, the stair-

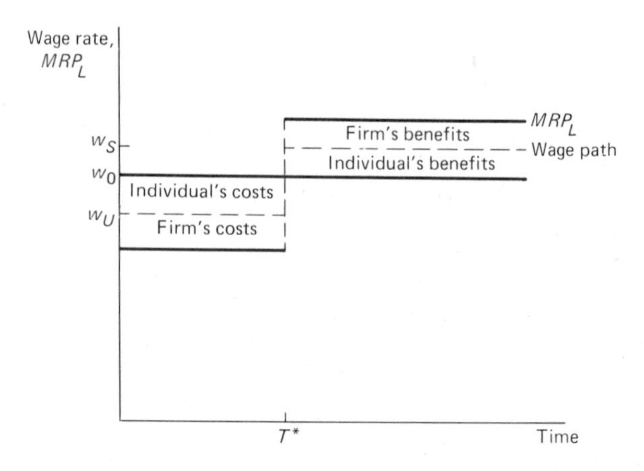

FIGURE 6.7 The Wage Effects of Specific Training: Costs and Benefits Shared by a Worker and a Firm

step wage path of Figures 6.5 and 6.7 might be smoothed out into something resembling AA' or BB' in Figure 6.8. A graph such as this, showing actual earnings measured against a person's age or years of work experience is called an **age–earnings profile** or an **experience–earnings profile**. The difference between the two profiles in Figure 6.7 is in the amount of training acquired. The lower wage during training and higher wage after training along AA' reflects the larger amount of training involved in that job. The gradual rise in earnings is an interesting and important result, because actual career earnings paths do tend to resemble AA' or BB'. That is, the wage effects of on-the-job training are consistent with one of the basic empirical regularities of individual earnings.

Not everyone will find that a job which provides ample on-the-job training is a sensible investment. The same factors that operated to influence an

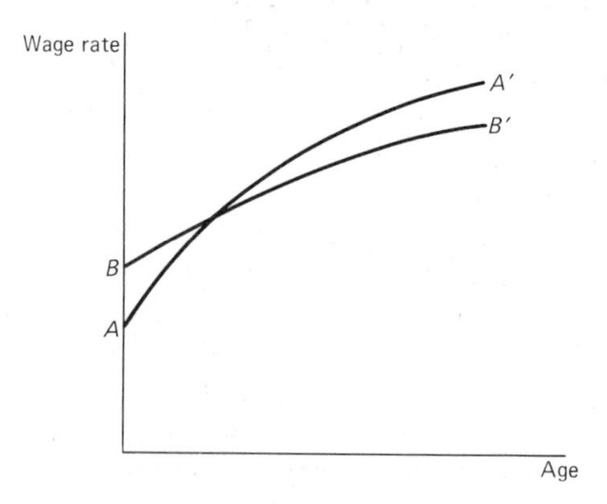

FIGURE 6.8 The Effect of Training on Age–Earnings Profiles

individual's rate of return to education are relevant here as well. The longer the period of time over which benefits are received, the greater will be the return to training. As a result, investment in training should be greatest for workers at the beginning of their career and it should decline thereafter. The same would be true for people who expect to work less continuously throughout their lifetime. As we will see in detail in Chapter 9, exactly that argument is often to account for the lower average earnings of women. When specific training is involved, firms might be reluctant to make an investment in older workers or in workers they expect to work less continuously—the benefits might not justify the costs. Ability may also play a role by reducing the costs of acquiring training. It may be true that smarter people are able to learn more per time period. Finally, discrimination may also be a relevant factor, if it is more severe for persons with more training.

Does this investment approach to job choice make sense to you in terms of your own experience or plans? Would you ever consider accepting a lower-paying job over a higher-paying one if you thought the long-term prospects were better? If so, you are adopting an investment perspective, extending your time horizon from the current period to include the future. What is it about a lower-paying job that might make its future prospects brighter? Is it the opportunity to learn and to advance? If so, you are making an investment in on-the-job training.

It may be useful to summarize here some of the basic ideas about on-the-job training developed thus far, because we will return to them frequently:

1. Both general and specific training involve costs and benefits. In the case of general training, a person both bears the costs and later receives the benefits, whereas with specific training costs and benefits are shared by the firm providing the training and the person receiving it.
2. In either case, people pay for training by accepting a wage lower than they might earn elsewhere in a job without training. The costs are an opportunity cost.
3. In jobs with specific training, workers earn more than their *MRP* during training and less thereafter. In jobs with general training, workers always earn a wage equal to their *MRP*, but their *MRP* rises as they receive training.
4. The gradual accumulation of on-the-job training in the beginning stages of a person's career helps explain the typical career growth in a person's earnings.
5. Current earnings may be a misleading indication of "true earnings," especially if a person is receiving a large amount of on-the-job training.
6. Rate-of-return analysis suggests that on-the-job training may be a better investment for some people than for others.

Application: Training and Wages in Professional Baseball

Major league baseball provides an interesting example of on-the-job training and its associated wage effects. What makes this situation particularly interesting is that the recent change in the legal structure of employment contracts in baseball had the effect of transforming what had been completely specific training into general training. That should have predictable effects on wages during and after training.

There is no question that baseball players do receive a great deal of on-the-job training, in the minor leagues, in spring training, and even in the major leagues. Most players find that their skills do increase, substantially, especially in the early stages of their career. Prior to 1976, those skills undoubtedly fell into the specific training category. Until that year, baseball operated under a contract provision called the *reserve clause*, which effectively prevented a player under contract to one team from negotiating with any other team. Thus, although training certainly did make players more productive to other baseball teams, those teams were prevented from making a contract offer. As for nonbaseball employment, it seems unlikely that even an improved ability to hit or pitch or field is a very marketable skill. The net result was that the acquisition of training had essentially no impact at all on a player's productivity in any firm besides the one providing the training. In circumstances such as that, we would expect the firm to pay the players more than their *MRP* during training in the minor leagues—and less afterwards—in the major leagues.

In 1976, the reserve clause was declared invalid by an arbitrator. Any player with at least six years of major league experience could become a free agent and negotiate with a large number of teams. With that structural change, the training that baseball players received now became general training. Trained players were more valuable not only to their own team, but equally to other teams as well.

How will this affect wages? Since workers receive the benefits of general training, we would certainly expect this change to increase the wages of trained players who are able to take advantage of free-agency. This would be true whether these players actually became free agents or, instead, sign long-term contracts with their original team. Indeed, the median salary rose more than fourfold between 1976 and 1982.

That, however, is not the end of the story. There must also be an effect on the wages of players during the time period when they are receiving training. If players can now expect to receive the benefits of training, it follows that they must also bear the costs. Certainly, the teams would not want to bear the costs, since they cannot count on reaping the benefits. Thus we would expect that the advent of free-agency would decrease the wages of players during their training period.

Direct evidence on this is not easy to find. Detailed salary information is not available. But there is some indirect evidence that is consistent with an effect like that. Prior to 1976, most major league teams operated as many as six minor league teams, organized according to the skills of the players. Class D and Class C contained the youngest and least skilled players, while Class AAA contained the more seasoned, more skilled minor league players.

Since then the number of minor league teams has shrunk substantially. Only the top four classes now exist. At the same time, in what appears to be a related development, a much greater proportion of players now enter the minor leagues after attending college and after playing several seasons of college baseball. (Previously, most players were signed directly out of high school.) Thus the training that might otherwise (and was previously) provided in the low minor leagues is more often received at college, where the trainees receive at most the relatively low wage of an athletic scholarship. The effect of this is to shift some of the costs of training from the various major league baseball teams to their players.

SUMMARY

The human capital model covers a vast amount of territory. There is no doubt that it is an important and useful set of ideas. It has reshaped the way economists analyze labor markets and the labor market behavior of both firms and individuals. Considering these new ideas together with the labor demand concepts of Chapters 2 and 3 and the labor supply analysis of Chapters 4 and 5, we now have a reasonably complete picture of how a simplified labor market operates. Taken together, these three elements—demand, supply, and human capital—are the main parts of the neoclassical economic theory of labor markets.

Among the many new ideas in this chapter, three stand out especially. First, there is the recognition that a person's productivity is not forever fixed, but rather can be improved. Second, there is a theory of individual behavior regarding their own human capital: that people make deliberate, purposeful investments in their own human capital in the form of education, training, migration, and so on. Evaluating these investments on economic grounds involves the use of discounting to adjust for the different time frames surrounding the cost and benefits. Third is the idea that a person's wage depends on the amount of human capital that he or she possesses. More carefully, in a situation of equilibrium in the labor market, the wage differential associated with any particular human capital investment will be just large enough (in present-value terms) to compensate for the costs involved. We saw the application of these ideas to investments in education and training.

These ideas form the beginning of a theory of the personal distribution of income, an answer to the question of why some people are rich and others are poor and why some occupations have high salaries and others much lower. The human capital explanation is this: Earnings differ among individuals or groups of individuals because the amount of human capital they possess differs, often as a result of previous decisions about human capital investment. That idea is an important one. It figures prominently, for example, in the human capital explanation of why women and blacks in the United States earn less than white males, an issue we examine closely in Chapter 9.

New Concepts

Endogenous versus exogenous
Human capital
Consumption versus investment
Positive time preference
Future value
Present value
Compounding
Discounting to present value
Discount factor
Internal rate of return
Opportunity cost of education
Positive externality
Overinvestment in education
On-the-job training
General training
Specific training
Age–earnings profile
Experience–earnings profile

7

Human Capital Theory: Extensions and Alternatives

INTRODUCTION

Chapter 6 presented the basic ideas of human capital theory, with special attention to its two most common forms, education and on-the-job training. We saw there that human capital theory provides an explanation of individual behavior regarding investments in human capital and of the resulting distribution of earnings. In this chapter we take a second look at some of those issues. Most of this chapter is devoted to a reconsideration of alternative explanations of the relationship between education, work experience, and labor market earnings. Some of the ideas presented here are best regarded as extensions or modification of human capital theory, whereas others are more antagonistic to the basic approach. The intent is to develop a more even-handed understanding of the strengths and weaknesses of human capital theory.

The chapter begins with a brief overview and critique of the human capital model. The human capital model does have some weaknesses that permit alternative explanations of some of its central predictions. We then look at some of these alternatives, beginning with the relationship between education and earnings. Two ideas, the credentialist argument and the educational signaling model, are considered. The next section presents the dual labor market model, which while incorporating some features of human capital theory, strongly rejects its emphasis on the competitive nature of the labor market and the importance of individual choice. The topic of the last section is the economics of internal organization. This is a new area of research in labor economics, linked to both human capital theory and to some of the descriptive features of the dual labor market model.

Human Capital Theory: Overview and Critique

It is useful to start with an overview of the human capital model and, in particular, attempt to isolate its "core" ideas and implications. The basic premise of this approach is that individuals (and others) make deliberate, purposeful investments in human capital and that these investments result in both higher productivity and higher labor market earnings. A companion assumption is that there are no special impediments or restrictions to human capital investments. People decide on a course of action concerning education or on-the-job training on the basis of an expected rate of return and then are able to execute that plan.

Several important implications follow directly from these assumptions. First, labor market earnings depend directly on the amount of human capital an individual possesses. Second, the resulting earnings distribution reflects, at a deeper level, the voluntary, self-interested human capital investment decisions of individuals together with the underlying distribution of initial ability. It is not a very large leap to the assertion that the distribution of labor market earnings is, in some general sense, "fair."

Critics of the human capital model have taken issue with virtually all of these ideas. They argue that the direct evidence linking human capital investments with increases in productivity is weak at best. It is undeniable that education and age (or, better, work experience) have systematic effects on average earnings. We saw that clearly in Chapter 6. But the key intervening link—the alleged increase in productivity—is rarely, if ever, observed. Moreover, the actual acquisition of human capital is itself also unobserved. No one has ever seen a unit of human capital, or measured the amount of human capital acquired in college or on-the-job training. Rather, investment in human capital must be indirectly inferred from the amount of time spent on activities such as education and work experience which are associated with higher income.

There is nothing inherently wrong with this procedure and, in fact, it is not uncommon in economics. One of the purposes of economic theory is precisely to extend our knowledge beyond what can readily be discerned. In this case, assumptions about maximizing behavior by firms and by individuals, together with the important concept of equilibrium, allowed us to deduce things that could not be seen.

Nevertheless, the lack of observability does cause problems. First, it makes it difficult to devise appropriate tests of whether or not the human capital model is an important explanation of the actual differences in earnings that exist among individuals or groups of individuals. The correspondence between human capital theory and the empirical research based on those ideas is weaker than in many other areas of economics. We look at those issues in Chapter 11.

Second, some critics accuse the human capital model of employing circular reasoning: Human capital investments encompass anything that increases a person's earnings, while the subsequent observed increase in earnings is taken as proof that an otherwise unobservable investment in human capital has occurred. Critics offer alternative interpretations that are also consistent with the observed empirical phenomena.

A separate set of criticisms focuses on the assumption that people are able to make unrestricted investments in human capital. Critics cite the existence of discrimination, large differences in family income, institutional arrangements, and other market imperfections. They argue that these factors often impinge in important ways on a person's ability to acquire human capital. If this is true, the resulting distribution of labor market earnings could not reasonably be regarded as fair.

EDUCATION AND EARNINGS: ALTERNATIVE EXPLANATIONS

The human capital model regards education as the classic example of investment in human capital. It interprets the well-established positive relationship between education and income as evidence of the productivity-enhancing effects of education. But there is little evidence for this other than the increased earnings themselves. Direct evidence of the effect of education on worker productivity is relatively rare. Is it possible, then, that the observed relationship between education and earnings reflects something else altogether? There are at least two alternative explanations of that relationship, both of which describe situations in which education affects earnings despite having little or no effect on productivity.

Education as a Credential

The first of these two explanations goes by the name **credentialism**, implying that it is the credentials of a college degree that are valuable and not any skills actually acquired.[1] Whether or not people actually learn valuable things in college is, in this model, immaterial. The important point is that at least some of the return to a college degree is *unrelated* to any productivity effect and due only to acquisition of the credential. For simplicity, then, it is convenient to think of education as having no effect at all on productivity, with its entire wage effect due to credentialism.

There is, in fact, some empirical evidence that provides support for this view. Rates of return are apparently much higher for "diploma years"—high school and college graduation—than for nondiploma years of schooling. This indicates that employers are apparently willing to pay an *extra* increment for workers with a degree compared to workers who have completed, say, three-fourths of the work for the degree. It is, of course, possible that much more is learned in diploma years, relative to the additional cost, thus accounting for its higher rate of return. But that does not seem terribly likely and there is no good evidence one way or the other. The rate-of-return differential is at least consistent with a credentialing effect.

It is not hard to cite anecdotal evidence that supports a credentialing effect of education. There are, for instance, some employment situations where additional course work translates automatically into a higher salary, irrespective of what may or may not have been learned. Nevertheless, as a general proposition, the credentialist argument does not seem strong under plausible assumptions about the behavior and competence of employers. If college graduates earn more than high school graduates, there must be sufficient employers who think the pay differential is warranted by the difference in productivity. If education was purely a credential, firms could lower their costs without reducing their output by substituting the equally productive, uncredentialed workers for the more expensive, college-educated ones. (This would be equally true if only part of the wage effect of education were due to its value as a credential. Even then, there remains an economically un-

[1] A major proponent of this argument is Ivar Berg. See his *Education and Jobs: The Great Training Robbery* (New York: Praeger Publishers, 1970).

justified relationship between education and income.) Unless all firms are completely unable to make any meaningful assessment of the productivity of workers, the return to education as a pure credential should be eliminated. Thus the existence of equilibrium wage differentials almost forces us to conclude that education must have effects that firms find valuable.

Even if the credentialist argument were true, education would, nevertheless, have value as a private investment in human capital. It still entails costs and provides benefits. Only the explanation of its benefits is different than in the more conventional version. From the social standpoint, though, the rate of return would be affected. If education were purely a credential, it would provide no social benefits at all, since no increase in output occurs as a result of education. In that case its rate of return would be zero. In a less extreme version of the credentialist argument in which education does have some effect on productivity, the social return would be lower than the private return.

Education as a Signaling Device

A more sophisticated version of this argument is the *signaling hypothesis*, a new and important set of ideas developed by the economist Michael Spence.[2] In this model, college-educated workers are more productive than workers without a college education, but not because they went to college. Rather, the value of a college education is that it reveals or signals information about a worker's productivity, even though it does not necessarily enhance it.

Spence's argument begins by noting that firms find it very difficult to predict accurately the future productivity of workers they are considering for employment. Similarly, prospective employees have a difficult time communicating their true productivity to employers. To some degree these problems are almost inevitable, given that workers are heterogeneous and that productivity is not directly observable. Suppose, however, that productivity is correlated for any reason whatsoever with an observable trait such as education. In that event, firms might be willing to pay new college-educated workers more because they expect that on average they will be more productive.

Spence calls a trait like education in this example a **signal**. It is a way for people to communicate to prospective employers their otherwise unobservable productivity. To be an effective signal, however, education must have one additional special characteristic. If more educated workers are paid more because on average they are likely to be more productive, what would prevent less skilled persons from acquiring the signal (a college degree) and then passing themselves off as more productive? If that happened, education

[2] A readable exposition of Spence's ideas is "Job Market Signalling," *Quarterly Journal of Economics* (August 1973).

would no longer have value as a signal, since it would no longer predict productivity.

For education to serve as a signal, it must be true that the costs of acquiring the signal are inversely correlated with true productivity—that is, higher for less skilled individuals than for more skilled individuals. For example, in the case of education, less skilled individuals might take longer to finish college or they might find the psychic costs too high. In any event, if the costs differ appropriately, less skilled individuals might find that, given the expected wage differential, it is not advantageous to attend college. Only the more skilled would attend college and thus a college diploma would be an effective signal of productivity. Spence calls a situation like that a **signaling equilibrium**.

Note that in the signaling model of education, it does not matter whether education actually makes people more productive or merely provides an easy way to identify those workers who are more productive, independent of their experience in college. Even if education had no effect whatsoever on individual productivity, it could still have economic value both for individuals and for society at large. Individuals benefit via higher incomes and society benefits through a better match between people and jobs. Education may be a credential, but it is a productive, information-revealing credential.[3]

Spence's signaling model is undeniably clever. It avoids the pitfalls of the credentialist explanation, while capturing some of its flavor. Still, one cannot help but wonder whether there might not be a better or cheaper way to signal true productivity than by acquiring a college degree. The costs to a person for a college degree are certainly in excess of $50,000, which seems like a large expenditure for the purpose of signaling true productivity. Why couldn't a person agree to take—and, indeed, offer to bear the cost of—an extensive series of tests designed to measure expected future productivity? To this economist, at least, the fact that students choose, instead, to attend college and that firms continue to offer wage premiums to college students suggests that higher education must have some important effects on productivity.

THE DUAL LABOR MARKET MODEL

The **dual labor market model** (DLM) was developed in the late 1960s by two economists, Peter Doeringer and Michael Piore, as an explicit challenge to human capital theory.[4] Their own research on the operation of the

[3] Can you provide a signaling explanation of the higher rates of return to diploma years? What information is revealed by the signal "started, but did not complete high school or college"?

[4] Peter Doeringer and Michael Piore, *Internal Labor Markets and Manpower Analysis* (Lexington, Mass.: Lexington Books, 1971).

low-wage labor market in Boston had convinced them that human capital explanations were inadequate for understanding the low earnings of the workers they studied. They felt that there was little difference in terms of apparent human capital between workers who were doing reasonably well and those who were either chronically unemployed or employed at very low wages. Their explanation of the situation they observed adopted some aspects of human capital theory, especially the idea of specific training. But they also stressed the importance of institutional features of contemporary labor markets, labor market discrimination, and the resulting immobility of labor. The orientation of their model is very different from the human capital approach.

Doeringer and Piore began by arguing that it was useful to think of the labor market as being divided into two distinct sectors—hence the designation "dual labor market model." They called these the **primary sector** and the **secondary sector**. The two sectors were defined not in terms of specific occupations or industries, but rather by a set of general characteristics. Thus jobs in the secondary sector "tend to have low wages and fringe benefits, poor working conditions, high labor turnover, little chance of advancement, and often arbitrary and capricious supervision."[5] In contrast, jobs in the primary sector have many of the opposite characteristics: employment is steady, working conditions are better, wages are higher, and there are significant opportunities for advancement. A further important difference between the two sectors concerns on-the-job training. Jobs in the secondary sector offer little or no training—they are "dead-end" jobs—whereas those in the primary sector provide extensive training, most of which, in their view, is usually specific rather than general.

Doeringer and Piore argued that the structure of the labor market in the two sectors was markedly different. The secondary sector was essentially a competitive market, not very different from a simple textbook supply and demand model. Wages tended to be at equilibrium levels, which were often quite low given the low skill requirements and lack of training.

The primary sector, though, was not a competitive market of the usual sort. Most jobs in this sector were part of an **internal labor market**,[6] that is, a labor market internal to, or entirely within, a large firm. An internal labor market typically had three characteristics. First, it was highly structured and regulated. Doeringer and Piore described it as "an administrative unit within which the pricing and allocation of labor is governed by a set of administrative rules and procedures."[7] The rules and procedures substitute for supply and demand forces. Second, an internal labor market conferred privileged status

[5] Doeringer and Piore, pp. 165–166.

[6] The concept of an internal labor market was developed by Clark Kerr in his article, "The Balkanization of Labor Markets." Kerr's article appeared in *Labor Mobility and Economic Opportunity*, ed. E. Wight Bakke (Cambridge, Mass.: Technology Press of MIT, 1954), pp. 92–110.

[7] Doeringer and Piore, pp. 1–2.

on "insiders"—those already hired—as compared to outsiders. Once a person was safely ensconced within an internal labor market, he or she was largely immune from regular competition from outsiders. Outsiders could enter an internal labor market only at a limited number of low-level positions termed **ports of entry**. Vacancies in other positions were usually filled from within by promotion. Often there was a well-defined "job ladder" which described a sequence of jobs that a person might reasonably expect to hold over a period of years. Third, wages within the internal labor market were often set above equilibrium levels. Doeringer and Piore suggested, without much explanation, that the rules and procedures of the internal labor market were influenced relatively little by conditions in the external labor market.

Finally, they asserted that there was limited worker mobility from the secondary sector to the primary sector. For one thing, the importance of firm-specific training created a natural division between workers in the two sectors. Workers without training are not in a position to compete with specifically trained workers for jobs within an internal labor market. Second, Doeringer and Piore argued that employment in the secondary sector often made a workers unsuited for subsequent employment in the primary sector. Secondary-sector employment created (or reinforced) a set of work habits—lack of promptness, inattentiveness to task, absenteeism, lack of respect for authority, petty theft—which were tolerated there but were quite inappropriate in the primary sector. The behavioral norms in the two sectors were so different that once a person became accustomed to secondary-sector employment, there was little chance of finding primary-sector employment.

In this view of how the labor market operates, the key to success is gaining access to entry-level jobs in the primary sector. Here noncompetitive elements are important. Wages in the primary sector remain above equilibrium, even though there is a continuous excess supply of qualified workers. Employment must be rationed among the queue of eligible workers and it is in that process, according to Doeringer and Piore, that discrimination, nepotism, personal contacts, or even luck play a major role. Human capital considerations are, they argue, less important. The fortunate ones who do gain primary-sector employment will enjoy the many benefits of the internal labor market. But those people who are "rationed out" must seek employment in the secondary sector instead.

Doeringer and Piore argued that, in practice, the workers most likely to be rationed out were the traditional victims of discrimination—blacks, Hispanics, recent immigrants, illegal aliens, teenagers, and many women. They became the predominant work force of the secondary labor market. An individual's labor market earnings reflect not so much his or her choices about human capital investment as the institutional structure of labor markets and

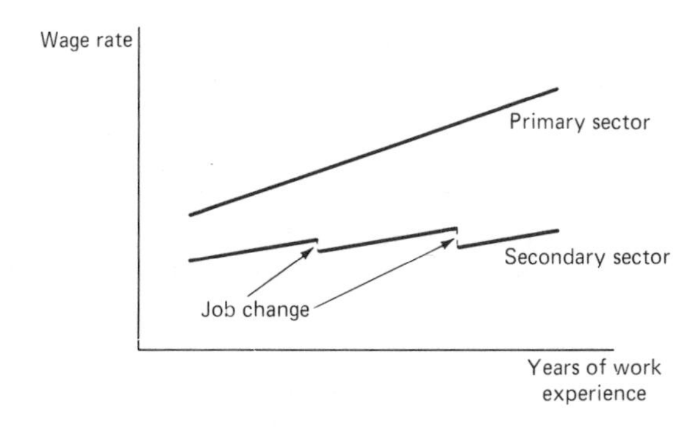

FIGURE 7.1 Typical Experience—Earnings Profiles in the Primary and Secondary Sectors

the operation of discrimination. Typical experience earnings profiles in the two sectors are illustrated in Figure 7.1.

More recently, economists working within this approach have relaxed the strict primary–secondary labor market distinction somewhat, resulting in what is known as the **segmented labor market model**. Piore, for example, has argued that within the primary sector there is an important distinction between an *upper tier* and a *lower tier* of jobs.[8] The upper tier apparently consists of professional and managerial jobs, while the lower tier includes stable blue-collar employment. Interestingly, there are similarities between the upper tier and the secondary sector. According to Piore, both operate without elaborate work rules and formal administrative procedures and in both there is a great deal of movement from job to job. In the upper tier, however, job changes are advancements (think of the often-rapid movement of corporate executives), whereas in the secondary sector it is just "drifting." Although this new version is less rigid, it does not alter the basic approach of the DLM model.

In the decade following the publication of these ideas, the DLM model enjoyed support from a number of economists. It was regarded as a serious challenger to the "competition plus human capital model" as the accepted model of labor market behavior. Today, its support among economists is much weaker. Students, though, invariably seem to like the segmented market approach, and so do researchers in other disciplines.[9] All are disturbed to find that most economists do not share their enthusiasm. There are two basic

[8] Michael Piore, "Notes for a Theory of Labor Market Stratification," in Richard C. Edwards, Michael Reich, and David M. Gordon, eds., *Labor Market Segmentation* (Lexington, Mass.: D. C. Heath and Company, 1975).

[9] For an example of its use by sociologists, see William J. Wilson, *The Declining Significance of Race* (Chicago: The University of Chicago Press, 1980), chap. 6.

reasons for its declining popularity among economists. First, there is, frankly, little empirical evidence in favor of its major propositions. Indeed, it is not always easy to tell what the propositions are. Even after 15 years, no one has offered a definitive statement about which jobs belong to the primary sector and which to the secondary sector, so it is not clear how to assess whether conditions are drastically different in the two sectors. Many of the early studies advanced in support of this approach were later shown to have serious statistical flaws. Research since then to test predictions about the lack of mobility across market segments (somehow defined) or to examine whether income varied sharply across sectors have not been very supportive.[10] The idea that the labor market is split into two distinct parts does not appear to be correct.

Second, and more fundamentally, this approach does not draw very much on the ideas of economics. It is primarily descriptive, rather than explanatory, an attempt to categorize broad sectors of the labor market, but not to analyze them. There is virtually no discussion of the behavior of firms or individuals that explains or is even consistent with the development of market segments. How does any of it fit with utility maximization by individuals or profit maximization by firms? Why are wages persistently set above equilibrium in the primary sector? Why do firms resort to the use of internal labor markets? Even after more than a decade during which such criticisms have been made, there is still no response.

In spite of that, this approach is not without value. First, it serves as a kind of antidote to the human capital model. Economists working with that approach frequently seem to regard individual choices as completely unrestricted and labor markets as if they were in a continual state of long-run equilibrium. Probably, neither proposition is true or essential to the human capital approach. Second, the segmentation approach is attractive, if only as a casual description of labor markets. It is not difficult to think, on the one hand, of people who spend their entire working career on a series of related jobs for the same large corporation; on the other hand, there certainly is a group of jobs that are unattractive in almost every way. Finally, its emphasis on the idea of internal labor markets forced other economists to think more carefully about what happens *inside* a firm, rather than just treating a firm as a "black box" which mysteriously transformed inputs into outputs. Firms do have a structure that is vastly more complex than is accounted for in conventional models of labor supply and labor demand; and that structure may be important for understanding labor market outcomes.

[10] See Glen Cain, "The Challenge of Segmented Labor Market Theories to Orthodox Theory: A Survey," *Journal of Economic Literature*, 14, no. 4 (December 1976), 1215–1257, and Greg J. Duncan, *Years of Poverty, Years of Plenty* (Ann Arbor, Mich.: Institute for Social Research, 1984), especially Chapter 4.

THE ECONOMICS OF INTERNAL ORGANIZATION

The Development of Internal Labor Markets

It is hard to deny that something like internal labor markets do exist.[11] Workers do, in many instances, move through a progression of jobs within a firm. Sometimes the progression is standardized enough to constitute a job ladder or what economists now call an **implicit contract**. Current employees are often treated differently from prospective employees—they do not compete on even terms for a new job opening. Where the DLM model theorists seemed to take these phenomena as given, other economists have attempted to provide economic explanations for them. The resulting body of literature, developed primarily in the last ten years, is known as the **economics of internal organization**, and it is on the frontier of labor economics research.

Labor economists working along these lines have focused on two general questions. First, what accounts for the development of internal labor markets? Why are they found in some circumstances but not in others? Second, what are some of the implications of internal labor markets for labor market analysis? For example, what things may change when we recognize the long-term employment relationships that typically characterize internal labor markets?

Why would employers ever choose to establish internal labor markets?[12] After all, in doing so, they are giving something up: their absolute right to make decisions about employment, promotion, or work procedures. That right, which implicitly exists in a perfectly competitive labor market, is now sacrificed to the rules and procedures of the internal labor market. What does the employer get in return? If we can identify the possible benefits to the employer and the circumstances in which those benefits are likely to be larger, we may be able to understand why and where internal labor markets develop.

Most analyses of this have stressed the informational problems that may exist within firms, particularly as related to the employment, promotion, and training of workers. To see why this might matter, consider first the opposite case where an employer has perfect knowledge of everything that occurs within a firm. That knowledge would include at least the following things: (1) the ability to evaluate perfectly the productivity of each worker, (2) the

[11] If you skipped the preceding section, an internal labor market is a highly structural, formal labor market which may exist entirely within a large firm. Typically, it has an elaborate set of rules and procedures that guide employment decisions. A key feature is that workers in an internal labor market are treated preferentially relative to workers in the external (competitive) labor market. For more details, see page 187–8.

[12] The discussion here draws heavily on A. Michael Spence, "The Economics of Internal Organization: An Introduction," and Oliver E. Williamson, Michael L. Wachter, and Jeffrey E. Harris, "Understanding the Employment Relation: The Analysis of Idiosyncratic Exchange." Both papers appeared in the *Bell Journal of Management Science*, 6, no. 1 (1975), 163–72, 250–78.

ability to regularly monitor the effort level and performance of each worker, and (3) complete information about the best way to perform all work tasks. In such a situation the employer would probably be unwilling to accept constraints on his or her authority. The firm could do better by treating each worker on an individual basis rather than establishing rules or procedures that would apply to the group of workers as a whole. An internal labor market is not likely where there are no informational problems.

Suppose, instead, that the firm's information is quite limited. The firm cannot easily determine a worker's skills nor easily monitor the level of effort. Moreover, suppose that the necessary tasks that workers must master are highly specialized; to use the expression commonly used, there is **job idiosyncrasy**,[13] meaning that the employment tasks are unique rather than standardized. Successful worker performance then would involve acquiring a great deal of very specific training about the characteristics of machinery, of co-workers, of group processes, and so on. Think of these things as the "tricks of the trade," not recorded in any job description, but instrumental for successful, highly productive work. Finally, it may well be true under these circumstances that current employees are far better informed about the essential features of tasks than the employer is.

In a situation like this, a great deal depends on the willingness of currently trained workers to share their knowledge with untrained workers. Only they can provide on-the-job training, and unless they do, productivity will suffer. The problem is that trained workers may have little incentive to assist in the training process if they believe that the newly trained workers may ultimately compete with them for subsequent promotions. Indeed, the incentive might well be to conceal or hoard information. Clearly, the firm has a potential problem.

One possible solution involves making a more formal employment bargain with the entire group of workers as a whole. In effect, an implicit employment contract is established which defines the rules and the rights and responsibilities of all parties. For example, the firm might agree to use seniority as the dominant criterion in promotion, even if it means not always promoting the best person. Employees might then be willing to facilitate the process of training workers. Since the firm cannot determine worker productivity perfectly, it might also establish more or less standard pay rates for each job category and then not concern itself with the exact productivity of each person in each job. Of course, there would be a limit to the firm's tolerance of poor work, and some performance criteria would have to be established. Rules and procedures concerning evaluation, promotion, and dismissal might be developed and with them, personnel departments, grievance procedures, and so on. The net result of all of this is that something quite like an internal labor market may develop. Its economic rationale is

[13] This expression comes from the article by Williamson et al.

clear—it is an efficient response to an employment situation in which there is imperfect information.

Effects of Internal Labor Markets

How does the existence of internal labor markets change some of our simpler ideas about the labor market? What results or conclusions will differ?

One thing that could change is the relationship between a worker's wage and his or her *MRP* in each time period. In an internal labor market, where long-term employment is the norm, both the employer and the employee can be forward-looking rather than exclusively present-oriented. What should matter to the worker is the present value of earnings over an expected sequence of positions stretching over a number of years rather than just today's wage. If the wage is a bit lower to start, but is expected to be correspondingly higher in the future, that should not be a problem—as long as the prospect of being laid off or fired is slim. As for the firm, it might actually gain by instituting a career wage profile that reduced wages below a worker's *MRP* initially and raised them later. The offer of higher pay, available only at the end of one's career, provides workers with an incentive to perform well enough to warrant continued promotion into these positions. Perhaps the implicit employment contract states that subject only to events beyond the firm's control (such as unforeseen demand changes) and to the performance of one's job competently and reliably, promotion is to be expected. If the present value of wage payments is no more than under an alternative system in which wages equaled *MRP* in each period, the firm gains through the incentive effects. If the incentive effects are large enough, the firm might even be able to offer a career wage profile with a slightly higher present value. In that case, both the firm and the workers benefit from this wage payment arrangement.

Figure 7.2 shows how this might work. Suppose that curve AA' represented a wage path corresponding to a person's productivity over time. Earnings rise because on-the-job training is acquired. Curve BB' represents a wage profile of equal present value, but with some earnings shifted for incentive purposes from early years to later ones. Earnings no longer correspond to productivity on a year-to-year comparison, but they do correspond (in present-value terms) over the worker's entire career. Curve CC', which represents a larger present value of lifetime earnings than the other two, could be the result if the incentive effects cause total lifetime productivity to rise.

There are a number of possible extensions of this basic idea of a career wage profile differing from a career productivity profile. An interesting one, suggested by the economist Edward Lazear, concerns mandatory retirement.[14]

[14]See Edward A. Lazear, "Why Is There Mandatory Retirement?" *Journal of Political Economy*, 87, no. 6 (December 1979), 1261–1284.

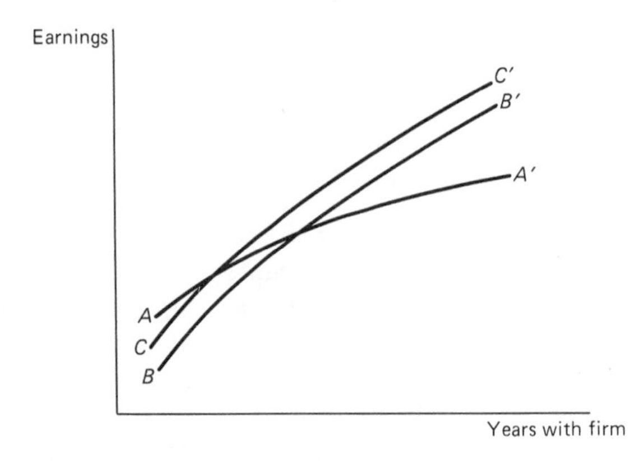

FIGURE 7.2 Possible Wage Effects of an Internal Labor Market

If wages are highest at the end of one's career and exceed one's current productivity, a worker might never want to retire. The firm, however, needs to know the retirement date so that it can determine how much to "underpay" a worker earlier in his or her career. If it did not know, it might end up paying more than it intended in present-value terms, perhaps enough more to nullify the incentive benefits of the wage scheme. The solution, according to Lazear, is a mandatory retirement provision that specifies the maximum age of retirement. That provides the certainty which is essential for the firm to implement this wage policy.

Application: Pay Differentials in an Automobile Assembly Plant

An especially interesting and apt example of these ideas was described to me by a former student who worked at an automobile assembly plant. An automobile assembly plant is a good candidate for an internal labor market. There are a wide variety of tasks that must be performed, each with a very specific skills component. Much of the job skills must be learned either by "observing" or "doing." Although many of the tasks require roughly comparable skill, a few, such as wiping cars clean at the end of the line, are less demanding. There are also a few jobs that are widely regarded as being less desirable for other reasons. Welding and spray painting are apparently especially disliked. Welding is very hot work and there is a real possibility of suffering burns; spray painters must wear a mask over their nose and mouth and smear the rest of their face with Vaseline to prevent exposure to the paint and paint fumes.

Pay, job assignment, and promotion policy are all covered by a labor contract between the United Auto Workers union and the automobile company. One possible contract would specify the exact rate of pay for each job, differentiating appropriately by skill and by desirability. Presumably, there is a set of relative wages that would lead to competent workers performing all the tasks, including the less desired ones. In effect, that would simply be a set of equilibrium wage rates. Such a contract would, to be sure, be difficult to negotiate since it would have to specify perhaps as many as 500 distinct wage rates. Indeed, given the normal difficulty in reaching contractual agreements, it might be almost impossible in a situation as complex as that.

The actual contract is quite different. It is much simpler, specifying a standard rate of pay with only small differentials for those few easier or less desirable jobs. There are no wage premiums for more experienced workers. Nevertheless, seniority does play an important role. Workers are permitted to choose their specific task on the assembly line by order of seniority. According to my source, the wage premium for the undesirable jobs are too small, so they are never voluntarily selected. Senior workers typically opt for the least demanding, least undesirable jobs within the standard-pay-rate group, while the lower-paid, lower-skilled jobs and the higher-paid, less desired jobs go to workers with the least seniority.

If we were to evaluate this situation solely in terms of the current time period, it would certainly seem inequitable. Rates of pay are not in strict accord with the nature of the task performed. In relative terms, some are overpaid and some underpaid. (In absolute terms, they are all probably making more than the competitive equilibrium wage rate for their skill level.) Why, then, don't the exploited workers complain and compel the union to represent their interests? The reason is straightforward. Workers are forward looking. They recognize that they can expect to enjoy the fruits of seniority themselves at a later time. Perhaps they also think it is wiser for the older workers to have the easier jobs. The wage scheme does not change the present value of their earnings over the many years they may expect to be employed. It just rearranges it. The firm may gain as well, as it now provides workers with an incentive both to remain with the firm and to assist in the training of new workers.

SUMMARY

The human capital model provides a reasonable and internally consistent explanation of how education and job experience increase earnings. But the crucial intervening effect—an increase in productivity—is itself unobserved. In this chapter we surveyed alternative explanations of these relationships.

Two explanations about the effects of education on earnings were discussed in the first part of the chapter. The credentialist argument ultimately founders because it seems to require that employers be absolutely unable to make judgments about individual productivity. If college-educated workers are no more productive than workers with less education, why are employers willing to pay them more? The signaling model argues that workers with a college education are more productive than those with less education, but not necessarily because of that education. Rather, education acts as a filter, distinguishing the more productive workers from the less productive. In Spence's terms, it is a signal.

The dual labor market borrows some ideas from human capital theory, but it differs by adding institutional structure and constraints on individual human capital investment behavior. The result is that a person's earnings are not primarily determined by his or her human capital, but by the sector of the labor market in which employment occurs. Moreover, the assignment of workers to the two sectors is "unfair."

The dual labor market model is known by virtually all economists, but accepted on its own terms by relatively few. As a description, it is often useful; as an explanation, it is much weaker. Empirical studies have not provided much support for its basic propositions. Nevertheless, its emphasis on the importance of internal labor markets is an important, lasting contribution.

The economics of internal organization approach attempts to explain what the dual labor market took for granted—the existence of internal labor markets. Specific training, informational problems, and job idiosyncrasy are key elements of its description of the internal structure of firms. It suggests that internal labor markets may be an efficient response where those conditions exist. The "solution" of internal labor markets may involve long-term employment relationships—and perhaps also a rearrangement of a worker's career earnings profile.

New Concepts

Credentialism
Signal
Signaling equilibrium
Dual labor market model (DLM)
Primary sector
Secondary sector
Internal labor market
Ports of entry
Segmented labor market model
Implicit contract
Economics of internal organization
Job idiosyncrasy

8

Further Topics in Labor Market Analysis

INTRODUCTION

This chapter surveys two topics that are part of traditional wage theory and a third which represents a completely different point of view. The first two are among the oldest ideas in wage theory, predating by a century or more the ideas developed in Chapters 2 to 7. The first of these is the theory of economic rent, which, as we noted at the beginning of Chapter 6, concerns the pricing of unique or highly specialized resources. That idea nicely illuminates a small but always interesting segment of the labor market—people with skills so unusual that they command incredibly high salaries. The second topic, the theory of compensating wage differentials, is even older. It concerns the effect on wages of differences in the nonmonetary characteristics of jobs—their degree of desirability or riskiness, for instance.

The last section presents an introduction to the economics of Karl Marx, especially as it is applied to labor and the labor market. The plight of labor in capitalist society was one of Marx's major concerns. He, and others working in a Marxist tradition, have written extensively, and often perceptively, about that. The section begins with a brief survey of Marxist wage theory and then considers a more recent Marxist contribution, the analysis of the labor process under capitalism.

ECONOMIC RENT AND THE LABOR MARKET

The Theory of Economic Rent

The concept of **economic rent** was developed by the economist David Ricardo early in the nineteenth century. Ricardo conceived of it as an explanation of land prices on parcels of different quality or location, but in fact, its application is more general than that. Technically, economic rent is defined as any payment to a factor of production (land, labor, or capital) that is in excess of the minimum price at which it would be supplied. In shorthand, it is the difference between the payment received by a factor and its "supply price." In the case of land, it is frequently true that its supply price is essentially zero. After all, land does not have to be produced in a factory, so there are no costs that must be covered to assure its supply. Landowners would, of course, prefer a higher price to a lower one. But because there are no costs involved in its supply, it will be supplied to the market no matter what its price is. By the definition of economic rent, then, all of the payment to land as a factor of production—which we commonly call rent—is what economists regard as economic rent.

Like all other prices, the actual market price for the use of land is determined by the interaction of supply and demand. If the **supply price** of a piece of land is really zero, as Ricardo assumed, its supply curve will be a vertical line, extending all the way down to the point where the price is zero. If the land has some alternative value, that value establishes its minimum supply price to this potential use and the supply curve is zero below that and vertical above it. In either case, the important point is that the supply curve is perfectly inelastic above its supply price. To construct the demand curve, we would ask what fraction of the land parcel would each demander be willing to use at each possible price. Each user's demand is, as always, a derived demand, since the value of having the parcel of land depends on the revenues that can be obtained from its use.

Figure 8.1 illustrates these ideas for a particular parcel of land. The supply curve is vertical; for simplicity, the supply price is shown as zero, but that is not essential. The demand curve is downward sloping, representing the usual negative relationship between price and quantity demanded. The equilibrium price would be p^*, since only there does the quantity demanded match the fixed amount available. The total economic rent received by the owner of the land parcel is represented by the shaded rectangle AP^*ON.

The important point about a factor that earns economic rent is that whether the price is outrageously high or ridiculously low, it is a long-run equilibrium price. Here is why. In the case of producible goods, the existence of profits (or losses) leads to entry (or exit) from the industry. The net effect of these movements is that in long-run equilibrium, all firms producing in an industry earn a normal rate of return on their investment. But this process of adjustment cannot apply to land, since land cannot be produced in a factory or moved from one location to another. Whenever a factor of production is in fixed supply, it must accept, for better or for worse, what the market will bear. Its market price is solely determined by the position of the demand curve.

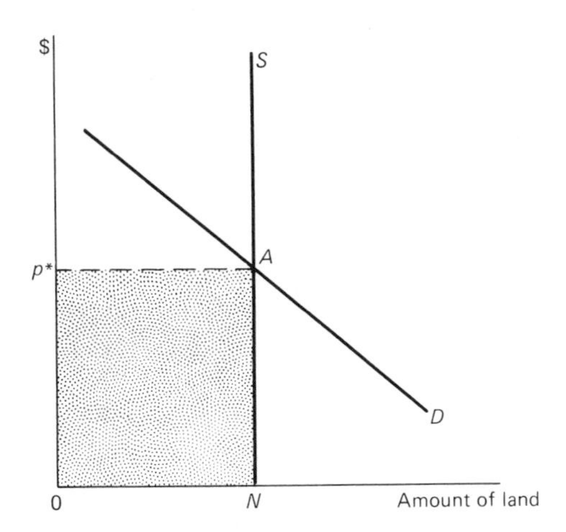

FIGURE 8.1 The Determination of Economic Rent

Economic Rent in Labor Markets

You may well be wondering what all of this has to do with labor and the labor market. In fact, it serves very well as an explanation for the determination of the labor market value of a certain class of labor skills. That class includes skills that are inherently in (relatively) fixed supply because they are unproducible and unlearnable by all but a very small group. Professional athletes, movie stars, opera singers, fashion models, and so on, all fall into this category. They share two characteristics with Ricardo's parcel of land—they are available in fixed supply (there is only one Julius Erving, one Marlon Brando, one John Travolta, one Luciano Pavorotti, one Cheryl Tiegs, etc.) and their services are supplied inelastically above their supply price. From an economic standpoint, these people are not very different from a parcel of land along Fifth Avenue in New York City or ocean-front property in Atlantic City. The combination of limited supply and large demand assures each a very handsome income. As economists, we would recognize that their income is an example of economic rent. Indeed, most of the truly enormous labor incomes in the economy are probably best classified as economic rent.

To see the idea more clearly, take a specific example—say, John Travolta or Cheryl Tiegs. They are genuinely unique labor resources and, quite fortunately for them, the market demand for their particular bundle of skills is quite high (at least as of the fall of 1985). Because they could be working in other less lucrative professions, their supply price to the film and modeling industry respectively is not zero, but neither is it anything close to their actual incomes. If John Travolta or Cheryl Tiegs clones could be readily produced in a factory, the price for their services would tend to settle at about the average cost of production. Because they would no longer be unique, their economic rent would be eliminated. They would have to be content, like most of the rest of us, to earn a normal rate of return on the costs of acquiring their skills. Until such cloning becomes feasible, however, John and Cheryl can relax and enjoy their rents—at least until the demand for their services falls.

Application: *Quasi-Rents in the Labor Market*

Economic rent figures in wage theory in a second, related way. Human capital theory tells us that in a situation of long-run equilibrium, wages will be proportional to the amount of human capital a person possesses. People with the same amount of human capital should, therefore, earn the same amount regardless of the exact nature of their skills. When, however, the labor market is not in long-run equilibrium—which is most of the time—the exact nature of a person's skills does matter. If the demand for computer programmers suddenly rises, programmers' wages will increase above that for equally skilled workers not trained as computer programmers.

How should we interpret the higher earnings of people fortunate enough to have been trained as computer programmers? One way is to think of their earnings as having two distinct components, one part representing a normal return of human capital and a second part due to the temporary scarcity of the skills they possess. The additional payment is something like economic rent, a demand-determined payment to a factor whose supply cannot be increased. Here the situation is only temporary, lasting just until the next group of computer programmers is trained. Thus the rents are also only temporary. Economists call them **quasi-rents**.

These differences in the returns to human capital can also exist for two other related reasons. First, if workers are geographically immobile, the same skills may be more valuable in one area than in another. Second, and of greater concern, is the situation in which the number of persons acquiring the necessary skills or entering an occupation is restricted. The most common form is one in which the current members of an occupation gain the exclusive right to train, license, or accredit new entrants. The stated purpose of these practices is usually to assure professional standards or to maintain order, but it is not too hard to imagine that regulating labor supply to assure the income of current members of the occupation might also get occasional consideration. If so, people in this occupation would earn quasi-rents that might exist for an extended time.

THE THEORY OF COMPENSATING WAGE DIFFERENTIALS

Theoretical Analysis

Suppose that two jobs required the same level of skill, but that one job was generally regarded by workers as being more desirable even when the wage rates were identical. One job could be more tedious or more demanding or more dangerous or less prestigious or more (or less) of anything that workers care about. In such a situation, could the equilibrium wage rates in the two jobs be the same? Clearly not, since if the wage rates were the same, no one would choose the less desirable employment. In labor market equilibrium, then, the wage rate for that job would necessarily be higher to compensate for its undesirable features.

Economists call these features of a job its **nonpecuniary job characteristics**, and the wage differences they create are called **compensating** or **equalizing wage differentials**. The important point is that the wage differences make the overall conditions of employment equal when the nonpecuniary characteristics are unequal. Indeed, equal wage rates would be unequal and unfair in such a case.

Adam Smith was one of the first economists to consider this aspect of wage determination. His book *The Wealth of Nations*, published in 1776, includes a full chapter entitled "Of Wages and Profit in the Different Employments of Labor and Stock." He noted there in a famous passage that "the whole of the advantages and disadvantages of the different employments of labor . . . must, in the same neighborhood, be either perfectly equal or continually tending to equality."[1] Smith's point was that it was "the whole of the advantages and disadvantages" and not just wages that must "tend to equality."

The examples cited by the early economists as evidence of this principle were extremely colorful, if not bizarre. Smith commented that "the most detestable of all employments, that of public executioner, is, in proportion to the quantity of work done, better paid than any common trade whatever." Nassau W. Senior, a nineteenth-century British economist, went a step further.[2] "To Adam Smith's instance of a public executioner," he wrote, "may be added that a common informer . . . paid not so much for encountering toil as for being pelted and hissed." As a final example, he noted that "there are employments, as for instance the slave trade, which imply fatigue, hardship, and danger, public execration, and if a slave trader can be supposed to reflect on the nature of his occupation, self-reproach. When almost all that renders life agreeable, or even endurable, is sacrificed to profit, the profit must be great."

Exactly which job characteristics will lead to compensating differentials and how large those differentials will be are, in general, not things that can be determined a priori by theoretical inquiry. The ultimate source of the differentials is the subjective preferences of workers and there is simply no scientific way to conclude what preferences should be, let alone what they are. When it comes to preferences, the rule is "de gustibus non disputandum est"—there can be no quarreling about matters of taste.

It is possible, nevertheless, to describe the effect of different assumptions about preferences on the determination of compensating wage differentials. The simplest assumption is that all workers have identical preferences—they all like or dislike features of a job equally. To see the effect of this, consider two jobs, A and B, which require exactly the same amount of human capital. If there were no relevant differences in job characteristics, wages in A and B would necessarily be equal. (We assume, for simplicity, a situation of long-run equilibrium). Graphically, this is illustrated in Figure 8.2, which shows the supply of workers to A as a function of the wage in A relative to the wage in B (w_A/w_B). Supply curve S_1 represents the situation of identical preferences and no differences in job characteristics. It is positioned at a relative wage of 1 ($w_A = w_B$) because there are no relevant differences in either required

[1] This passage is from pp. 99–100.

[2] These quotations appear on pp. 201–202 of Nassau W. Senior, *An Outline of the Science of Political Economy*, first published in 1836.

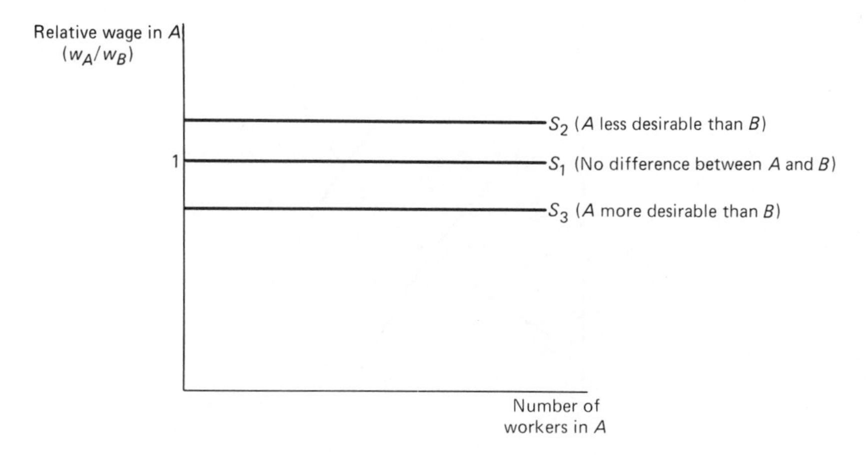

FIGURE 8.2 Compensating Wage Differentials with Uniform Preferences

skill or job characteristics; it is horizontal at that wage because preferences are uniform. If job *A* were, instead, judged to be uniformly less desirable, the supply curve would be higher (but still horizontal). This is shown as S_2. The resulting wage premium is the compensating differential necessary to induce people to bear the less pleasant working conditions in *A*. Exactly the opposite would happen if *A* were the more desirable job. Now the supply curve to *A* would be positioned lower, as in S_3. The compensating wage differential is received by workers in job *B* instead. Note that in all three cases, the equilibrium relative wage will be independent of the demand for labor.

Now suppose that all workers dislike something about job *A*, but that the strength of their dislike differs. In that case, the supply curve of workers to *A* will be upward sloping, as shown in Figure 8.3. The curve starts at some relative wage, greater than 1, which is just large enough to satisfy the worker whose dislike for *A* is the weakest. In the same way, every other worker is included in the supply curve at the lowest wage at which he or she would be willing to work in *A*. In this case, the demand curve for labor does affect the equilibrium wage rate, because a higher relative wage is necessary to attract additional workers. It is the preferences of the marginal worker that matter, not those of the workers with weaker preferences. Figure 8.3 includes two possible demand curves. The effect on the equilibrium relative wage is easily seen.

There is one final, interesting possibility which is a variation on the two preceding cases. Suppose, again, that preferences differ, but that now some workers have no dislike for working in *A*. (Don't forget: De gustibus non disputandum est; perhaps the public executioner enjoyed his work or, at least, didn't mind it.) Now the supply curve has a horizontal position at a relative wage of 1, representing the workers with no distaste for *A*, and an upward-

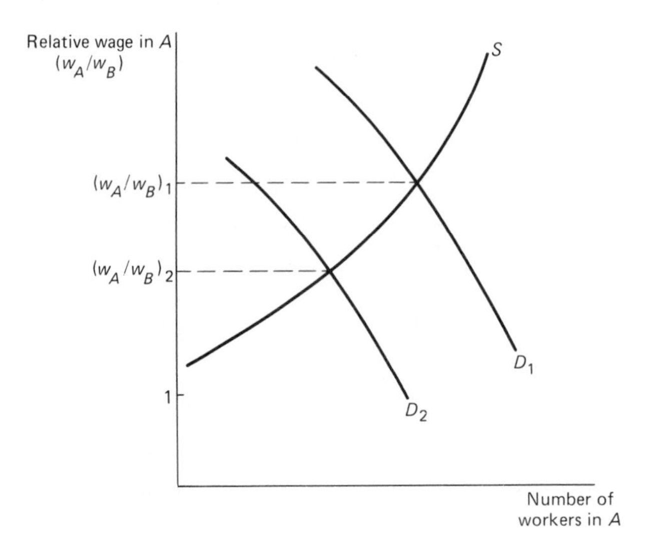

FIGURE 8.3 Compensating Wage Differentials When Workers Have Different Preferences

sloping portion thereafter for the other workers. If the demand curve for labor is D_1, then as shown in Figure 8.4, there will be a compensating wage differential received by all workers there, including the ones for whom additional compensation is unnecessary. If, however, the demand is much smaller, as at D_2, it is clearly possible that no compensating differential will exist, despite the fact that most workers dislike working in A. If enough workers are indifferent to working the midnight shift or to frequent traveling or even to various risks, occupations that have those characteristics will not need to pay compensating wage differentials.

Thus far, we have a consistent explanation for every conceivable result, a situation that makes empirical testing of the theory of compensating wage differentials difficult. There is, however, one clear and important prediction of this analysis. If there is a *change* in the relevant characteristics of a job—it becomes, say, less dangerous—the compensating wage differential will change accordingly. The underlying mechanism is a shift in the supply curve. Figure 8.5 shows the basic idea. Suppose that given the current characteristics of A and the preferences of workers, the relevant supply curve is S_1. The corresponding relative wage is $(w_A/w_B)_1$. If the undesirable features were somehow diminished, the curve would shift out to S_2. At each relative wage, more workers than before will now find employment in A desirable. The corresponding equilibrium wage falls to $(w_A/w_B)_2$. Exactly the opposite would occur if the undesirable features of A became more severe.

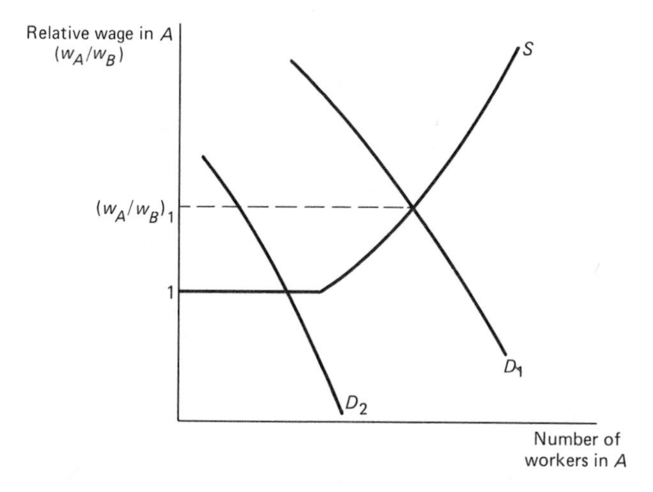

FIGURE 8.4 The Possibility of No Compensating Differential When Workers Have Different Preferences

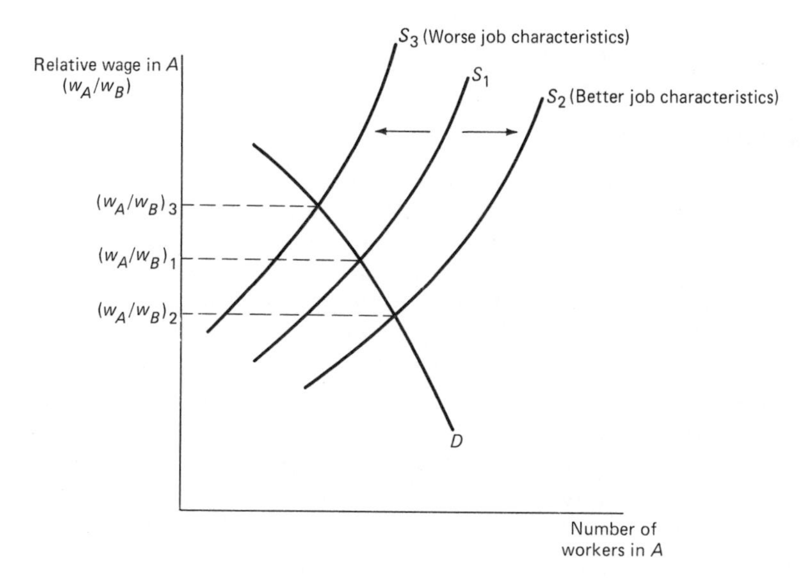

FIGURE 8.5 The Effect of Changes in Nonpecuniary Job Characteristics

Application: *Regulating Occupational Health and Safety*

The idea that jobs with undesirable job characteristics provide compensating wage differentials leads to one very important policy implication. That concerns the regulation by government agencies such as OSHA (the Occupational Safety and Health Administration) of health and safety on the job. Simply put, the prediction is this: Where job risks are well understood by workers, workers who choose hazardous jobs receive compensating differences. Attempts to improve health and safety standards will, at best, result in a reduction in equilibrium wage rates, just as in Figure 8.5. If the regulation is poorly implemented, as many economists contend of OSHA regulations, its costs may well exceed the benefits.

The key issue here is whether job risks are, in fact, clearly understood by workers. A tragic example concerns the exposure to asbestos of tens of thousands of workers for many years *prior* to the recognition by the scientific community of its link to cancer. They received no compensating differential at all, although now, if negligence can be proved, they may be entitled to payments.

In practice, it is not easy to determine how much information workers have and utilize in their job choice. How, then, can we know whether workers really are receiving compensating differentials? One reasonable possibility is that workers might well have better information about safety issues than about health issues, since the latter are more technical and may require scientific study. If this idea about worker information is correct, OSHA might more usefully regulate occupational health standards than safety standards.[3]

Empirical Evidence

Despite the straightforward nature of the theoretical arguments, testing the theory of compensating differentials has turned out to be a formidable task. One problem is created by the diversity of individual preferences noted above. It simply is not clear—with a few notable exceptions—which job characteristics might reasonably be expected to result in compensating differentials. Presumably, a high risk of a fatal or disabling injury is a characteristic that most persons would regard as undesirable. But beyond characteristics such as that, there are relatively few obvious candidates. Personally, I would require a compensating differential to work as a lawyer, but I suspect most lawyers feel the same way about being an economics professor. In any event, it is not even sufficient, as we saw in Figure 8.4, that most people find a job characteristic undesirable. It is the preference of the marginal worker that matters.

[3] For an interesting discussion of these ideas, see Albert L. Nichols and Richard Zeckhauser, "Government Comes to the Workplace," *Public Interest*, no. 619 (1977), pp. 39–69.

A second problem involves making the correct kind of comparison. To isolate compensating differentials, it is necessary to compare jobs that are identical in all other respects, including the skills that are required. That trash collectors and warehouse workers earn less than computer programmers or corporate vice-presidents and have less desirable working conditions as well is not disproof of the theory of compensating differentials. Clearly, there are human capital differences among the jobs as well which explain the differences in wages. If it were possible to measure a worker's human capital perfectly, there would be no problem. Comparisons could then be made after adjusting for any wage difference due to differences in human capital. But, in fact, human capital is measured quite imperfectly. As a result, it is possible that the wage effects of nonpecuniary job characteristics may be confounded with the wage effects of human capital differences. It could even appear that more desirable job characteristics are associated with higher, not lower wages, as in the example above.

There is certainly no shortage of anecdotal evidence in support of the theory of compensating differentials. But statistical studies that attempt to relate wages, skills, and working conditions for broader samples have not always been conclusive. One finding which has been confirmed in many studies is that, other things the same, jobs with a higher risk of a fatal accident do pay higher wages. The magnitude of the compensating differential ranged in the various studies from $200 to $3500 per year for each one-thousandth percentage point increase in the probability of being killed.[4] But for less dramatic characteristics, the evidence is mixed. One author who surveyed the literature concluded that there was "some clear support for the theory" but also "an uncomfortable number of exceptions."[5] It is not clear whether the inconclusive results reflect the problem noted above or indeed do refute the theory.

A recently published study by Greg J. Duncan and Bertil Holmland managed to avoid some of these common empirical problems and, in so doing, provided much stronger evidence for the compensating differentials hypothesis.[6] The unusual feature of their study was the fact that they had information on wages, skill measures, and working conditions for a representative sample of Swedish men at two different points in time. This allowed them to compare the change in a person's wage with the corresponding change in his working conditions, as in the analysis described in Figure 8.5. The measures of working conditions were extremely detailed; they included three measures of the in-

[4] See Robert S. Smith, "Compensating Wage Differentials and Public Policy: A Review," *Industrial and Labor Relations Review*, 32 (April 1979), 339–52.

[5] Charles Brown, "Equalizing Differences in the Labor Market," *Quarterly Journal of Economics*, 94 (February 1980), p. 118.

[6] Greg J. Duncan and Bertil Holmland, "Was Adam Smith Right After All? Another Test of the Theory of Compensating Wage Differentials," *Journal of Labor Economics*, 1 (October 1983), 366–79.

flexibility of working hours, three measures of the extent of hard physical labor, four measures of whether work was dangerous and why, and two measures of whether it was stressful. Of the ten working condition measures tested, nine had the predicted positive effect on wages. This represents some of the strongest systematic evidence to date.

A MARXIST APPROACH TO LABOR MARKET ANALYSIS

Karl Marx's ideas about the working of a capitalist economy and of the role of labor in it are too important to overlook. There is, of course, much disagreement about the value of his ideas, particularly for microeconomic analysis, and in truth, his impact on "mainstream" economics has been quite small. Still, there is no denying the influence his ideas have had on non-mainstream economists in the United States and Western Europe and on mainstream economists in much of the rest of the world. His influence has spread far beyond economics, into fields such as sociology, anthropology, political science, history, and literary criticism. The impact of his ideas on contemporary political activity throughout the world is undeniable. Few other writers in history can claim such a strong and diverse following more than a century after their death. Whether one agrees with him or not, his ideas are worth understanding. Needless to say, the contrast with the ideas of mainstream labor economics—the ideas of Chapters 2 to 6—is striking indeed.

It is not possible to do justice to the range or complexity of Marx's ideas in just a few pages. He wrote many articles, pamphlets, and books, including the famous *Communist Manifesto* and his three-volume economics treatise, *Capital*. In addition, there has been an enormous amount of work by others following in his tradition. Moreover, it is difficult to take just a piece of Marx, because his ideas are part of an interrelated system. The best we can do here is focus on some of the most important ideas, particularly those that relate to labor and the labor market in a capitalist society.[7]

Fundamentals of Marxist Economics

To begin, we should consider Marx's analysis of the basic features of capitalism. Marx categorized societies by their characteristic **social relations of production**, a term that he used to summarize the dominant form of organization of production in a particular society. For example, in a slave society, there is the relationship between master and slave in which one group,

[7] A good source on Marx's economic analysis as well as his broader viewpoint is John G. Gurley, *Challengers to Capitalism: Marx, Lenin, Stalin, and Mao* (New York: W. W. Norton & Company, Inc., 1979).

the masters, owned the other much larger group of slaves and had an absolute right to whatever was produced. In feudal society there was the different relationship between lord and serf. The distinctive feature of capitalism, according to Marx, was the creation of two new groups, the **bourgeoisie** or capitalists and the **proletariat** or workers. These two groups were classified according to their relationship to what Marx called the **means of production**, which in the case of capitalism, were capital goods. (In feudal society, land was the important means of production.) Thus the bourgeoisie were the owners of capital and the proletariat were persons who possessed only their own labor. Indeed, another distinctive feature of capitalism was the emergence of what Marx called **wage labor**—what we would call a labor market.

The social relations of production lead, in turn, to the related idea of the **class structure** of a society. In each society, classes are created consisting of people grouped according to their relationship to the means of production. Thus, under capitalism, the two classes are the bourgeoisie and the proletariat. Finally, Marx's conception of the relationship between classes was quite different from the harmonious situation usually depicted in mainstream economics. Marx believed from his study of history that there was an inherent and inevitable antagonism between classes. He wrote in *The Communist Manifesto* that "the history of all hitherto existing society is the history of class struggles . . . the epoch of the bourgeoisie possesses . . . this distinctive feature. . . . Society as a whole is more and more splitting up into two great hostile camps, into two great classes directly facing each other—bourgeoisie and proletariat."[8]

Marx also had a very different notion of how the equilibrium wage rate was established in a capitalist economy. The ideas of labor demand and labor supply, as we presented them in Chapters 2 to 5, had not yet been developed, so Marx worked within a different tradition of economic analysis.[9] Marx believed that the value or price[10] of every good in the economy was determined by the amount of socially necessary labor used to produce it. That labor included both the amount of labor directly used in the production of a good and the amount of "congealed" labor embodied in the capital goods which were used. For example, Marx reasoned that if the production of one commodity required twice as much labor as some other commodity, its price would be twice as high. By adding that price depended on the "socially necessary" labor, Marx meant to eliminate the ridiculous situation in which the amount of labor used in the production of a commodity would be large and thus its labor value high only because production was inefficiently or-

[8] *The Communist Manifesto*, pp. 1–2.

[9] The tradition is called the *classical* school, as compared to contemporary economics, which is referred to as *neoclassical*.

[10] In Marx's system, there is a difference between a commodity's value or inherent worth and its price. In neoclassical economics, value and price are identical since a commodity's price is taken as a measure of its value.

ganized. Thus the phrase, "socially necessary" really meant "efficient according to prevailing standards."

This approach to price determination is called the **labor theory of value** and it was not original with Marx. Adam Smith had used it in a famous example to describe the equilibrium rate of exchange between beaver and deer.[11] Marx's contribution was to extend the idea to production with capital goods—which turned out to cause problems he never satisfactorily resolved—and, more important, to apply the concept to labor itself. Its price (or wage), then, would, like all other commodities, reflect the amount of socially necessary labor used to produce it. In the case of labor, that would be the amount of labor needed to maintain a worker and his or her family at a socially accepted standard of living. Notice again the idea of socially necessary labor and the corresponding idea of a socially accepted standard of living. In a poor country, this may be only the bare necessities, but in more affluent societies, it could provide a much higher standard of living. The important point is that in a Marxist world, a worker's wages are determined not by supply and demand forces, but by societal norms about what is socially necessary.

Finally, Marx demonstrated how workers were exploited under capitalism. A worker might, during the mid-nineteenth century, work a 12-hour day, thus producing commodities with a total value equal to 12 hours of labor time. But if only 6 hours per day were required to produce the goods that provide a socially accepted standard of living, that is what the worker is entitled to and what he or she receives. The difference between the value of what a worker produces and what the worker is paid, which Marx called **surplus value**, goes to the capitalist. The exploitation, according to Marx, lay in the fact that the capitalist was enriched by the efforts of labor. More crucially, this was a fundamental property of capitalism, since as Marx had shown, labor was exploited even when the price of all commodities was exactly equal to the value of the labor time necessary to produce them. The **exploitation of labor** was one of the inner laws of capitalism.

There is much more to Marx's analysis of capitalism, not the least of which is his notion of its inevitable collapse. Only the briefest outline must suffice. Marx believed that capitalists had an inherent drive to "accumulation," that is, to acquire more capital in an effort to stay ahead of the competition. One result of this was to reduce the amount of labor needed in production and thus to create what Marx in a memorable phrase called the "reserve army of the unemployed." Over time, Marx foresaw two ominous trends. The first was the relative impoverishment of the working class. Second, and somewhat paradoxically, is the fall of the capitalist class as well. The very drive for accumulation is the source of their downfall, since by replacing

[11] In Smith's example, it took one day to catch a deer and two days to catch a beaver Thus he reasoned that the equilibrium exchange ratio of deer for beaver would have to be two deers for one beaver, since that represents equal labor values.

labor with capital, the production of surplus value is reduced. Surplus value comes only from labor, not from capital. Ultimately, Marx expected a collapse of the capitalist system after which first socialism and then communism would take its place. Communism would be a truly classless state with collective ownership of the means of production. Its fundamental principle was to be "from each according to his ability, to each according to his needs."

A Marxist Analysis of the Labor Process under Capitalism

Marx's contributions to contemporary economics are quite different than he probably imagined they would be. His crowning theoretical achievement, the labor theory of value, and his explanation of the origin of surplus value and the exploitation of labor, is little used. At best, the labor theory of value is a cumbersome mode of analysis, strictly correct only in special circumstances and after extensive mathematical exercises. It is much more complex and much less general than neoclassical microeconomics. At worst, his analysis is wrong, gravely weakened by difficulties in correctly calculating the value of congealed labor and by the task of transforming labor values into prices. In fairness to Marx, remember that he worked out his ideas over a century ago, before some of the central ideas of modern economics were developed. Other microeconomists of his time were not any better.

Marx's more lasting contributions to labor economics have been derived from his analysis of class structure and class conflict. In this section we focus on one application as an example of contemporary Marxist research and as an illustration of the Marxist approach. This application concerns what is called the **labor process** and it emphasizes the way in which class antagonism, coupled with the distinctive feature of labor as a factor of production, have influenced the development of technology and the organization of work. The major work here is *Labor and Monopoly Capital* by Harry Braverman; a shorter piece that develops similar ideas is "What Do Bosses Do?" by Stephen Marglin.[12] Both are eminently readable and require little prior exposure to Marxist ideas.

By the phrase "labor process" Marxists mean the detailed way in which work is organized. Think for a moment about the modern factory system through Marxist eyes. The organization of work is strictly hierarchical, not democratic. There are bosses and there are workers; a typical organizational structure looks like a pyramid. Tasks are subdivided to an almost extraordinary degree by means of the division of labor and the specialization of task. Technology rules supreme and job satisfaction is sacrificed to profit. A worker

[12] See Harry Braverman, *Labor and Monopoly Capital* (New York: Monthly Review Press, 1974), and Stephen A. Marglin, "What Do Bosses Do?" *Review of Radical Political Economy*, 6, no. 2 (Summer 1974), 60–112.

has become an "operative," tending to a machine, rather than a craftsman exercising and developing his or her skills. Workers are so compartmentalized that there is no longer any feeling for the commodity being produced. To use a famous Marxist phrase, the worker is "alienated" from the environment and the product of his or her labor. Labor has become "the most wretched of commodities."

A mainstream neoclassical economist might dispute a few items on the list but would attribute the rest to the pressures of competition and the technical requirements of efficient production. After all, they reason, why would work be organized that way if it were not more efficient? If there were an alternative, more humane production system that was at least as efficient as this one, it would be adopted, since it would also be more profitable. (For one thing, capitalists could reduce the compensating wage differentials they would have to pay workers to take on such undesirable work.) The apparent similarities of the production system in the Soviet Union and in the United States is regarded as another piece of evidence in favor of the efficiency argument. If technology is independent of the political system, the underlying rationale is likely to involve efficiency criteria. As a final argument, there is Adam Smith's famous example of the effects of the division of labor which he observed in a pin factory. There, as he recounted in great detail, he found ten men making 4800 pins a day. They were able to do so, he argued, because the many tasks were divided among the men and each became specialized in a specific part of the production process. Without such a division of labor, he suspected that they could make no more than 20 pins a day. If Smith is to be believed, the returns to the division of labor were truly enormous, at least in this case.

Braverman presents a Marxist explanation of the labor process under capitalism. The basic idea stems from a critical distinction, drawn only by Marxists, between **labor** and **labor power**. Labor power is defined as the capacity to do work, whereas labor is the actual amount of work done by an individual. For machinery, no such distinction is necessary, because a machine cannot withhold its effort, it cannot shirk; nor for that matter, can it exert itself with special purpose or intensity. But workers, of course, can do all these things. That leads to the predicament of capitalists, because what is bought and sold in the labor market is not labor itself but rather labor power. In hiring a worker, a capitalist agrees to pay so many dollars for so many hours of work, and the worker, in return, agrees to spend those hours at the employment site. But the actual amount of labor expended by the worker and received by the capitalist is never certain and cannot be readily specified.

The development of the labor process under capitalism, is, in Braverman's view, dictated by the labor/labor power distinction. For the capitalist, the objective of employment is, naturally, to maximize the amount of labor actually obtained from labor power. However, because of the fundamental class conflict between capitalists and workers, the workers can be expected to withhold their labor in every way possible. That is where technology and the labor process enter the picture. Braverman argues that the development of technology and the organization of work have been guided by the attempt by capitalists to continuously reduce the gap between labor and labor power. In Braverman's words, "technology . . . is *produced* by the social relations" of capitalism,[13] which consist of the class conflict between capitalists and workers.

Braverman's book consists primarily of a detailed historical exposition of this thesis. For example, he begins with the development in the late eighteenth century of the centralized factory system in the textile industry. Prior to that, production occurred in a decentralized manner, with each worker producing at home under the putting-out system. (Recall the discussion of this in terms of labor supply in Chapter 4.) The purpose of centralization, Braverman argues, was not efficiency per se, but rather the transfer of control over work hours from labor to capital. The role of the division of labor and specialization of task is to assure the capitalist of an essential role in production as the person who alone has knowledge of the entire process. Workers can never become bosses if they are systematically denied knowledge of some of the essential parts of the production process.[14]

Scientific management or Taylorism is given an especially extensive treatment by Braverman. Scientific management was a set of techniques developed in America in the late nineteenth century by Frederick W. Taylor and then successfully applied by him to the steel industry. Although it was regarded as an important tool in improving the efficiency of the workplace, it is also considered as a dehumanizing approach and its excesses have been widely parodied (Charlie Chaplin's movie, *Modern Times*, is a famous example). The basic idea was to specify in exact detail each and every task that a worker would perform. Each task was analyzed by Taylor and then broken down into standardized elements—for example, lifting, turning, or bundling. Each was then assigned a prescribed execution time according to Taylor's scientific principles. The intent was to eliminate to the greatest extent possible the variability of performance by workers and increase productivity. In Braverman's terms, this step, in which workers are treated as if they were robots, marked an elaborate attempt to control labor power and thus extract the maximum amount of useful labor from it.

You may by now be able to anticipate Braverman's argument about the rise of assembly-line production and other automated, externally controlled production processes. These are, according to Braverman, simply further logical developments in the continual effort by capitalists to strip workers of any control over their own labor.

Braverman's argument is much richer than outlined here and his book is full of fascinating historical details. One need not subscribe to a Marxist view of the labor market to find it interesting and rewarding.

[13] Braverman, p. 20.

[14] This point is heavily emphasized by Marglin.

SUMMARY

The theory of economic rent and the theory of compensating wage differentials identify further sources of wage differences. Economic rent is earned in the labor market whenever a person possesses skills that are both in demand and unproducible. Because they are unproducible, the supply response that makes returns to human capital reasonable does not operate. Economic rent can be the source of very high earnings. Compensating wage differentials are the results of differences in job characteristics. Much depends on the nature of individual preferences, and that introduces uncertainty about the expected outcomes. A general conclusion might be that if enough people have a similar opinion about the characteristics of one job relative to another job that requires equivalent skill, a compensating wage differential will arise. Changes in job characteristics, perhaps via regulation, will lead to changes in wages in the opposite direction.

The Marxist approach, described in the last section, offers a different way to look at the labor market and at labor market outcomes. Its perspective and even its vocabulary are quite different from that of the neoclassical approach to labor markets. Marx's attempt to analyze a capitalist economy is flawed in a number of respects, but the Marxist approach has been usefully applied by many researchers. The distinction between labor and labor power is a good example, since it follows naturally from Marx's theory of class and inherent class antagonism.

New Concepts

Economic rent
Supply price
Quasi-rent
Nonpecuniary job characteristics
Compensating wage differentials
Social relations of production
Bourgeoisie and proletariat
Means of production
Wage labor
Class structure
Labor theory of value
Surplus value
Exploitation of labor
Labor process
Labor versus labor power

9

Labor Market Discrimination and Earnings Differences by Sex and Race

INTRODUCTION

Consider the following facts. In 1983 the median annual earnings of males who worked full-time, year-round was $22,508. For women, also full-time, year-round workers, the comparable figure was $14,479—just 64.3 percent as much. That 1983 figure actually represented a sharp and sudden improvement in the earnings ratio. During the previous two decades the earnings ratio had been virtually unchanged, ranging between 58 and 60 percent each year. So steady was the ratio that the National Organization of Women adopted the slogan "59¢" as its symbol of economic discrimination against women.[1]

There are also large earnings differences between black and white workers. Also in 1983, the median wage and salary earnings of black males who were full-time, year-round workers was $16,410, just over 71 percent of what white males in the same category earned. Back in 1959, however, the ratio had been much lower—just 61 percent.[2] In between, it had reached 66 percent in 1964, 70 percent in 1970, and 77 percent in 1978, before dropping. Similar comparisons for black and white families show a rather different pattern. The median income of a black family was only 56 percent of that of a white family in 1983—$14,510 versus $25,760. This ratio had fallen substantially since the mid-1970s, when it peaked at 62 percent.

How can these earnings and income differences be explained? Why do women earn less than men and blacks less than whites? Are they less valuable to employers, or are they subject to unfair treatment? Why has the earnings ratio risen steadily for black men compared to white men, but moved in such a narrow range without any trend for women compared to men? Why is the situation of black men and black families so different? What kind of policies are called for on behalf of the government?

That is a long list of very serious questions. Few issues in contemporary American society have generated as much political activity as these or been as hotly contested. The Civil Rights movement and the women's movement, affirmative action and the Equal Rights Amendment, have become familiar terms that have changed both the political system and the labor market in fundamental ways.

In this chapter we bring the many tools of labor economics to bear on these questions. As always, we begin by developing the economic theory that is relevant to the problem—in this case, the economic analysis of labor market

[1] There is at least literary evidence that the earnings ratio has been steady for longer than a decade. *Leviticus* 27:1–4 (New English Version) contains this passage: "The Lord spoke to Moses and said, 'When a man makes a special vow to the Lord which requires your valuation of living persons, a male between twenty and sixty years old shall be valued at fifty silver shekels. If it is a female, she shall be valued at thirty shekels.' "

[2] The figures for earlier years refer to whites versus nonwhites, rather than whites versus blacks. Blacks account for about 90 percent of nonwhites.

discrimination. A central idea is whether or not practicing discrimination increases a firm's profits or reduces them, since that will indicate something about the relationship between discrimination and competition. Following that, we turn to the statistical measurement of discrimination. With these preliminaries out of the way, we then look at the evidence on earnings differences by sex and by race in the third and fourth parts of this chapter. The last section looks at government policy and some of the current legal issues.

THE ECONOMIC ANALYSIS OF LABOR MARKET DISCRIMINATION

To begin, we should define terms, because discrimination is an often-misused term. Economists define **labor market discrimination** very precisely. *Discrimination is the difference in earnings between individuals who are in all economic respects identical.* They are equally productive, differing only with respect to some noneconomic, personal characteristic—for example, race, sex, national origin, religion, or sexual preference—which gives rise to a difference in treatment. To repeat, discrimination involves the unequal treatment of economic equals. That average earnings differ by race or by sex is, by itself, not sufficient proof of discrimination, since men and women or blacks and whites may not, in fact, be identical in all relevant economic respects. Much of the economic research into these issues is directed toward determining the importance of discrimination in accounting for these earnings differences.

The conventional economic approach to the analysis of discrimination is a limited one in some respects. Economists devote little attention to the types of issues studied by researchers in other disciplines: Why does discrimination exist? What is its source, its nature, its function? Why is it more prevalent in some societies than in others? Why is it directed against some groups and not others? Instead, economists focus on the economic effects of those attitudes, without attempting to analyze the discriminatory attitudes themselves. This separation actually follows the standard practice in economic analysis of taking as a given of the situation to be analyzed the tastes, preferences, feelings, attitudes, and even prejudices of the persons involved. An economist studying the demand for bananas or sports cars does not question why people seem to want bananas or sports cars, or whether those wants are legitimate. To an economist they are simply part of the data of the problem to be analyzed.

The same approach goes for feelings of prejudice held by one group of people against people of another group. One of the first economists to analyze labor market discrimination, Gary Becker,[3] used the phrase **tastes for dis-**

[3] Gary S. Becker, *The Economics of Discrimination*, 2nd ed. (Chicago: The University of Chicago Press, 1971).

crimination to emphasize that in terms of economic analysis, they were on a par with other tastes and preferences of individuals. Morally, of course, we may find discriminatory feelings offensive; that is a normative issue, although one about which most people would agree. The purpose of the economic analysis of discrimination is to show how those feelings are translated into the economic realm and how they influence labor market behavior and labor market outcomes.

Why should we bother with a theoretical approach to labor market discrimination? Why not just recognize that discriminatory feelings do exist and then attempt to measure the impact and extent of discrimination? Why waste time with economic theory?

The basic reason is simple. Unless we know how discrimination operates in the labor market, it is not possible to design appropriate and effective policies to remedy it. To do that, we need to analyze discrimination at two levels. First, we need to look again at the behavior of firms and workers and see how it might change if they had discriminatory tastes. Put more formally, we need to incorporate those tastes into the basic labor market model and see what difference it makes in the results. Second, we need to look beyond the firm to the market as a whole. Do market forces tend to strengthen or weaken the position of firms who practice discrimination? Is discrimination a profitable strategy or an unprofitable one? Does it matter whether the market is competitive or one with monopolistic elements? One famous economist put the issue this way: "Under what circumstances is it possible for groups with identical economic characteristics to receive different wages in a market equilibrium?"[4] Economic theory can help in identifying those circumstances.

In the next section of this chapter we examine several well-known economic models of labor market discrimination. We start with those in which personal prejudice plays a role and consider separately three sources of that prejudice: employers, employees, and customers. These models, developed primarily by Gary Becker and Kenneth Arrow, lead, as you will see, to some surprising predictions. After that, some alternative explanations are considered, including imperfect competition and imperfect information.

Employer Discrimination

Suppose that some employers have a subjective preference for one group of workers or a distaste for another, independent of the skills of the workers. How will that affect the wages of workers in the two groups? How will that affect the firm's profits?

To analyze this situation, start with a competitive labor market and a

[4] Joseph E. Stiglitz, "Approaches to the Economics of Discrimination," *American Economic Review*, 63, no. 2 (May 1973), p. 287.

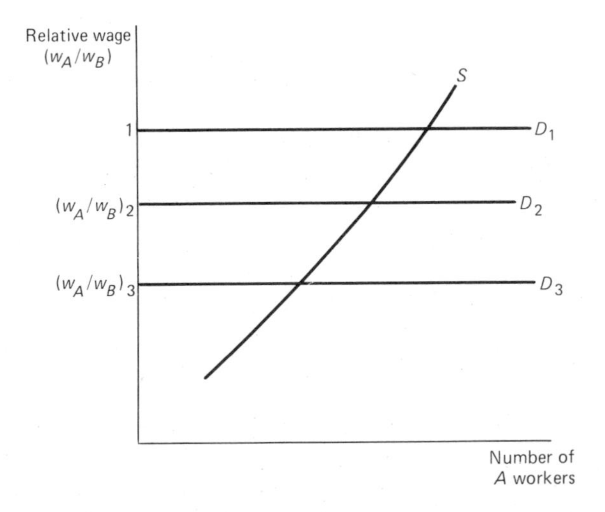

FIGURE 9.1 Labor Market Discrimination with Uniform Preferences

competitive product market. There are two groups of workers—call them *A* and *B*—who are identical in all economic respects, including productivity, except that *B* employers dislike *A* workers.[5] For the moment, assume there is no antidiscrimination legislation, so the employers are free to act as they please.

In the absence of any prejudice, the wages of *A* and *B* workers would always be exactly the same, since otherwise firms would hire only the less expensive workers. By the same logic, if *A* workers are uniformly disliked by all employers, their equilibrium wage will necessarily be less. At equal wages, no employer would be willing to hire them. But unless the distaste for *A* workers is infinitely large, there must be some wage differential just large enough to make employers regard *A* and *B* workers equally again. For example, employers might be willing to hire *A* workers if their relative wage was 3/4 that of *B* workers, or 1/2, or 1/4, or 1/10, depending on the strength of their own discriminatory taste.

A convenient way to represent this idea and its effects is shown in Figure 9.1, which shows the market supply of and demand for *A* workers expressed in terms of their *relative* wage, w_A/w_B. If there were no discrimination, the demand curve for *A* workers would look like D_1, horizontal at a relative wage of 1, which is where $w_A = w_B$. (Remember: *A* and *B* workers are equally productive.) If, instead, all firms had a uniform dislike of *A* workers, the demand curve might look like D_2, which gives a lower relative wage, $(w_A/w_B)_2$. At a relative wage higher than this, employers are unwilling to hire *A*

[5] Implicitly, this model assumes that there are no *A* employers or very few of them.

workers at all, but given the strength of their prejudice, the wage differential at $(w_A/w_B)_2$ is just large enough to induce them to hire A workers. With a stronger dislike for A workers, the demand curve would be lower yet, as at D_3. As you can readily see, dislike of A workers does appear to result in discrimination, with the extent of the discrimination depending on the strength of the dislike.

The analaysis is more complicated, but more interesting and more realistic, if some employers have stronger discriminatory feelings than others. For example, some employers may have no preference for A versus B workers and their demand curve would be like D_1 in Figure 9.1. Others would have demand curves like D_2 or D_3, and so on. The total market demand curve for A workers would then look something like the one shown in Figure 9.2. It is constructed by adding in each firm's demand at the relative wage at which it is just willing to hire A workers. The small horizontal portion at a relative wage of 1 represents the combined demand of the firms with no prejudice against A workers. The downward-sloping part includes the firms who do have discriminatory tastes, starting from those with the weakest preference at the top of the curve down to those with the strongest distaste at the bottom. Thus the curve gives the total number of A workers demanded at each relative wage. If the supply curve is S_1, the equilibrium relative wage will be $(w_A/w_B)_1$ so that again A workers suffer wage discrimination.

There are some important and surprising ideas in this model. First, labor

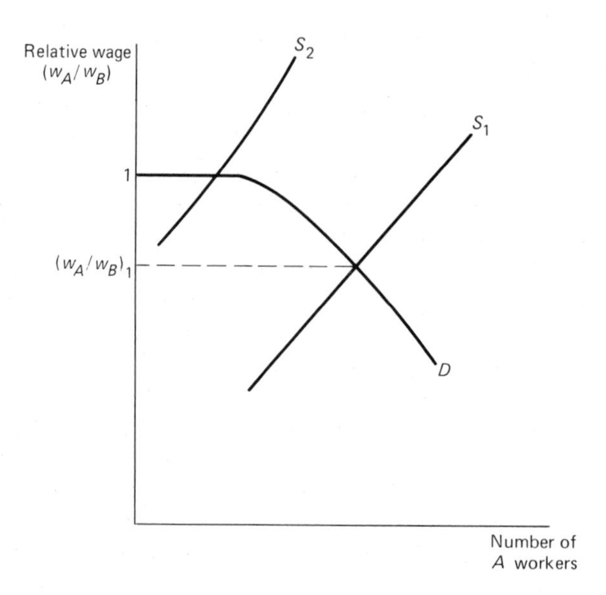

FIGURE 9.2 Labor Market Discrimination When Firms Have Different Discriminatory Preferences

supply now matters in determining the wage of A workers. If the supply curve had been considerably smaller, like S_2, then employment of A workers could have been confined to the employers who had no prejudice or preferences. There would, in that event, have been no wage discrimination even though most of the employers were potential discriminators.[6]

Second, it is no longer true that at the market equilibrium, all employers are just indifferent between hiring A and B workers. Now, those employers represented on the demand curve above the equilibrium point will hire only A workers, since they were willing to hire A workers at a relative wage *above* the equilibrium wage. Similarly, those employers represented on the demand curve below the equilibrium hire only B workers. For them, the wage differential between A and B workers in equilibrium is not large enough to compensate for the strength of their dislike for A workers. Only those firms (if any) who are *just* willing to hire A workers at $(w_A/w_B)_1$ will hire both A and B workers.

This last result is a crucial one. Suppose that there are some firms in an industry which hire only A workers, whereas others hire only B workers. By our original assumption, A and B workers are equally productive. Since w_A is less than w_B, it follows that the firms that are unwilling to hire A workers will have higher costs than those that are willing to do so. But because the product market is competitive, all firms must sell at the same price. Thus this model suggests that those firms that are unwilling to hire A workers at the equilibrium wage will pay for that in terms of reduced profits. *Discrimination is not consistent with profit-maximizing behavior.* This is a conclusion whose importance should not be underestimated.

This result applies at a specific point in time, with the current distribution of firms and the current size of each firm. But since different firms earn different amounts of profits, it is probable that the structure of firms in an industry will change over time. The more profitable firms—those who have weak discriminatory preferences—will expand and/or other firms will enter and establish production. The less profitable, more discriminating firms would then account for a smaller share of the market. In time, they might be driven out of business altogether if their higher costs caused them to suffer losses.

This adjustment process is illustrated in Figure 9.3. The labor supply and labor demand curve from Figure 9.2 are included. The initial relative wage is $(w_A/w_B)_1$. With entry by new firms and/or expansion of old ones, the demand curve for A workers shifts out as shown. It might rise first to something like D_2 and then ultimately to D_3 if competitive pressure is strong enough. The key point is that profit maximization in a competitive market with free entry should tend to eliminate discrimination. Because discrimi-

[6] A workers might still be considered worse off, because they would have fewer employment options than B workers.

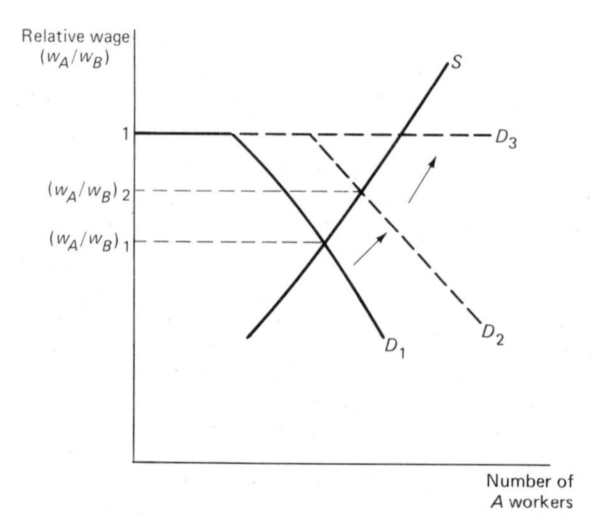

FIGURE 9.3 The Effects of Entry in a Discriminatory Labor Market

nation reduces profits, it should be untenable in the long run. Needless to say, this is a surprising result. Arrow concludes that the model "predicts the absence of the phenomenon it was designed to explain."[7]

Application: Discrimination and Profit Maximization

The idea that discrimination reduces profits is so surprising that a few examples may be useful.

1. This example is not from labor economics, but it shows the idea clearly. It concerns an incident of alleged discrimination in the renting of commercial retail space which occurred in a small college town. It is a true story.

   In this town there was a clothing store adjacent to the university. It was extremely popular with students and it appeared to be quite successful. Nevertheless, the store's lease was not renewed and it closed. There were rumors that the landlord had refused to renew the lease because of the sexual preference of the owners.[8]

   Try to analyze the situation coldly from an economic standpoint. A landlord interested only in profit would rent to the tenant willing to pay the highest rent. Race, sex, religion, sexual preference, or even the potential

[7] Kenneth J. Arrow, "Some Mathematical Models of Race Discrimination in the Labor Market," in Anthony Pascal, ed., in *Racial Discrimination in Economic Life* (Lexington, Mass.: Lexington Books, 1972).

[8] Incidentally, discrimination against persons on the basis of sexual preference is not illegal under federal antidiscrimination legislation. Some local ordinances do make such discrimination illegal.

use of the land would be irrelevant. Prospective tenants would bid for the space on the basis of their ability to best use that space to create something of value to consumers. Maximizing the rent means that the land is allocated to the tenant whose prospective use is most highly valued. That is an inadvertent but very desirable function of using a price systems to allocate scarce resources.

In this case, if the clothing store was the highest-valued use, both the landlord and the students suffered losses. The landlord received a lower rent than was otherwise possible and the land was allocated to a less valuable use. Insufficient concern with profit is the cause.

2. For the first 60 to 70 years of its existence, the major league baseball industry consisted of firms (teams) that employed only white workers (athletes). At the same time, there was a separate league for black baseball players, called the Negro League. Many of the players in that league were as good as those in the "majors," but their salaries and working conditions were considerably worse. Certainly, they were subject to discrimination.

   Then, just as now, entry into the major leagues by new teams was strictly regulated. No entry at all was permitted until 1960, although teams were sold or moved on occasion. With entry restricted, even the existence of some potentially nondiscriminating employers (those in the Negro League) was not sufficient to affect conditions in the majors.

   Today, major league baseball is fully integrated. The Negro League no longer exists. There is no indication that there is still discrimination against black players. How did this happen?

   The historical facts are these. In 1947, the Brooklyn Dodgers, under employer Branch Rickey, hired the first black major league baseball player, Jackie Robinson. The American League was integrated shortly thereafter, and all other teams followed suit. After 80 years of segregation, fairly complete integration was achieved within a relatively short span of years.

   From an economic standpoint, Mr. Rickey and the Dodgers were a nondiscriminating employer. At the current relative salary for white and black players of equal quality, they alone were willing to hire blacks. In this case it seems that they hired very skilled black players such as Jackie Robinson (who quickly became one of the best players in the league) at relatively lower salaries, rather than simply hiring equally skilled but less costly blacks. Why did the others follow? Possibly, they now realized that fears of fan nonacceptance of black players were ungrounded. Additionally, however, they now faced competitive pressure to hire skilled players, irrespective of race. Failure to do so would undoubtedly have caused a team's competitive position to decline. How do you think a team would fare today if it persisted in hiring only white players or, for that matter, indulged its preference for any kind of player on grounds unrelated to performance? What do you think would happen to such an employer?

The general points of these two examples should be clear. Discrimination is a costly practice for those who indulge in it. It may, nevertheless, persist if entrepreneurs such as the landlord place other values above profits. The role of entry of new firms is crucial. Where entry is restricted, as it was in both examples, the competitive pressures that economists count on to eliminate discrimination may work very slowly.

Employee Discrimination

Now consider the case in which it is the employees rather than the employers who have discriminatory tastes. Suppose that *B* workers dislike working with *A* workers, but that the reverse is not true. As before, the labor and product markets are competitive and *A* and *B* workers are identical in terms of productivity.

The simplest way to analyze this situation is to think of the composition of the work force as a nonpecuniary characteristic of a job. *B* workers, then, would require a compensating differential in an integrated work setting, but *A* workers would not. Thus a discriminatory wage differential would exist in an integrated situation. But would integration occur? Probably not. Why wouldn't an employer choose instead to hire all *A* workers or all *B* workers and thus avoid the compensating differential? The expected result here is not discrimination with integration, but segregation without it.

There is one way in which employee discrimination can lead to both an integrated work force and wage differentials. Suppose that there was a second group of *B* workers who were more skilled than the other *A* and *B* workers. Call them *B*' workers and assume that they are *complements* with the less-skilled workers. (Recall that in the case of complements, more of one factor increases the marginal product of labor schedule of the other.) In that case, productivity will be higher if both *A* and B' workers are employed together. Against that must be set the compensating differential paid to the B' workers in an integrated setting. It is certainly possible that the best solution, from the standpoint of the firm, would involve an integrated setting in which productivity is higher and a discriminating wage differential exists.

Customer Discrimination

A third possibility is that customers have preferences and prejudices about *A* and *B* workers. This would be unlikely to have an effect on production workers, but in direct sales and service it would operate along the lines discussed above. If *B* customers dislike *A* workers, *A* workers can gain employment only by offering their services at lower wages than otherwise similar *B* workers. Discriminating customers do pay more than otherwise, but there is nothing to prevent them from continuing to do so forever, if they like. Only their utility is involved, rather than profits as in the case of employer discrimination.

Alternative Sources of Discrimination

Economists have also developed a series of other explanations for discrimination. Most of these involve modifying the assumptions of the previous models, especially those concerning the degree of competition and the extent of information about individual productivity. We consider these arguments in turn.

Imperfect Competition. This designation refers to a series of explanations, all of which begin by assuming that competition is lacking in some crucial respect. One example is pure monopoly, in which there is no competition at all. If there is only a single firm and if there is no possibility of entry by new firms, the usual competition pressure is absent. Since a monopoly typically earns above-average profits, it could decide to sacrifice some of its potential profits and practice discrimination. The serious question, then, is how common these textbook cases of monopoly are.

A related version of this focuses on discrimination in financial markets and its effects on labor market discrimination. Suppose that banks and other financial institutions, which are typically controlled by members of the discriminating group, are unwilling to provide financing to nondiscriminating firms. After all, if workers who suffered from discrimination could borrow money without excessive difficulty, they could enter an industry in which there was discrimination and earn profits as long as they were not otherwise inefficient. In time, that entry should eliminate the discriminatory wage differential. If, however, that form of entry is prevented, discrimination may persist. Anything that restricts entry strengthens discrimination, as we saw in the baseball example.

The possibility of this kind of discrimination is real and the development in the 1970s of banks owned by blacks or women was a response to this. So, too, was the passage of legislation prohibiting discrimination in lending practices. You should recognize, however, that just as labor market discrimination is costly to employers, financial market discrimination is costly to those institutions that practice it. The cost here is in passing over the more profitable loans that could be made to nondiscriminating firms.

Another version is the **conspiracy model**, which attempts to explain discrimination as the result of an agreement among employers to keep wages down for a certain group of workers. Economists tend to be extremely suspicious of this kind of explanation whether it is used to explain labor market discrimination or the behavior of cartels. The problem is that sticking to the agreement always requires forgoing profitable opportunities. Policing the agreement is difficult at best, and if the group is relatively large, it may be impossible. Economists assume that every band of conspirators has some members who will ultimately choose increased profits over group loyalty, thus weakening the conspiracy. Entry by nondiscriminating firms is another obvious problem. In a country such as South Africa, where the conspiracy agreement is sanctioned by law and blacks have extremely limited access to financial capital, a conspiracy might be sustainable. Perhaps, too, it made sense in certain parts of the American South in earlier times. But it does not seem likely to be a strong explanation for the presence of discrimination today in the United States.

A final example is the dual labor market model, which we discussed in Chapter 7. As we emphasized there, that model was originally developed to account for the unfavorable labor market situation of women, blacks, and other minorities in urban labor markets. It argues that discrimination in the labor market operates to keep these workers out of the secure jobs in the primary sector and in dead-end jobs in the secondary sector. There, wages are low and there is little or no opportunity to learn job skills. In this case the imperfect competition lies in the barrier between the two sectors of the labor market. This approach is generally consistent with the discrimination models described above, except for the idea that the discrimination is not eliminated by competitive pressures. The model does not, however, explain why this happens. As we noted before, the approach is descriptive, not analytical.

One interesting extension of this approach does seek to explain the *origin* of labor market segments by adopting a Marxist orientation. According to this argument, capitalists deliberately introduced race and sex distinctions into the labor market to weaken feelings of class unity among workers.[9] If workers viewed themselves as being different from one another and even in opposition to each other, they would be less likely to recognize their common class position vis-à-vis the capitalists. That would tend to strengthen the position of the capitalists.

Imperfect Information. More and more often, we have begun to emphasize the implications of imperfect information in the labor market. A person's future job performance is very difficult to predict beforehand and mistakes may be costly to correct afterward. It is not inconceivable, then, that firms might attempt to predict future job performance on the basis of easily observed characteristics such as race or sex rather than the less easily observed characteristics that actually determine job performance. As long as the observable characteristics are correlated with performance on average, this might make sense for the firm.

This situation is called **statistical discrimination**. It is a form of discrimination because it can lead to the unequal treatment of equals. In effect, all individuals are assumed to have the average productivity of everyone else in their group. Even if a man and a woman or a black and a white were equally productive, they would be treated differently if the average productivity of men and women and blacks and whites was different. The discrimination is "statistical" because the productivity of an entire group of workers is described by statistical measures such as the mean and the variance.

[9] See Richard C. Edwards, Michael Reich, and David M. Gordon, *Labor Market Segmentation* (Lexington, Mass.: D. C. Heath and Company, 1975), Introduction.

This form of discrimination does not necessarily stem from tastes for discrimination. It may not be deliberate and it may not be practiced with the *intent* to harm one group. But it could be important, especially if employers are not well informed about the average characteristics of the groups. That could be true when those characteristics are changing relatively rapidly, so that information adjusts only after a considerable time lag. A good example might be the increased labor force participation and career orientation of women in the last decade or two. If employers still believe that women are more likely to quit jobs in order to raise a family, they might make employment decisions on that basis.

MEASURING DISCRIMINATION

Average earnings differences between groups can exist for many reasons. There could be differences in human capital or in rent-producing skills, differences in the nonpecuniary characteristics of their jobs, in the incidence of monopsony or unionization, and so on. Alternatively, there might be differences in the treatment that equally skilled persons receive depending on which group they belong to—in other words, discrimination.

These two general explanations have very different interpretations. In the first case, we would probably conclude that the earnings differences were not the "fault" of the labor market and did not reflect current labor market discrimination. Rather, the earnings difference could be *explained* or *accounted for* by the differences in those factors. If, however, men and women or blacks and whites receive different earnings even though they had the same skills and were the same in terms of everything else that was relevant, there is reason to suspect discrimination. But note that this means that discrimination is measured indirectly. Economists do not typically observe the process of discrimination. Rather, they infer its presence from the inequality of results in the face of the equality of all relevant conditions.

Subject only to the inherent problems of measuring human capital, nonpecuniary job characteristics, rent-producing skills, and so on (as well as qualifications noted below), it is possible to determine the relative importance of these two explanations of earnings differences. The total difference in average earnings between any two groups can always be divided up into two parts, where one part summarizes the effects of differences in all the relevant (measured) characteristics that have economic value to employers, and the other part represents the importance of discrimination.

A specific example may help to illustrate how this technique works. Suppose that there is a one-year average difference in the amount of education between black men and white men and suppose that each year of education increases the earnings of white men by $900 per year. Then the difference in education "accounts for" or "explains" $900 of the difference in earnings.

That $900 difference would exist even if there were no current discrimination.[10] Following that procedure for each variable gives the total amount of the earnings difference that is due to differences in important characteristics. The portion of the earnings gap that cannot be explained by differences in these characteristics is then attributed to discrimination. If the explained portion is large, current labor market discrimination is not important. Conversely, the smaller the explained portion, the more important is discrimination. To repeat: *Discrimination, as measured by economists, is that portion of the average earnings gap between any two groups that cannot be otherwise explained by differences in skills or other relevant characteristics.*

The two parts of the earnings gap are usually expressed as a proportion of the actual difference in earnings. Together they must add up to 100 percent—there is nothing left over. Thus, if the total earnings gap was $4500 per year and $1500 was due to differences in all of the measures taken together, one-third of the earnings difference can be explained and two-thirds unexplained. Exactly the same procedure can be applied to each variable by itself in order to identify the exact source of earnings differences. The $900 earnings difference due to education would tell us that educational differences by themselves account for 20 percent ($900/$4500) of the earnings difference.

This is a useful and commonly used procedure, but it has two weaknesses of which you should be aware. The first concerns *measurement*. For the economist's usual measure of discrimination to be meaningful and to be used with confidence, it is necessary that the effects of *all* relevant factors be accounted for fully. If some important factor that influences earnings is omitted from the empirical analysis, this could easily reduce the size of the "explained" category and thus *automatically* increase the size of the "discrimination" category. (It could also have exactly the opposite effect if the omitted factors tended to increase the relative earnings of the group with lower earnings.) The possibility of mismeasurement is genuine. It is impossible to measure all the things that influence a person's labor market value.[11]

The second problem concerns *interpretation*. The basic procedure is fine as far as it goes. Leaving aside the measurement problems, it does indicate the importance of current labor market discrimination on average earnings differences. That, however, is a relatively narrow definition of discrimination. It ignores the possibility that *prior* discrimination, either in the labor market or in the public schools or elsewhere, might itself be the cause of the current differences in human capital or other characteristics. If black men today have, on average, less human capital than white men because their parents were

[10] Alternatively, $900 of the earnings gap would be eliminated if the difference in education could be eliminated.

[11] The measurement difficulties cause a problem only if the omitted factor is both important to earnings and if the average amount of that factor is different for the groups whose earnings are being compared. Even then it is not always clear whether the effect is to overstate or understate the importance of discrimination.

poorer, because they were often educated in underfunded, segregated school systems, and because they made human capital investment decisions in a more discriminatory environment, should the earnings differences that result be interpreted as reflecting discrimination or human capital differences? In the typical statistical measure, it would appear in the "explained" category; in a broader accounting, however, it would almost certainly be regarded as part of the discrimination component of the difference in earnings.

There is nothing wrong with the typical measure—it is just narrower and exclusively present-oriented. It measures only current labor market discrimination, rather than discrimination interpreted more broadly. If public policymakers want to know whether policies intended to reduce discrimination in the labor market could substantially reduce earnings differences between groups, it, not the broader concept, is exactly the right measure. But even if discrimination in the narrow sense were unimportant, it does not follow that discrimination in the broader sense has no impact on earnings differences.

EARNINGS DIFFERENCES BETWEEN MEN AND WOMEN

Characteristics of Female Earnings

Two features of female earnings stand out prominently. The first is the remarkable stability over time in the ratio of median female earnings to those of men. Even though the labor force participation and commitment of women has increased tremendously, the women's movement has become a powerful political and economic force, sex discrimination in employment was made illegal by the Civil Rights Act of 1964, affirmative action programs are in place, and a woman has been nominated for vice-president of the United States, still median female earnings are not much higher, relative to men, than they were 25 years ago. Table 9.1 presents the earnings information for selected years from 1960 to 1983.

The second characteristic feature is the still large differences in the types of jobs that men and women hold. Put more formally, there is a great deal of **occupational segregation** by sex. Table 9.2 shows the proportion of female full-time wage workers in major occupational groups as of 1982. As you can see, nearly 40 percent of all wage and salary workers were women, but that percentage holds in very few occupations. The typical finding is that the more detailed the job classification, the more likely it is to be dominated by either men or women. "Female occupations" include, to no one's surprise, nursing, teaching, most clerical jobs, health service workers and personal service workers, and private household workers. Those five broad categories alone account for 35 percent of all women's employment. On the other side are the occupations dominated by men—engineering, law, economics, most skilled craft

TABLE 9.1 Median Annual Earnings of Year-Round Full-Time Workers 14 Years and Over by Sex, 1960–1983

YEAR	WOMEN	MEN	RATIO (%)
1960	$ 3,293	$ 5,417	60.8
1962	3,446	5,794	59.5
1964	3,690	6,195	59.6
1966	3,973	6,848	58.0
1968	4,457	7,664	58.2
1970	5,323	8,966	59.4
1972	5,903	10,202	57.9
1974	6,970	11,889	58.6
1976	8,099	13,455	60.2
1978	9,350	15,730	59.4
1980	11,197	18,612	60.2
1981	12,001	20,260	59.2
1982	13,014	21,077	61.1
1983	14,479	22,508	64.3

Source: U.S. Bureau of the Census, Current Population Reports, Series P-60, Nos. 37, 41, 47, 53, 66, 80, 90, 101, 114, 123, 132, 142, 145, U.S. Government Printing Office, Washington, D.C.

jobs, and managers. No doubt you can add to the list from your own observation.

Recognizing the fact of occupational segregation leads to an important and frequently misunderstood idea. We know that in 1983, women who worked full-time, year-round about 64 percent as much as men. But what exactly does that mean? Does it, for instance, mean that women earn 64 percent of what men earn doing the same job? In general, the answer is "no." The major source of male–female earnings differences is the very large difference in the types of jobs they hold. Even if it were possible to eliminate all earnings differences for men and women doing the *same* job, the male–female earnings gap would change relatively little. Most of the difference in earnings between men and women exists *between* job categories, not *within* them. The 64% ratio refers only to the median earnings of men and women, given their current jobs, and does not serve as a comparison of earnings for any specific job. You will see later that this fact has enormous implications for designing effective antidiscrimination policy.

Explaining the Male–Female Earnings Gap: The Human Capital Approach

Are there any reasons to believe that women actually deserve to earn less than men? Are they less qualified or less skilled, on average, than men? Are they less valuable to employers? If so, why? What accounts for the difference?

There is a well-known and quite controversial economic argument which

TABLE 9.2 Occupational Segregation By Sex in 1981 for Full-Time Wage and Salary Workers

OCCUPATION	PERCENT FEMALE WORKERS
Total	39.5
Professional and technical	42.8
Engineers	4.7
Lawyers and judges	20.7
Nurses, dieticians, and therapists	90.9
Teachers, college and university	29.2
Teachers, all other	67.1
Economists	27.1
Managers and administrators	28.4
Sales workers	33.0
Clerical and kindred workers	78.4
Bank tellers	94.0
Secretaries	99.3
Bookkeepers	90.6
Craft and kindred workers	5.6
Carpenters	1.4
Machinists	3.6
Operatives (except transport)	38.8
Textile operatives	61.7
Assemblers	52.7
Transport equipment operatives	4.9
Bus drivers	27.7
Truck drivers	2.1
Nonfarm laborers	10.4
Service workers (except private household)	50.3
Cleaning service workers	32.9
Food service workers	61.2
Health service workers	87.4
Personal service workers	66.8
Private household workers	94.6

Source: Nancy F. Rytina, "Earnings of Men and Women: A Look at Specific Occupations," *Monthly Labor Review,* April 1982, Table 1.

suggests that women do deserve to earn less than men because they tend to acquire less human capital. This argument was first advanced by two economists, Jacob Mincer and his student, Solomon Polachek, and it soon found its way into the pages of the 1974 Economic Report of the President.[12] The argument goes this way. In many families a traditional division of labor on the basis of sex still exists. Women typically assume primary responsibility for home activities, including childbearing, "raising a family," and "keeping house." Men, on the other hand, tend to specialize in labor market activities. This need not be true in every case, just often enough for it to be true on average. Indeed, it is true that men usually work more continuously than women in the labor market.

Why there is such a specialization is a thornier subject to resolve. Social norms about the definition of sexual identity and the appropriate economic and social roles of men and women are undoubtedly relevant. It is also possible that it is economically sensible to specialize in tasks in the sense that each can then do the designated task more efficiently. (It does not, however, follow that it is women who should specialize in nonmarket work.) It is difficult to believe that biology plays more than a minor role. Discrimination itself may be a factor; if women earn less than men for any reason whatsoever, a family can increase its standard of living by having the husband work in the labor market and the wife work in the home.

Actually, for the argument made by Mincer and Polachek, it does not matter *why* the division of labor and specialization of task exists. Whatever the reason, it may affect the human capital investment decisions of both men and women, since the value of an investment depends on the number of years in which benefits will be received. If women expect to spend fewer years working in the labor market, it will be sensible for them to acquire less human capital than otherwise similar men.[13] This argument is thought to apply especially to investment in general training on the job, since the costs of that are borne entirely by the individuals. If so, women will have fewer skills than men and will have lower labor market earnings.

This specialization of functions within a family may have other effects as well. Women may find that the skills they do possess become "rusty" from disuse during periods of time in which they are not employed. If so, women might be even less valuable to employers than they look on paper. Additionally, it is possible that many women may seek out jobs that allow them some individual scheduling flexibility or which fit into their family's schedule. If they do place restrictions on their job choice, this

[12] See Jacob Mincer and Solomon Polachek, "Family Investments in Human Capital: Earnings of Women," *Journal of Political Economy,* 82, Vol. 2, II (March–April 1984), pp. 76–108.

[13] This effect is made even stronger, since the years of nonparticipation are early in a woman's career when the present value is larger.

could limit their opportunities and thus result in reduced earnings.

Finally, firms may be less willing to offer jobs with specific training to women. Remember that firms and individuals share the costs and benefits of specific training. If a firm reasoned that a woman was less likely to work continuously, it might be reluctant to offer employment. Of course, future employment plans can rarely be known with certainty, and it is difficult to elicit truthful accounts from prospective employees.[14] Firms might then resort to statistical discrimination, in effect assuming that all women have the same, less desirable, pattern of labor force participation.

There are several important implications that follow from this argument. First, it is possible to use this argument to explain the observed pattern of occupational choice by sex. Women might seek out employment in those occupations that facilitated or, at least did not heavily penalize, intermittent labor market activity, in which skills did not deteriorate too rapidly during periods of nonemployment, and in which there was relatively little general or specific on-the-job training. They might well end up being concentrated in a few occupations that meet those criteria.

Second, in this view, differences in human capital and thus differences in labor market earnings are interpreted as being "voluntary." That is, the differences reflect the organization of families and the resulting decisions of both men and women about what best serves their interests. Their often different decisions are alleged to reflect primarily their different roles, not labor market discrimination.

This last idea leads to a striking policy recommendation as well as to a forecast of the male–female earnings gap in the future. If the source of earnings differences is the family and not the labor market, antidiscrimination policy directed at the labor market is misguided and inappropriate. The "cure" is a change in the way families choose to allocate tasks and responsibilities. As for the forecast, that depends on future trends in labor force participation by married women. If, however, husbands and wives begin to specialize less and share tasks more, differences in human capital investment should disappear and the earnings gap between men and women should gradually erode.

This human capital explanation of the male–female earnings gap is a plausible and, in some respects, persuasive one. It would be surprising if differences in labor force participation and career orientation had *no* labor market effects. It does not, however, necessarily follow that *all* of the earnings gap is due to human capital factors. To find out how important this explanation is, we need to look at empirical studies of earnings differences between men and women.

[14] What would you say if a prospective employer asked you whether you were planning to quit your job?

Empirical Evidence on the Male–Female Earnings Gap

There have been many studies of the male–female earnings gap in the past 10 to 15 years.[15] Most of them have attempted to measure the importance of differences in human capital investments along the lines suggested by Mincer and Polachek. One of the earliest and best known studies is that of Mincer and Polachek themselves, based on a national sample of men and women age 35 to 44 in 1967. The major contribution of their empirical work was in looking more carefully at different segments of a woman's work history. They reasoned that women would be less likely to invest in on-the-job training during periods of employment before the birth of their children and more likely during periods of employment thereafter. In the earlier period, women may be planning to take time off to raise a family, whereas in the latter case, they are likely to be more permanent workers. In fact, Mincer and Polachek found that work experience in the latter segment did appear to be more valuable, which was consistent with their argument. By their calculations, differences in the amount and continuity of work experience accounted for nearly half of the earnings gap.

Subsequent studies, however, cast some doubt both on the data and on the analytical techniques used by Mincer and Polachek.[16] One follow-up study found a much smaller effect of experience differences on earnings differences, after correcting for some data problems and altering the techniques used. In addition, the sample Mincer and Polachek used is now somewhat dated and it included women from only a narrow age range.

A more recent and broader study was done by Mary Corcoran and Greg J. Duncan.[17] They analyzed information from a 1976 national survey of working men and women of all ages. The survey itself was specifically designed to measure many of the frequently cited differences in labor market skills and commitment. In addition to the usual information, this study included a detailed work history for each person. With that, accurate measures of the extent and continuity of previous work experience could be constructed.[18] For example, Corcoran and Duncan knew how many times each person had stopped working and how long he or she had stayed out of the labor force since finishing school. They also knew whether a person had taken his or her current job because of self-imposed schedule restrictions.

[15] For a good summary, see the chapter by Francine Blau in William Darity, ed., *Labor Economics: Modern Views* (Boston: Kluwer Nijhoff Publishers, 1984).

[16] See the article "An Exchange: The Theory of Human Capital and The Earnings of Women," *Journal of Human Resources*, 13, no. 1 (Winter 1978), 103–134.

[17] Mary Corcoran and Greg Duncan, "Work History, Labor Force Attachment, and Earnings Differences between Races and Sexes," *Journal of Human Resources*, 14, no. 1 (Winter 1979), 3–20.

[18] Most previous studies lacked direct information about a woman's work experience.

TABLE 9.3 Explaining Earnings Differences between White Men and White Women

	AVERAGE AMOUNT		FRACTION OF WAGE GAP ACCOUNTED FOR (%)
	White Men	*White Women*	
Years of education	12.9	12.7	2
Work history (years)			
Years in current job	8.7	5.7	16
Other work experience	11.3	8.1	4
Proportion of years part-time	9%	21%	9
Work continuity			
Years out of labor force since school	.5	5.8	3
Percent with two or more work interruptions	2.8%	11.8%	1
Work restrictions			
Percent who placed schedule limitations on current employment	15%	34%	3
Other (urban location, southern residence, absenteeism)			−2
Total			36

Source: Greg J. Duncan, *Years of Poverty, Years of Plenty,* (Ann Arbor, Mich.: Institute for Social Research, 1984), Chapter 6, Table 1.

Table 9.3 summarizes their findings about the source of earnings differences between white women and white men. The first two columns show the average amounts of the various factors. As you look down those columns, you will notice that for most of the measures, there are substantial differences between men and women. The only exception is years of education completed. Women, on average, have worked fewer years with their current employer; in addition, a larger fraction of their work experience was at part-time work. There are also large differences in work continuity. On average, women had spent nearly six years out of the labor force since finishing school, ten times more than men, and they were five times more likely to have spent two or more periods out of the labor force. There was also a very large gap in the proportion who reported that they had imposed some kind of scheduling limitation when they looked for and then accepted their current job. No survey is perfect and this one, like all others, lacks measures of the actual amount of human capital each person has acquired as well as some other things. But if differences in work experience and labor force commitment are important, this study should provide a reasonable estimate.

Following exactly along the lines of the statistical procedure for measuring discrimination described earlier, Corcoran and Duncan computed the importance of each factor in accounting for or contributing to the earnings gap. Those numbers, expressed as a proportion of the total earnings gap, are shown in the last column of the table. Each figure shows how much of the earnings gap can be related to differences in the amount of the factor being considered. As always, the larger the total explained portion, the less important is current labor market discrimination.

In spite of the large differences shown in the first two columns, Corcoran and Duncan found that they were not able to explain average earnings differences very adequately. Differences in work experience were by far the most important factor, accounting for 29 percent of the earnings gap. Differences in seniority on the current job accounted for 16 percent of the earnings difference by itself. Work continuity, however, was not important over and above its direct effect on work experience. This suggests that the problem that skills might become rusty during periods of nonemployment is not very severe. The same is true for the imposition of work limitations. In all, Corcoran and Duncan concluded that their expanded list of factors explained 36 percent of the wage gap between white women and white men. The other 64 percent remained unexplained. They concluded that "the wage advantages enjoyed by white men cannot be explained solely or even primarily by superior qualifications or greater attachment to the labor force."[19]

We began our analysis of male–female earnings differences by asking whether women deserved to earn less than men. The answer to that question, based on the studies of Mincer and Polachek, Corcoran and Duncan, and many others is "yes." Differences in work experience do affect earnings and even if there were no current discrimination at all, women would earn less than men. As long as there is a specialization of tasks within families on the basis of sex, there are likely to be differences in average labor market earnings. Looked at another way, however, it seems clear that the earnings difference between men and women is much larger than can be explained on the basis of human capital differences. Women do deserve to earn less than men—at least for now—but not nearly as much less as they currently do.

It is frustrating, but accurate, to report that economists are, as yet, unable to explain why women earn so much less than men. It is always possible that relevant factors have been overlooked in the empirical analyses. Their impact would, however, have to be very dramatic to alter the conclusions drawn thus far. The empirical analysis suggests the importance of discrimination, but it does not specify the mechanisms. How does it occur? Why isn't it eliminated by profit-seeking behavior? We simply do not know.

[19] Corcoran and Duncan, p. 19

EARNINGS DIFFERENCES BETWEEN BLACK AND WHITE WORKERS

Differences by race in economic opportunity and economic status have become a matter of major concern in the past decades. Prior to 1954, segregation in public education was a matter of law in southern states; prior to 1964, discrimination in housing, education, and employment on the basis of race was not illegal in virtually all parts of the country. Since then, assuring equal opportunity and improving the economic status of black workers and black families have been major policy goals.

There is no doubt that some progress has been made. The earnings gap between black and white workers has fallen considerably, as Table 9.4 shows. Black men now earn, on average, over 70 percent of what white men earn, compared to about three-fifths 25 years ago. Black women earn close to 90 percent of what white women earn, up from just under 70 percent in 1960. The extent of occupational segregation by race has also declined.

There are, however, a number of areas in which equality has not been achieved and race remains an important factor. Except for a few categories, earnings of blacks still lag behind. Unemployment rates are about twice as high for black men as white men; in 1983, one out of every six black men over age 20 was classified as unemployed. For black teenagers, unemployment rates are regularly over 40 percent and sometimes over 50 percent. As we saw in Chapter 5, labor force participation rates have fallen over time for

TABLE 9.4 Median Annual Earnings of Year-Round Full-Time Workers 14 Years and Over by Race and Sex, 1960–1983

YEAR	MEN			WOMEN		
	Black	*White*	*Ratio (%)*	*Black*	*White*	*Ratio (%)*
1960	$ 3,789	$ 5,662	66.9	$ 2,372	$ 3,410	69.6
1962	3,799	6,025	63.1	2,278	3,601	63.3
1964	4,285	6,497	66.0	2,674	3,859	69.3
1966	4,528	7,164	63.2	2,949	4,152	71.0
1968	5,603	8,014	69.9	3,677	4,700	78.2
1970	6,598	9,373	70.4	4,674	5,490	88.1
1972	7,548	10,786	70.0	5,320	6,131	86.8
1974	9,082	12,343	73.6	6,611	7,025	94.1
1976	10,225	14,071	72.7	7,724	8,295	93.1
1978	12,485	16,194	77.1	8,889	9,578	92.8
1980	13,547	19,157	70.7	10,672	11,277	94.6
1982	15,503	21,602	71.8	12,132	13,160	92.2
1983	16,410	23,114	71.0	13,000	14,677	88.6

Source: U.S. Bureau of the Census, Current Population Reports, Series P-60, Nos. 37, 41, 47, 53, 66, 80, 90, 101, 114, 123, 132, 142, 145.

prime-age black males, so that a substantial race gap now exists. Family income relative to whites has actually fallen since the mid-1970s. Poverty rates have risen. In this section we take a closer look at many of these statistics.

Explaining the Black–White Earnings Gap

We begin by considering why the average earnings of black men are lower than those for white men. The statistical approach is exactly the same as the one used to analyze male–female earnings differences. That is, we want to know how much of the difference in average earnings reflects differences in labor market skills and how much is unrelated to that and thus presumably due to discrimination. Two points are worth mentioning in advance. First, no subtle human capital argument, like that of Mincer and Polachek, is necessary here. Both black and white men are regular labor force participants and, other than discrimination, there is no reason to think that incentives to acquire human capital differ. Second, the results of this exercise refer only to current labor market discrimination. Some of the current differences in skills may reflect previous discrimination in the public schools or elsewhere.

There have been many studies of this kind, focusing on different age groups or different years. Virtually all find that the most important factor accounting for earnings differences is the difference in the average amount of education. The study by Corcoran and Duncan referred to earlier found that this difference was just under two years and that by itself it accounted for 43 percent of the wage gap. A few other miscellaneous differences, mostly concerning geographic location, typically explain another 10 percent or so of the difference. Roughly, then, 50 to 60 percent of the earnings gap between black and white men can be explained by differences in their characteristics. Black men and white men would not have equal earnings today even if there were no discrimination. Again, it is necessary to be careful in placing the 43 percent due to educational differences in the nondiscriminatory category. That is correct only as far as labor market discrimination is concerned. The educational differences may well reflect the effects of prior discrimination—less access to educational facilities and much lower family income.

Explaining the Increase in the Black–White Earnings Ratio

As far as black–white earnings are concerned, the more interesting question is why the earnings ratio has risen over time. There are a number of explanations, all of which are probably partially correct. First, there has been a narrowing of the historical differences in skills, especially among new labor market entrants. Not only have young blacks attained more education than in the past, but the relative quality of that education has probably improved as well. Second, there has almost certainly been a reduction in discrimination as the result of more than a decade in which antidiscrimination legislation has been applied. This shows up in the form of much higher payoffs to college completion for blacks now than in the past. This type of effect would cause the earnings ratio to rise even if skill differences had not narrowed.

There are two other less straightforward explanations, both of which involve changes in the composition of the working population over time. The first focuses on the effects of the decline in labor force participation by black men on observed median or average earnings.[20] The decline is relevant, because studies of earnings differences usually consider the earnings only of working persons or, even more narrowly, of year-round, full-time workers. As a result, changes in the composition of the working population over time can affect the average earnings of the group, depending on which persons are no longer working. Specifically, it is the potential labor market earnings of the nonparticipants that matter. If the nonparticipants would have had low earnings, their nonparticipation *raises* the average of those that remain. Exactly the opposite would happen if the nonparticipants would have had high incomes. There is, of course, no foolproof way to know for certain what the earnings of nonworkers would have been, but common sense suggests that it probably was not too high. After all, if their earnings prospects had been good, they probably would have been working. If so, the average earnings of the working population would rise over time as a larger fraction of low-income workers no longer work.[21]

To explain the rising ratio of black–white earnings, we need to take this argument one step further. The rate of nonparticipation must be rising more rapidly for blacks than whites, so that the effect on black average earnings is greater than on white average earnings. In fact, that much appears to be true; between 1969 and 1979, the proportion of the population with any work experience in the previous year fell by 10 percentage points for blacks compared to a 3-point drop for whites. One estimate, based on strong assumptions about the likely earnings of nonparticipants, concluded that up to half of the increase in the black–white earnings ratio could be attributed to changes by race in nonparticipation rates.[22]

A final explanation emphasizes the natural changes that occur in a

[20] Richard Butler and James Heckman, "The Government's Impact on the Labor Market Status of Black Americans: A Critical Review." Industrial Relations Research Association Series, 1977.

[21] This general problem is called **selection bias**, referring to the idea that the sample itself may be biased (nonrandom) because of the deliberate behavior of individuals. As a good example, think about why the college grades of a sample of juniors and seniors are usually higher than for a sample of freshman and sophomores. Who has dropped out of the sample over time?

[22] See Charles Brown, "Black/White Earnings Ratios since the Civil Rights Act of 1964: The Importance of Labor Market Dropouts," *Quarterly Journal of Economics*, vol. XLIX, no. 1 (1981), 31–44.

working population over time as older workers retire and younger ones enter the labor market. That natural process turns out to be very important for understanding changes in the black–white earnings ratio, because earnings ratios for the retirees were much lower than the average. Older black men were frequently educated in a segregated school system with very low expenditures per student, and they spent much of their careers working in an environment in which legal and social sanctions concerning discrimination were quite different from those of today. It is not very surprising, therefore, that their earnings suffered. As the passage of time eliminates the older workers from the group of black and white workers whose earnings are compared, the earnings ratio naturally rises. In addition, however, they are "replaced" by groups of younger workers for whom the earnings ratio is much higher than the average. Thus, over time, the earnings ratio will rise, even if nothing else happens, as older workers with below-average earnings ratios are replaced by younger workers with above-average earnings ratios.

How important is this effect? Duncan and Hoffman found that almost 60 percent of the increase in the earnings ratio between 1967 and 1978 was due to the retirement of older workers and the entry of younger ones.[23] In the future, however, this source of growth in the earnings ratio will be weaker, since the older groups of black workers no longer have such low earnings compared to white workers of the same age. Thus the retirement of these workers will no longer impart an upward bias to the trend in aggregate earnings.

Although the overall trend in the earnings ratio has been upward, not all black workers have shared equally in the gains. Most studies find that older black workers have not experienced much improvement.

Instead, the gains have gone primarily to younger workers, especially those just entering the labor market. Even among this group, the gains have been enjoyed mostly by those with more education, especially college graduates. One economist called them the "black elite,"[24] and it seems clear that they are nearly on a par with young white college graduates. On the other hand, the black–white earnings ratio for young workers with a high school education or less actually fell during the 1970s.

The result of these various changes is that the earnings distribution for black men has become more unequal in the last decade. It is a mistake to look only at the rising trend in the median earnings of black men and conclude that all segments of the black population have been able to improve their economic status.[25] The

[23] Greg J. Duncan and Saul D. Hoffman, "A New Look at the Causes of the Improved Economic Status of Black Workers," *Journal of Human Resources*, 18, no. 2 (Spring 1983), 268–82.

[24] This phrase comes from Richard E. Freeman, *Black Elite* (New York: McGraw-Hill, 1976).

[25] Indeed, it is a serious mistake to think of blacks and whites as internally homogeneous groups. Income differences within race groups are much larger than average income differences between them.

falling labor force participation rates for black men and the very high unemployment rates are grim statistics which emphasize that fact.

Income Differences among Black and White Families

Finally, as we noted in the introduction to this chapter, the relative income of black families has not increased along with the earnings of black workers. In 1983 the median income of black families was only 56 percent as large as that of white families, not only down from its all-time high of 62 percent in 1975 but not very much higher than in the mid-1950s. It is also substantially lower than the corresponding ratio of earnings by race for men and women.

There are two important factors contributing to this decline. First, family structure differs significantly by race and these differences have increased in the past decade. In 1983, two out of every five black families were headed by a single woman, compared to less than one out of eight for white families. Second, recall that the labor force participation rate for white women, especially married women, has risen sharply since the early 1960s. In the past, the participation rate had been much higher for black women; now the two rates are virtually identical.

The combined result of these two trends is that black families now tend to have fewer earners than white families. In 1967 nearly 60 percent of black families had two or more earners; by 1977 this was down to 46 percent and by 1983 it was 43 percent. Meanwhile, the proportion of white families with two earners rose from just over half in 1967 to 55 percent in 1977 and to 56 percent in 1983. It is not hard to see how that arithmetic leads to lower relative incomes for black families.[26] Since living standards and the welfare of children depends on family income rather than individual earnings, this is a matter of great concern.

FEDERAL ANTIDISCRIMINATION LEGISLATION

The Civil Rights Act of 1964

The major piece of antidiscrimination legislation in the United States is the Civil Rights Act of 1964. **Title VII** of that act refers to employment practices. Its key passage declares it unlawful "to refuse to hire or to discharge any individual, or otherwise to discriminate against any individual with respect to his compensation, terms, conditions, or privileges of employment because

[26] A recent study found that the average economic status of black children in two-parent families was actually lower than that of white children in one-parent households. See Martha S. Hill, "Female Household Headship and the Poverty of Children," *Five Thousand American Families,* vol. 10 (Ann Arbor, Mich.: Institute for Social Research, 1983).

of that individual's race, color, religion, sex, or national origin." The provisions of the Act applied to all employers who were engaged in interstate commerce and who employed at least 15 persons. The **Equal Employment Opportunity Commission** (EEOC) was established to administer Title VII. Initially, EEOC had authority only to mediate complaints and to encourage people to file private lawsuits, but in 1972, it was given the power to bring lawsuits on its own.

There has been a lengthy dispute among economists about the effectiveness of EEOC. One well-known study concluded that cumulative EEOC expenditures had had a positive effect on the black–white earnings ratio.[27] The initial emphasis of EEOC on resolving individual cases of alleged discrimination probably had little impact on anyone other than the parties directly involved. Subsequently, EEOC changed its emphasis and began initiating broad "systemic" suits, aimed at practices within an entire company. An early, celebrated case involved AT&T and provided for over $50 million in back pay and the establishment of new company employment and training procedures. In another major EEOC case settled in 1983, General Motors agreed to spend $42.5 million to hire, train, and promote more women and minorities. A major, innovative feature of the settlement was the creation of a $15 million educational package of endorsements and scholarships to be used for the more than 100,000 women and minorities (and their families) either currently employed by GM or on layoff. It is worth noting, however, that it took ten years to reach a settlement even without a time-consuming trial.

Like many laws, it is easier to show what Title VII says than what it means. Almost from its adoption, two widely divergent interpretations developed and it was not until 1979 that the Supreme Court finally decided the issue. By one interpretation, Title VII required that the protected categories—race, color, religion, sex, and national origin—must from that time on be treated as irrelevant. They could no longer be used in employment decisions, unlike the situation in the past when they had been used to the detriment of blacks, women, and so on. Preferential treatment of *any* kind was to be eliminated.

According to the alternative interpretation, however, those categories could still be used in employment decisions as long as they were used to *help* groups who were the victims of previous discrimination. In this view, the intent of the law was to help disadvantaged groups rather than merely to eliminate discrimination. If preferential treatment was required to achieve that goal, that would be acceptable. For example, the adoption of employment quotas to increase employment of women or minorities should, by this rea-

[27] Richard B. Freeman, "Black Economic Progress after 1964: Who Has Gained and Why?" in Sherwin Rosen, ed., *Studies in Labor Markets* (Chicago: The University of Chicago Press, 1981).

soning, be tolerated, but the quotas commonly used in the past to limit their numbers would not be acceptable.

There is a world of difference between these two views. The first prohibits the use of quotas, targets, and other employment or wage practices made consciously on the basis of race, color, religion, sex, or national origin. The other view sanctions the use of those techniques in certain cases. What did the Congress intend to do in Title VII?

What the Congress may have intended will never be known. We do know that one of the strongest supporters of the bill, Senator (and later Vice-President) Hubert Humphrey apparently offered to eat the pages of the bill one by one if anything in the bill could be interpreted as advocating preferential treatment of any kind. In any event, the U.S. Supreme Court finally resolved the argument in *Steelworkers* v. *Weber*, a case involving alleged "reverse discrimination." The facts were these. The United Steelworkers and the Kaiser Aluminum Company had voluntarily agreed to implement a race-conscious quota plan in which half of all new entrants into a craft training program were to be black. At the time, 39 percent of the local work force was black, but only 2 percent of the craftsmen were black. Both parties agreed that there had been discrimination in the past and the quota system was their proposed remedy. Weber, who was white and who was not selected into the training program, sued on the basis of Title VII. He claimed that he was the victim of "reverse discrimination."

The Court reasoned that the legislative history of Title VII and the historical context in which it was passed "make clear that an interpretation . . . that forbade all race-conscious affirmative action would bring about an end completely at variance with the purpose of the statue." As a result, they argued that quotas designed to remedy previous discrimination did not violate the intent of the law, thus accepting the second interpretation of the law. Weber's charge of reverse discrimination was rejected and the voluntary use of quotas was permitted.[28]

Two other features of Title VII deserve mention. First, notice the inclusion of sex as a protected class. No doubt that seems perfectly natural now that sex discrimination and women's rights have become important issues. But in 1964 when the legislation was passed, there was little awareness of sex discrimination as a serious problem. Was the inclusion of sex in Title VII an example of unusually enlightened and far-seeing legislative wisdom? Indeed, by most accounts, it was just the opposite.[29] Sex was added to the bill at the last minute through an amendment proposed on the floor of the Senate not by supporters of the bill, but by its opponents. They hoped that adding a

[28] In June 1984, the U.S. Supreme Court apparently restricted the use of race-conscious classifications in a case involving firefighters in Memphis. As of this writing, the law on this issue is very much in flux.

[29] This account is based on Donald A. Robinson, "Two Movements in Pursuit of Equal Employment Opportunity," *Signs*, 4, no. 3 (Spring 1979), 413–33.

"frivolous" category such as sex to the bill would ensure its defeat. Who, they thought, would vote for a bill that required that men and women be treated equally? Much to their surprise, the amended version of Title VII was passed and thus sex discrimination came to be included in the bill. As a consequence of this procedure, there was never any legislative discussion about how the sanctions against discrimination on the basis of sex should be interpreted. The lack of any legislative history has enormously complicated the subsequent process of interpretation by the courts.

Second, the traditional interpretation of the law was that it applied only to situations in which different workers perform the same job. The reason was a technical one, involving the way in which the provisions of an earlier piece of legislation, the Equal Pay Act, were linked to Title VII. That legislation had forbidden pay differences between men and women "for equal work on jobs the performance of which requires equal skill, effort, and responsibility, and which are performed under similar working conditions." The key word was "equal" and it had generally been given a narrow interpretation by the courts. Only on jobs that were very similar, if not identical in work content could the provisions of the Equal Pay Act be used.

If the same interpretation applied to Title VII, its impact would be substantially weakened, especially as it applied to cases of alleged sex discrimination. The reason is the one we noted earlier: most of the difference in earnings between men and women reflects the very different kinds of jobs they hold and the pay that is associated with those jobs, rather than differences in pay for men and women holding the same job. Thus, under this narrow interpretation, Title VII was not a particularly strong tool for combating sex discrimination.

The Legal Theory of Comparable Worth

If the application of Title VII was restricted to cases involving equal jobs, its usefulness would be sharply limited. The recognition of that led finally to the development of a new and controversial legal argument, known as the theory of **comparable worth**. Instead of arguing for "equal pay for equal work," this new theory argued for the broader idea of "equal pay for jobs of comparable worth." Technically, it involved a reinterpretation of the link between Title VII and the Equal Pay Act. Its implications, especially for the labor market, are potentially far-reaching.

The theory of comparable worth says that if two jobs require the same level of skill, they should receive the same pay. According to this theory, this result should prevail even if the actual skills required in the two jobs are themselves quite different. The jobs need only be of comparable worth, not identical in all respects or even any respect. For example, in one court case, female clerical workers at the University of Northern Iowa argued that it was illegal for the school to pay them less than janitors and groundskeepers. In another case, city nurses in Denver argued that their jobs were undervalued in comparison with other predominantly male job classifications such as plumbers and maintenance workers.

In these two examples, the courts ruled against the women, but in 1981, the U.S. Supreme Court opened the door to this new legal theory.[30] The case involved the pay of women who guarded women prisoners in an Oregon jail. The women were paid substantially less than a group of men who guarded the male prisoners. Both sides agreed that the jobs were not identical since the men guarded more prisoners. But the women argued that the pay differential was not in proportion to the difference in tasks. The Supreme Court decision did not actually endorse the theory of comparable worth; indeed, the written opinion emphasizes that the case did not involve comparable worth. But the judges did agree that Title VII could be used even when the jobs in question were not identical. Most legal experts believe that future claims of discrimination based on the theory of comparable worth will be favorably received. Since that decision, a U.S. District Court judge ruled that the state of Washington was guilty of discrimination because female occupations were paid less than "comparable" occupations that were primarily male. The American Federation of State, County, and Municipal Employees, a union that represents public sector employees (40 percent of whom are women) has filed similar suits against the cities of San Jose, Los Angeles, Chicago, and Philadelphia, and the states of Connecticut, Hawaii, and Wisconsin. The Supreme Court has not yet ruled on the merits of any of these cases.

So much for its legal aspects. What might its economic effects be? For one thing, it may cause enormous budgetary problems for cities and states. Preliminary awards against the state of Washington were over $800 million and the state claimed that the effects would be "devastating."

A more important problem for labor economists is the idea of worth and how it might be measured. In Chapter 2 when we considered "What Are Baseball Players Worth?", we touched on some of the complications involved in measuring worth. Are poets worth more or less than baseball players? What about nurses compared to plumbers? The essence of the problem is that in economic terms, worth or value is ultimately a subjective, not an objective concept. It does not reside in a person. Rather, it depends on consumer preferences as expressed through the market and summarized in the market price. Economists count on those prices to direct the allocation of scarce resources to their most valuable or worthy uses.

What valid comparisons can be made about the comparability of dissimilar jobs? The simplest point is that the wage, like any price, provides a subjective evaluation of the worth of a job. If a particular job pays $10 per

[30] The case is *Gunther* v. *County of Washington*, Oregon, U.S. Supreme Court, June 8, 1981.

hour and if the employer is maximizing profits in a competitive economy, we can be confident that an hour's use of labor time creates additional value of at least $10. From human capital theory, we also know this: In the long-run, equilibrium wages are proportional to the human capital required. (We abstract here from possible differences in nonpecuniary characteristics.) Thus, if two jobs carry the same wage, then no matter how dissimilar they are in terms of the exact skills required, we can infer that they are of equal worth—that is, create equal value. Conversely, where wages differ, then no matter how similar the jobs may appear, we can similarly conclude that the jobs are not of comparable worth.

The problem, though, is what to do when market prices are distorted, as they are if discrimination exists. Proponents of comparable worth theory argue that precisely because of labor market discrimination, the wage rate must be rejected as a measure of the worth of a job. They propose to substitute an "objective" measure of the worth of a job, based on an evaluation of job content and required job skills.[31] Ultimately they suggest that it is possible to establish the comparability or noncomparability of such diverse occupations as nurses and truck drivers, secretaries and maintenance workers, and then set wages and salaries accordingly.

Most labor economists regard that proposal with great skepticism. The issue is primarily one of practicality and implementation. Can job evaluation techniques accurately measure the required skills of a job, let alone its subtle nuances? Is the opinion of a single job evaluator or, for that matter, a judge, likely to be better than that of the market as a whole? Would the resulting set of relative wages operate, as prices must, to allocate resources efficiently?

Suppose, nevertheless, that it is possible to determine the true worth of each job and that what emerges is something like a set of long-run equilibrium pay scales. As long as nothing changes, everything is fine. But it is not sensible to talk about an economy without change. Supplies and demands change regularly as consumer tastes shift and new technology and new products are developed. How could these changes be accommodated? Would salaries be permitted to rise to establish a new equilibrium if it meant that comparable jobs would no longer have comparable pay? If not, labor shortages would develop. What about declines in demand for some kind of labor? In this case, employment will fall if wages are fixed and cannot change.

At best, pay based on the inherent worth of a job is an appropriate concept for long-run equilibrium in the labor market. Even there, measurement problems may be unsurmountable. But long-run equilibrium is not the usual state of affairs. In the interim, wages can and should differ, reflecting

[31] For a full account of these issues, see Donald J. Treiman and Heidi I. Hartmann, eds. *Women, Work, and Wages: Equal Pay for Jobs of Equal Value* (Washington, D.C.: National Academy Press, 1981).

not only the skills used on a job, but also the balance between supply and demand. Unless wages are allowed to change to establish an equilibrium, labor market problems are certain to arise. If comparable worth leads to inflexible, administered prices—a disguised form of price controls—economic efficiency will be impaired.

As virtually always in discussions of discrimination, we are left in an uncomfortable position with no clearly preferable choices. It is true that wage differences do appear to reflect discrimination, although the evidence of that is indirect. It is true that the strict interpretation of Title VII is not a very strong legal tool to combat discrimination. It is also true that comparable worth theory, if implemented, could dramatically correct wage inequities. But it would also have potentially serious labor market effects and it might be both unworkable and inequitable.

Application: Comparable Worth among University Professors

One example often emphasized (for obvious reasons) by economists involves the issue of university salaries. It remains true that professors in fields such as engineering, physics, law, and economics are mostly male, whereas professors in nursing and home economics are usually female. Their job duties are remarkably similar, as are their academic credentials. Standard job evaluation techniques would probably rate them as comparable.

Salaries, however, are often quite different. It will probably surprise few of you to learn that engineers, lawyers, and even economists are more highly paid than nursing professors even within the same university. (They are also paid more than some other predominantly male fields—agriculture and various other disciplines in the humanities and social sciences.) Indeed, the salary disparity holds even in the uncommon situation in which an engineering or law professor is female and a nursing professor is male.

This sounds like a classic comparable worth case.[32] If the jobs are comparable, why are the wages different? The answer is that the jobs are really not comparable, whatever the apparent similarities. Universities pay engineers well because they are immensely useful to private industry, which, by offering them high salaries, establishes a fairly high floor on the salary of engineering professors. As for their value to private industry, it reflects the ultimate value of their skills to consumers—that is, to society at large. The alternative demand for nurses' services is much weaker, and that accounts for much of the salary difference. The same thing is true for economists and

[32] A case like that was filed by the American Nurses Association on behalf of female faculty in the School of Nursing at the University of Pittsburgh.

English professors. It is not that economists are smarter—they are not. But society apparently values their services more highly.[33]

Any university that established comparable pay for professors in engineering, economics, law, physics, nursing, and home economics would find one of two things happening. If it equalizes pay by "leveling down," it would be unable to attract competent professors in the previously more highly paid fields. If it "leveled up," it would face an enormous excess supply of labor in what were previously the low-paying fields.

SUMMARY

The economic analysis of labor market discrimination and of earnings differences by race and sex presents a host of ideas and findings that are important and complex, but also incomplete and occasionally inconsistent. There are many insights, but few unqualified and definitive conclusions.

The theoretical analysis of labor market discrimination yields two extremely important ideas. First, the exercise of discrimination is inconsistent with profit maximization. If a firm insists on hiring only a certain kind of worker and refuses to hire other equally skilled, but lower wage workers, its production costs will be higher and its profits will be lower. Second, in a competitive market with free entry, high-cost firms tend to be weeded out over time. That is, normal competitive pressures should operate to drive discriminating firms out of business and, in so doing, eliminate wage differences due to discrimination.

Discrimination could persist where entry was restricted or profit incentives are weak. Imperfect information, leading to statistical discrimination, is another possibility.

In empirical work, it is standard practice to decompose average earnings differences between groups into two parts—one part due to unequal treatment of equals and a second part due to differences in relevant labor market characteristics. The latter portion is usually regarded as "explained." It is the part not due to current labor market discrimination, although it may be due to prior labor market discrimination or to prelabor market discrimination involving such things as education and training.

A plausible argument can be made that traces male–female earnings differences back to the traditional division of labor within households. If women expect to work fewer years in the labor market, their incentives to invest in human capital may be reduced. This human capital explanation is

[33] As of this writing, starting university salaries for economics professors were considerably lower than for professors of finance. Sex discrimination is irrelevant here and the training and skills are extremely similar. (Some finance professors are actually trained in economics departments.) To the dismay of economists, it appears that just as in the case of the engineers, the large nonacademic demand for would-be finance professors is the source of the wage disparity.

popular among many economists, but careful empirical studies show that it accounts for only about one-third of the average earnings difference between white men and white women.

Empirical studies of earnings differences by race for males document the importance of educational differences in explaining the earnings gap. Something over half of the wage gap can be related to differences in individual characteristics. The rise in the earnings ratio over time is related to a series of factors: convergence in the quality and quantity of education, reduction in discrimination, and two different sources of upward bias due to sample composition change. Finally, we noted the rather different level and trend of family income comparisons by race.

In the final section, we examined federal antidiscrimination legislation. The Civil Rights Act of 1964 outlaws discrimination in employment on the basis of both sex and race. Although the legal interpretation is still subject to change, the prevailing opinion is that it permits race-and sex-conscious employment practices if the intent is to help racial minorities and women. If the law is interpreted to apply only to situations involving equal or identical work, its impact is sharply reduced, especially insofar as earnings inequality by sex is concerned. The legal theory of comparable worth was developed to remedy that problem; it asserts that jobs need only be comparable, not identical, for the provisions of antidiscrimination law to apply. This is a powerful tool that potentially may have a major impact on the labor market. It may well have adverse consequences, especially if, as many economists assume, job evaluation is done quite imperfectly and the resulting wage standards are imposed in an inflexible way.

New Concepts

Labor market discrimination
Tastes for discrimination
Employer discrimination
Employee discrimination
Customer discrimination
Conspiracy model
Statistical discrimination
Selection bias
Occupational segregation
Title VII
Equal Employment Opportunity Commission (EEOC)
Comparable worth

10

Labor Unions

INTRODUCTION

Thus far we have analyzed wages and employment exclusively from the standpoint of market behavior. Whether we considered the very simple supply and demand model of Chapter 2 or the more complicated versions of Chapters 6 to 9, we always focused on the ways in which supply and demand forces interacted to determine a market equilibrium. Except for the discussion of minimum wage legislation in Chapter 3, we have not yet considered the possibility that wages could be established other than by that supply–demand interaction. In this chapter, then, we look at the most widespread alternative wage-setting mechanism—unions and the collective bargaining process.

It is sometimes assumed that wage setting via supply and demand and wage setting via collective bargaining are two entirely different approaches with no common ground at all. In fact, however, many aspects of collective bargaining are greatly illuminated by the basic economic theory of labor markets. The point to bear in mind is that the factors underlying labor supply and labor demand curves continue to apply even in the presence of collective bargaining. Those forces are the basis for analyzing the labor market effects of unions.

The real-world process of collective bargaining is enormously complex and it has become the subject of an entire course of study of its own, usually called **labor and industrial relations**. Unions are studied not only by economists, but also by sociologists, political scientists, historians, and lawyers. Unions are certainly much more than just economic institutions. But they do have definite economic effects on the labor market, and in this chapter we identify them, concentrating especially on their impact on wages and employment. In doing so, we largely ignore not only the noneconomic characteristics of unions, but also the process of collective bargaining itself. A good book in labor and industrial relations can fill in the gaps if you are interested in those aspects of unions.[1]

There are three major topics covered in this chapter. The first is an overview of unions in the U.S. economy, with attention to their declining importance in the past two decades. The second concerns the economic impact of unions, drawing on the basic ideas of economic theory. The goals and behavior of unions are considered, together with an analysis of their labor market effects in different market structures. In the last part of the chapter, empirical studies of the labor market effects of unions are examined. We focus on two issues: the impact of unions on wages and their effect on productivity.

[1] See, for example, Arthur B. Sloane and Fred Whitney, *Labor Relations* (Englewood Cliffs, N.J.: Prentice-Hall, Inc., 1983).

LABOR UNIONS IN THE UNITED STATES

Labor unions are an important institutional feature of the U.S. economy, but they have never been as powerful or as pervasive as unions are in much of Western Europe. It is easy to exaggerate their importance, something that is regularly done both by union supporters and union critics.

In this country the earliest labor union is traced back to the late eighteenth century. The modern labor movement began to develop in the latter part of the nineteenth century and by 1900, about 5 percent of nonagricultural employees belonged to unions. The development since then is traced in Table 10.1.[2] Unions grew at a moderate rate through 1920, actually declined in importance during the 1920s, and then grew rapidly between about 1935 and 1950. The key to the success of unionization during the latter period was the passage in 1935 of the **National Labor Relations Act**, a landmark piece of legislation that established a supportive legal framework for collective bargaining. Union membership increased by over 10 million persons in this period, as many of the heavy manufacturing industries—automobiles, steel, rubber and tires, electrical equipment—were successfully unionized. As a proportion of nonagricultural employment, union membership peaked in 1954 at about 35 percent, but it has fallen steadily since then. In 1980, the last year for which complete data are available, about 20 million workers—just under 22 percent of the nonagricultural work force—belonged to a union.

The degree of unionization varies considerably across sectors of the economy. Table 10.2 summarizes that information for the period 1960 to 1978. Two features of American unionism are evident. First, unionization is much stronger in mining, construction, manufacturing, and transportation

TABLE 10.1 Union Membership in the United States, 1900–1980

YEAR	UNION MEMBERSHIP AS A PERCENTAGE OF: *Nonagricultural Employment*	*Labor Force*
1980	21.9	18.6
1970	27.3	22.6
1960	31.4	23.6
1950	31.5	22.3
1940	26.9	15.5
1930	11.6	6.8
1920	18.4	12.1
1910	9.8	5.7
1900	5.2	2.8

Sources: U.S. Bureau of Labor Statistics, *Handbook of Labor Statistics*, selected years.

[2] The table shows union membership. The percentage of workers covered by union contracts is slightly larger.

than elsewhere in the economy. Second, the extent of unionization has actually fallen in the more heavily unionized industries, whereas it has increased slightly in the "all other" category. That increase reflects primarily increased unionization of public-sector employment, which is one of the few areas where unionization has increased in the past two decades.

Why have unions fared poorly in the last few decades? There are several common explanations. First, the composition of employment in the United States has undergone substantial change, much of which has been disadvantageous to the union movement. Services and other white-collar work, which have always been difficult to organize, have grown rapidly, whereas manufacturing and other heavily unionized sectors have declined in relative importance. Even if unionization rates within industries had been constant, these changes alone would have led to a decline in the proportion of the work force that is unionized. Second, as Table 10.2 indicates, unionization rates have, in fact, declined in the heavily unionized industries. This means that even if the composition of employment had not changed (which it did), these changes alone would have caused the unionization rate to fall. A recent study that investigated the importance of these two effects concluded that the change in unionization rates within an industry was the more important factor in accounting for the decline in unionization since 1956.[3]

That finding leads to the further question of why the within-industry unionization rates have fallen. Again, there are a number of contributing factors. Much of the employment growth has occurred in geographic areas such as the South and the Sunbelt which have been traditionally resistant to unionization. Most of these states have **right-to-work laws**, which prohibit union contracts from requiring that all employees in a unionized firm became members of the union and contribute to its financial support.[4] Right-to-work legislation makes it more difficult for a union to establish a secure financial base and thus tends to impede unionization.

In a recent study, Neumann and Rissman advanced another possible

TABLE 10.2 Unionization by Industry (%), Selected Years, 1960–1978

YEAR	MINING	CONSTRUCTION	MANUFACTURING	TRANSPORTATION	OTHER
1978	50.3	68.2	39.6	35.5	15.3
1970	59.1	72.8	47.4	54.1	14.3
1960	55.2	77.6	51.2	64.1	14.2

Source: U.S. Bureau of Labor Statistics, *Directory of National Unions and Employee Associations*, selected years.

[3] George R. Neumann and Ellen R. Rissman, "Where Have All the Union Members Gone?" *Journal of Labor Economics*, 2, no. 2 (April 1984), 175–92.

[4] Section 14B of the Taft-Hartley Act, passed by Congress in 1947, gave states the authority to enact right-to-work legislation. Twenty states currently have such legislation.

TABLE 10.3 Membership of the Ten Largest Unions, 1982

UNION	NUMBER OF MEMBERS
Teamsters (IBT)	1,800,000
Teachers (NEA)	1,641,354
Steelworkers (USW)	1,200,000
Autoworkers (UAW)	1,140,370
Food, commercial (UFCW)	1,079,213
State, county (AFSCME)	950,000
Electrical (IBEW)	883,000
Service (SEIU)	700,000
Carpenters (CJA)	679,000
Machinists (IAM)	655,221

Source: Bureau of National Affairs, *Directory of U.S. Labor Organizations, 1982–83.*

explanation.[5] They suggested that unions are less attractive to workers now because the public sector now provides substitutes for some of the services previously provided exclusively by unions. Unemployment compensation, workers' compensation, and regulation of occupational health and safety were cited as examples of the public-sector substitutes. The result, according to Neumann and Rissman, is that the demand for union representation by workers has decreased.

Finally, as will be explained more fully later, government deregulation of industry has, in some cases, contributed to a decline in unionization rates.

Table 10.3 provides a list of the ten largest unions in the United States as of 1982. The importance of unions in transportation, manufacturing, and in the public sector is evident.

THE LABOR MARKET EFFECTS OF UNIONS: THEORY

Unions and Their Objectives

It would be both useful and satisfying to be able to develop a model of how a union behaves and what bargaining objectives it seeks. The ability to describe the objectives and constraints of firms and individuals is the key to our being able to predict their probable behavior in a variety of circumstances. Unfortunately, the attempt to model behavior remains an unresolved problem

[5] Neumann and Rissman.

in labor economics.[6] It is tempting to postulate that unions are trying to maximize something, but exactly what that something is has not yet been determined to the general satisfaction of economists. None of the obvious, simple candidates for the thing being maximized stand up to scrutiny. For example, a policy of trying to *maximize* wages would *minimize* employment, not a very likely goal. A policy of trying to maximize total wages paid does give consideration to both wages and employment. But if the labor demand curve is elastic at the current wage, this policy would call for a negotiated decrease in wages. (The increase in employment would outweigh the decrease in wages.)

It is possible to argue that unions choose their objectives to maximize the utility of their members, but by itself that is not very helpful, because it is too vague. What do union members want?[7] Higher wages, secure employment, improved working conditions? But how much of each?

One common but inappropriate argument about union behavior likens them to a "labor monopoly." No doubt this idea originates from the observation that some unions do enjoy market power, rather like a monopoly does in the sales of its product. There, however, the similarities end, because unlike a monopoly, unions do not actually have anything to sell. They do not, for example, directly sell the services of employees as a labor contractor does. Instead, unions are one participant in the collective bargaining process which determines the wages, hours, and working conditions under which employment takes place. Applying the monopoly model to the behavior of unions is not a productive exercise.

In the theoretical discussion that follows, we assume that unions seek to increase wages for their members and that they are successful in doing so. (In the last part of the chapter, we examine whether that assumption is correct.) The analysis focuses on the labor market effects of that wage policy under a variety of circumstances. It is worth noting that in a model of union behavior, these labor market effects would be an integral factor in determining a union's wage objectives in the first place.

We consider first the effect of a union in a competitive market and then examine the quite different case in which the labor market is monopsonistic. Along the way, we identify the circumstances in which unions are likely to be strong and note some of the actions they may take in their own behalf to help create those conditions.

[6] There was an active intellectual debate in the late 1940s concerning whether "political" or "maximizing" models were more appropriate for the analysis of union behavior. The major participants were Arthur Ross, who presented the political argument in his book, *Trade Union Wage Policy* (Berkeley, Calif.: University of California Press, 1948) and John Dunlop, who developed economic models of union behavior in his book, *Wage Determination under Trade Unions* (New York: Augustus Kelley, 1950).

[7] Samuel Gompers, president of the American Federation of Labor (AFL) from 1886 to 1924, is reported to have once answered that question, " More, more, more—now!"

Union Effects in a Competitive Labor Market

The basic analysis of union effects in a competitive labor market is quite simple. As we have seen repeatedly, labor demand curves are always downward sloping when the labor market is competitive. Thus, if unions are effective in increasing the wages of their members, they will simultaneously have a negative impact on employment.

Although that prediction is straightforward, the nature and magnitude of a union's labor market impact will vary in different situations. There are two general cases worth analyzing, one in which only a single firm is unionized and the other in which an entire industry is unionized. The two situations differ, because in the latter case there are price effects to consider as well. This alters the labor demand curve in a way that is advantageous to a union, but it also sets in motion forces that tend to erode a union's strength.

The case in which a single firm is unionized is shown in Figure 10.1. We assume here that the labor market is initially competitive and that the product market is also competitive. The firm is, by definition, a price taker in the product market; if it tried to increase its price singlehandedly, its sales—and thus its employment—would fall to zero.

Suppose that the firm becomes unionized and the wage consequently rises from the initial equilibrium wage, w^*, to w^u. A union contract typically specifies the wage rate and perhaps also certain work rules and working conditions, but it does not specify *who* is to be hired nor *how many* workers are to be hired. (Exceptions to that will be considered subsequently.) The firm, then, has two employment options. It can choose to upgrade its hiring standards, perhaps hiring workers whose equilibrium wage is equal to w^u.

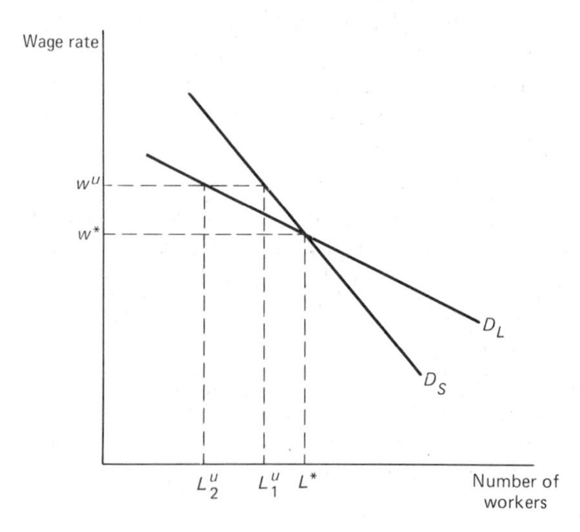

FIGURE 10.1 Short and Long-Run Employment Effects of a Union-Negotiated Increase in Wages

Alternatively, it can continue to hire workers of the same skill level, but reduce employment to the point where the MRP_L just equals w^u.

This latter option is illustrated in Figure 10.1, which includes both the firm's short-run and long-run labor demand curves, designated as D_S and D_L, respectively. In the short run, the firm will reduce its employment from L^* to L_1^u, moving along D_S. For all workers between L_1^u and L^*, the *MRP* is less than w^u, and it is therefore no longer profitable to hire them. The long-run effect is, as always, greater—in this case, an additional decline in employment to L_2^u.

Just as in the case of minimum wage legislation, the *magnitude* of the employment effect depends both on the difference between w^u and w^* and on the elasticity of the labor demand curve. Unless the demand curve is completely inelastic (vertical), negotiated wage increases always reduce employment. In general, the more elastic the demand curve, the greater will be the adverse employment effects of any wage increase—note, for instance, the difference between the short-run and long-run effects. That leads to an important prediction: *Union power will tend to be greater the more inelastic the demand curve for labor*. Where demand curves are elastic, the more severe employment consequences of a wage increase may serve to moderate a union's wage objectives.

Observing these effects in real labor markets is complicated by the fact that other factors influencing employment are changing along with wages. One such situation, which was perhaps more common during the 1960s than today, is shown in Figure 10.2. Suppose that the demand curve for labor is increasing (shifting out) from one year to the next at a regular rate as a result of increased demand for the product or productivity growth.[8] In the figure, D_0 is this year's demand curve and D_1 is the demand curve for the following year; w^* and w^u again represent the original wage and the union wage. If the wage had increased and demand had not, employment would have fallen from L_0^* to L_0^u. If demand had increased and wages had not, employment would have increased to L_1^*. The actual result, reflecting both changes, is L_1^u—both wages and employment have increased. The correct measure of the employment effect, though, is the difference between L_1^* (which is unobserved) and L_1^u.

It is worth noting that a situation like this is ideal for unions. The adverse effect on employment involves workers who are never hired rather than current workers who must be laid off.

In the preceding analysis, we assumed that a firm was always free to choose its desired level of employment once the wage rate was set via collective bargaining. In some cases, though, this is not the case. A union contract may

[8] The U.S. auto industry in much of the 1950s and 1960s is a good example of this situation. Economic growth and suburbanization were two underlying factors contributing to the increase in the demand for automobiles.

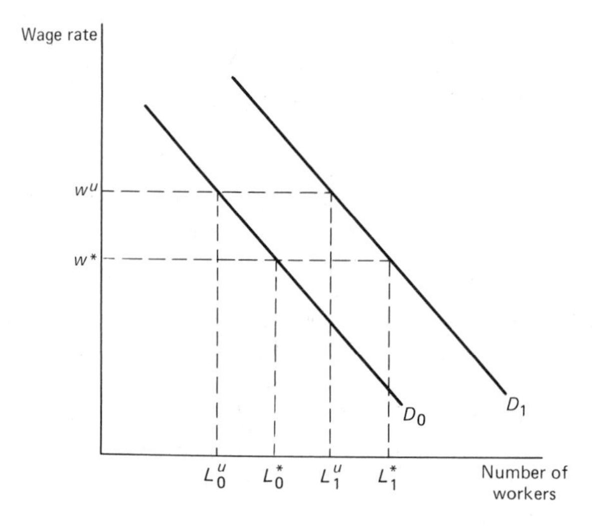

FIGURE 10.2 The Effect of Unions on Employment When Labor Demand Is Increasing

specify both the wage rate and the amount of employment, typically in an attempt to increase employment by pushing a firm off its labor demand curve. The general practice is called **featherbedding**.[9]

There are several famous historical examples of featherbedding. Probably the best known involved the railroads in the nineteenth century. The union contract continued to require the employment of a coalman even after the railroads switched from coal to diesel fuel and left the coalman with nothing to do. The International Typographical Union also succeeded in including a featherbedding practice in their contract with the newspapers. In this case, the problem was the development in the late nineteenth century of a new printing technology that reduced the demand for typesetters. The "solution" called for the making of a duplicate printing plate which, once completed, was immediately discarded.

The practice of featherbedding still exists today, even though it is widely criticized. The contract that governs the use of musicians in Broadway musicals specifies the minimum allowable orchestra size. The producer may, of course, choose to use fewer musicians, but the full complement must be paid in any event. The current contract of the International Longshoremen's Association guarantees workers a minimum number of hours of work each year. In some other cases, the issue is cloudy. Are teachers' contracts that place maximum limits on class size featherbedding or an attempt to maintain the quality of education?

In any case, the classic practice of featherbedding can be depicted as

[9] Featherbedding is also used to refer to the related practice of limiting the amount of work that an employee can perform.

shown in Figure 10.3 At a contract wage of w^u, the firm would, if allowed, choose to hire L^u workers. A contract with featherbedding would specify a point such as A, off the demand curve to the right. The difference between L^u and L^A indicates the extent of featherbedding.

Application: *Shifting the Demand Curve for Union Labor*

Sometimes a union is subject to a decrease in demand that is beyond its control. The United Auto Workers could do little to prevent OPEC from increasing gasoline prices, despite the serious impact that had on sales and employment in the U.S. auto industry. But in other cases, a union need not be a passive observer of its demand curve. It can—and often does—attempt to increase the demand curve it faces, either by increasing the demand for the final product or by affecting the way in which production is carried out. Frequently, this is done through the political process rather than through the collective bargaining process.

A few examples will illustrate the general point. The Copyright Act in the United States denies certain copyright protections to books that are written in English by authors living in the United States if they are printed outside the United States. Why? This increases the demand for domestic printing services, which, in turn, increases the demand for unionized printers. Similarly, the Hotel Employees and Restaurant Employees International Union strongly (and successfully) opposed a proposed tax reform in 1982 that would have limited the deductibility of business-related meals. The proposal would

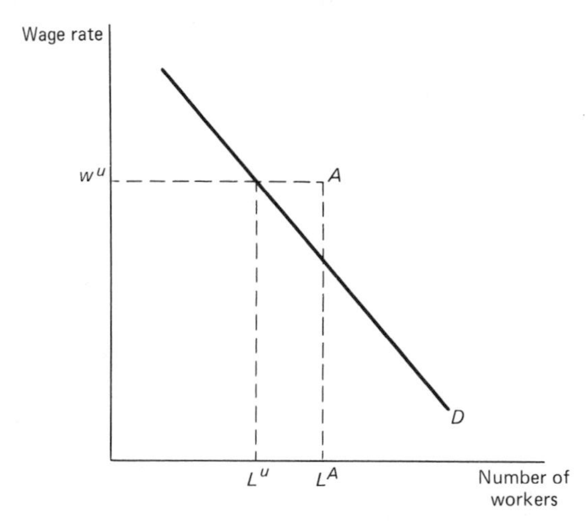

FIGURE 10.3 Featherbedding: Pushing a Firm Off Its Labor Demand Curve

have had the effect of raising the price of business meals, thereby reducing both the amount of meals and the amount of labor demanded.

Probably the most far-reaching demand-shifting proposal is **domestic content legislation**, which was proposed by the United Auto Workers in response to the sharp decline in employment in the U.S. auto industry. (Employment in 1983 was 23 percent below the 1978 level, representing a loss of 170,000 jobs.) A domestic content bill was actually passed by the House of Representatives in 1983, but it died when the Senate failed to consider it. As of this writing, it was still under active consideration by Congress.

Under the provisions of the 1983 version of the bill, a specified amount of the production cost of a car sold in the United States would have to be incurred in the United States. In 1985, the required percentage of domestic content would range from 3.3 percent for automakers who sold 100,000 units (smaller firms would be exempt) to 30 percent for companies selling 900,000 cars or more. By 1987, when the bill was to be fully implemented, the specified percentages would range from 10 percent to 90 percent.

The striking feature of this bill is that it applied not only to American auto manufacturers who had been increasing their own production in foreign countries of autos or parts intended for the U.S. market,[10] but applied equally to foreign firms who sold automobiles in the United States. Based on 1982 sales figures, Toyota would have to increase its domestic content from 5 percent to 67.5 percent by 1987, Nissan from 5 percent to 57.8 percent, and Honda from 5 percent to 36.5 percent.

The proposed domestic content legislation differs from the other two examples in that it affects the use of labor in production rather than the demand for the final product. That is, it would increase the demand for U.S. autoworkers rather than the total demand for autos in the United States. Figure 10.4 shows the effect of this legislation from two perspectives. Panel (a) represents the demand for autoworkers in the United States. Three demand curves are included, one for 1978, another for 1983, and the third for 1987, assuming domestic content legislation was in effect. Panel (b) shows the same situation from the standpoint of Japanese autoworkers. The effects are exactly reversed. Domestic content legislation would sharply reduce the demand for labor there.

It is possible that the effect of a union on employment in competitive markets may be more severe in this case than is indicated by conventional labor demand curves. Those curves, whatever their elasticity, show the profit-maximizing employment level assuming that the firm remains in business. It is, however, not clear that that should always be expected. If a union suc-

[10] The general practice is called **outsourcing** and, at least for domestic manufacturers, it can be addressed through the conventional mechanism of collective bargaining.

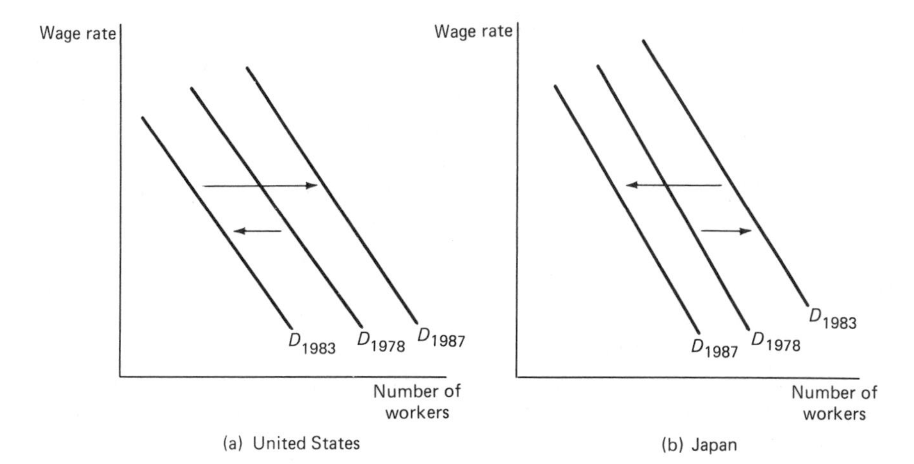

FIGURE 10.4 The Effect of Domestic Content Legislation on the Demand for Labor in the United States and Japan

cessfully raises wages above the level that would otherwise exist and if the firm is unable—as we assume—to increase the price of the product it sells, the firm's profits will almost certainly fall. (To argue otherwise, you must assume that the firm was not minimizing its production costs initially and that the wage increase will spur the firm into such an increase in efficiency that total costs actually fall despite the wage increase.) The question, then, is whether profits are affected strongly enough to cause the firm to cease production.

In the case of a single unionized firm operating in a competitive product market, it is quite possible that this will, in fact, occur. If the entry and exit of firms from the industry are not restricted, the long-run equilibrium price in the industry will be one in which firms earn zero **economic profits**. Earning zero economic profits means that a firm's revenues are just large enough to cover all its out-of-pocket production costs as well as the opportunity cost of remaining in business. Put differently, it is doing at least as well as in its best alternative line of business. If firms are able to earn more profit than that, new firms will enter the industry, thereby driving down the price, and if they earn less, some will exit to take advantage of their better opportunities elsewhere, raising the price in the process. Exit and entry thus guarantee that in long-run equilibrium firms will earn zero economic profits.

If a unionized firm is, prior to unionization, earning zero economic profits, any increase in its wage costs will cause its economic profits to be negative. Unless the firm is shocked into new-found efficiency or rescued by an increase in demand or some kind of cost-reducing technological change, it will eventually exit the industry and seek the more profitable opportunities available in other industries. Long-run employment in the firm may, therefore, fall to zero if a union does manage to raise wages.

We now turn to the situation in which an entire industry is unionized. Wage changes will now typically lead to price changes, since all firms now have higher production costs and all are willing to supply less output at any price. The new long-run equilibrium price will be just high enough so that firms can once again earn zero economic profits.

This situation is unambiguously better for a union for two separate reasons. First, there is no longer the problem of a unionized firm exiting an industry because its economic profits are negative. The increase in price permits firms to remain economically healthy. Second, the resulting labor demand curve is always less elastic than when only a single firm is unionized and it is unable to increase its price.

Figure 10.5 shows the latter effect. The initial situation is represented by point *A*. If the wage rose to w^u and if the output price were constant, employment would fall to L_1^u along demand curve D_1 (point *B*), exactly as in the analysis for a single firm. With the increase in price, however, the demand curve shifts up to D_2 (the MRP_L curve is higher) and employment rises to L_2^u (point *C*). Nevertheless, employment always falls even after the price increase, because the higher price reduces the amount of output demanded and because each unit of output will now be produced with more capital and less labor than before. The resulting labor demand curve for the firm is *DD*, which is less elastic than the two underlying demand curves. The industry labor demand curve is derived from demand curves such as *DD*.

This result also follows directly from the third Hicks–Marshall elasticity rule. The product demand curve for an entire industry is always less elastic than that for a single firm; the industry as a whole has a downward-sloping

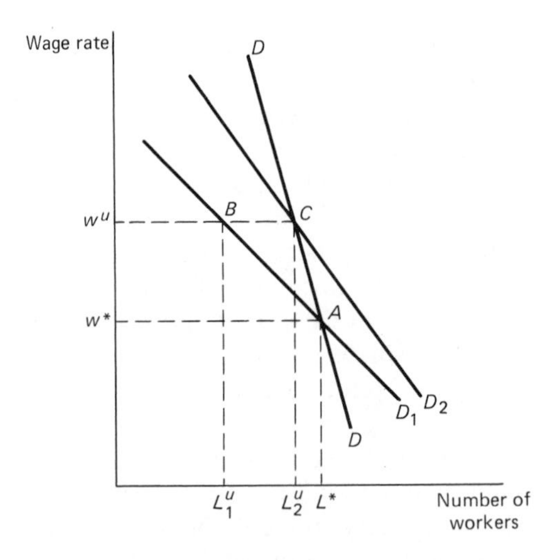

FIGURE 10.5 The Effect of a Wage Increase on Employment When All Firms in an Industry Are Unionized

demand curve, whereas for each firm it is horizontal. Since the elasticity of labor demand depends positively on the elasticity of the product demand curve, it follows that the industry-wide demand curve for unionized labor will be less elastic than the labor demand curve of a single unionized firm.

This is a general rule, useful not just for showing the difference in demand curve elasticity between a single firm and an entire industry. If, for instance, two different unionized industries are compared, the labor demand curve will, all else the same, be more elastic in the industry with the more elastic product demand curve.

It is clearly advantageous for a union to organize an entire industry. Not surprisingly, unions usually try to do exactly that and many have been successful. The problem, though, is in maintaining that degree of unionization. Since both wages and prices are increased in a unionized industry, a potentially profitable opportunity exists for new firms to enter that market, hire equally productive nonunion workers at a lower wage, produce at lower cost, and undercut the output price of the unionized firms. It is important to recognize that this entry could occur in two quite different ways. First, new nonunion firms could attempt to operate within the domestic market. Second, international trade provides a mechanism by which nonunion firms producing in foreign countries can "enter" the domestic market. If entry in either form occurs, unionized firms will be unable to successfully maintain their higher prices. The labor demand curve will become more elastic and the unionized firms may no longer be able to earn economic profits. Entry outside the sphere of influence of an existing union poses a serious threat to that union's strength.

Application: *Entry in the Meat-Packing Industry*

For many years, meat packing was a stable industry dominated by two large firms, Armour and Swift. The United Food and Commercial Workers International Union represented workers throughout the industry. Workers were well paid and firms were profitable.

In 1960, the situation began to change. A firm called Iowa Beef Processors (now IBP) entered the industry and instituted radical changes that would transform the industry. They introduced new "slaughtering" technology and, more important, established plants in meat-raising areas rather than in Kansas City and Chicago, which were the traditional homes of the industry. By locating outside the union's geographic sphere of influence, they were able to employ nonunion labor at a considerable savings.

In a relatively short time, IBP became the leading firm in the industry. Other new, efficient, primarily nonunion packers followed IBP into the industry. In recent years, the industry has been marked by plant closings and by substantial concessions by unions on wages, benefits, and work rules.

What, then, can a union do in order to maintain its position? There are a number of possibilities. First, it could attempt to convince consumers to buy union-made goods rather than otherwise similar nonunion goods. "Buy union" advertising campaigns are an example of that. Several years ago, the International Ladies Garment Workers Union tried that with television commercials that encouraged consumers to "look for the union label." If effective, a strategy like that acts rather like a barrier to entry. New firms cannot effectively enter the relevant market without first becoming unionized. It is, however, unclear how effective this strategy is likely to be.

Second, a union can attempt to organize the workers in the new firms, thereby imposing the same wage costs on all of them. Even if this is successful, however, it has no impact on the wages paid by producers in foreign countries.

A third strategy involves an attempt to limit entry via international trade by seeking controls over imports. A union cannot, of course, do this by itself; it needs the help of the federal government. The most common forms of import protection are a **tariff**, which is a tax on imported goods, and an **import quota**, which establishes a legal maximum on the amount of imports permitted. The effect is the same in either case: The price of the imported goods rises.[11] A highly publicized recent example of this is the "voluntary" quota on imports of Japanese automobiles between 1981 and 1985. It has been estimated that the quota increased the price of an automobile by between $600 and $1000, with a total cost to consumers of $4.3 billion.[12]

Finally, there are some situations in which entry by new firms in the domestic market is impeded. Here we need to distinguish two cases. Sometimes, market structure is the source of entry restrictions. In oligopolistic industries, technological factors frequently create barriers to entry by new firms, whether they are unionized or not. In contrast, there is no such protection provided in competitive markets. It is probably not a coincidence that unions tended to be stronger (at least until very recently) in the heavy manufacturing industries—automobiles, steel, rubber, and tires, for instance.[13]

In other cases, though, the lack of entry and the resulting union strength has been a by-product of government policy. Government regulation of the trucking industry through the Interstate Commerce Commission (ICC) is a classic example. Since 1935, when the ICC first began to regulate trucking, it has chosen to protect the industry from normal competitive pressures. The ICC's regulatory objective was to maintain the profitability of the industry, and one of the ways they did this was by prohibiting entry by new firms.

[11] There is one difference between quotas and tariffs. With tariffs, the increase in the price is received by the government, while with a quota, foreign producers receive the increase in price. Of the two policies, most economists would support tariffs.

[12] Robert Crandall, "Import Quotas and the Automobile Industry: The Cost of Protectionism," *Brookings Review,* 2, no. 4. (Summer 1984) 8–16.

[13] Even in these cases, entry has occurred in recent years through imports. Technological barriers to entry were not as severe as had been supposed.

Entry was allowed only in those few situations where it could be shown that existing firms were unable to provide satisfactory service. Neither the price at which that service was provided nor the resulting profits were considered as sufficient grounds for entry. In short, ICC regulations transformed a potentially competitive industry into a protected industry with restricted entry. In so doing, it greatly strengthened the position of the Teamsters Union, which represented the truck drivers. According to a study by the economist Thomas Moore, the increased cost of trucking regulation in the mid-1970s was about $4 billion per year. He estimated that $1.2 billion of that went to the truckers in the form of higher wages.[14]

There is one more development in this story which serves to emphasize further the roll of entry. In 1979, three new members, including two economists, joined the ICC, with a mandate from President Carter to promote the deregulation of the industry. In 1980, Congress passed the Motor Carrier Act. Entry restrictions were eased and price competition was permitted for the first time. In March 1983, with over 25 percent of its membership laid off, the Teamsters union agreed to forgo all wage increases, except for cost-of-living payments, for a period of 37 months.

The recent deregulation of the airlines provides another example of the importance of entry restrictions in establishing union strength. Under regulation there was relatively little entry, but deregulation has led to the appearance of new, lost-cost, nonunion airlines. People's Express and Muse Airlines are two prominent examples. The pressures caused by deregulation and entry have compelled unions in some of the established airlines to accept substantial wage concessions. In 1983, unionized workers at Eastern Airlines accepted an 18 percent pay cut, saving the airline $360 million, in exchange for stock. Wage adjustments also took place at Western Airlines and at Continental Airlines.[15]

Union Effects in a Monopsonistic Labor Market

The effects of a union operating in a monopsonistic labor market are drastically different from those that occur in competitive markets. In the monopsony case, unions find themselves in the unusual position of being able to increase both wages *and* employment, at least within some range of wage rates.

Figure 10.6 presents the basic monopsony diagram, exactly as first developed in Chapter 3. The monopsony market equilibrium without a union is w_m and L_m. Notice what happens when the industry becomes unionized.

[14] Thomas Gale Moore, "The Beneficiaries of Trucking Regulation," *Journal of Law and Economics*, 21 (October 1978), 327–44.

[15] Continental Airlines declared bankruptcy and unilaterally broke its union contracts.

Unionization does two things. First, it typically raises the wage above w_m. Second, and more crucially, it provides the firm with a new supply curve of labor which is *perfectly elastic* over most of its range. If the wage were set at w_1, the new labor supply curve facing the firm would be horizontal at w_1 up to the point of its intersection with the original supply curve (point A), and it would be upward sloping thereafter. The corresponding MLC curve will also change. Along the horizontal portion of the supply curve, the cost of hiring each additional worker is constant—it is equal to w_1. Thus the MLC curve will also be horizontal, coinciding with the supply curve through point A. There, where the supply curve becomes upward sloping, the MLC curve will jump up to point B and follow the original MLC curve thereafter. (The sudden jump in the MLC from A to B reflects the cost of hiring an additional worker at a wage greater than w_1 and increasing the wage of *all* previously hired employees.) No matter what the new union wage is, the labor supply curve and MLC curve will be horizontal up to the intersection with the supply curve and will have their original positions after that.

In effect, unionization eliminates a large portion of the upward-sloping supply curve which characterizes monopsony and replaces it with a horizontal supply curve, just as if the labor market were competitive. In so doing, it eliminates the differential between the wage and the MLC.

Figure 10.6 shows what happens when the labor market is unionized and wage increases are negotiated. If the wage were set at w_1, the firm would be willing to hire not just the original L_M workers, but rather, a larger amount, L_1. Even though the wage is higher than in the pure monopsony case, the MLC curve is actually lower in the relevant range of employment—beyond L_M. For workers between L_M and L_1, the MRP_L now *exceeds* the cost of

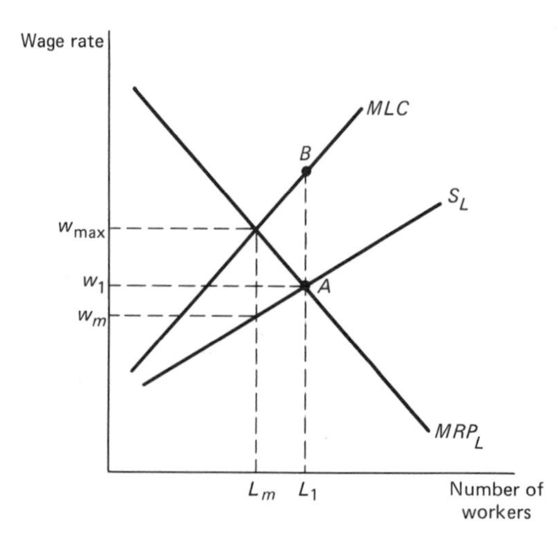

FIGURE 10.6 Union Effects in a Monopsonistic Labor Market

hiring them. This gives a quite remarkable result: Wage increases lead to increases in employment. Indeed, this is true for any wage between the monopsony wage (w_M) and the competitive wage (w_1), a result that you can prove to yourself by sketching in the appropriate *MLC* curve.

For wages greater than w_1, the conventional negative relationship between wages and employment once again holds. Still, the union could push the wage all the way up to w_{max} without reducing employment below the original level, L_M.

It is quite possible that some of the turn-of-the-century unionization efforts took place in monopsonistic labor markets. Workers in that setting were a natural focus of unionization, since they earned depressed wages (compared to a competitive market) and faced a single common employer. Thus the early effects of unionization may have been closer to those outlined by the monopsony model than the competitive model. But as monopsony has become less common and as some earlier monopsony markets have become unionized, it is likely that the situation now conforms more closely to the competitive market analysis.

THE LABOR MARKET EFFECTS OF UNIONS: EMPIRICAL EVIDENCE

The Effects of Unions on Wage Rates

The empirical question we would like to answer is this: Have unions been able to increase the wages of their members above what they would otherwise have been? The observation that unions do secure wage increases for their members is not proof that the unions *cause* the wage increases. Wages tend to increase over time in nonunionized firms too, reflecting the economy-wide increase in productivity.

To measure the union impact on wages properly, information is required not only about the current union wages, which is simple enough to acquire, but also about what the wage would have been in the absence of a union. The latter piece of information is, however, unobservable—it no longer exists once a union is in place. (You may recall that a very similar problem existed in computing the rate of return to education; a person's wage in the absence of education could not be observed. Attempts to determine the effect of minimum wage legislation also ran into this problem.) In practice, then, most researchers attempt to measure the difference in wages between union and nonunion workers who are otherwise as similar as possible. In effect, the wages of the nonunion workers are taken as a reasonable estimate of what the union workers would otherwise have earned. A technique such as this would provide an estimate of the average union wage effect. Certainly, some unions might have larger effects and others smaller effects.

This approach is not quite as straightforward as it sounds for a number of reasons. (Often, it seems like nothing in economics research is.) It is possible that unionization affects the wages of nonunion workers so that the wages of nonunion workers are no longer an accurate guide to what the wages of union members would otherwise have been. To make matters more confusing, there are two quite different plausible effects of unions on the wages of nonunion workers.

The first of these is called the **spillover effect** and is illustrated in Figure 10.7. Part (a) refers to the unionized sector and part (b) to the nonunion sector. If the workers being compared are identical except for the fact of unionization, their wages would in equilibrium have been the same in the absence of any union effect. This requires only that the worker be sufficiently mobile across jobs so as to eliminate any disequilibrium wage differences. The initial situation (without a union) is shown as a wage of w_0. With unionization, assume that the wage rises in the union sector to w^u and that employment falls to L^u. With less employment now availabie in the unionized sector, some workers, who are unsucessful in finding employment there, may now move to the nonunion sector to seek employment. This would shift the supply curve in the nonunion sector out to S_1. To absorb the now larger supply of labor, the equilibrium wage there would have to fall to w_1.

Thus one possible effect of higher wages in the union sector is to depress wages for otherwise similar workers in the nonunion sector. In this case the measured union–nonunion wage difference is, expressed in percentage terms, $(w^u - w_1)/w_1$. The true impact of unions on the wages of their own members is a smaller amount, $(w^u - w_0)w_0$. Where spillover effects operate in this way, the union–nonunion wage differential overstates the actual ability of unions to increase the wages of their members.

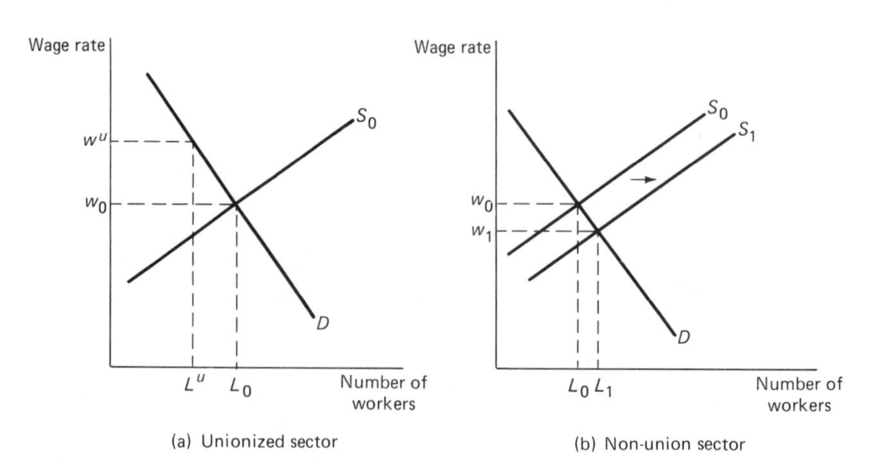

(a) Unionized sector

(b) Non-union sector

FIGURE 10.7 The Spillover Effect

The second possibility is called the **threat effect**. If a union is able to increase wages for its members, nonunion firms may react by raising the wages paid to their workers in order to ward off the threat of unionization. This would have two consequences. First, the increase in wages there would reduce employment in that sector. Second, the measured union–nonunion wage differential would now be an underestimate of the ability of a union to increase the wages of its own members.

It is possible for the spillover and threat effects to operate simultaneously. Some firms in the nonunion sector may perceive a genuine threat of unionization and may respond accordingly. Others may not be concerned about unionization, and there the spillover effect could operate.

There are at least two other important factors that complicate the task of measuring union wage effects. First, it is not easy to identify workers who are in all respects identical except for unionization. The measures of a worker's skill that are available to researchers are fairly crude—a person's age, education, and perhaps occupation and/or industry. There are frequently also some unmeasured skills and traits which are relevant in determining a person's productivity and wage rate. This would cause a problem only if unionized workers differed systematically—were either better or worse—from nonunion workers in terms of these unmeasured dimensions of skill. It is conceivable that union workers may, in fact, be better in this respect than workers who are otherwise similar in terms of measured characteristics. After all, if union wages are higher, there will be an excess supply of labor for unionized employment, and employers could be more selective in their hiring decisions. If so, some of the impact of these unmeasured skills would be mistakenly attributed to unionization.

Second, there is usually no information available on working conditions, a factor that we know affects wage rates through the theory of compensating wage differences. This would create a problem only if there were a systematic difference in working conditions between the union and nonunion sector. That, however, is quite possible, since unions are more likely to arise in situations in which working conditions are relatively poor. Even today, thinking about mining or working in the steel mills or automobile plants, it is possible that such differences still exist. If union workers do, on average, have less desirable working conditions, their wages would be higher even without unionization. Again, this effect would incorrectly be attributed to the effect of unionization.

What do the studies suggest about the effect of unions on wages? There have been many studies, each slightly different in form and with slightly different findings. A consensus estimate would be that as of the mid-1970s, unionized workers earned, on average, between 15 and 25 percent more than otherwise similar nonunion workers.[16] Some studies using more sophisticated techniques have found effects only about half that size. The estimated effect is smaller than both unions and their critics regularly suggest. The current figure might well be somewhat lower as the result of the unprecedented wage cuts that occurred in the early-1980s for unionized workers in trucking, in airlines, and in the automobile and steel industries. The Bureau of Labor Statistics reported that new major collective bargaining contracts in 1983 called for an average wage increase of just 2.8 percent annually over the life of the contract. This was the lowest figure reported since the mid-1960s; the previous low had been set in 1982.

A few other findings about union wage effects stand out. It appears that unions have a greater impact on the earnings of black men than on those of white men. This is because the labor market situation of nonunion black workers remains poorer than for white nonunion workers. One study[17] of the union effects in the mid-1970s found a 34 percent union wage advantage for black workers compared to a 14 percent wage advantage for whites. Another interesting study by Stafford and Duncan[18] provided some support for the compensating differentials hypothesis noted above. They found that including measures of work effort and job inflexibility *reduced* the estimated union wage effect substantially—from 31.3 percent to 18.9 percent in their analysis.

Finally, there is some evidence that the union wage effect varies across unions in ways that are consistent with the predictions of economic theory. A recent study by Freeman and Medoff showed that in manufacturing industries, the union wage effect was larger the larger the proportion of the industry that was unionized. That result is quite consistent with the earlier discussion about the effect of nonunion firms on union strength.

Unions in industries facing continued import competition have tended not to seek large wage increases, presumably in recognition of the large negative employment consequences. Unionized workers in the textile and garment industry are good examples of that. They are among the lowest paid unionized workers and earn little more than their nonunionized counterparts. Recent wage concessions in the auto and steel industries are undoubtedly due to the increased penetration of imports.

[16] The figures in the text are from Orley Ashenfelter, "Union Relative Wage Effects: New Evidence and a Survey of Their Implications for Wage Inflation," in Richard Stone and William Peterson, eds., *Econometric Contributions to Public Policy* (New York: St. Martin's Press, 1979), Daniel J. B. Mitchell, *Unions, Wages, and Inflation* (Washington, D.C.: Brookings Institution, 1980), and Greg Duncan and Saul D. Hoffman, "A New Look at the Causes of the Improved Economic Status of Black Workers," *Journal of Human Resources,* (Spring 1983). A famous work containing estimates of the union wage effect through the early 1960s is H. Gregg Lewis, *Unionism and Relative Wages in the United States* (Chicago: University of Chicago Press, 1963).

[17] Duncan and Hoffman.

[18] Frank P. Stafford and Greg J. Duncan, "Do Union Members Receive Compensating Wage Differentials?" *American Economic Review*, 70, no. 2 (June 1980), 355–71.

The Effect of Unions on Productivity

In addition to negotiating about wage rates, unions also bargain with management over working conditions and work rules. Because of that, there has long been interest and concern over whether unions might have a negative effect on worker productivity. For many years, the answer, based almost exclusively on anecdotal evidence, was thought to be "yes." Now, however, new thinking and new studies suggest that, in fact, unions may actually improve worker productivity.

It is not hard to see how unions might have a negative effect on productivity. Work rules and other restrictive practices may impede the firm's choice of how to utilize its work force most efficiently or about the introduction of new technology. They may also give seniority protection to inefficient workers. We have already noted the practice of featherbedding, which certainly decreases productivity by increasing the amount of labor necessary to produce a given amount of output. There are many other famous examples and, although anecdotes do not prove an argument, they are illustrative. The railroad unions (the original source of featherbedding) are a prominent example. When railroad speeds averaged no more than 10 miles an hour, 100 miles was recognized as a day's work. Remarkably, that is still the case, even though that is no more than several hours' work, and thus every 100 miles, the railroad must either change crews or pay an extra day's wages. There are also a long list of so-called "arbitraries"—routine maintenance tasks, for example—which require extra pay. The railroads estimate that the arbitraries alone cost between $250 and $445 million annually.[19] Work restrictions in unionized construction are also legendary. No unionized craftsworker can perform any task in another's jurisdiction—a plumber removing a nail, for example. Invariably, this causes additional labor to be used, which is one reason for the rule in the first place.

Is it nevertheless possible that unions increase the productivity of workers? One line of reasoning suggests that unions do so by providing a **collective voice** mechanism for discussing employment issues and problems with employers.[20] Why is that important? There are, it is argued, many work rules and policies that must be set in any firm concerning such things as heating, lighting, safety, promotion, vacations, job assignments, and so on. The unique characteristics of all of these is that once they are set, they affect all workers identically; economists call them **public goods** because of their shared "public" character. Firms could, if they wanted, simply unilaterally impose these rules

[19] This information comes from "Will Cabooses Ride Off into the Sunset? Railroads Hope So," which appeared in the *Wall Street Journal*, March 18, 1982.

[20] These ideas are drawn from "The Two Faces of Unionism" by Richard B. Freeman and James L. Medoff, which appeared in *Public Interest*, 57 (Fall 1979), 69–93. The original source of the collective voice concept is Albert Hirschman, *Exit, Voice, and Loyalty* (Cambridge, Mass.: Harvard University Press, 1973).

and policies, leaving workers with only a "take it or leave it" choice. If workers quit at an overly rapid rate, that would indicate that the terms were not satisfactory and the firm could then revise them. But, in fact, that approach is usually a bad idea: "leaving" or quitting is costly to the firm, since it must then hire and train new workers. In many cases it would be better for firms if they could learn what their employees preferences really are and attempt to accommodate them where that is feasible.

That is where unions enter the story. Unions, it is argued, can facilitate that communication process by acting as a collective voice mechanism on behalf of employees. It is likely that workers will express their preferences to union representatives more freely than they could directly to management. The result might well be a reduction in quit rates compared to a take-it-or-leave-it policy, as well as an improvement in worker morale. Neither result necessarily leads to higher productivity, but the connection is plausible. There is, in fact, evidence that quit rates are lower for unionized workers, even compared to workers with similar wages.[21]

There is another, older argument about possible positive effects of unions on worker productivity. We have already come across this argument, known as the **shock effect**, in connection with the imposition of minimum wage legislation. Higher union wages, it is argued, "shock" an inefficient firm into taking the necessary steps to become efficient, things it should have done before, but had not. As in the case of minimum wage legislation, there is no way to know how important this effect might be.

There have been some recent attempts to quantitatively assess the importance of these arguments about union effects on productivity. One important study, by Charles Brown and James Medoff,[22] compared productivity per worker for twenty manufacturing industries on a statewide basis in 1972 to determine whether workers in unionized firms were more productive. As factors that might influence the amount of value added per worker, they included the amount of capital per worker, the average skills or labor quality of the workers, the size of the firm, and the fraction of workers who were unionized in each industry in each state. They found that between otherwise identical firms that were completely unionized, on the one hand, and completely nonunion on the other, there was a 22 percent difference in productivity in favor of the unionized firm. Interestingly, that 22 percent effect was virtually identical to the union–nonunion wage differential, which they computed independently using the standard research approach described above.

[21] See Richard E. Freeman, "The Exit–Voice Tradeoff in the Labor Market: Unionism, Job Tenure, Quits, and Separatisms," *Quarterly Journal of Economics*, 94 (June 1980), 644–73.

[22] See Charles Brown and James Medoff, "Trade Unions in the Production Process," *Journal of Political Economy*, 86 (June 1978), 355–79.

This study is not definitive—more work of a similar nature is needed—but it is suggestive.[23]

SUMMARY

This chapter has examined an important institutional feature of labor markets. In many instances, wages are determined not by the impersonal supply and demand forces of the market, but by the very personal forces of collective bargaining between a labor union and management. Even where collective bargaining exists, supply and demand forces remain important. As always, if negotiated wages exceed the market equilibrium wage, negative employment consequences follow. A monopsonistic labor market is an exception to this, however. Unions can, within some range, increase both wages and employment in a monopsonistic labor market.

The ability of unions to raise wages without suffering substantial employment losses is greater when labor demand is increasing and/or when the labor demand curve is inelastic. Unions often take deliberate actions, frequently with the assistance of government, to create those desirable conditions. The ability of a union to maintain any wage advantage depends crucially on whether or not nonunion firms are able to enter the industry. Again, government policy has had an important effect in preventing entry into certain industries, thereby strengthening the unions involved.

In the theoretical section of the chapter, it was assumed that unions were able to increase the wages of their members. In fact, empirical studies confirm this, finding a union wage effect of between 15 and 25 percent. Union effects on productivity are less clear. There are arguments for both a positive and a negative productivity effect. Some recent econometric evidence suggests that the overall effect may be positive, but these findings are still tentative.

New Concepts

Labor and industrial relations
National Labor Relations Act
Right-to-work laws
Outsourcing
Featherbedding
Domestic content legislation

[23] Other evidence of positive effects of unions on productivity as found by Kim Clark in a study of cement firms that became unionized. Clark found a 6 to 10 percent increase in productivity, together with a 12 to 18 percent increase in wage rates. See Kim B. Clark, "The Impact of Unionization on Productivity: A Case Study," *Industrial and Labor Relations Review*, 33, no. 4 (July 1980), 451–69.

Economic profits
Tariff
Import quota
Spillover effect
Threat effect
Collective voice
Public goods

11

Labor Market Earnings and the Distribution of Income

INTRODUCTION

We have, thus far, discussed a large number of factors that influence a person's labor market earnings—from simple supply and demand to human capital to nonpecuniary job characteristics to unionization, discrimination, and internal labor markets. This chapter focuses on what is known empirically about earnings and about the determinants of these earnings.

Since about the mid-1960s, there have been hundreds, if not thousands, of articles and books analyzing earnings differences. The literature on this topic has crossed over from economics into disciplines such as sociology, and it has also crossed over from technical papers in professional journals to popular and polemical best-sellers.[1] This research is not as closely related to the economic theory of wage determination as we would like, but it is an interesting, important, and sometimes controversial body of research. In the first part of this chapter, we look at some of those research findings.

The last two sections in this chapter are concerned with the distribution of income. We look first at the **personal distribution of income** in the United States, including the characteristics of the poverty population. In considering the personal distribution of income, all income from whatever source received by an individual or family is included. An alternative approach is to consider income distribution in terms of the different sources of income. This approach is called the **functional distribution of income** and it is briefly discussed in the last section.

WAGE AND EARNINGS DIFFERENCES: A SURVEY OF EMPIRICAL FINDINGS

The Earnings Function Approach

Most empirical studies of the determinants of labor market earnings employ an **earnings function** approach. In this approach, an individual's earnings are related to—more formally, they are expressed as a *function* of—a set of relevant personal characteristics. Letting X stand for this set of characteristics, an earnings function can be expressed as

$$W = f(X) \tag{11.1}$$

where f is the function relating X to W.

[1] Books by noneconomists that have attracted a wide audience include Christopher Jencks and others, *Inequality* (New York: Basic Books, Inc., 1972), and George Gilder, *Wealth and Poverty* (New York: Basic Books, Inc. 1981). Jencks's book is written from a liberal perspective, Gilder's from a conservative one.

With information on an individual's wage and on the relevant characteristics, the statistical technique of **multiple regression analysis**[2] can be used to determine the best estimate of the effect of each characteristic on wages. Regression analysis also indicates the extent to which all of the characteristics taken together can explain the variation in wages. The statistical formulation is

$$W = B_0 + B_1X_1 + B_2X_2 + \ldots + B_kX_k + \varepsilon \qquad (11.2)$$

where ε represents random, unmeasured factors that affect wages. In equation (11.2), $B_1 \ldots B_k$, called the **regression coefficients**, take the place of f in equation (11.1). These coefficients are the best estimate, based on the data, of the effect on earnings of a 1-unit change in $X_1 \ldots X_k$, holding constant the amount of all the other characteristics. Thus, if X_1 was education and B_1 = \$900, then among persons who are the same in all other respects ($X_2 \ldots X_k$), one extra year of education accounts, on average, for a \$900 difference in earnings.

Ideally, the role of theory in statistical analysis is to identify the hypothesis that is to be investigated. In this case, that means specifying the relevant factors that belong in X. The economic theory of labor markets provides a lengthy list of potentially important factors:

1. The amount of physical capital to which a worker has access
2. The amount of human capital a person possesses
3. The amount and kind of rent-producing skills a person has
4. Nonpecuniary job characteristics
5. Aspects of market structure—whether the labor market is competitive or monopsonistic, whether there are barriers to entry
6. Unionization
7. The existence of internal labor markets
8. Labor market discrimination

No research has ever attempted to consider all these factors simultaneously, mostly because of the difficulties of compiling the relevant information. Most empirical economic studies of earnings relate wages to measures of a person's human capital and ignore the other items on the list.[3]

Even here, there are difficulties. In principle, studies like these link a worker's stock of human capital to his or her earnings. In fact, as we noted

[2] If you are unfamiliar with multiple regression, see the Appendix to this chapter. It contains a nontechnical summary of regression analysis.

[3] In previous chapters we have looked at the empirical research on some of these topics—monopsony, unions, nonpecuniary job characteristics, and discrimination.

back in Chapter 7, no one has ever seen a unit of human capital, so direct measurement is impossible. What is known is the amount of *time* a person spent in activities in which human capital is usually acquired, especially years of school and years of work experience. The common empirical practice is to assume that the amount of human capital acquired is proportional to the amount of time spent at work and at school—the more time at school or at work, the more human capital a person has gained. The general relationship is probably correct, but it is certainly not perfect by any means. For example, a typical college graduate spends 16 years in school, 33⅓ percent more than a high school graduate. Does that mean that the average college graduate also has 33⅓ percent more human capital? Do all persons with the same amount of education also have the same amount of human capital? Similarly, does everyone receive the same amount of on-the-job training per year of work? The inevitable—and, often unappreciated—result is that relating a person's earnings to his or her years of education and years at work is not the same thing as examining the relationship between earnings and human capital.

In any event, the resulting earnings function, now usually called a **human capital earnings function**, is often of the general form[4]

$$W = B_0 + B_1 \text{ (years of education)} + B_2 \text{ (years of work experience)} + \ldots + \varepsilon \qquad (11.3)$$

In equation (11.3), B_1 gives the effect on earnings of an additional year of education for workers with the same amount of work experience and B_2 does the same for an additional year of work experience.

In addition to the basic economic explanations noted above, there are several other explanations of earnings differences which are not as closely or directly linked to labor economics. They are well-enough known, however, to warrant mention, and they have been used in earnings functions.

Inheritance of Ability. In the late 1960s and early 1970s, several psychologists argued that a person's ability was determined primarily by the genetic makeup inherited from one's parents.[5] This argument was part of the long-standing and still unresolved debate over whether nature or nurture—that is, genes or environment—was the more important determinant of one's IQ or ability. In this instance, however, the writers went further by arguing

[4] This specification was popularized by Jacob Mincer in his book, *Schooling, Experience, and Earnings* (New York: Columbia University Press, 1972).

[5] See, for example, Richard Herrnstein, "IQ," *Atlantic Monthly*, September 1971, pp. 43–64, and Arthur R. Jensen, "How Much Can We Boost IQ and Scholastic Achievement?" *Harvard Education Review*, 39 (1969), 1–123.

that labor market earnings depended on ability in a direct way. Thus they concluded that observed earnings differences were biological in origin. The distribution of earnings among individuals could then be seen as reflecting the underlying distribution of genetic endowments.

The notoriety of these ideas arose from their very conservative policy implications. If it is true that ability is biologically determined, government social programs designed to help disadvantaged children, usually by increasing their human capital, would be useless. The distribution of ability and earnings, however unequal, is a biological fact, not subject to change.

Few economists place much weight on this argument and, indeed, it is now clear that even the scientific evidence for the heritability of genetic traits is weak.[6] Much more important is the evidence that IQ plays a minor role in earnings determination. Ability, as measured by test scores, has only a weak influence on labor market earnings.

Social Class Background. Many sociologists have stressed the importance of social class and family background on a person's earnings.[7] Do people born into wealthier families have higher earnings than people from poorer families? Is America a society where economic status is readily passed on from one generation to the next?

There are really two distinct hypotheses here. First, there is the purely empirical issue of *whether* earnings are related to social class background. What is the correlation between the earnings of parents and the earnings of their children? Second, there is the issue of *how* family background affects earnings. It is probably not often true that social class or family background affect one's earnings *directly*. Will an employer pay you more just because your last name is Rockefeller, du Pont, or Vanderbilt? More likely, a person's background affects earnings *indirectly* by affecting the amount of human capital that he or she acquires. This could take the form of a "richer home environment"—access to the finer things in life—or a better education, made possible by high family income or family connections.

The latter approach is broadly consistent with the human capital approach to labor market earnings. Its distinctive feature is in emphasizing factors that may influence a person's opportunities to acquire human capital. The former implies a very different view of wage determination.

Studies of the effects of these factors on earnings usually include some measure of intelligence (IQ scores) and a measure of family background

[6] See Paul A. Taubman, "Earnings, Education, Genetics, and Environment," *Journal of Human Resources*, 11, no. 4 (1976), 447–61, and Leon J. Kamin, *The Science and Politics of IQ* (New York: Lawrence Erlbaum Association, 1974).

[7] Representative of this approach is William Sewell and Robert Hauser, *Education, Occupation, and Earnings: Achievement in the Early Career* (New York: Academic Press, Inc., 1975), and Christopher Jencks and others, *Who Gets Ahead?* (New York: Basic Books, Inc., 1979), Chapter 3.

(parents' education, occupation, or income) together with human capital variables. Thus the earnings function is

$$W = B_0 + B_1(\text{years of education}) + B_2(\text{years of work experience}) + B_3(\text{ability}) + B_4(\text{social class background}) + \varepsilon \quad (11.4)$$

Empirical Findings

There have been an extraordinary number of earnings function studies, each differing in some way and focusing on a slightly different feature of wage determination. Despite these differences, it is encouraging that a set of consensus findings has emerged.

First, years of education and years of work experience are both important determinants of individual earnings. An additional year of education increases earnings by about 6 to 10 percent, depending on the group studied and whether the education is at the secondary level or at college. Experience is also valuable. Most studies find that earnings increase quickly with experience near the beginning of one's career and then increase less rapidly later. This result fits in nicely with the notion that investments in on-the-job training are predominantly made early in one's career and then fall off sharply. This statistical evidence does not, however, tell us why education and work experience affect earnings. The findings are certainly consistent with a human capital explanation, but in the absence of direct information about a worker's human capital, alternative explanations (see Chapter 7) cannot be ruled out.

Second, it appears that neither IQ nor social class background are important direct influences on labor market earnings. The conventional wisdom about the link between intelligence and earnings—"if you're so smart, why aren't you rich?"—is not well founded. As for background, its important effects on earnings are indirect, rather than direct—and even here, its impact is not too strong.

Third, education and work experience together explain about one-fourth to one-third of the variation in earnings among individuals. With the aid of some technical (and perhaps questionable) assumptions, it is possible to increase that fraction to about one-half. That is definitely an upper-bound estimate of the importance of education and job experience on earnings.[8] It is hard to know exactly how to interpret that finding. If education and work experience explain one-third of the variation in earnings, is that a lot or a little? Does it suggest that labor market earnings are only weakly related to economic factors? On the one hand, given all the measurement problems and all the other omitted factors, even explaining as much as one-third of earnings

[8] That estimate comes from Mincer.

differences with such a limited set of factors is a substantial achievement. On the other hand, it is also true that about two-thirds of the variation in earnings is not explained by education and experience differences among workers. It would, however, almost certainly be wrong to conclude that the unexplained earnings differences are unrelated to economic factors.

Application: What Do Empirical Studies of Wages Mean?

Consider the task of trying to explain the quite substantial average income of doctors. Economic theory provides a series of possible explanations, each of which could well be operating simultaneously.

Begin with human capital considerations. Clearly, a doctor makes an enormous individual expenditure on human capital investments, first at college, then at medical school, and finally as an intern and resident. In long-run equilibrium, the return on this investment would surely yield a considerable salary. Economic rent may also be relevant. Perhaps the number of even potentially capable brain or heart surgeons is small relative to demand. Compensating wage differentials may also play a small part, if, on average, potential M.D.'s find a doctor's work schedule unappealing or dislike close contact with blood and disease. Finally, it is frequently argued that doctors, through the American Medical Association, have restricted the supply of doctors.[9] If that were true, human capital in the form of medical education would be more valuable than an equivalent amount of human capital in some other form.

In a typical statistical analysis of earnings, a doctor is distinguished only by his or her education and years in practice. Is it surprising that education and experience do not fully explain earnings in this case?

The situation is much the same for the special skills that lead to economic rent—there are too many possibilities. A professional athlete earning several hundred thousand dollars annually would show up in a survey as just another young worker, perhaps one with a college degree. Needless to say, he or she earns much more than the average college graduate.

The basic point here is straightforward. A human capital earnings function does not really do justice to the human capital model, let alone to the full range of economic explanations of wage differences. The arguments of economic theory are much richer than is represented by statistical work. That work is interesting and important, but one needs to interpret it with care.

[9] The classic article on this topic is Reuben A. Kessel, "Price Discrimination in Medicine," *Journal of Law and Economics*, 1 (1958), 263–82. A key fact, cited by Kessel, was the power, assigned to the AMA, to certify medical schools. Between 1906 and 1944, the number of certified schools fell from 162 to 69.

THE PERSONAL DISTRIBUTION OF INCOME

In this section we examine the distribution of income among families in the United States, first by looking at the distribution as a whole and then by examining the poverty population. This changes our emphasis in two important ways. First, we will now usually focus on families rather than on individuals. Families are collections of two or more persons who typically share resources. Family income thus depends on the number of income recipients in a family. A family with two persons, both earning moderate salaries, may have a higher total income than a family with one person with a higher salary. Second, we are shifting from earnings to income, which is a broader concept. Labor economists have much more to say about earnings than about income, but because income is a more comprehensive measure of a family's economic well-being,[10] it is worth considering.

The Distribution of Income in the United States

Tables 11.1 and 11.2 present basic descriptive information about the distribution of income among families in 1982, the most recent year for which statistics are available. The income information comes from the Current Population Survey (CPS), a monthly survey of about 65,000 households conducted by the Bureau of the Census. Each March, information is collected on family income in the previous year. Income includes money income from all sources, but the value of goods and services received directly, such as Medicaid,

TABLE 11.1 The Distribution (%) of Family Income by Income Bracket in 1982

INCOME LEVEL	ALL FAMILIES	WHITE	BLACK AND OTHER
Less than $5,000	6.0	4.6	15.1
$5,000– $9,999	10.6	9.3	19.6
$10,000–$14,999	12.4	12.1	14.9
$15,000–$19,999	12.1	12.3	11.1
$20,000–$24,999	12.3	12.6	10.7
$25,000–$34,999	19.5	20.3	14.5
$35,000–$49,999	16.0	16.9	9.6
$50,000 and over	10.9	11.9	4.6
Median	$23,433	$24,603	$15,211
Mean	$27,391	$28,603	$19,282

Source: U.S. Bureau of the Census, Current Population Reports, Series P-60, No. 140, Table 2, *Money Income and Poverty Status of Families and Persons in the United States: 1982 (Advance data from the March 1983 Current Population Survey),* U.S. Government Printing Office, Washington, D.C., 1983.

[10] Even income is far from a perfect measure. Wealth holdings are excluded and so is the value of leisure time, just to cite two obvious problems.

TABLE 11.2 The Distribution of Aggregate Income in 1982 by Income Quintile

	INCOME RANGE OF QUINTILE	PERCENT DISTRIBUTION OF AGGREGATE INCOME
Lowest quintile	0–$11,200	4.7
Second quintile	$11,201–$19,334	11.2
Third quintile	$19,335–$27,750	17.1
Fourth quintile	$27,751–$39,992	24.3
Highest quintile	$39,993–	42.7
Top 5 percent	$64,000–	16.0
		100.0

Source: U.S. Bureau of the Census, Current Population Reports, Series P-60, No. 140, Table 4, *Money Income and Poverty Status of Families and Persons in the United States: 1982* (*Advance Data from the March 1983 Current Population Survey*), U.S. Government Printing Office, Washington, D.C., 1983.

Medicare, food stamps, and public housing, are not included. All of the figures refer to income before taxes.

Table 11.1 shows the distribution of income for all families together and separately by race. Median family income in 1982 was $23,433, which means that half of all families were above and half below that. Average income was about $4000 higher, because of the presence of some people with very high incomes. The distribution is not symmetric. Instead, it is skewed to the right—the lower tail of the distribution must stop at zero, but the high-income tail has no maximum. This "right-skewing" has long been noted as a characteristic feature of the distribution of income in most economies.

As you can see in the table, the distribution of income for nonwhite families is much more heavily concentrated in the lower-income ranges. There are two factors at work here—lower earnings and fewer earners per family as compared to whites. Median income for nonwhite families was about 55 percent of that for whites. In terms of mean income they did a bit better, at 60 percent.

Table 11.2 organizes the same basic information differently in order to illustrate the extent of inequality in income. Suppose that we take all families in the United States (61.4 million in 1982), rank them from lowest income to highest, and then place them in five *quintiles*, each containing exactly 20 percent of the total number. Then we can ask what share of the total income in the economy goes to each of the five groups. If there were perfect equality, each quintile would get exactly 20 percent of the total, so the difference between the actual percentage and 20 percent reflects the degree of inequality.[11] The actual figures for 1982 are shown in the table. To rank among

[11] A more precise measure of income inequality is the **Gini coefficient**. Its virtue is that it summarizes the entire distribution of income by a single number. It ranges from 0 in the case of perfect equality to 1 in the case in which one person had all the income and all other persons had no income. The Gini coefficient for the United States is about 0.40.

the richest 20 percent of all families, your income would have to be about $40,000; you would need $64,000 to make it in to the top 5 percent. In contrast, the poorest quintile had money incomes ranging up to $11,200 per year.

You can see the degree of inequality in 1982 in the second column of the table. The poorest 20 percent of all families receive less than 5 percent of total income, and the bottom two quintiles together get only about 16 percent. A large share goes to richer families—nearly 43 percent to the top quintile and 16 percent to the very top 5 percent. Inequality was somewhat greater in 1982 than in recent years, because the high unemployment rate sharply reduced the income of some workers.

Some economists have argued that the figures in Table 11.2 greatly overstate the true extent of income inequality.[12] They point out that some of the inequality is the result of observing different persons at different points in their careers. We expect young workers to have lower earnings than more experienced workers, but for most of them the condition will be only temporary. As they acquire more on-the-job training, their earnings will tend to increase. By this reasoning, the degree of inequality should either be considered in a life-cycle context or be adjusted for the income differences associated with age. Although the appropriate way to do this has been the subject of much debate, the basic point is well taken.[13]

It is difficult to interpret the numbers in Table 11.2 without having some standard of comparison. Does the United States have a great deal of inequality or a moderate amount? There are at least two obvious standards we could use. First, we could ask how inequality in the United States compares to other countries. Second, we could consider how inequality in the United States has changed over time. Has it gotten more or less unequal?

Relative to other industrialized countries, the United States is near the middle of the pack. One study of *after-tax* income in the United States and nine countries in Western Europe concluded that France and Spain had the most inequality; Sweden and the Netherlands the least. Inequality in the United States was then about the same as in Canada and Austria. Taken as a group, the industrialized countries tend to have less inequality than the developing countries. Not too surprisingly, the capitalist economies usually have more inequality than do socialist countries. One study of the Soviet Union found a considerable amount of income inequality there, despite the ideological commitment to equality.[14]

As for the trend in inequality over time, the results are not absolutely

[12] See Morton Paglin, "The Measurement and Trend of Inequality: A Basic Revision," *American Economic Review*, 65, no. 3 (September 1975): 598–609.

[13] For some criticisms of the approach, see the set of articles in *The American Economic Review*, June 1977.

[14] Gur Ofer, "The Distribution of Income of the Urban Population in the Soviet Union," paper presented at the Second World Congress of Soviet and East European Studies, October 1980.

clear. If we look at data like that in Table 11.2 for previous years, there appears to have been very little change since World War II. In 1947, for example, the income share of the bottom three quintiles was within a percentage point of the 1982 figure, while the fourth and fifth quintiles had gained and lost about 1 percentage point, respectively. The apparent stability is puzzling, especially in light of the enormous increase in government expenditures designed to equalize incomes, including both direct cash payments and a series of compensatory education and training programs. How can it be that they have failed to help?

As usual, economists have found much to complain about concerning the data that are available. A major conference on income inequality[15] concluded that because of measurement problems the level of inequality was overstated and reductions in inequality over time were understated. Without trying to do justice to an extensive literature, a few of the major measurement problems and their likely effects can be noted.

Exclusion of Nonmoney Income. As we noted above, the data on income exclude the value of public housing, Medicaid, food stamps, subsidized school lunches, and all other programs that provide goods or services to persons directly rather than providing them with income. In 1981, 20 percent of all families in the United States received benefits from at least one of those four programs. The total market value was estimated at $12.5 billion, none of which is reported as money income in the income distribution statistics. Since the size of these government programs and the benefit levels have increased throughout the postwar period, and since most goes to lower-income families, their omission undoubtedly masks some reduction in inequality, more broadly defined.

Demographic Changes. There are two issues here. First, as a result of the postwar baby boom, the age distribution of families has changed over time. There are now relatively more families concentrated in the earlier, lower-income stages of their careers. Moreover, the large size of the group has reduced their income relative to older workers. There has also been a sharp increase in the number of families headed by a single adult. Both effects would tend to increase reported income inequality.

Exclusion of Taxes. All the income data are measured before taxes. Most studies show that the overall tax system, including the individual and corporate income taxes, sales and property taxes, and payroll taxes, is mildly progressive. This means that the after-tax distribution of income is somewhat more

[15] "Conference on the Trend in Income Inequality in the U.S.," Institute for Research on Poverty, Special Report 11, 1978.

equal than the pretax distribution, although the difference is not that large.[16] But this bias has probably gotten smaller as nonprogressive taxes, such as sales tax and payroll taxes, have increased in importance. Thus, as far as the trend on inequality is concerned, this problem would give the appearance of diminished inequality.

Poverty in the United States

Let's look more closely at the bottom part of the distribution of income—those families and individuals classified by the Census Bureau as living in poverty. In the United States a family is considered to be living in poverty if its cash income (not counting the value of any in-kind transfers it may receive) falls below an officially designated income standard. That standard is not a particularly generous one by U.S. levels, although it certainly is compared to much of the rest of the world. The basis of the standard is the Department of Agriculture's Economy Food Plan, which is its least costly, nutritionally adequate diet. The cost of that diet is adjusted for family size and then multiplied by three on the assumption that food expenses should account for no more than one-third of household expenses. The resulting number is the poverty standard. In 1983 it was about $5060 for a single person and $10,180 for a family of four.

Poverty first became an issue of national concern in the United States in the mid-1960s. At that time, the United States, which regarded itself as an affluent society, discovered the extent of poverty in its midst. In 1965, over 17 percent of all persons and over 20 percent of all children were classified as poor, and for blacks the corresponding figures were 40 percent and 50 percent, respectively. The eradication of poverty became a high national priority. President Johnson declared a "war on poverty" and initiated a large number of federally funded Great Society programs designed to eliminate the causes of poverty and to alleviate its effects. Federal spending for income support programs increased sharply and became the fastest-growing part of the federal budget.[17] In 1981 total expenditures amounted to $295 billion, including $140 billion for Social Security and $76 billion for various welfare programs.

The effectiveness of all these programs is a hotly debated topic, especially in the context of the recent attempt to reduce the growth of the federal budget and to curtail spending for social programs. The percent of people in

[16] One of the best studies of the effects of taxes in the distribution of income is Joseph A. Pechman and Benjamin A. Okner, *Who Bears the Tax Burden*? (Washington, D.C.: The Brookings Institution, 1974).

[17] The category social welfare programs include social insurance programs (Social Security and public employee retirement payments plus unemployment insurance and workers' compensation), welfare programs, health and medical programs, veterans' programs, and spending for education and housing.

poverty fell steadily from 1965 through 1973, when it reached its all-time low of 11.1 percent. Through the rest of the 1970s, the rate fluctuated, mostly in the 11.4 to 11.8 percent range, then rose substantially from 1980 to 1983. The official poverty count in 1983 was 35.3 million people, representing 15.2 percent of the population.[18] The rise between 1980 and 1983 reflects both the prolonged recession and high unemployment rates of that period and the reductions in social welfare expenditures. It is not yet clear whether the increase represents an upward trend.

Table 11.3 presents basic information on *families* in poverty in 1982, the last year for which complete data are available. In all, 7.5 million families, 12.2 percent of all families were poor that year. (The poverty rate for families is lower than the poverty rate for individuals because poor families tend to be larger than average.) As the table shows, the poverty rate is much higher for black and Spanish-origin families than for white families, and it is quite high for female-headed families of any race or ethnicity. The **feminization of poverty** is now a major concern. Well over half of all black and Spanish-origin female-headed families were in poverty in 1982, and for black families, with

TABLE 11.3 The Incidence of Poverty among Families in 1982

FAMILY CHARACTERISTICS	POVERTY RATE (%)
All families	12.2
White families	9.6
Black families	33.0
Spanish origin	27.2
Married couple	7.6
Female-headed family	36.3
White	27.9
Black	56.2
Spanish origin	55.4
Educational attainment of householder	
8 years or less	23.0
9–11 years	20.0
12 years	10.2
College (1 year or more)	4.8

Source: U.S. Bureau of the Census, *Current Population Reports,* Series P-60, No. 140, Tables 14, 18.

[18] Recall that the poverty rate is based on an income definition which excludes the value of noncash benefits. A Census Bureau report that attempted to include these benefits and compute their value by alternative methods found that the official estimate of poverty in 1979 would have been 12 to 42 percent lower. See *Alternative Means for Valuing Selected In-Kind Transfer Benefits and Measuring Their Effect on Poverty*, Bureau of the Census, Technical Report 50, 1982.

a female head under age 25, the figure is over 80 percent. Female-headed families accounted for about 45 percent of the poverty population, even though only 15 percent of all families are headed by women. Finally, as the last set of entries in the table show, poverty status is strongly related to the education level of the household head. Over 20 percent of families headed by persons with less than a high school education were in poverty, compared to less than 5 percent for families with a college-educated head.

Recent research has discovered some very surprising characteristics of the poverty population. It had originally been thought that poverty status was likely to be a permanent condition for persons classified as poor in any single year. Underlying this belief was the idea that poverty was largely the result of a deeply ingrained system of personal values and attitudes which made it difficult for families to change their behavior so as to escape from poverty. According to this idea, called the **culture of poverty thesis**,[19] families in poverty this year would almost certainly be in poverty next year and for much of the rest of their lives as well. Two quite pessimistic scenarios grew out of this. One was the possibility that the poverty population might constitute an **underclass**, a large, well-defined group permanently outside the mainstream of American economic life.[20] The other was the concern that poverty status might be passed on from one generation to the next, forming a cycle of poverty that was extremely difficult to break.

It now appears that this conception is not accurate, at least not for most of the poverty population. This new information comes from the Panel Study of Income Dynamics, a national study that followed a representative sample of families for 10 consecutive years (1969 to 1978) to monitor changes in their economic status. That study has provided detailed information about the poverty population, especially about the dynamics of poverty. Three main findings stand out.[21]

1. *Poverty is much less permanent, but far more pervasive* than had previously been thought. The relative constancy of the aggregate poverty rate during the 1970s did *not* reflect stability in the poverty population. Over the 10 years of the study, more than one-fourth of all persons fell into poverty at least once. In contrast, less than 1 percent were poor all 10 years and only 5.4 percent were poor at least half of the time. Less than two-thirds of the persons who were poor in any single year were also poor the next year and

[19] This phrase comes from Oscar Lewis, an anthropologist, who studied poverty families in Latin America and then in the United States. Among the attitudes and values emphasized by Lewis were a strong orientation toward the present, a sense of resignation and fatalism, and low self-esteem. Lewis's ideas are presented in *La Vida* (New York: Random House, Inc., 1965). For another use of that concept, see Edward A. Banfield, *The Unheavenly City* (Boston: Little, Brown and Company, 1969).

[20] The idea of an underclass has been popularized recently in Ken Auletta, *The Underclass* (New York: Random House, Inc., 1981).

[21] These findings are reported in Greg J. Duncan and others, *Years of Poverty, Years of Plenty* (Ann Arbor: Institute for Social Research, 1984), Chapter 2.

of all persons who were ever poor, almost 40 percent were poor in only a single year. The notion of a large underclass appears to be incorrect.

2. *Persistent poverty is more a matter of demographic circumstances than of labor market deficiencies.* The study characterized persons who were poor in 8 years out of 10 as "persistently poor." In all, 2.6 percent of the population—about one-tenth of persons ever poor—fell into this category. The important finding about this group is that it is predominantly composed of people who probably cannot be expected to have strong labor market ties. About one-third of the persistently poor are elderly, and 65 percent of the nonelderly live in households headed by women. Still others are disabled. Only about one-sixth of the persistently poor live in households headed by able-bodied, nonelderly men.
3. *Family composition changes are the most important and the most common factors affecting changes in poverty status.* Divorce and remarriage were the most common routes by which women and children fell into and climbed out of poverty.

THE FUNCTIONAL DISTRIBUTION OF INCOME

A different way to examine the distribution of income in an economy is to look at the share of national income received by each factor of production, taken as a group. Traditionally, land, labor, and capital were the factors of production treated in this way and the distribution of income among the three factors is called the **functional distribution of income**. These three groups were identified because of their distinct functions as inputs in the production process.

The analysis of the functional distribution of income is an old and famous subject in economics. In the first part of the nineteenth century, it was regarded as *the* major task of economic analysis. (Its importance has fallen somewhat recently, as economists have given more of their attention to the personal distribution of income.) Consider these words from *The Principles of Political Economy and Taxation*, written by David Ricardo, the most famous economist of his time:

> The produce of the earth . . . is divided among three classes of the community, namely, the proprietor of the land, the owner of the stock of capital necessary for its cultivation, and the laborers by whose industry it is cultivated. To determine the laws which regulate this distribution is the principal problem in Political Economy.[22]

The functional distribution of income is easily represented with a labor supply and demand curve, as in Figure 11.1. For expositional ease it is convenient to treat land and capital together as a single fixed factor and analyze

[22] David Ricardo, *The Principles of Political Economy* (London: J. M. Dent and Son, 1965), p. 1.

only the distribution of income between workers, on the one hand, and landowners plus capitalists, on the other. To show the functional distribution of income, we need to identify graphically the total income in the economy and the portions received by the factors of production. It is always true that the total amount of income received by all factors of production is equal to the total value of output produced. This is a basic proposition in macroeconomics and also follows directly from the circular flow of income proposition. Since the total value of output is always the sum of the MRP_L for each worker, the total income in the economy is the area under the demand (= MRP_L) curve up to the equilibrium level of employment.

In Figure 11.1 the total value of output or income is the trapezoid *CBAO*. The share going to workers is the shaded rectangle created by the equilibrium wage and employment level. Finally, the remainder, below the labor demand curve and above the wage line, is the share of national income that is received by the owners of land and capital in the form of land rent, interest, and profits. It is always possible to divide total income up in this way to show the relative shares of labor and the other factors of production.

On what does the functional distribution of income depend? What determines whether labor's share is large or small? Two factors are important. One is, not too surprisingly, the relative positions of the supply and demand curves, since that determines the level of the wage rate. The other is the rate at which the MRP_L falls as more workers are employed. Why should that matter? Remember that the equilibrium wage equals the *MRP* of the last worker. But for all previous workers, the MRP_L exceeds the wage and that difference is the source of the income of the owner of the fixed factor. When

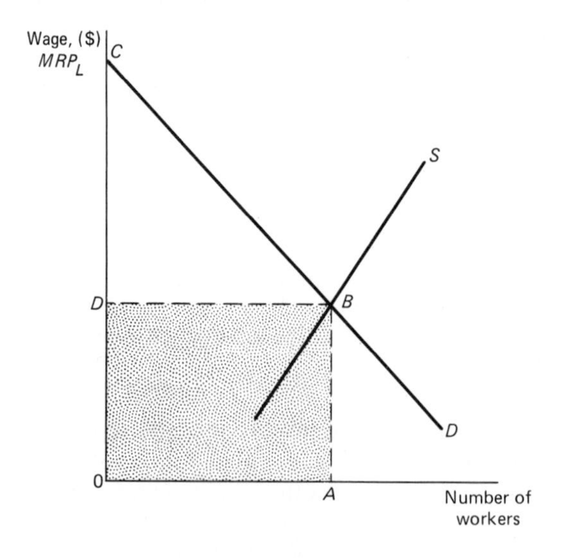

FIGURE 11.1 Functional Distribution of Income

the demand curve is very steep, meaning that the MRP_L of previous workers was much higher, the income share of landowners and capitalists will be larger in relative terms. Graphically, imagine that the demand curve in Figure 11.1 was steeper but intersected the supply curve at the same point. Then the area under the demand curve and above the wage line would be larger. Exactly the opposite holds when the demand curve is flat, so there is not much excess of MRP_L over the wage on previous workers.

Application: Labor Market Discrimination and the Functional Distribution of Income

In Chapter 9 we looked at how discrimination might operate in the labor market and at how it has affected different groups in the United States. Here, we focus on a simpler question: how a strong form of discrimination affects the functional distribution of income. Another way to put that is to ask: Who gains from discrimination? Who loses?

As a specific example of discrimination, consider a stylized model of an economy something like South Africa. South African society operates under an official policy of apartheid, which calls for maximum separation of races. In practice, the laws are quite complex. For simplicity, assume that the labor market effect of the laws is to restrict the employment opportunities of black workers to a designated geographic area (called the "reserves" or tribal homelands) or to a limited number of jobs. Assume also that black and white workers are equally skilled. The result of the apartheid law is to establish one labor market for black workers and a separate one for whites.

The labor market and income distribution effects of this policy are shown in Figure 11.2. The two panels represent the black and white sectors, respectively. First consider what would happen in the absence of discrimination.

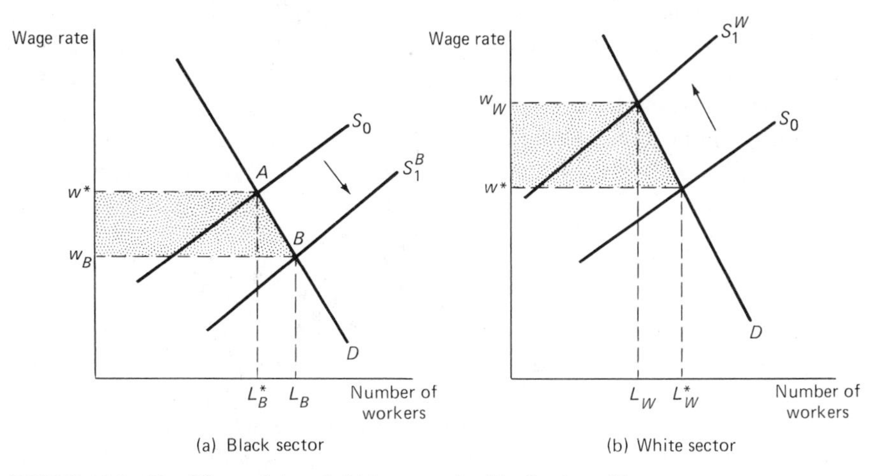

FIGURE 11.2 The Effects of Apartheid Laws on the Distribution of Income

In that situation, with homogeneous workers and no employment restrictions, there would be a single, uniform wage throughout the economy. This is shown as w^*; the labor supply curves (S_0) adjust to guarantee that wages are equal. The area under the demand curves and above the wage line represents the collective income of the capitalists in each sector. Total wage income is the rectangle formed by the equilibrium wage rate and the corresponding amount of employment.

We assume that the apartheid rules are severe enough to require adjustments in labor supply. More labor is crowded into the black sector than would otherwise work there and correspondingly less in the white sector. This is shown by supply curves S_1^B and S_1^W. Wages fall—predictably—in the black sector to W_B and rise in the white sector to W_W.

Note what happens to the income of the capitalists. It rises in the black sector by an amount equal to the shaded area ABW_BW^* and falls by the corresponding shaded area in the white sector. Thus the apartheid restrictions harm not only black workers but also white-sector capitalists, whereas they aid the white workers and white capitalists in the black sector. The important point is that apartheid does not increase the income of all segments of the white population.

SUMMARY

Economic theory provides a series of explanations for the labor market earnings of different individuals. Human capital, rent, market structure, nonpecuniary job characteristics, and discrimination are among the most important ideas. One problem with these many explanations is that there is no easy and accurate way to take account of them in empirical work. The many studies of individual earnings functions relate a person's earnings to his or her personal characteristics. Both years of education and years of work experience stand out as important factors explaining the differences in earnings among individuals. Collectively, the commonly measured traits of individuals explain about one-third of the variation in individual earnings. It is, however, impossible to say exactly how important human capital or rent or even internal labor markets are in determining earnings. The necessary data do not exist.

In the second section of the chapter, we looked at aggregate statistics on family income and on the incidence of poverty. Families in the richest 20 percent of all families had about four times as much income as those in the lowest 20 percent. Overall, the degree of income inequality in the United States is on a par with most industrialized countries. It is important to remember that most measures of income and of income inequality do not take account of goods and services received directly rather than as income. They also do not account for the income inequality associated with being at various stages of one's career.

We also noted that there is still a quite substantial poverty population—15.2 percent of all persons in 1983. Poverty is very strongly associated with family status. Female-headed families have a poverty rate over 36 percent, and for black female-headed families it was 56 percent in 1982. Nevertheless, poverty appears to be more pervasive but less permanent than earlier researchers had hypothesized. Most spells of poverty are brief.

The chapter closed with a brief look at the functional distribution of income, which has the distinction of being one of the oldest topics in labor economics. The impact of discrimination on the functional distribution of income was also noted. The surprising finding there is that not all members of the discriminating class gain.

New Concepts

Personal distribution of income
Functional distribution of income
Earnings function
Multiple regression analysis
Regression coefficients
Human capital earnings function
Feminization of poverty
Culture of poverty thesis
Underclass
Functional distribution of income

APPENDIX: An Introduction to Regression Analysis

Regression analysis is the most commonly used statistical technique to discover the effects of one thing on another. What follows is a nontechnical introduction to the basic ideas of regression analysis.

Suppose that you had information on the education and earnings of a sample of people and you wanted to determine the effects of education on earnings. A person's earnings would be called the **dependent variable** and education is the **independent variable**. One way to do this is to draw a graph of the relationship between education and earnings, using the information from the sample. A typical graph like that, which is called a **scattergram**, is shown in Figure A11.1. It is common practice to place the independent variable (education) on the horizontal axis and the dependent variable (earnings) on the vertical axis. Each point then represents the earnings and education for one person in the sample.

A conventional way to summarize the relationship between earnings and education is by drawing the "best-fitting" straight line through the scatter of points. The dashed line in Figure A11.1 is a line like that and it is called the **regression line**. Formally, "best-fitting" means that the line minimizes the sum of the squared difference between actual earnings and the earnings estimated for each person from the regression line. In the figure, the arrow between point *A* and the regression line shows that difference (unsquared) for one person.

The most important feature of the regression line is its slope. The slope shows the effect, on average, of each additional year of education on earnings—which is what we wanted to know.

A more sophisticated way to do the same thing is to omit the scattergram and instead, express the regression model in algebraic form as follows:

$$Y_i = B_0 + B_1 \text{ (years education)}_i + \varepsilon_i \tag{A11.1}$$

In equation (A11.1), Y_i stands for the earnings of each person, "years education" is the corresponding amount of education, and ε_i, called the **error term**, reflects all other random influences on Y_i. Regression analysis calculates the values of B_0 and B_1 that give the best fit—that is, they explain individual earnings better than do any other values of B_0 and B_1 in the formal sense explained above. These estimates are called **regression coefficients**. Just as in the scattergram, this estimate of B_1 shows the effect of an additional year of education on earnings.

Regression analysis is not limited to the relationship between two variables. In **multiple regression analysis**, the same ideas are applied to the

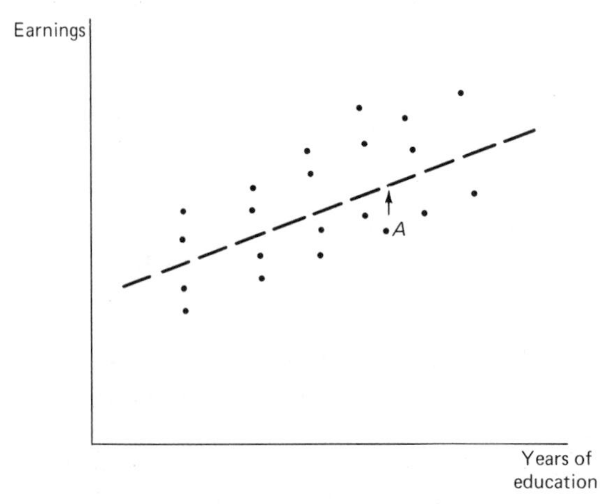

FIGURE A11.1 A Regression Model of the Relationship between Education and Earnings

relationship between a dependent variable and several independent variables. Once more than a single independent variable is used, the scattergram technique becomes useless, because we cannot draw in that many dimensions. The expanded regression model would be written this way:

$$Y_i = B_0 + B_1 \text{ (years education)}_i + B_2X_{2i} + B_3X_{3i} + \ldots + \varepsilon_i \quad \text{(A11.2)}$$

where X_{2i} and X_{3i} are the values of the other independent variables. Multiple regression analysis gives the best estimates of B_0, B_1, B_2, B_3, and so on. Each coefficient gives the independent effect of a change in that variable in the dependent variable, holding the other independent variables constant. For example, if X_2 were years of work experience, B_2 would tell us the value of an additional year of work experience for persons with the same level of education and all other variables.

There is one more useful piece of information that can be derived from a regression analysis. Suppose that we wanted to know not only the separate effect of each independent variable, but also how well, all together, they explained differences in earnings. To see how this idea might be measured, look at Figure A11.1. Suppose that instead of the actual scatter of points shown there, each person with a specified amount of education had exactly the same earnings. The best-fit regression line would then pass through each point and thus would explain each person's earnings perfectly. Clearly, the regression line shown in Figure A11.1 explains the actual scatter of points much less perfectly than that. If the scatter had been wider yet, the fit would have been still worse.

The standard measure of **goodness of fit** is based on the distance of each point from the regression line. It is called the R^2 and it measures the proportion of variance in the dependent variable explained by the independent variables. Its range goes from 0 to 1. It would be 0 if earnings were completely unrelated to education, and it would be 1 if earnings were perfectly explained by education, as in the hypothetical case above when the regression line passed through all the points.

There is actually a great deal of debate over whether the R^2 is a very useful piece of information. Economists typically believe that it is not, whereas sociologists attach greater importance to it. There is no straightforward way to decide whether the R^2 of any particular equation is high or low, and its value has no bearing whatsoever on the estimated values of the regression coefficients. A low R^2 simply means that the independent variables collectively explain only a relatively small portion of the variation in the dependent variable, and that other factors, summarized in the error term of the regression model, are also important.

12

Unemployment

INTRODUCTION

In this chapter and the next, we change our focus to examine a topic we deliberately set aside in Chapter 1—the issue of unemployment. In the past, this change in focus might have been described as a shift from microeconomics to macroeconomics. Indeed, until fairly recently, unemployment was not considered a major topic in labor economics, but was covered instead in macroeconomics courses. The analysis of labor economics took for granted the economic performance of the economy as a whole. Returning the favor, macroeconomists did their analysis on the basis of very simple assumptions about the operation of the labor market.

Today, those traditional distinctions are much less meaningful. Labor markets have become an important topic in macroeconomics; unemployment is a major issue in labor economics. When the unemployment rate averaged about 4 percent, as it did through the 1960s, it could be omitted in reasonably good conscience from a course in labor economics. When the unemployment rate began to edge up to about 6 percent in the early 1970s, to 7 to 8 percent in the late 1970s, and reached a postwar high of 10.8 percent in December 1982, it could not.

At the same time and for similar reasons, macroeconomics underwent a substantial intellectual reorientation, a process often described as a search for the "micro-foundations of macroeconomics." One effect was that the dividing line between microeconomics and macroeconomics became blurred. Another was that unemployment came to be widely regarded as being much more of a microeconomic problem than it had been in the past. Microeconomists invaded the traditional turf of macroeconomists and began to offer explanations for unemployment. These explanations were based on microeconomic analyses of the behavior of firms and individuals regarding wages, employment, and unemployment. Today, the microeconomics of unemployment is well-enough established to constitute a "new view" of macroeconomics, in contrast to the older approach associated with John Maynard Keynes and his followers. Some of the most important research in economics is currently being done in the intersection of labor economics and macroeconomics.

Reporting on a topic that is of enormous national interest, as unemployment certainly is, and which is also in the midst of a major intellectual transformation, is not a simple task. It was much easier 15 to 20 years ago to teach about unemployment. It was probably also much easier to learn about it. Then, economists knew the answers—or thought they did. Today, we have learned that unemployment is an extremely complex and varied phenomenon. It is certainly a mistake, as you will see shortly, to think of unemployment as a single thing, with a single cause, and a single remedy—a description that characterizes the older view of unemployment reasonably well. Instead, we know that unemployment is a composite of many factors.

Different people become unemployed and remain unemployed in different ways, for different reasons, and with different effects. There is no single, easy solution to the problem of unemployment. Certainly, economists are now much less confident of the ability of conventional macroeconomic policy to manage and control unemployment.

In this chapter we look carefully at the issue of unemployment. We begin by presenting a brief historical overview of unemployment in the U.S. economy. After that, we first consider how unemployment is officially measured and then examine a subtle but important issue about the appropriate interpretation of the unemployment rate. We go on to consider the conventional explanations of unemployment. The most important idea here is that there is some unemployment that inevitably exists even when the labor market is in an equilibrium situation. Finally, in the last section, we examine some of the details of the unemployment insurance system and how they might affect the equilibrium unemployment rate. The analysis of the relationship between unemployment and inflation is deferred to Chapter 13.

UNEMPLOYMENT IN THE U.S. ECONOMY

Let's begin by simply describing the historical record of unemployment in the U.S. economy. Then we will move on to measurement, interpretation, and explanation.

Any account of unemployment in the United States must begin with the experience of the Great Depression. The causes of that event are well beyond the scope of this text—it is a course of study all by itself. Here we need only note the grim statistics. In 1929, the year of the stock market crash, the unemployment rate was 3.2 percent. Four years later it was 24.9 percent—nearly 13 million unemployed persons in a labor force of 52 million. The gross national product fell by half between 1929 and 1933, and it did not reach its pre-Depression level until 1939. Unemployment remained well above 10 percent until 1941 and then fell sharply when the United States entered World War II. In 1944, with over 11 million persons in the armed forces, the unemployment rate dropped to a record 1.2 percent.

Figure 12.1 shows the unemployment rate for the U.S. economy over the period 1954 to 1983. There is both a cyclical pattern to the unemployment rates and a time trend. On five occasions since 1954—in 1958, 1961, 1969, 1975, and 1981—the unemployment rate increased sharply, corresponding to a decline in economic activity over the business cycle. These declines, or recessions, were extremely severe and unusually long in 1975 and again in 1981. Starting in the late 1960s, there is a discernible upward trend in the unemployment data. Beginning with the low rate of 3.5 percent in 1969, achieved during the Vietnam war, the unemployment rate has edged upward, even ignoring the three cyclical jumps. More important, in the recovery period

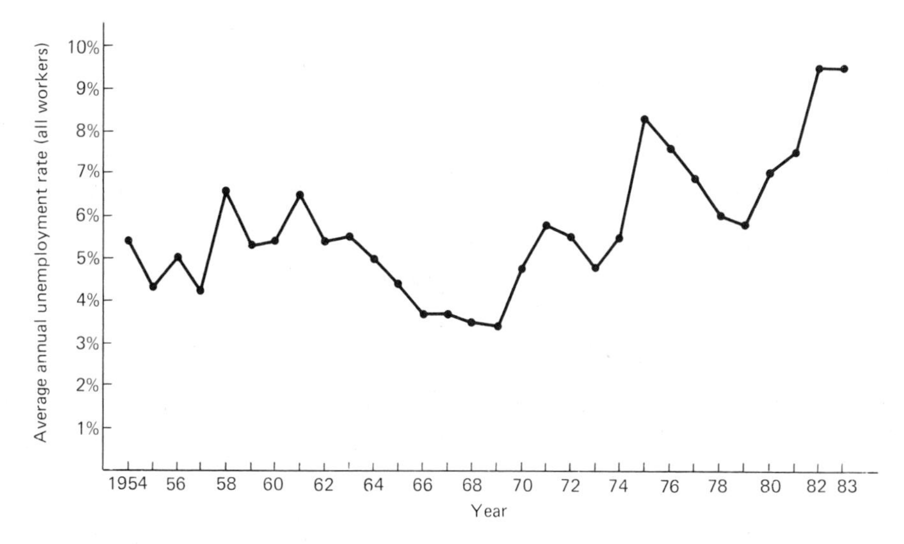

FIGURE 12.1 Unemployment in the United States, 1954–1983

after the first two recessions (the third recovery is still in progress as of the date this was written), the unemployment rate fell, but not back to its previous level. By any standard the unemployment rates of the 1970s and 1980s look conspicuously worse than those of the 1960s.

UNEMPLOYMENT STATISTICS AND WHAT THEY MEAN

Measuring Unemployment

In the United States, the unemployment rate and other labor force statistics are derived from a regular monthly survey of about 65,000 households all across the country. That survey, called the Current Population Survey, provides information on the labor market activity in the week just before the survey of each person age 16 or older. A set of official definitions is then used to classify each person into one of three labor force categories: employed, unemployed, or not in the labor force. It is worth looking briefly at the way those categories are defined, because the official unemployment rate is unavoidably dependent on those definitions.

It is important to emphasize that there is no single, perfectly objective way to measure unemployment. Underlying the definitions currently used by the Bureau of Labor Statistics (BLS) are two basic ideas: that the labor force categories should be market-oriented and that the primary purpose of the unemployment rate should be to assess the state of the economy rather than to measure individual economic hardship.

Here is how the three labor force categories are currently defined. To be considered as *employed*, a person must in the week before the survey either have worked one hour or more for pay or at least 15 hours without pay in a family-operated business. Persons who are temporarily absent from work because of illness, vacation, an industrial dispute, or bad weather are also counted as employed, even if they do not meet the standard criteria. Their absence from work does not reflect on the state of the economy, so they are properly classified as employed. Finally, note what is not considered. Whether people work part-time or full-time does not matter. Also, persons engaged in nonmarket work—caring for a house or family—are not counted as employed, no matter how many hours a week they spend at it. Employment must be market oriented to count in the official statistics.

Unemployment is much more difficult to measure, precisely because it is harder to establish the market orientation. To be counted as *unemployed*, a person must both be without a job in the preceding week and have made a specific effort to find employment within the last four weeks. The latter provision is called the **job search requirement**. It is intended to make the concept of unemployment market oriented and thus limit unemployment to persons who are actively seeking work.[1] Persons without jobs who do not meet the job search requirement are not counted as unemployed, but are, instead, classified as *not in the labor force*. There are, however, two groups of people who are counted as unemployed whether or not they search for work—people on temporary layoff and people waiting to begin a new job within 30 days. Note that it does not matter *why* a person became unemployed. Whether a person quit a job, was laid off, or is looking for a first job, is irrelevant as long as the other criteria are satisfied.

The line between unemployment and not being in the labor force is the fuzziest of all the concepts. The job search requirement is by far the most controversial of the definitions currently in use. On the one hand, some critics argue that the requirement is too weak. They contend that the specific job search actions may often not be very substantial or very effective. People with little serious interest in obtaining a job may qualify as unemployed, they argue, thus inflating the reported rate. On the other hand, others argued that the requirement is too strict, since it fails to count as unemployed some persons who truly do want to work, but who have given up looking for work. These are the so-called **discouraged workers**, persons who might look for work if they thought conditions were better and prospects brighter. Current BLS practice is to count them as not in the labor force rather than as unemployed,

[1] Job search activities include such things as interviewing for a job, registering with an employment office, answering an employment advertisement or placing one, or checking with friends or relatives.

but to publish information on the number of discouraged workers on a quarterly basis.

With these definitions, the basic labor force statistics can be readily calculated. Let E stand for the number of employed persons, U for the number of unemployed persons, and NLF for those classified as not in the labor force. Together, $E + U$ is equal to the labor force (L), and $E + U + NFL$ is the noninstitutional population (P). The **unemployment rate** (UR) is $UR = U/(E + U)$, that is, the proportion of the labor force that is unemployed. The **labor force participation rate**, which we encountered in Chapter 5, is simply $(E + U)/P$. A final measure is the **employment rate** measured as E/P.

The breakdown of the civilian noninstitutional population in 1983 into the various categories is shown in Figure 12.2.[2] All the figures are averages for the entire year. The civilian noninstitutional population age 16 or older included 174.2 million persons—100.8 million were employed, 10.7 million were unemployed, and 62.6 million were classified as not in the labor force. The overall civilian unemployment rate was, therefore, 9.6 percent [10.7/(100.8 + 10.7)], up sharply from 7.6 percent in 1981. You should be able to confirm that the civilian LFPR was 64 percent and the employment rate about 58 percent.

Figure 12.2 also shows the four paths into unemployment. In 1983, nearly 60 percent (6.3 million) of all unemployed persons had lost their last job, while another 8 percent quit theirs. (In 1981, when the economy was better, quits were up a bit and job losers down, a common finding.) The remaining third came from out of the labor force—2.4 million as persons reentering the labor force and about half that number seeking their first job. On the other side of the figure, you can see that about 90 percent of the people not in the labor force did not want a job, but 6.6 million of them said they did, even though they were not actively searching for work. Of that group, 1.6 million were ultimately classified as discouraged workers, people who were no longer looking for work because they thought they could not get a job. The rest were in school, caring for a home and family, were having health problems, or had other miscellaneous reasons. Not too surprisingly, the number of discouraged workers increases as the unemployment rate rises; between 1981 and 1983, for example, the number rose by about half a million.

As is usually the case, there was a great deal of variation in the unemployment rates for different groups in the economy. That information is summarized in Table 12.1. The unemployment rate was higher for blacks and Hispanics than for whites—over twice as high for blacks than whites, with the rate for Hispanics in the middle. Although men historically have had lower unemployment rates than women, this was not the case in 1983. This

[2] Two excellent sources of data on employment and unemployment are the *Monthly Labor Review* and *Employment and Earnings*, both published monthly by the BLS.

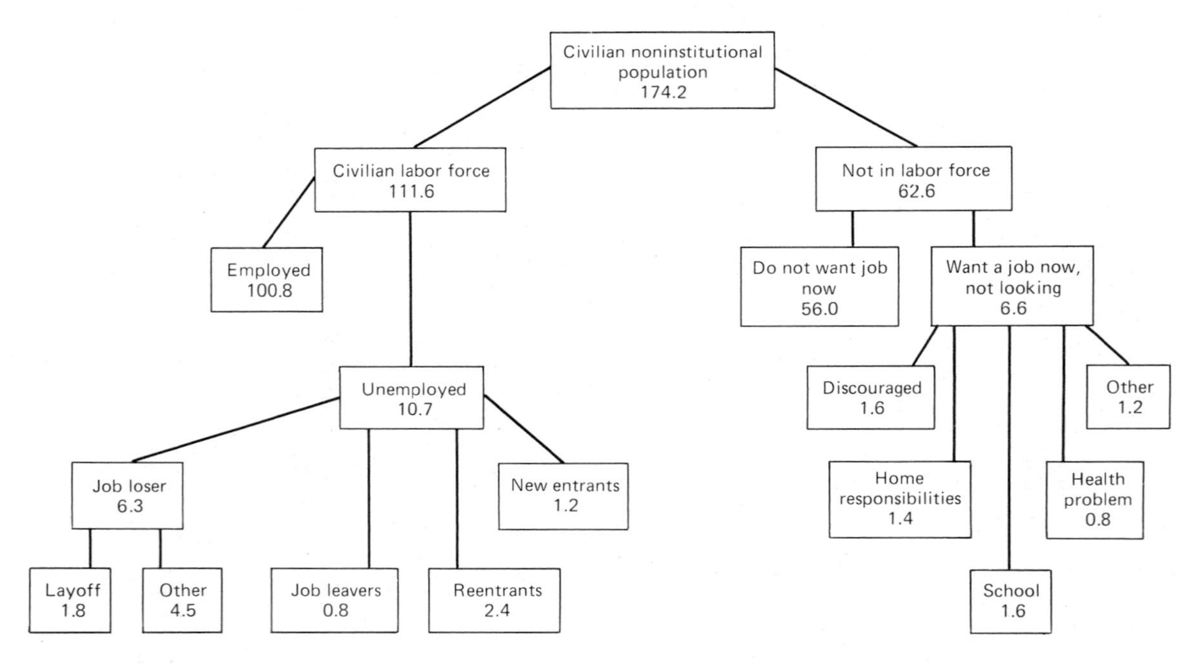

FIGURE 12.2 Employment Status of the Civilian Noninstitutional Population in 1983 (All Figures in Millions)

TABLE 12.1 Selected Unemployment Rates (%), 1983

GROUP	RATE
All	9.6
Men	9.9
Women	9.2
White	8.4
Men, age 20+	7.9
Women, age 20+	6.9
Men, 16–19	20.2
Women, 16–19	18.3
Black	19.5
Men, age 20+	18.1
Women, age 20+	16.5
Men, 16–19	48.8
Women, 16–19	48.2
Hispanic	13.8

reversal actually reflected the degree of occupational segregation by sex in the U.S. economy. The industries with the highest unemployment rates in 1983 were among the ones that are still predominantly male—automobiles, steel, construction, and trucking. Finally, unemployment rates were much higher for teenagers than for adult workers. For black teenagers, the unemployment rate in 1983 reached 48 percent, an all-time high.

The numbers in Table 12.1 illustrate an important point. There is no such thing as a single unemployment rate in the economy. Rather, the aggregate unemployment rate is best regarded as a weighted average of the unemployment rates of the different groups, where each group is weighted by its share of the labor force. The dispersion of unemployment rates is itself meaningful. It is the first clue that the unemployment rate may reflect something other than just the state of the economy.

A Closer Look at Teenage Unemployment

The very high rates of unemployment among teenagers shown in Table 12.1 have served to focus a great deal of attention on their labor market problems. Taking a closer look at the problem suggests how much complexity and diversity lies behind a single unemployment rate.[3]

[3] An excellent source of information on teenage labor market problems is Richard B. Freeman and David A. Wise, eds., *The Youth Labor Market Problem: Its Nature, Causes, and Consequences* (Chicago: The University of Chicago Press, 1982).

A bit of historical perspective is useful here to identify the nature of the current problem. First, teenage unemployment rates have always been well above the rates for adults. From 1964 to 1974, teen unemployment rates were, on average, nearly five times higher than the rates for adults, aged 25 and older. Since then, the teen rate has risen, but it is actually a much smaller multiple of the adult rate now. Since 1980, youth unemployment has been about $3\frac{1}{2}$ times the adult rate. So what we are seeing in the 1980s are teenage unemployment rates that are high in absolute terms but actually lower in relative terms.

Second, the most conspicuous feature of teenage unemployment is the enormous race differential—well over two to one. The race disparity is actually larger since the late 1960s than it was prior to then. Since we generally regard the more recent period as one in which labor market discrimination eased and employment opportunities improved, the evidence of deterioration is both puzzling and disturbing.

Actually, the race differential in *employment* is even larger than the unemployment rates suggest. There is also a very substantial difference in teenage labor force participation rates by race. Those rates had been virtually identical in the mid-1950s, but since then the rate for black teens has declined steadily to about 37 percent in 1983; the corresponding rate for whites was about 57 percent. The combined result of the lower labor force participation rate and higher unemployment rate for black teenagers is that the fraction of black teenagers who were employed in 1983 was about 20 percent. For white teenagers, the employment rate was 45 percent.

In spite of these rather bleak figures, some economists believe that the problem of teenage unemployment is often exaggerated. For one thing, many unemployed teenagers are in school, an activity that is usually regarded as worthwhile. In many cases, they are looking for no more than part-time work. Although the unemployment of teenagers still in school is not unimportant, it is probably reasonable to regard it as less serious than the unemployment of adults seeking full-time work. The number of teenagers who are unemployed and not enrolled in school is surprisingly small. In 1979, which was admittedly a year of relatively low unemployment, well under 5 percent of all teenagers fell into that category. Even for black teenagers whose official unemployment rate was 38 percent that year, less than 7 percent were unemployed and not enrolled in school. The notion that unemployment is pure idleness is probably inappropriate for the teenage population as a whole.

It also appears that the high teenage unemployment rates are caused in large part by a relatively small group. A study of teenage unemployment in 1976 (when the aggregate unemployment rate was 7.7 percent and the teenage rate was 19 percent) found that among teenagers not enrolled in school, over half of all weeks of unemployment was caused by less than 10 percent of them who were unemployed for six months or more. Thus teenage unemployment is not a widespread problem. It is a severe problem for a relatively small group who are, the study concluded, predominantly black high school dropouts living in poverty areas.

There is one more finding which is, at least, not negative. One concern about teenage unemployment is that it leads to poorer job prospects in the future—that it has a "scarring effect." Although this line of research is still continuing, the consensus thus far is that it does not have a negative effect. This does not, however, mean that teenagers who experience unemployment do just as well in later years as do teenagers who are never unemployed. Some of the traits associated with a higher probability of unemployment—factors such as low education, low family income, and race—also affect later success in the labor market. What the research does suggest is that, in and of itself, the experience of unemployment has no appreciable negative effect.

It would, nevertheless, be a mistake to treat teenage labor market problems too lightly. Although the causation is not well understood, nonemployment does appear to be correlated with criminal and gang activity, drug use, and youth suicide. Labor market ties of teenagers not in school are often very weak. Among black youths not in school, only about 60 percent were classified as in the labor force in 1979 and only 40 percent were employed. The loose connection to the labor market of out-of-school teenagers is a matter of much current concern.

Interpreting the Unemployment Rate: The Incidence and Duration of Unemployment

Suppose that the unemployment rate were a steady 8 percent each month for a year. If you think about it, there are many different ways in which that steady 8 percent rate could be achieved. One way is for the same people to remain unemployed for the entire year. In that case, the **incidence of unemployment**—that is, the proportion of the labor force that experiences any unemployment—would be low. The **duration of unemployment**—the average length of time a spell of unemployment lasted—would, however, be quite long. A very different way to have that constant 8 percent unemployment rate is if a completely different group of people were unemployed each month. In this situation, the duration of unemployment would be short (exactly one month), but its incidence would be very high—just the opposite of the first case. A whole series of intermediate cases are, of course, also possible.

As the two examples suggest, any unemployment rate which is measured over an extended time period such as a year is consistent with very different combinations of incidence and duration. As far as any given unemployment rate is concerned, the two are always inversely related to each other. This is not true, though, when the unemployment rate changes from one time period to the next. Indeed, if the unemployment rate rises, it must be true that either incidence is higher or duration is longer or both.

Recognizing the role of incidence and duration makes interpretation of the unemployment rate more precarious. The same rate—8 percent in the example above—can reflect two entirely different underlying situations. Where duration is long and incidence is low, as in the first example, unemployment is primarily a matter of a small group of hard-core unemployed persons. The labor market is completely static—no one ever changes his or her employment status. In the other version, the labor market is characterized by steady movements or flows from one employment status to another. Employed persons become unemployed and unemployed persons become employed. Unemployment might seem a bit less of a problem in the sense that virtually everybody gets it, but everybody gets out of it quickly enough. Unemployment here is something like catching a cold—many of us get it, but the pain and inconvenience are temporary.

Which of these two unemployment scenarios best characterizes the U.S. economy? One study[4] examined unemployment in 1979 and found that in that year, when the average unemployment rate was 5.8% (approximately 6 million unemployed persons per month), there were a total of 37 million distinct spells of unemployment. Nearly 57% of these spells lasted 5 weeks or less while, at the other extreme, only 6% lasted 6 months or more. The average duration of a completed spell of unemployment in 1979 was just about 2 months. In years when the average unemployment rate is higher, duration tends to rise, but the same general pattern holds.[5] Most spells of unemployment in the United States economy are relatively short.

It might seem, then, that the evidence favors the second version, since the duration of unemployment is relatively short and its incidence is relatively high. Indeed, that interpretation of these facts is common. Martin Feldstein, a well-known economist who served as chairman of the Council of Economic Advisors under President Reagan from 1982 to 1984, argued on the basis of findings like these that there was "an active labor market in which almost everyone who is out of work can find his usual job in a relatively short time.[6] This emphasis on unemployment as a frequent but short-lived event in the lives of many people is an important part of the "new" view of unemployment.

There is clearly a great deal of truth to this interpretation. The older view of unemployment, which emphasized unemployment as a long-term problem for a small group of people, misses the regular movements in the labor market—the flow of people from one employment status to another. Nevertheless, this new view has some weaknesses. First, spells of unemployment can be ended by a period out of the labor force as well as employment.

[4] The figures discussed here are from Norm Bowers, "Probing the Issues of Unemployment Duration," *Monthly Labor Review*, 103, no. 7 (July 1980), 23–32.

[5] G. A. Akerloff and B. G. M. Main, "Unemployment Spells and Unemployment Experience," *American Economic Review*, 70, no. 5 (December 1980), Table 2, p. 388.

[6] Martin Feldstein, *Lowering the Permanent Rate of Unemployment* (Washington, D.C.: Joint Economic Committee, U.S. Congress, 1973), p. 11.

A single person might well account for several short spells of unemployment by failing to meet the job search requirement in the middle of a longer spell of nonemployment. There is some evidence to support that idea. In a typical year, about a third of all persons with some unemployment are unemployed more than once. Sometimes this is due to the characteristics of the industry in which a person works; for instance, construction workers are much more likely to have more than one period of unemployment. But in many other cases, movements between being unemployed and being not in the labor force may help account for both the large number of spells and the short duration of many of them.[7]

Second, and closely related to this point, the average duration of a *spell* of unemployment typically understates the average amount of unemployment experienced by *persons* who are unemployed in a year. Akerloff and Main showed that this was true both for those persons who were unemployed only once in a year and for those with multiple spells of unemployment.[8] If you are wondering how everyone who is unemployed can have more unemployment than the average length of a spell of unemployment, here is why it is possible. Akerloff and Main found that the average duration of unemployment was shorter for those persons who were unemployed two or more times than for persons unemployed only once. As a result, both groups suffered more unemployment than is indicated by duration statistics—the "single-spell" persons because the duration of their spell of unemployment was long and the "multiple-spell" persons because they have multiple spells. In 1977, for example, the average duration of a spell of unemployment was 9.5 weeks; for persons with one spell, though, the average duration was 13.6 weeks, and for persons with two or more spells, it was about 18 weeks.[9] Akerloff and Main concluded that the burden of unemployment is greater than is indicated by conventional duration statistics.

Moreover, to complicate things further, consider the following seemingly self-contradictory fact. Although most spells of unemployment over a year are relatively short, most people who are classified as unemployed in a specific month will remain unemployed for a relatively long time. The explanation for this apparent anomaly is straightforward if you think about it carefully. The longer a person's total period of unemployment, the more likely it is that he or she will be unemployed in any given month. As a result, the population of currently unemployed persons is always disproportionately composed of those persons whose unemployment is of relatively long dura-

[7] This argument has been made by Kim Clark and Lawrence Summers, "Labor Market Dynamics and Unemployment: A Reconsideration," *Brookings Papers on Economic Activity*, no. 1 (1979); pp. 13–72.

[8] See Akerloff and Main, "Unemployment Spells and Unemployment Experience," pp. 885–93.

[9] Akerloff and Main, Table 2, p. 388.

tion.[10] Akerloff and Main found that for the period 1948 to 1978, the average duration of unemployment for currently unemployed persons ranged from 20 to 30 weeks—about three times the average duration of all spells of unemployment in a year.[11]

These ideas about duration and incidence add several layers of complexity to any attempt to understand and explain unemployment. It is possible for (1) most spells of unemployment to be short, (2) most persons unemployed in a given month to be in the midst of a long spell of unemployment, and (3) most unemployed persons to be unemployed longer than the average duration of a spell of unemployment.

TYPES OF UNEMPLOYMENT

It has long been standard practice among economists to identify four general types of unemployment: frictional, structural, seasonal, and cyclical. The first three belong together in that they are not fundamentally due to the macroeconomic problem of inadequate aggregate demand. Indeed, it is hard to imagine a functioning labor market in a complex, dynamic economy in which there would not be some unemployment from these three sources—although the amount is by no means fixed. Cyclical unemployment, on the other hand, was the focus of Keynes's *General Theory of Employment, Interest and Money,* and it is neither necessary nor desirable. It has been one of the major subjects of macroeconomics ever since.

Frictional Unemployment

Even when the economy is growing rapidly, the normal flows of people from one job to another, from one city to another, and from school or home to work will cause some unemployment. The process of matching workers and jobs inevitably takes time, even if job vacancies and unemployed workers are in rough balance in number, in skills, and in location. That searching time is what is called **frictional unemployment.**

Consider yourselves, for example, at the time you graduate from college. Some of you may be fortunate enough to arrange suitable employment prior

[10] Exactly the same kind of relationship exists in the length of hospital stays. Measured over a year's time, most spells in the hospital are of short duration and the average duration of a spell is relatively low. But a survey of all patients in a hospital on a particular day would show that a large proportion were in the midst of an extended stay and that the average duration for that group is much higher.

[11] G. A. Akerloff and B. G. M. Main, "An Experience-Weighted Measure of Employment and Unemployment Durations," *American Economic Review*, 71, no. 5 (December 1981), 1003–1011.

to graduation. In that case, you will move from out of the labor force to employment without any intervening period of frictional unemployment. But, realistically, many of you will go through a period—a short one, we hope—of looking for work, of learning what you want, of trying to see that your interests and abilities are well matched to your employment. During that time you would be officially classified as unemployed. Unless that period stretches out too long, it is probably not a matter of great concern.

The same kind of searching occurs on the other side of the labor market as well. Job vacancies are not filled at once in part because firms are looking for the "right person." They do not necessarily hire the first person who applies for a vacancy anymore than a person necessarily accepts the first available position.

The fundamental cause of frictional unemployment is that workers and jobs are heterogeneous, that information is imperfect (or costly to acquire, which amounts to the same thing), and that neither firms nor workers are instantaneously mobile. If all firms and workers were perfectly omniscient and mobile, there would be no purpose in searching for work, since everything would already be known. The lack of information and lack of mobility are the frictions that cause this type of unemployment.

The existence of frictional unemployment is perfectly consistent with equilibrium in the labor market. We regularly say that at the equilibrium wage, labor supply and labor demand just balance, which, taken literally, suggests that there will be no unemployment at all. That, of course, is untrue, although it is a useful assumption for the microeconomic analysis of wages. Rather, it is more accurate to say that at the equilibrium wage, it is *arithmetically possible*, but *economically impossible* to have zero unemployment, especially in a decentralized market economy. Even when the labor market is in equilibrium in the sense that the labor supply and labor demand curves do not require any wage adjustment, there will always be some job vacancies and some unemployment of the sort described above. The corresponding unemployment rate is now often called the **natural unemployment rate** or the **full-employment unemployment rate**.

The idea of a natural unemployment rate is extremely important, but it needs to be understood and used carefully. The natural unemployment rate is not "natural" in the sense that it is inevitable or unchangeable. Nor is it optimal in any economic sense or even necessarily desirable. It is not hard to image circumstances in which the natural rate could be too high or even too low. Rather, the word "natural" is used to suggest a link to equilibrium in the labor market and to the rational economic behavior of firms and individuals given the actual characteristics of the economy.

Milton Friedman, who coined the phrase, suggested that the natural rate would depend on "the actual characteristics of the labor and commodity markets, including market imperfections, stochastic variability in demands and supplies, the cost of gathering information about job vacancies and labor availabilities, the costs of mobility, and so on."[12] Thus the natural unemployment rate could be altered by changing any of those things. But given those characteristics, the resulting equilibrium unemployment rate is natural in the same way that a specific supply and demand curve lead "naturally" to an equilibrium price. The natural rate reflects the self-interested behavior of firms and individuals, operating under the actual constraints and characteristics of the economy. Later in this chapter we look closely at the way in which the unemployment insurance system affects the behavior of individuals and firms and thus potentially influences the natural unemployment rate.

In recent years, some economists have formalized the idea of frictional unemployment under the name of **search theory**. One of the early, important contributions of this work was the idea that searching for work and being unemployed was a rational economic activity with costs and benefits that could be identified and analyzed. Although a full exposition of the ideas of search theory would take us too far afield, it is worth looking briefly at the basic approach.

Why do people search for a job rather than always accept the first available job? Common sense suggests that rational persons will continue to search only if they believe that the benefits of continued search outweigh the costs. Similarly, they stop searching and accept an offer of employment when that is no longer true. The benefits of continued search are straightforward. People continue to look for work because they expect to find a better job, one with higher pay and other more desirable characteristics. The economic benefit of search is the higher pay, added up over the expected tenure of a job, all discounted to present value. An inevitable complication exists because people never know with certainty what will be available to them if they continue to search. Rather, they must form some rough estimates and then make decisions on the basis. Thus the benefits of search are really the expected benefits. As for the costs, they include the income forgone by continuing to search for work—that is, the forgone income on the best job not accepted.

There is an extensive—and still growing—literature on how people form estimates of likely wage offers and how they develop optimal search strategies. For our purposes here, we can ignore those developments and focus instead on the broad implications of this approach. First, it subtly changes the conception of frictional unemployment. Frictional unemployment is now understood not just as a problem of finding a job, but rather of selecting the right job. It may well be optimal not to accept the first available job or even the second.

Second, it suggests how the natural rate of unemployment could be too high or too low. Suppose that some kind of extreme penalty were imposed

[12] Milton Friedman, "The Role of Monetary Policy," *American Economic Review*, 58, no. 1 (March 1968), p. 8.

on individuals who remained unemployed for more than, say, two weeks, no matter why they became unemployed in the first place. No doubt that could reduce the unemployment rate by drastically raising the cost of continued job search. But it might well lead to a very poor allocation of labor, as workers scurried to take any available job. That resulting inefficiency is the sense in which the natural rate could be too low.

Finally, this approach shows clearly that anything that affects the costs or benefits of search may affect search time and thus affect the unemployment rate. An obvious and much studied example is the provision of unemployment compensation to unemployed workers, which reduces the costs of search. The accuracy of labor market information held by individuals may also be a factor. Where expectations of likely benefits are overly optimistic, the resulting period of job search unemployment will be inappropriately extended. It is possible that this contributes to the high unemployment rates of teenagers and also of entrants and reentrants to the labor market, since those groups might well have less accurate labor market information.

Structural Unemployment

In any real-world economy, there will be regular demand shifts in both product and labor markets. New products appear, reducing the demand for substitute goods. New technologies develop, changing labor demands directly. Changing patterns of foreign trade will also contribute to the demand shifts. The net result is that employment will grow in some industries and decline in others. Labor must be reallocated from industry to industry and from place to place.

Most of the unemployment that is caused by the process of labor market adjustment falls into the frictional unemployment category. But when the persons unemployed in the declining sector are not suited to the jobs available in the expanding one, **structural unemployment** exists. The most conspicuous example is a mismatch of skills, in which the available employment requires skills that the unemployed workers lack. The recent loss of employment in the "smokestack" industries is a good example, since very few new job opportunities require the skills those workers possess.[13] Structural unemployment can also exist if there is a geographic imbalance between available jobs and unemployed workers.

It is common to think of structural unemployment as being of longer duration than frictional unemployment. It is hard to imagine frictional unemployment regularly lasting for six months or more. Unemployment that lasts that long probably reflects structural unemployment, although there are other possibilities. It is also common to think of structural unemployment as

[13] This problem is compounded by the fact that most available jobs pay considerably less than the wage these workers had been receiving.

being concentrated among persons with few labor market skills or living in economically unattractive areas where few job opportunities exist.[14]

This category of unemployment is not quite as straightforward as it may seem. It is reasonable enough that workers laid off in, say, heavy manufacturing, may not successfully find jobs as computer programmers. But why are they unable to find employment in jobs that do require the kind of skill and training they have? One possible explanation is that the wage in the labor market for workers of that skill level is for some reason stuck above the equilibrium wage. Minimum wage legislation, a union contract, or just the often-noted downward rigidity of wages could all have that effect.

Sometimes, the term "structural unemployment" is now used to refer to people who are unemployed due to the structure of the labor market. Looked at in this view, structural unemployment also fits into the category of natural unemployment as described by Friedman.

Seasonal Unemployment

Seasonal unemployment is the least important of the normal types of unemployment. Some kinds of production tend to be organized on a seasonal basis with high labor demand at one time during the year and low demand at others. Agricultural employment is a good example. Other examples include construction work (employment falls during bad weather) and automobile manufacturing (plants often close down entirely for retooling for model changes).

In some instances, seasonal unemployment cannot easily be reduced, because the underlying production process requires large variations in output and employment. In this case, workers may come to expect some unemployment. If so, the theory of compensating wage differentials predicts that workers would be compensated for bearing the risk of unemployment. The high wages of construction workers are often interpreted in this light. Sometimes, however, firms have considerable discretion about their employment and unemployment decisions. In those situations, a firm's decision about how to organize production over the course of a year may be influenced by, for instance, the characteristics of the unemployment insurance system. We look at this possibility in detail in the next section. The point for now is that it is not correct to think of the amount of seasonal unemployment as a fixed feature of an economy.

Cyclical Unemployment

The last type of unemployment is **cyclical** or **demand-deficient unemployment**. A full exposition of these ideas is beyond the scope of this book. As we noted earlier, explaining cyclical fluctuations in output and employment is one of the major topics in macroeconomics.

[14] Appalachia was often used as the standard example of this in the past. The rash of steel mill closings in the Steubenville–Youngstown area makes that a current example.

The basic idea, first advanced by Keynes, is that the economy is subject to large, unexpected shifts in the level of aggregate demand and that those shifts ultimately affect both employment, unemployment, and output. Aggregate demand, as defined by Keynes, consisted of the total planned spending of three broad sectors of the economy: the consumption spending of households, the investment spending (including inventory adjustments) of firms, and the spending of the government sector. Keynes believed that the level of investment spending was especially unstable. Because investment was inherently future oriented—it involved incurring costs now in the anticipation of *future* profits—it was, he argued, highly dependent on psychological factors. Investors were subject to bursts of enthusiasm and bouts of pessimism, with no clear basis in objective economic facts; in a famous phrase, Keynes referred to the "animal spirits" of investors as an important factor in investment decisions.

In any event, the distinguishing feature of the Keynesian analysis is not so much the instability of demand as the way in which the economy responds to that instability. To appreciate the Keynesian perspective, it is useful to consider first the view of the classical economists who preceded Keynes and against whom he was reacting. Figure 12.3 presents a highly simplified model of the economy, with the product market shown in panel (a) and the labor market in panel (b). (*Note:* In macroeconomics, it is conventional to assume that labor is homogeneous, so there is only a single wage rate to consider.) In panel (a), the curves labeled *AD* and *AS* are the aggregate demand and aggregate supply curves of output for the economy as a whole. Note that the position of the *AS* curve depends on the wage rate, since the wage, operating through the marginal cost curve, determines how much output it is profitable for a firm to produce at each price. (See the discussion of the output effect in Chapter 3 for more on this.) If the wages were higher and everything else

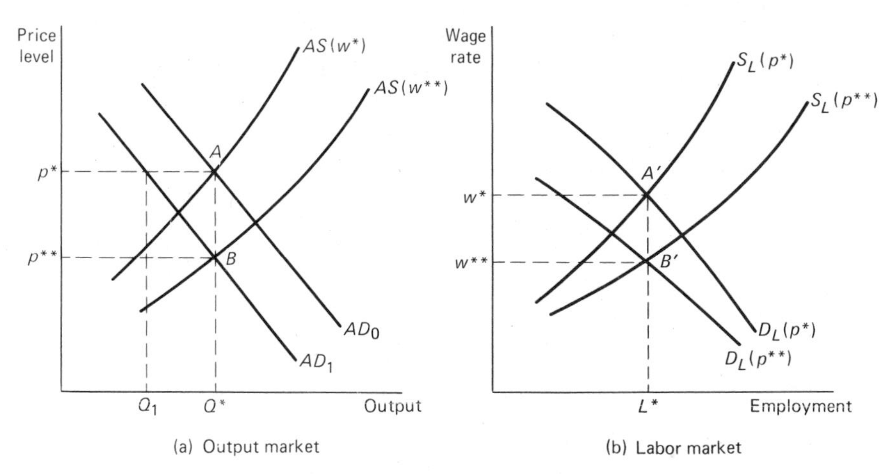

FIGURE 12.3 The Output and Employment Effects of a Decrease in Aggregate Demand—The Classical Analysis

were the same, the curve would shift in; if it were lower, the supply curve would shift out. With a wage of w^*, the relevant supply curve is $AS(w^*)$. If AD_0 is the aggregate demand curve, the product market is in equilibrium at price p^* and the equilibrium output of the economy is Q^*

The same situation, now represented in terms of the labor market, appears in panel (b). The wage measure on the vertical axis is the money wage rate, w. Both the labor demand curve and the labor supply curve are functions of the price level. A lower price level would shift the labor demand curve downward, because MRP would be lower. A lower price level would also shift the labor supply curve out, an effect which is less obvious. A lower price level, holding the wage constant, is equivalent to a higher wage, holding the price level constant.[15] Either way, it is now possible to obtain more goods for each hour worked. When the labor supply curve is upward-sloping, as it is in Figure 12.3, either change would increase desired labor supply. In the case of a change in the price level, this effect is represented graphically as a shift in the labor supply curve. A lower price level shifts the supply curve out: at each money wage rate, workers now desire to supply more hours of labor. A higher price level would shift the curve in.

Given a price, p^*, the relevant labor supply curve is $S_L(p^*)$. The equilibrium wage is w^* and the amount of employment is L^*, which represents full employment in the economy. (There is, of course, an associated rate of unemployment—the natural unemployment rate—reflecting the other three sources of unemployment.) Point A' in panel (b) corresponds exactly to point A in panel (a). In fact, given the amount of capital in the economy and the underlying technology of production, the equilibrium output, Q^*, can just be produced with the full-employment level of employment, L^*.

Together, the two diagrams give a w,p pair that results in simultaneous equilibrium in both the product market and the labor market. What matters for labor market equilibrium is the **real wage**, w/p, rather than the specific values of w and p. Once either the wage or the price is set, there is only a single possible value for the other, consistent with equilibrium in the labor market. Changes in the price level do *not* change the equilibrium value of the real wage.

Once that idea is recognized, the effect of macroeconomic fluctuations on the equilibrium level of employment and output can be readily shown. Suppose that there is a fall in aggregate demand for any reason whatsoever; this is represented in panel (a) by curve AD_1. According to the classical economists, the decline in aggregate demand would result in excess supply equal to $Q^* - Q_1$ in the product market at the initial price level, p^*. The price level would, therefore, fall. Since there is only a single real wage consistent with labor market equilibrium, the money wage must fall as well. In

[15] Economists refer to this as the absence of "money illusion."

practice, this occurs because the lower price level reduces labor demand and increases labor supply exactly as explained above. The fall in the wage has the further effect of causing the aggregate supply curve to shift outward.

In the new equilibrium, the price level falls to p^{**} and the wage rate to w^{**}. The new aggregate supply curve is $AS(w^{**})$ and the corresponding labor demand and labor supply curves are $D_L(p^{**})$ and $S_L(p^{**})$. The new equilibriums in the product and labor market are represented by points B and B', respectively.

Notice what happens to the variables of interest. Output and employment are unchanged, as is the real wage, which is now equal to w^{**}/p^{**}. Put differently—and more dramatically—the decline in aggregate demand does not cause a decline in equilibrium employment or an increase in unemployment. All the adjustments are in prices, none in quantities. Implicitly, the classical economists assumed that the economy moved relatively quickly from one equilibrium to another, so there was no need to inquire into what was occurring in the interim—when there was disequilibrium in at least one market.

Keynes's analysis was based on a different set of assumptions. Where the classical economists had assumed that prices and wages were both perfectly flexible, even in a downward direction, Keynes argued that wages tended to be relatively inflexible when downward adjustments were required for equilibrium. He claimed that workers were concerned about their money wages rather than their real wages. No matter what happened to prices, they resisted a wage cut, but increases in the price level had no impact on labor supply. "Whether logical or illogical," he wrote, "experience shows that this is how a laborer in fact behaves."[16]

Keynes's version of the effect of a fall in aggregate demand is shown in Figure 12.4. Again, the initial equilibrium is represented by points A and A' with a real wage of w^*/p^*, employment of L^*, and output of Q^*. The fall in aggregate demand is shown as the shift from AD_0 to AD_1. There are two important differences, though, between this version and the classical one. First, note that the labor supply curve in panel (b) is *not* treated as a function of the price level, in keeping with Keynes's claim about the unimportance to workers of real wages. Second, the diagram shows the case of complete wage rigidity, even in the face of a decline in labor demand.

With inflexibility in wages, the burden of adjustment to the decline in aggregate demand is now reflected in the quantities of output and employment

[16] John Maynard Keynes, *The General Theory of Employment, Interest and Money* (New York: Harcourt, Brace & World, 1964), p. 9. He attributed this downward wage inflexibility to the concern of workers for preserving their real wage relative to other workers. Changes in the price level, which affected the real wage of all workers, would leave the real wages of different workers in the same relation to one another. In contrast, changes in money wages would typically occur in piecemeal fashions, one industry at a time, for example. Workers in one industry who agreed to a wage cut could not be sure that others would also do so. Thus changes in money wages had the potential to disturb the distribution of relative real wages and, Keynes's view, that was why the money wage was inflexible.

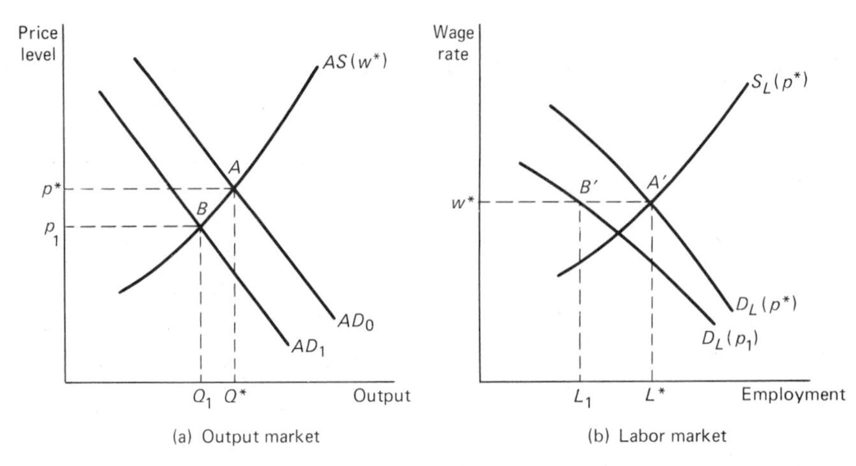

FIGURE 12.4 The Output and Employment Effects of a Decrease in Aggregate Demand—The Keynesian Analysis

in the economy. Equilibrium in the product market occurs at B, but the labor market is in disequilibrium at the corresponding point B'. With nominal wages stuck at w^*, the real wage is now too high for a full-employment equilibrium. The result is a decline in employment from L^* to L_1 and a decline in output to Q_1. There is also an increase in unemployment equal to $L^* - L_1$. Keynes termed this kind of unemployment "involuntary unemployment" in the sense that it represented workers who were willing to work at the prevailing real wage. Clearly, the impact of the decline in aggregate demand is quite different than it is in the classical case.

Figure 12.4 represents the extreme case of completely inflexible wages. A less stringent assumption which also leads to cyclical swings in employment, unemployment, and output is that wages adjust slowly to a decline in demand. In this case, the major difference between the Keynesian and classical models concerns how quickly the economy moves from one equilibrium to the next. Keynesian economists could concede the existence of an eventual equilibrium, but argue that the new equilibrium was not reached quickly enough to be useful for economic policy. In the interim—which might be very long—unemployment would exist. As Keynes commented in a different context, "in the long run, we are all dead."[17]

The analysis above leads directly to the standard solution for cyclical unemployment advanced by Keynesian economists. The key is for the government to stabilize the level of aggregate demand by adjusting its own spend-

[17] This famous quote actually comes from an earlier work by Keynes, *A Tract on Monetary Reform* (London: Macmillan Co., 1923). The full quotation is: "But this long run is a misleading guide to current affairs. In the long run, we are all dead. Economists set themselves too easy, too useless a task, if in tempestuous storms they can only tell us that when the storm is long past, the ocean is flat again" (p. 80).

ing level to compensate for any shifts in private spending. When private-sector spending is too low, government spending should increase, and conversely, it should fall when private spending appears to be too high. The general Keynesian prescription, then, is that government spending should be countercyclical in order to maintain full employment.

Explanations of Wage Rigidity

The least satisfactory feature of the Keynesian analysis is its assumption about the behavior of wages. Why is it that wages are sticky at best and completely inflexible at worst? What prevents the labor market from clearing at an equilibrium wage rate? It would certainly seem to be advantageous to a firm to cut wages when there is excess supply. Why, then, doesn't it do so? Why do quantity adjustments (i.e., employment changes) dominate wage adjustments in the labor market?

Keynes himself is not very helpful on these matters; he took wage rigidity as a factor to be used in a model rather than something to be explained. Since the time of Keynes—and especially in the past decade—economists have devoted a great deal of effort to that task of explanation. Much of the recent research has sought to explain wage rigidity in terms of the explicit, optimizing behaviors of firms and workers. It is, for instance, not sufficient to point to union contracts as a source of wage rigidity, since the union contracts could just as easily require wage flexibility. It is the underlying behavior of firms and workers that economists want to understand.

It is fair to say that most economists agree that wages and, for that matter, prices are less than perfectly and instantaneously flexible, especially where equilibrium requires downward adjustments. There is, however, less agreement on the reasons for this and the current state of understanding is far from satisfactory. The following are among the more important current explanations. They are not mutually exclusive; each may be operating at the same time and accounting for wage inflexibility in different parts of the economy.

Demand Instability and Risk Shifting.[18] Suppose that a firm's demand curve is subject to large, frequent, and unpredictable shifts which cause a worker's value to the firm to fluctuate over time. In this economic environment, the firm could adopt either of two wage and employment policies. It could adjust its wage whenever demand changed, always paying a wage that would just permit it profitably to employ its entire work force. The wage would rise in good times and fall in bad times, but employment would be stable. Alternatively, it could pay a constant wage, perhaps equal to the average value of a worker over the business cycle. In this case, wages in good

[18] This explanation is due primarily to Costas Azariadis, "Implicit Contracts and Underemployment Equilibria," *Journal of Political Economy,* 83 (December 1975), 1183–1202.

times are lower than they would otherwise be, and in bad times they are higher. Since wages are rigid, the demand fluctuations would lead to variations in employment and unemployment.

Figure 12.5 shows the effects of the two policies when there is a fall in demand from D_0 to D_1. With a flexible wage policy, the wage falls to w_1 and employment remains at L_0. With a rigid wage, employment falls to L_1, but the wage is, of course, unchanged.

If the wage rate in the constant-wage policy is chosen appropriately, the firm should be indifferent between the two policies. In contrast, it is often suggested that most workers will prefer the constant-wage policy. The main reason is that the instability of their earnings stream is thereby reduced. Workers no longer bear the risk that their earnings may fall precipitously, an event they could not well plan for, since the timing and magnitude are unknown ahead of time. The risk is shifted to the firm, which is in a better position to bear it.[19]

There are, of course, some workers who do not gain from the constant-wage policy: namely, those who will suffer the unemployment that results as an inevitable consequence of that policy. Even so, the constant-wage policy might well be adopted. For one thing, *most* workers are better off; perhaps no more than 10 to 20 percent would ever suffer unemployment. If layoffs follow a prescribed rule ("last hired, first fired"), those who are protected from layoff could easily outweigh those who will bear the brunt of it. That might be especially important in setting union contracts, where explicit voting with decision making by majority rule is the common practice.

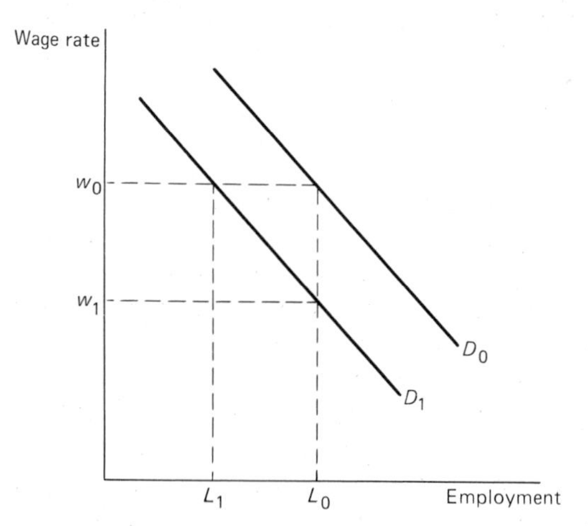

FIGURE 12.5 Comparing the Employment Effect of a Flexible-Wage Policy and a Rigid-Wage Policy

[19] Individuals have less access to capital markets than firms do. Thus individuals are less able to "smooth out" their income fluctuations through borrowing and lending.

Even workers who do experience unemployment may be willing to accept the constant-wage policy. If they are forward-looking, they may realize that they will someday be in a position to benefit from the policy. Other workers will have taken their place in the group that is subject to layoff. Also, if the expected period of unemployment is relatively short and if unemployment compensation is available, it may not be too severe a problem.

The notion that workers might themselves choose wage stability in the face of demand instability is intriguing. The ad hoc Keynesian assumption of wage rigidity now appears as the outcome of an economic process of maximization. Economic fluctuations now result in fluctuations in employment and output.

Demand Instability, Goodwill, and Long-Term Employment Relationships.[20] Suppose again that a firm's demand curve is subject to frequent and unpredictable fluctuations. Suppose further that, except for these fluctuations, both the firm and its workers anticipate that there will be an ongoing, long-term employment relationship. This could be due to specific training or to the development of an internal labor market, although the actual reason is unimportant.

In this situation a firm might itself choose a constant-wage policy because of its symbolic content. If demand falls and the firm lowers wages accordingly, it may be seen as "taking advantage of the workers" and perhaps even benefiting from its action via the lower wage. If, instead, it holds the wage constant and adjusts its employment, it cannot be accused of capitalizing on bad times. Workers do not feel devalued as they might with a general decrease in wages. Viewed in terms of its effects on the worker morale and trust necessary to maintain the long-term employment relationship, the constant-wage policy may well appear desirable. The result, once again, would be fluctuations in employment and unemployment.

The difference between the two wages and employment policies is even clearer in the case where it is difficult for workers or their union to verify whether the firm is facing good times or bad times. This is not quite as farfetched as it may seem. The firm, not the workers, receives customer orders and has knowledge of its current financial status. If the workers are completely uninformed, they might not trust the firm to implement a variable-wage policy. The firm, after all, would always benefit if it were able to employ the same number of workers at a lower wage. It might, therefore, not necessarily reveal truthfully whether times were, in fact, good or bad. The firm might, for instance, deliberately exaggerate its assessment of the bad times

[20] This section draws on George A. Akerloff, "A Theory of Social Custom, of Which Unemployment May Be One Consequence," *Quarterly Journal of Economics,* 94, no. 4 (June 1980), 749–75, and Joseph E. Stiglitz, "Theories of Wage Rigidity," paper prepared for Conference on Keynes' Economic Legacy, University of Delaware, 1984.

and similarly understate the good times, thereby holding wages down in both instances.

The point is that a firm clearly can benefit by misrepresenting the state of its demand curve. Realizing that, the workers would probably prefer the constant-wage policy in the first place. Demand fluctuations would then lead to fluctuations in employment, but—and this is the crucial point—the firm no longer has an incentive to misrepresent how good or bad things are. No matter what its current demand curve is, it would always want to hire the profit-maximizing number of workers (i.e., where $w = MRP_L$). To do otherwise—say, exaggerating the bad times by hiring less than that amount—would be like "cutting its nose to spite its face."

This idea is shown in Figure 12.6. Suppose that D_0 and D_1 are the true labor demand curves in two time periods. With wages of w_0 and w_1, the firm would be willing to maintain employment at L_0 even with the fluctuation in demand. The firm, though, might claim that the actual demand curves were d_0 and d_1 and insist that wages w_0' and w_1' were necessary to maintain employment at L_0. In contrast, if a rigid wage of w_0 is specified, the firm will have no incentive to misrepresent the demand curve. When D_0 is the relevant demand, it is profit maximizing to hire L_0, not L_0', workers; at L_0', the MRP_L is still greater than w_0. When demand falls to D_1, the firm will hire L_1 workers.

Imperfect Information and Shirking Behavior. In a recent paper, Shapiro and Stiglitz[21] linked rigid wages and involuntary unemployment to the inability of employers to observe costlessly the on-the-job effort of workers. They reason this way. Where a worker's own actual work effort can be monitored

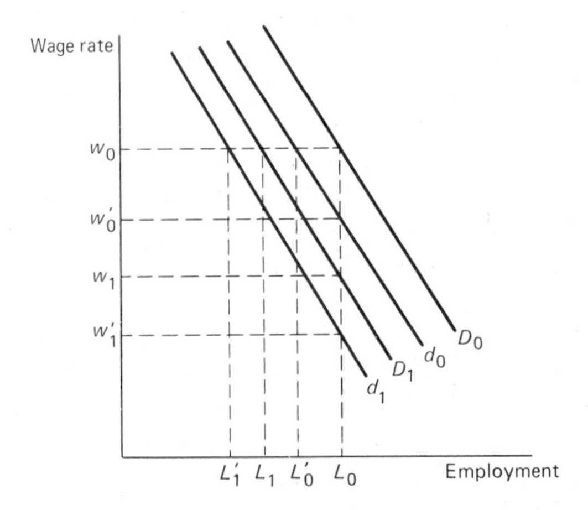

FIGURE 12.6 Flexible-Wage and Fixed-Wage Policies When Workers Cannot Observe Changes in the Labor Demand Curve

[21] Carl Shapiro and Joseph E. Stiglitz, "Equilibrium Unemployment as a Worker Discipline Device," *American Economic Review*, 74, no. 3 (June 1984), 433–44.

only imperfectly, that worker has an opportunity to **shirk**—that is, to put forth less effort. Like any activity, shirking has both benefits and costs. The benefits to a worker of shirking is an easier workday, while the cost depends on both the probability that shirking will be detected and the penalty that would be imposed.[22] The optimal (utility-maximizing) amount of shirking depends on a comparison of these costs and benefits. Formally, utility would be maximized where the marginal cost of shirking just equaled its marginal benefit.

From the firm's standpoint, there are two ways to reduce shirking. The first is to devote resources to monitoring worker effort, thereby increasing the probability of detection. The second is to increase the penalty if shirking is detected.

The issue considered by Shapiro and Stiglitz is what the firm's wage policy will be under these circumstances. Suppose, first, that all firms paid the equilibrium wage, that is, the wage consistent with full employment. With that wage policy, the costs of shirking would tend to be low. Even if a worker were caught shirking and were fired, another, essentially comparable job could be readily obtained. This is true precisely because each firm is paying the full-employment wage. The effect is that workers will have an incentive to shirk.

To reduce the amount of shirking, a firm could pay its workers more than the prevailing wage. A worker could then no longer find an equally good job if he or she were caught shirking and fired. It would seem that that should be effective in reducing the amount of shirking. Unfortunately, there is a difficulty with this solution. Since all firms have the same problem with shirking, they will all raise wages to increase the costs to workers of shirking. The result of this uncoordinated collective action is that all firms will pay the same wage and that this wage is above the equilibrium wage.

This equilibrium has three interesting features. First, because wages are above equilibrium, there is involuntary unemployment—an excess supply of labor at the prevailing wage. Second, the existence of unemployment reduces the amount of shirking, since now a worker who is fired may be unable to find *any* job. Unemployment thus acts as a "worker discipline device." Finally, it is an equilibrium, in the sense that firms do not have an incentive to lower the wage even though there are unemployed workers. The result is a rigid, above-equilibrium wage and unemployment even without cyclical fluctuations in demand.

UNEMPLOYMENT INSURANCE AND THE RATE OF UNEMPLOYMENT

In this section we examine the possible role of the unemployment insurance system in increasing unemployment, an idea we have referred to

[22] The cost of shirking would be equal to the probability of detection multiplied by the penalty.

several times already. It provides an excellent example of the way in which the natural unemployment rate may be influenced by government programs and other institutional features of the labor market.

The **unemployment insurance** (UI) system was established in 1935, with the primary purpose of protecting workers from undue economic hardship resulting from unemployment. Its basic structure involves raising revenues through a payroll tax on firms and subsequently providing benefits to eligible unemployed persons. Technically, the UI program is run by the states and each state sets up its own rules concerning eligibility, benefit levels, and financing. Some of the details of the program are important for understanding its potential effects on unemployment.

Let's begin by considering the benefit side. First, each state must decide who is eligible to receive UI benefits. It is impractical, if not financially impossible, to provide benefits to all unemployed persons. Suppose, for example, that a person could become eligible simply by entering the labor force and looking for work. Would it surprise you if the flow of persons into unemployment through that route was, as a result, very high? Most states, therefore, restrict eligibility to persons who have been employed for at least a specific number of weeks and/or have earned at least some minimum income over some previous period of time. Even then, most, although not all states deny eligibility to workers who voluntarily quit their jobs and to those fired with just cause. Overall, only about half of all unemployed persons are eligible for UI benefits.

A second benefit-related issue concerns the number of weeks that UI benefits can be received. This is determined by the federal government rather than by the states. Through the 1960s, 26 weeks was the standard period of eligibility, but in 1970 coverage was extended to 39 weeks, effective during periods of high national or state unemployment. Another 13 weeks of potential coverage was added in 1974 and yet another 13 weeks in 1975, making a grand total of 65 weeks. Since then, the duration of coverage has been scaled back. Maximum eligibility now ranges from 34 to 55 weeks, depending on the state.

Finally, actual UI benefits depend on an individual's earnings and on the state's **replacement rate**. The replacement rate is the fraction of previous earnings that an unemployed person receives. For example, if the replacement rate is 50 percent and a person earned $200 per week, he or she would receive $100 per week in unemployment compensation. Although the replacement rate varies from state to state, it is, with some important exceptions, uniformly applied within a state. Thus it is usually true that persons who had higher earnings when they were employed also receive higher UI benefits if they become unemployed. There is some variation in replacement rates even within a state, though, primarily because there are minimum and maximum payment levels to persons who are eligible for UI.[23] As a result, persons who qualify

[23] Many states also provide extra benefits based on the number of dependents that an unemployed worker has.

for the minimum payment face a higher replacement rate, whereas those at the maximum get a lower rate. Finally, UI income receives preferential tax treatment. Until 1978, UI income was completely free of tax. In that year, UI income became taxable if a family's income exceeded a designated threshold level. In 1983, one-half of unemployment insurance income was taxable for married couples with taxable income of $18,000 or more.

Because of the nontaxation of UI benefits, the actual replacement rates that an unemployed person faces is higher than the nominal rate in the state. The correct comparison is between after-tax income when employed and UI benefits available if unemployed. Martin Feldstein calculated an average replacement rate of 55 percent and most other estimates fall in that range.[24] For lower-income persons who may receive the minimum rate, the replacement rate may be as high as 75 percent. It is not difficult to construct examples of unemployed persons who, because of the features of their state UI system, their state income tax system, and their family size, may have replacement rates of 80 or 90 percent.

Feldstein, in particular, has argued that because many people receive high replacement rates, the UI system provides adverse incentives that increase unemployment. He has identified two distinct sources. First, UI benefits sharply reduce the cost of continued job search. Where replacement rates are quite high, the monetary costs of unemployment may be quite small. Most studies confirm that higher replacement rates lead to longer periods of unemployment. A common finding is that an increase in the replacement rate from 0.4 to 0.5 increases the length of a period of unemployment by one-half to one week.[25]

Second, and even more important, according to Feldstein, is the effect of UI benefits on the layoff policy of firms.[26] He argues that in the absence of UI, firms would be less likely to lay off workers in response to a *temporary* decline in demand. In considering a layoff, the firm would have to recognize that a worker might not be available for rehire later, which would result in the additional costs of hiring and training new workers. But given the current UI system, firms make excessive use of temporary layoffs precisely because they expect that workers will usually be available for rehire, as long as the layoff is relatively short. Because UI benefits make workers more willing to bear unemployment, they provide incentives to firms to organize production in a way that increases layoff unemployment. Feldstein provides evidence that up to half of all temporary layoff unemployment is accounted for by the benefits provided by the UI system.

[24] See Martin Feldstein, "Unemployment Insurance: Adverse Incentives and Distributional Anomalies," *National Tax Journal*, 27 (June 1974), 231–44.

[25] This estimate comes from Ronald G. Ehrenberg and Ronald L. Oaxaca, "Unemployment Insurance, Duration of Unemployment, and Subsequent Wage Gain," *American Economic Review*, 66, no. 5 (December 1976), 754–66.

[26] See Martin Feldstein, "The Effect of Unemployment Insurance on Temporary Layoff Unemployment," *American Economic Review*, 68, no. 5 (December 1978), 834–45.

There is also a potentially perverse incentive in terms of the financing of the UI system. In most states, different firms face different UI tax rates based on the financial burden their own unemployment has placed on the UI system in the recent past. Frequently, this is based on the industry in which a firm operates. For example, construction companies pay a higher tax rate because construction workers almost always have higher unemployment rates. Orthodontists, on the other hand, pay relatively low rates. This general practice is called **experience rating**—firms are "rated" for tax purposes on the basis of their recent unemployment experience. In principle, a firm's revenue contribution to the UI system is linked to the expected future benefits paid to its unemployed workers.

In practice, however, experience rating is *imperfect*, in the sense that the actual payments by different firms do not accurately reflect the differences in the financial burden they place on the system. The reason is that there is both a maximum and a minimum tax rate. No matter how much unemployment a firm is responsible for, it pays no more than the maximum. No matter how little unemployment it creates, it must pay at least the minimum. As a result, some firms pay much more than their share and others much less. High-unemployment firms are subsidized by low-unemployment firms.

To see how this might affect layoff behavior, consider a firm already paying the maximum rate and a firm paying a rate less than that. For the latter firm, each additional layoff will increase its tax rate. Thus the layoff involves additional costs to the firm which must be included in the layoff decision. For the firm already at the maximum, there are no additional costs to consider. Its rate is fixed; its marginal cost of a layoff in terms of its tax rate is zero.

Since the UI costs of a layoff are very different for these two firms, it is not hard to imagine that their layoff practices will also differ. A recent study by Topel[27] estimated that imperfect experience rating accounted for about 30 percent of all temporary layoffs. Topel concluded that a significant reduction in layoff unemployment could be achieved by improving experience rating without changing the benefit levels available to unemployed workers.

A few conclusions and caveats are in order. First, even if UI benefits do cause workers to search longer for work, that may not necessarily be all bad. One of the benefits of search is a better utilization of labor skills, and one of the expressed purposes of the UI system is to facilitate that search process. Would it necessarily be better to have a lower unemployment rate if it was achieved by having many unemployed persons accept the first available job? The findings about imperfect experience rating are more clear cut. It is hard to see why low-unemployment firms should regularly subsidize firms with high unemployment rates. Finally, this entire line of research reminds

[27] Robert H. Topel, "On Layoffs and Unemployment Insurance," *American Review*, 73, no. 4 (September 1983), 541–59.

us that unemployment is in some measure a function of the institutional arrangements and government policies that we adopt.

SUMMARY

In this chapter the problem of unemployment became the focus of analysis. Few topics in economics are more important; the unemployment rate is the subject of national attention and the object of national economic policy. There has been a tremendous amount of important empirical and theoretical research on unemployment in the past two decades. It is now recognized that unemployment is a far more complex and varied phenomenon than was thought in the 1960s. Still, the current state of understanding is far from complete and unemployment remains high on the agenda of continuing economic research.

The chapter began with measurement issues. The official unemployment rate accurately measures the extent of joblessness among currently active job seekers, but it is sensitive to its underlying definitions. The major controversies involve the job search requirement and the proper classification of discouraged workers.

More central and more complex are the issues of the duration and incidence of unemployment. Any unemployment rate is consistent with vastly different combinations of duration and incidence. The older view of unemployment had implicitly adopted a "long duration, low incidence" perspective, in which unemployment was thought to consist primarily of the long-term unemployed. In contrast, the new view of unemployment emphasizes the labor market flows of workers among the various labor force categories, a view that is consistent with a "high incidence, short duration" situation. Recent empirical studies show unmistakably that most spells of unemployment are short and the average duration of unemployment is relatively low. It is also clear that most persons unemployed in any given month are in the midst of a long spell of unemployment and that most persons who become unemployed in a year are unemployed for longer than the average duration of a single spell of unemployment. Both the old and new views of unemployment would seem to receive some support from these complex research findings.

Turning to theory, we looked at the traditional four-way classification of types of unemployment. Three of these—frictional, structural, and seasonal—will exist even when the economy is operating at "full employment." Collectively, they comprise what is now usually called the natural unemployment rate. This refers to unemployment that reflects the purposeful, maximizing behavior of individuals and firms on the basis of the actual characteristics of the economic environment.

The last type of unemployment is cyclical unemployment. It was attributed by Keynes to a fall in aggregate demand, given the fact of rigid or sticky wages. With prices unable to adjust to reach a new, full-employment equilibrium, the burden of adjustment is shifted to employment and output. The result is involuntary unemployment. Where Keynes simply assumed wage rigidity, more recent research has tried to explain why that behavior might be observed. This is important and fascinating research.

The final section discussed the operation of the unemployment insurance system, with emphasis on the way it affects the behavior of individuals and firms. Evidence suggests that the UI system increases both the incidence and duration of unemployment. Not all of the resulting unemployment is undesirable, but it is suggestive of the factors that influence the natural unemployment rate.

New Concepts

Job search requirement
Discouraged workers
Unemployment rate
Labor force participation rate
Employment rate
Incidence of unemployment
Duration of unemployment
Frictional unemployment
Natural unemployment rate
Full-employment unemployment rate
Search theory
Structural unemployment
Seasonal unemployment
Cyclical unemployment
Real wage
Wage rigidity
Shirking
Unemployment insurance (UI)
Replacement rate
Experience rating

13

Unemployment and Inflation

INTRODUCTION

In this chapter we move from the analysis of unemployment to the relationship between unemployment and inflation. In looking at that issue, we are really considering something slightly different: namely, whether the unemployment rate can be *permanently* reduced through the use of fiscal or monetary policy. The traditional wisdom about that, based on the famous Phillips curve, was that macroeconomic policy could effectively reduce unemployment. That belief was the basis of macroeconomic policy in the United States during the 1960s, a decade in which macroeconomic policy was generally deemed effective in controlling inflation, reducing unemployment, and promoting economic growth. When both unemployment and inflation rose sharply during the 1970s and macroeconomic policy became conspicuously less successful, the Phillips curve relationship came under fire from many economists. A new view about the relationship between inflation and unemployment emerged, based on the idea of the natural unemployment rate. The conclusion of this approach is exactly the opposite of the earlier view. It suggests that macroeconomic policy cannot permanently alter the rate of unemployment and it can do so temporarily only at the risk of accelerating inflation.

In the first part of this chapter we look at the original development of the Phillips curve. We then turn to the criticism of that approach and look at the alternative theory. Finally, we consider why the natural rate of unemployment may have risen in the past two decades and some general policy options to reduce it.

THE PHILLIPS CURVE AND THE RELATIONSHIP BETWEEN INFLATION AND UNEMPLOYMENT

At one level the Phillips curve is remarkably simple, a characteristic that undoubtedly contributed to its great popularity. In an article published in 1958, the economist A. W. Phillips examined the historical relationship between unemployment rates and the rate of change of money wages in Great Britain during the period 1862 to 1957.[1] He reported two important findings. First, he found that when the unemployment rate was high, the corresponding rate of change of money wages was relatively low or even negative. In other years, when the unemployment rate was lower, the rate of change of money wages tended to be larger. That is, it appeared that the unemployment rate and the rate of increase in money wages were inversely or negatively related

[1] A. W. Phillips, "The Relation between Unemployment and the Rates of Change of Money Wage Rates in the United Kingdom, 1862–1957," *Economica,* 25 (November 1958), 283–99.

to each other. Second, Phillips suggested that the relationship was stable over an extended period of time. In a famous part of his paper, he showed that the actual experience of Britain between 1948 and 1957 was very similar to the relationship that existed between 1861 and 1913. By implication, the Phillips curve was a characteristic and permanent feature of the economy.

Phillips presented his findings in the famous curve that bears his name. As shown in Figure 13.1, the unemployment rate is measured along the horizontal axis. On the vertical axis is the rate of change of money wages, denoted as $\dot{w}$. The curve is negative sloped, reflecting the inverse relationship between unemployment and the rate of change in wages. Note that it is not a straight line, but instead is convex to the origin, steeper at the top and flatter at the bottom. This means that when the unemployment rate is fairly high—for example, at point A—a 1 percentage point decrease in the unemployment rate is associated with a relatively small increase in money wages. But successive 1-point decreases in the unemployment rate causes larger and larger increases in wages.

The Phillips curve can be presented either in terms of $\dot{w}$, the rate of change of wages, or $\dot{p}$, the corresponding rate of change of prices—inflation, for short. Phillips used $\dot{w}$, but most economists since then have used $\dot{p}$, since the inflation rate is more important for economic policy. It makes no difference to the analysis which measure is used, since the two inflation rates differ by the rate of productivity growth. For example, if $\dot{w}$ equals 3 percent but producivity growth is also 3 percent, $\dot{p}$ will be zero; if the rate of growth of productivity were only 1 percent, $\dot{p}$ would be 2 percent. The same negative relationship between unemployment and inflation exists no matter which measure of inflation is used. Only the position of the curve, not its slope, is affected.

Phillips deduced his famous relationship from economic history rather than deriving it from economic theory. He did not explain what caused un-

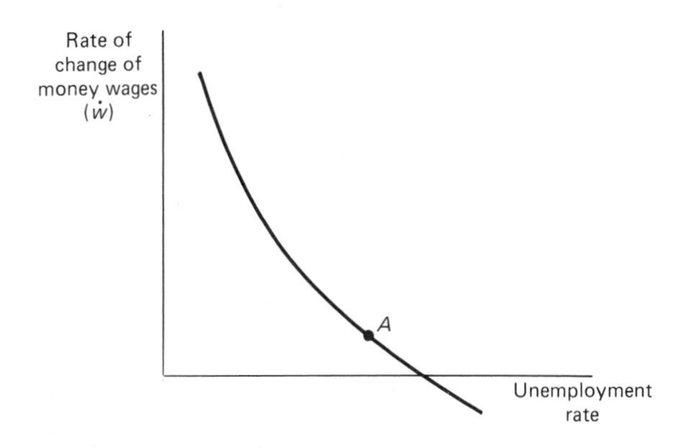

FIGURE 13.1 The Phillips Curve

employment and inflation to vary inversely. He simply presented an empirical observation, albeit a persuasive one.

Despite the lack of theoretical explanation, the Phillips curve gained wide and rapid acceptance among macroeconomists. It came to be interpreted as representing the set of feasible unemployment rate–inflation rate combinations which existed in an economy. According to this view, an economy could operate equally well anywhere along its Phillips curve, trading off lower unemployment rates for higher inflation rates, and vice versa. In a phrase that was popular, the Phillips curve presented a "menu of policy options." One needed only to discover the applicable Phillips curve for an economy, choose the desired combination, and then design and implement appropriate macroeconomic policy. It was almost that simple.

Discovering the Phillips curve for any particular country was not a difficult matter and by 1960, two famous American economists, Paul Samuelson and Robert Solow, provided one for the U.S. economy in the postwar period.[2] Their research confirmed the negative relationship between unemployment and inflation for the United States. So, too, did the actual experience of the U.S. economy during the 1960s, as shown in Figure 13.2.

Beginning in 1970, however, the simple Phillips curve relationship begins to look more complicated. Any unemployment rate now corresponds to a higher inflation rate than in the past—look, for example, at 1962 and 1963 compared with 1971 and 1972 or, even worse, with 1974 and 1979. It is still possible to find the traditional inverse relationship between 1970 and 1973 and again between 1976 and 1979. But the relationship is, at best, short-lived

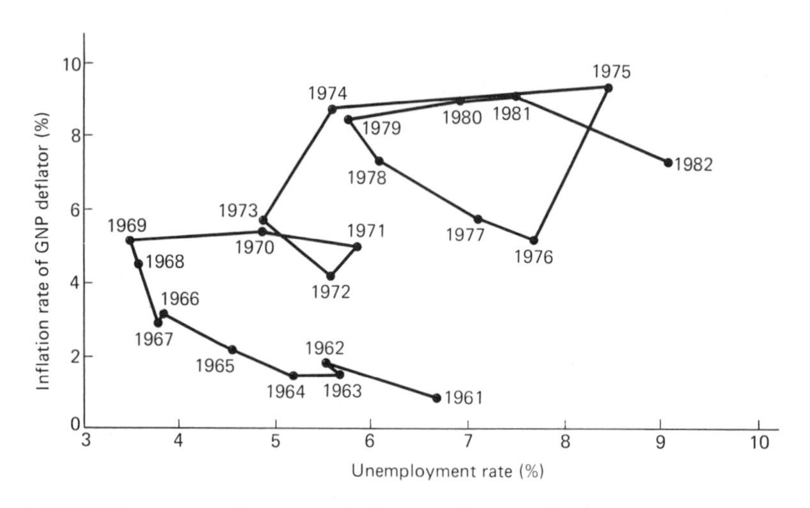

FIGURE 13.2 Unemployment and Inflation in the United States, 1961–1982

[2] Paul Samuelson and Robert Solow, "Analytical Aspects of Anti-inflation Policy," *American Economic Review Papers and Proceedings*, 50, no. 2 (May 1960), 177–94.

and the Phillips curve if it still exists, is steadily shifting outward. If the Phillips curve is not stable, it loses its value as a guide to economic policy. What good would it be if policymakers selected a desired combination off the Phillips curve menu and instituted the correct policies only to find themselves with a higher-than-expected inflation rate because the curve had suddenly shifted?

Just as disturbing are the apparent clockwise cycles in the data from 1970 to 1974 and again from 1976 to 1981. Look at the latter period more closely. Between 1976 and 1979, all looks well. True, the entire set of combinations is less desirable than previously, but the negative relationship does hold. But in 1980 and 1981, both unemployment and inflation rise. Comparing those two years with 1976 and 1977, it looks as if the unemployment rate has been unchanged, even though the inflation rate has increased substantially. Does that suggest that the Phillips curve relationship is invalid or obsolete?

Not too surprisingly, the macroeconomic experience of the 1970s led some economists to reconsider the Phillips curve. In particular, these economists turned to the economic theory that might explain the results represented by the Phillips curve. That led to some surprising ideas and a revised understanding of what the Phillips curve represents and how it might be used in macroeconomic policy.

ECONOMIC THEORY AND THE PHILLIPS CURVE

Labor Market Equilibrium and the Phillips Curve

Suppose, for the moment, that the famous negatively sloped Phillips curve relationship does hold. Since unemployment and employment are themselves inversely related, the Phillips curve relationship implies that inflation affects employment and output as shown in Figure 13.3. In panel (a), higher inflation rates increase employment by decreasing unemployment; in panel (b) the effect of increased employment is shown in terms of its effect on the amount of output produced. We can, therefore, represent the Phillips curve either in terms of the conventional negative relationship between inflation and unemployment or in terms of a positive relationship between inflation and both employment and output. The three formulations are equivalent.

Viewed in terms of Figure 13.3, however, the Phillips curve yields conclusions that are inconsistent with other widely held ideas. In Chapter 12 when we considered the equilibrium of an economy in the context of classical and Keynesian analyses of unemployment, we concluded that there was a single real wage (w/p) consistent with equilibrium in both the product and labor markets. We saw there that changes in aggregate demand could lead to change in the price level ($\dot{p} \neq 0$), but the corresponding changes in wage necessary to achieve equilibrium guaranteed that neither output nor employment would be changed. Put differently, equilibrium employment and output

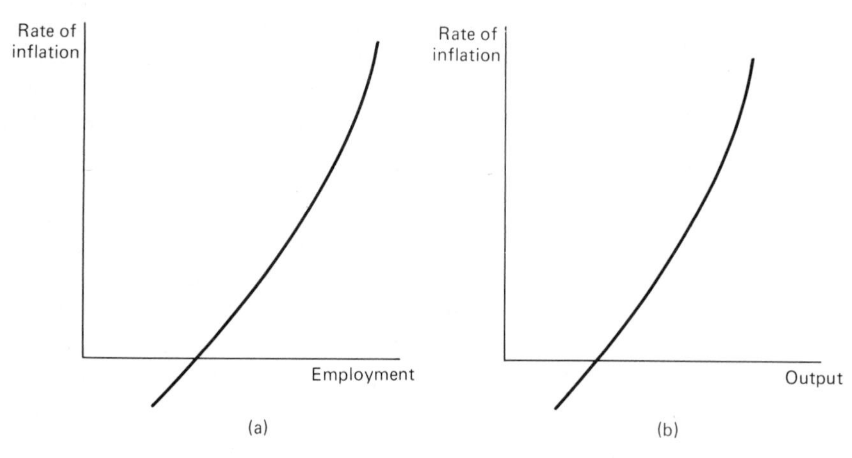

FIGURE 13.3 The Relationship between (a) Inflation and Employment and (b) Inflation and Output If the Phillips Curve is Negatively Sloped

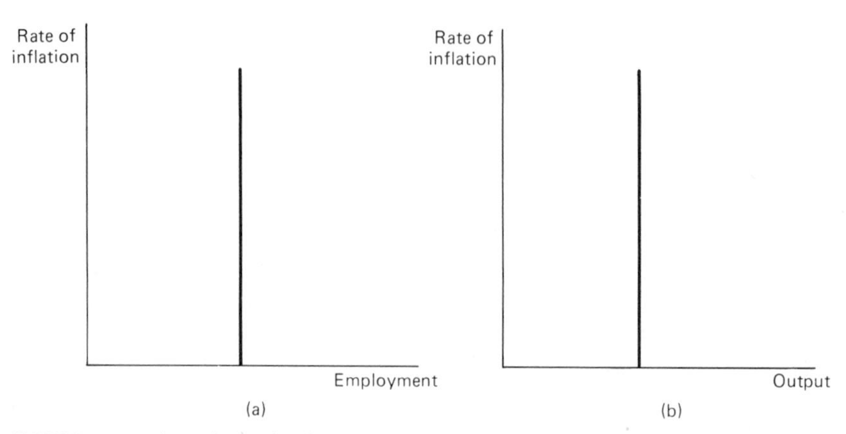

FIGURE 13.4 The Relationship between (a) Inflation and Employment and (b) Inflation and Output When the Labor and Product Markets Are in Equilibrium

are *unaffected* by the rate of inflation. Reversing the logic used above, it follows that the Phillips curves depicting the relationship between inflation, employment, and output *when there is equilibrium in the product and labor market* will be vertical, as shown in Figure 13.4(a) and (b).

An argument like this, but put in the slightly more difficult context of a growing economy, was made by Milton Friedman in his famous 1967 presidential address to the American Economics Association.[3] Friedman reasoned

[3] Milton Friedman, "The Role of Monetary Policy," *American Economic Review*, 58, no. 1 (March 1968), 1–17.

this way. Every economy has an equilibrium real wage rate which ultimately reflects the factors underlying the labor demand and labor supply curves—such things as the amount of capital, the productivity of labor, and the size of the population. As we saw in Chapter 12, there is also a natural rate of unemployment which is consistent with equilibrium in the labor market. Over time, the real wage in the economy will typically increase, with its exact rate of increase depending on the changes in the factors that underlie the labor supply and labor demand curves. In each time period, though, there will be a single, determinate real wage consistent with equilibrium. Finally, along this time path of equilibrium real wages, the natural unemployment rate will be constant. That rate is a feature of labor market equilibrium, given the characteristics of the economy, and does not depend on the particular equilibrium real wage that exists.

To make things concrete, suppose that conditions are such that equilibrium real wages can grow at 2 percent per year on average. That, however, tells us almost nothing about the rate of growth of nominal wages or prices, except for the necessary relationship between the two growth rates. Wages could increase by 2 percent and prices by 0 percent, or by 12 percent and 10 percent, or any other arithmetic combination in which $\dot{w} - \dot{p} = 2\%$. There are an infinite set of combinations of wage and price growth, all of which are consistent with maintaining equilibrium in the labor market.

The upshot of Friedman's argument is this: If wages and prices move together to maintain equilibrium in the labor market, there will be no trade-off between unemployment and inflation. In an economy where the equilibrium real wage is growing at 2 percent per year, an inflation rate of 100 percent together with a wage increase of 102 percent would have no more effect on reducing unemployment than an inflation rate of 0 percent and a wage increase of 2 percent. Both preserve labor market equilibrium and in both cases, the unemployment rate will equal the natural unemployment rate. Of course, if prices increased by 100 percent and wages by 90 percent or 110 percent, the unemployment rate might well change temporarily—an idea we will consider in a moment. But in those cases, the labor market would no longer be in equilibrium.

The resulting Phillips curve, now often called the **long-run Phillips curve** (LRPC), is vertical, positioned at the natural rate of unemployment, as in Figure 13.5. Bear in mind that it depicts an equilibrium relationship between inflation and unemployment.

Most economists now accept the logic of Friedman's argument, at least as a long-run proposition. Its implications for unemployment policy are quite strong, to say the least. The menu of policy choices that characterized the older approach has disappeared. In its place is the natural unemployment rate, which is compatible with any rate of inflation. Macroeconomic policy can affect the rate of inflation, but not the rate of unemployment. Only policies directed at the factors that determine the natural rate can be effective.

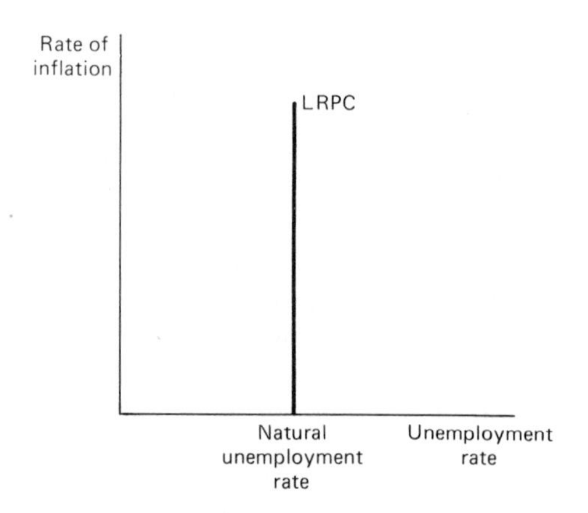

FIGURE 13.5 The Long-Run Phillips Curve

Imperfect Information and the Phillips Curve

If in the long run there is no trade-off between unemployment and inflation, what can be said about the alleged short-run relationship? What accounts for it? Why might there exists a trade-off in the short run, but none in the long run?

Explaining the **short-run Phillips curve** relationship satisfactorily is not as easy as it sounds. Suppose we accept the idea that the short-run relationship represents the situation where, for some reason, the changes in w and p cause the real wage to deviate from its long-run path. That must be true, because along its long-run path, there is, as we just saw, no unemployment—inflation trade-off. But the desired negative relationship between unemployment and inflation is by no means assured even in this case. If the real wage is temporarily "too low," firms would like to increase the amount of employment, but labor supply would fall. Actual employment would fall, not rise. Exactly the same thing would occur if the real wage were temporarily "too high." Now labor supply is larger, but firms are willing to hire fewer workers. For the negative Phillips relationship to hold, there must be some real wage at which both labor supply *and* labor demand are larger than they would be at the equilibrium real wage. It is not obvious that that is possible.[4]

One possible explanation was advanced by Friedman in his presidential address. He argued there that workers and firms might well have different information about changes in the price level; specifically, he suggested that firms might learn about those changes more quickly than workers. That is

[4] Some economists now question the validity of the negative relationship between inflation and unemployment on empirical grounds. See, for instance, Robert J. Barro, *Macroeconomics* (New York: John Wiley & Sons, Inc., 1984), pp. 440–46.

sufficient to generate a short-run negative relationship between inflation and unemployment. Whether it is a descriptively accurate representation of behavior is less clear.

The basic idea is shown in Figure 13.6. Suppose that initially the labor market is in equilibrium at point *A*, with a real wage of w_0/p_0, employment of L_0, and an unemployment rate of UR_N, the natural unemployment rate. For simplicity, let the current inflation rate be zero. As we have now seen several times, an increase in aggregate demand due, say, to government fiscal or monetary policy, will eventually cause both prices and wages to rise. Labor market equilibrium will be reestablished at point *B*, where the price level and money wage are both higher but the real wage is unchanged.

Suppose, however, that at first only the firms realize that the price level has increased. In that case, labor demand will shift up proportional to the increase in price; if the price level were 10 percent higher, every point on D_1 would be exactly 10 percent above the corresponding point on D_0. The labor supply curve, which would shift in to S_1 if the price level increase were recognized, is, however, unchanged. Thus equilibrium occurs at point *C*, with the nominal wage rising to w_2, employment rising to L_2, and unemployment falling below the natural rate.

Notice the peculiar features of the equilibrium at point *C*. Both wages and prices have increased, but the increase in the price level is greater than the increase in the wage rate. (The percentage increase in the price level is indicated by the vertical distance between points *A* and *B*; the increase in wages from w_0 to w_2 is clearly less than that.) Thus the real wage is actually

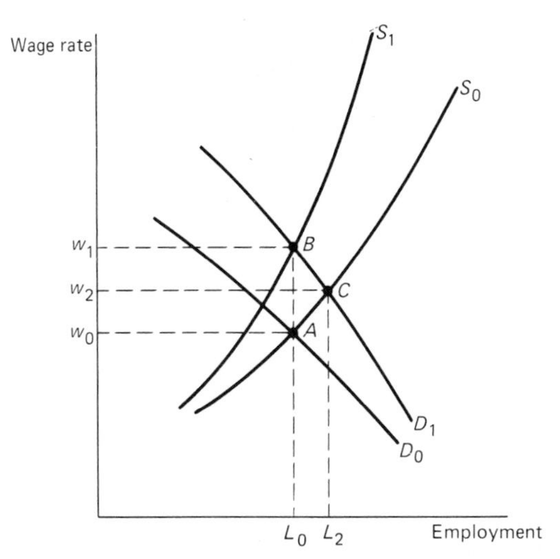

FIGURE 13.6 Friedman's "Fooling" Model: Wage, Price, and Employment Effects of an Increase in Aggregate Demand

lower at point C than at point A, but as perceived by workers, it is higher, since they see only the increase in wages, not the even larger increase in prices. With a lower real wage, firms are willing to hire more workers, while the higher perceived real wage leads to an increase in the number of workers willing to work.

Figure 13.7 shows what has happened in terms of a Phillips curve, drawn in terms of unemployment in panel (a) and employment in panel (b). The increase in the price level is represented by $\dot{p}_1$. As you can see, the two solid-line Phillips curves do have the characteristic slopes—negative in (a) and positive in (b). Points C' and C'' corresponds to point C in Figure 13.6.

Sooner or later, though, workers will inevitably recognize that the price level has increased and that the real wage has fallen. When that happens, the labor supply curve in Figure 13.6 will shift in, eventually causing the real wage to increase and, in the process, reducing employment and increasing unemployment. The two curves in Figure 13.7 will also shift; the new long-run equilibrium lies along the vertical, dashed lines in both diagrams. Friedman's "fooling model" thus has the attractive feature of being able to account both for a short-run trade-off between inflation and unemployment and the lack of such a trade-off in the long run.

Expectations and the Phillips Curve

The analysis of Figures 13.6 and 13.7 involved the special case in which the underlying rate of inflation (i.e., before the increase in aggregate demand) was assumed to be zero. The Phillips curve relationship then arose because of a discrepancy between the actual price level and the price level expected and perceived by workers. Equivalently, we can say that there was a difference

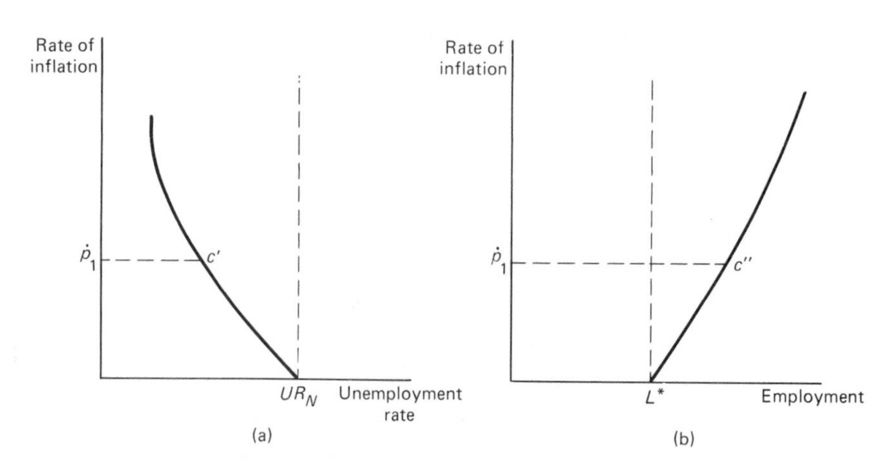

FIGURE 13.7 The Relation Between (a) Inflation and Unemployment and (b) Inflation and Employment When Workers Do Not Realize That the Price Level Has Increased

between the actual rate of inflation ($\dot{p}_1$) and the expected rate, which was, in this case, zero. Viewed this way, the negatively sloped Phillips curve in Figure 13.7(a) shows the relationship between inflation and unemployment when workers expected the inflation rate to be zero. Similarly, the vertical Phillips curve represents that same relationship when inflationary expectations are correct and the economy is in equilibrium.

This approach to the Phillips curve analysis is shown in Figure 13.8. Each of the three Phillips curves is based on a different underlying expected rate of inflation—namely, $\dot{p}^e = 0$ percent, $\dot{p}^e = 3$ percent, and $\dot{p}^e = 6$ percent. Note that on each curve, the inflation rate corresponding to the natural unemployment rate (UR_N) is also the one corresponding to the expected rate of inflation. Thus point A on PC_0 represents the situation where $\dot{p}^e = \dot{p} = 0$ and $UR = UR_N$; at B on PC_3, $\dot{p}^e = \dot{p} = 3\%$; and again, $UR = UR_N$; and so on, for point C on PC_6. That is no coincidence, but is rather an essential condition for equilibrium in the labor market. Only when $\dot{p}^e = \dot{p}$ will wages increase at a rate consistent with equilibrium in the labor market. When the labor market is in equilibrium, we know that $UR = UR_N$.

Suppose that the economy is initially operating at point A and is then subjected to an unanticipated increase in aggregate demand. The price level increases—inflation sets in. Following exactly the logic developed above, the unanticipated inflation causes employment to rise and unemployment to fall. The economy moves to a point such as, B, where, as is evident, $\dot{p} > \dot{p}^e$. For graphical convenience, the rate of inflation is assumed to be 3 percent at point B.

The important question for macroeconomic policy is whether, having

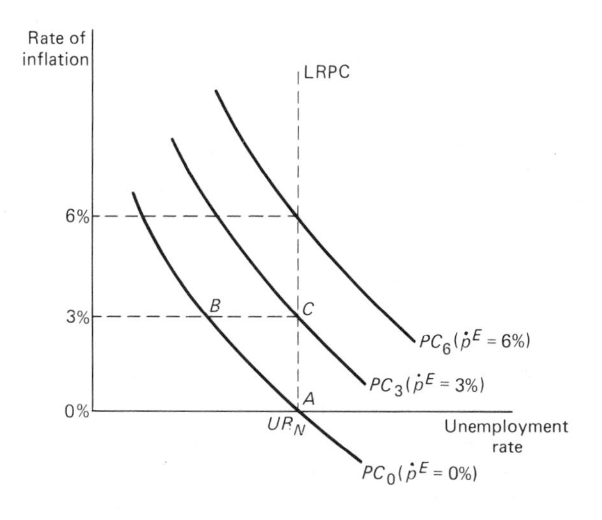

FIGURE 13.8 Inflationary Expectations and the Phillips Curve

gotten to point *B*, the economy can stay there. In other words, can the unemployment rate be permanently reduced by fiscal and/or monetary policy? The answer depends on what happens to **inflationary expectations**. As Figure 13.8 suggests, point *B* is stable only if expectations do not change. It is possible that people might cling stubbornly to incorrect expectations. But it would be surprising if that were true for very long, since expectations that are incorrect result in actions that will not turn out as anticipated. Exactly how expectations are revised is a complicated and important matter and one that is a major area of current research. But the general prediction, certainly, is that inflationary expectations will be revised upward, which, in turn, will lead to a more rapid growth in nominal wages. The result is that the economy no longer operates along PC_0, but instead along another, higher Phillips curve based on a higher expected rate of inflation.

Figure 13.8 illustrates the case in which expectations adjust fully to the change in the actual rate. The economy moves horizontally from point *B* to point *C* on the new Phillips curve PC_3. Point *C* represents a situation in which expectations are once again fulfilled and the labor market is again in equilibrium. As you can readily verify, the upward revision of inflationary expectations has resulted in a situation in which, relative to point *A*, there is no reduction in unemployment, but the inflation rate is higher.

Once again, we have derived the result that there is no permanent trade-off between unemployment and inflation. There is a second important idea here as well. To keep the unemployment rate below the natural rate, it will be necessary to have ever-higher rates of inflation. The reason is that in this model, it is not inflation that causes the unemployment rate to fall, but rather, a rate higher than what was expected. Thus, in Figure 13.8, when the expected rate was 0, an inflation rate of 3 percent was sufficient to reduce unemployment to UR_1. But when the economy has come to expect 3 percent and has moved to point *C*, a higher inflation rate—such as 6 percent—is now necessary. In time, even that higher rate would be insufficient to reduce the unemployment rate. Put in strong terms, a commitment to keep the unemployment rate below the natural rate requires an accelerating rate of inflation.

In this approach, we see that the vertical Phillips curve corresponds to the situation in which inflationary expectations are correct, and the negatively sloped curve the situation in which they are incorrect. That tells us that the actual shape of the Phillips curve depends on how accurately and how quickly expectations are revised.

Suppose, for example, that expectations adjust with a time lag or adjust only partially. In that case, movements up a short-run Phillips curve will still shift the curve out, but by less than in shown in Figure 13.8. If that were true, the long-run Phillips curve would be steeper than the short-run curve, but it would not be vertical. Some long-run trade-off between unemployment and inflation would still exist.

Another view about the formation of expectations, known as the **rational**

expectations hypothesis, holds that the expectations of workers and firms are never systematically wrong. In this use, "rational" means that the expectations are formed on the basis of all available relevant information, and saying that the expectations are not systematically wrong means that they are not persistently either too high or too low. Rather, the expectations are, on average, correct. The unemployment rate in the economy will, therefore, vary randomly around the natural rate, depending on whether expectations are too high or too low. But there would be no systematic relationship—no correlation—between the rate of inflation and the rate of unemployment.

The rational expectations hypothesis is highly controversial and there is, as yet, no conclusive evidence about the formation of expectations and its effects on the economy. Virtually everyone agrees that the economy is now much more sensitive to and informed about inflation than in the past. It is no longer as easy to fool people, which means that using the traditional Phillips curve is more precarious than in the past.

EMPLOYMENT AND UNEMPLOYMENT IN THE 1980S

The Natural Unemployment Rate

The new Phillips curve analysis shifts the focus of unemployment policy away from traditional macroeconomic policy and toward an understanding of the determinants of the natural rate of unemployment. Especially in the light of the high unemployment rates that the U.S. economy experienced during much of the 1970s and in the 1980s, a number of questions arise. First, how high is the natural unemployment rate? Is it 4 percent, 6 percent, 8 percent, or what? Second, has the natural rate risen over the past decade? Does that lie behind the higher unemployment rates of the 1970s? Finally, what kind of policies might be effective in reducing the natural rate?

Before we look at those ideas, we need to consider how the natural rate might be measured. Saying that it is the rate corresponding to labor market equilibrium is not helpful, since it is not easy to know whether or not an equilibrium exists. In practice, the natural rate is usually defined in terms of the associated rate of inflation. Specifically, the natural unemployment rate is the unemployment rate at which the inflation rate is constant—neither increasing nor decreasing. The basis for this definition is the result, which we saw in Figure 13.8, that unemployment rates below the natural rate can be maintained only through accelerating inflation rates. At the natural rate, however, since the expected and actual inflation rates are equal, there is no tendency for the inflation rate to rise. The natural unemployment rate is sometimes called the **nonaccelerating inflation rate of unemployment** or NAIRU.

By most accounts, the natural unemployment rate was in the vicinity of

4 percent through most of the 1960s, about 5.8 percent in the mid-1970s, and now is closer to 6.5 to 7.0 percent. Government policy now accepts that figure. The Council of Economic Advisors no longer calls for a fall in the unemployment rate to 4 percent.[5] Since an unemployment rate of 6.5 percent or higher is extremely high by our own historical standards, the obvious question is why the natural unemployment rate is so much higher now than in the past. We have some partial answers, but not definitive ones.

The Changing Demographic Composition of the Labor Force. As we saw in Chapter 12, different demographic groups in the labor force have different characteristic unemployment rates. There is nothing that guarantees that this should always be true, but historically it has been. It is useful to think of the aggregate unemployment rate as being a weighted average of the rate for each group, with each group weighted by its share of the labor force.

It follows that one way the natural rate could rise is if those groups with higher unemployment rates account for a larger share of the labor force. During the period of the late 1960s and most of the 1970s, that seems to be what happened. The baby-boom generation grew up and entered the labor market, swelling the ranks of inexperienced workers, first job seekers, and those looking for their niche in the labor market. The sheer size of that group placed additional pressure on the labor market. In addition, the labor force participation rate of married women rose sharply, thus increasing the number of reentrants into the labor market. The result was a fall in the share of the labor market accounted for by prime-age males, the group that traditionally has the lowest unemployment rate.

A crude way to assess the importance of these changes is to calculate the unemployment rate that would exist today if each group had its actual current unemployment rate, but its share of the labor force was the same as in the past. Using 1982 unemployment rates and 1958 labor force shares gives a hypothetical 1982 unemployment rate about $\frac{3}{4}$ of a point lower than the actual 1982 rate.

Demographic changes in the future may operate to reduce the natural rate. The size of the cohorts of young workers is projected to fall over the next decade. Even if their unemployment rates remain high, their declining importance in the labor force will pull the natural rate down.

Degree of Wage Rigidity. Anything that prevents equilibrium in specific labor markets by making wages more inflexible will tend to increase the natural rate of unemployment. One often-noted example is minimum wage legislation, even though research has not yet demonstrated a strong link

[5] The Humphrey–Hawkins Full Employment and Balanced Growth Act of 1978 called for a 4 percent unemployment rate in 1983, together with a 3 percent inflation rate. Policymakers concluded that the goals were unattainable.

between teenage unemployment and the minimum wage. Another is the role of labor unions in wage negotiations.

It is true that these factors also existed when unemployment rates were lower in the 1960s. But they may have had less impact then, because wages were rising due to productivity growth. Conditions in the 1970s and 1980s, however, placed more pressure on labor markets and required greater wage flexibility. The oil price increases changed relative prices of final goods and the costs of different production techniques. Both had an impact on labor markets. Certain key unionized industries—automobile, steel, and textiles—were subject to increased competition from lower-cost foreign producers. Deregulation of trucking and airline travel permitted price competition as well as the entry of low-cost, often nonunion firms. Unemployment in these sectors was partially the result of wage rigidity.

Social Welfare Spending. Does social welfare spending raise the natural unemployment rate by providing a safety net of income support? This is a highly controversial idea, to say the least. We saw in Chapter 12 that this is probably true in the case of unemployment insurance, both because of the benefit levels and the method of financing used. Economists who have studied these effects think that the UI system may account for up to a percentage point of unemployment. It is possible that other social programs, such as AFDC, food stamps, and Medicaid, increase unemployment by placing a wage floor on jobs that will be acceptable. That is, they may raise the *reservation wage*, the lowest wage at which a person will accept employment. The possible link between these programs and unemployment was discussed in the 1983 Economic Report of the President. But it is too early to assess the probable quantitative importance.

Employment Policy in the United States

During the 1970s the focus of employment policy shifted from the training programs of the 1960s to programs emphasizing direct employment on public works projects. Included among these public sector employment programs were the Emergency Employment Act of 1971, the CETA program, which ran from 1973 to 1982; the Local Public Works Capital Development and Investment Act of 1976; and the Public Works Employment Act of 1977.

Although this approach is generally popular among politicians, economists tend not to share their enthusiasm. There are serious practical and economic questions about the potential effectiveness of this approach. For one thing, there is an inevitable time lag in establishing public works programs. Congress must pass legislation and appropriate funds, government agencies must set up administrative procedures, and employment projects must be created and approved—all before employment begins. It is not uncommon to find a time lag of up to two years, which sometimes means that the program becomes effective just when it is no longer needed. One study found that 90 percent of all expenditures for public works designed to reduce unemployment during the 1974–1975 recession actually occurred more than $2\frac{1}{2}$ years *after* the low point of the recession was reached.

A second problem emerged in the 1970s as public-sector employment funds became available on a regular basis. It is argued that state and local governments had a natural incentive to substitute federally funded employment projects for projects they would otherwise have funded themselves. Why raise taxes to build a new road when the same project can be built with federal money instead? Economists call this a **fiscal substitution effect** and it suggests that the apparent employment effects of public works programs is far less than it appears. That is, it does not appear to be true that public works projects lead to large net increases in employment since some of the projects and thus some of the employment would have occurred even in the absence of the programs. Some estimates have placed the fiscal substitution effect from 30 to 50 percent of total program funding.

In the 1980s, employment policy has moved away from public-sector employment and toward policies that attempt to reduce the natural rate of unemployment. There have been two general approaches. One focuses on the unemployment problems of specific groups and attempts to increase their employment prospects through some combination of wage subsidies and/or job training. The two groups that are typically made the focus of these programs are unemployed workers who are less than age 24 and adult workers who suffer long-term employment. The other basic direction involves reforming those current policies that inhibit wage flexibility and labor mobility or that actually encourage unemployment. We look briefly at these two approaches next.

Targeted Employment Policy. One example of this approach, the Targeted Jobs Tax Credit, is designed to help young workers by providing tax incentives to prospective employers. This program has been operating on a relatively small scale since 1979. It applies to employers who hire economically disadvantaged youth aged 18 to 24. Employers are entitled to tax credits for two years—up to $3000 the first year and $1500 the second. The idea is to overcome the initial resistance to hiring these youths and to provide young workers, who often have had no previous work experience, with two years of subsidized employment. It is assumed that by then a worker will be productive enough to warrant conventional employment. Although the general approach seems reasonable, by most accounts this has not had a major impact.

Nevertheless, the program was extended in 1983 to provide subsidies for the summer employment of disadvantaged youths who were aged 16 to 17. In this case, the wage subsidy was 85 percent, which meant that youths who were employed at the minimum wage ($3.35 per hour) would cost a firm only about $0.50 an hour. It is hoped that this program would give these youths some job experience and enable them to establish an employment record. That, in turn, should help them subsequently when they look for career-oriented employment. It is much too early to know whether this program achieved even its short-term goal of increasing summer employment for these youths.

Training programs are now provided under the Job Training Partnership Act (JTPA), the program that replaced CETA. Previous training programs had been cricitized for not being closely linked to the private sector, where employment would ultimately occur. In principle at least, the JTPA establishes a formal partnership among private industry, the public sector, and vocational training institutions to design and provide federally financed training. The jobs targeted for training include economically disadvantaged youths, low-skilled and chronically unemployed adults, and even skilled workers who have lost jobs in declining industries. Again, it is too early to evaluate this program. Its success will depend on how well it can be implemented at the local level and whether it can identify needed skills and successfully teach them to the target groups.

Other proposed policies to enhance training and retraining include the following: (1) allow unemployed workers to take their extended unemployment payments in the form of vouchers good for training that they choose; (2) make training expenses borne by individuals tax-deductible; and (3) allow states to use a portion of their unemployment insurance taxes to support job retraining programs.

Policy Reforms. The most obvious candidate here is reform of the unemployment insurance system. As we saw earlier, there is substantial evidence that the UI system increases the incidence of short-term unemployment and somewhat weaker evidence that it affects the duration of unemployment as well. Probably the most important reform involves increasing the degree of experience rating of firms. That would make firms bear a greater share of the increased costs created by their own unemployment record. That kind of reform is attractive because it might be able to reduce unemployment without any effect on the benefits available to unemployed workers.

SUMMARY

The famous negatively sloped Phillips curve, once the cornerstone of macroeconomic policy, is now viewed as, at best, a temporary phenomenon. The economic performance of the decade of the 1970s showed that the traditional Phillips curve relationship was either unstable or nonexistent. Theoretical analysis suggested that the relationship was not consistent with labor market equilibrium.

The current view is that the negative relationship between inflation and unemployment exists only when the actual inflation rate differs from that which was expected and on which workers and firms based their plans. There is a separate short-run Phillips curve for each and every expected rate of inflation. Attempts to move along any single curve inevitably lead to compensating shifts from one curve to another as expectations are revised. A Phillips curve representing the relationship between inflation and unemployment when the labor market is in equilibrium shows no trade-off between inflation and unemployment. Instead, there is a single equilibrium unemployment rate—the natural unemployment rate—which is consistent with any correctly anticipated rate of inflation. The long-run Phillips curve is vertical.

Most estimates put the natural unemployment rate in the range 6.5 to 7.0 percent. Why the natural unemployment rate is so much higher now than in previous decades is not fully understood. Many of the factors that tend to increase unemployment were also operating in the 1960s. It is necessary to show that these factors are more important or more serious now than in the past. The changing demographic composition of the labor force and wage rigidity in the face of increased structural change in the economy are two commonly noted factors. The existence of an extensive set of social welfare programs such as UI and welfare is another possibility.

Employment policy has included job training, direct public-sector employment, and various wage subsidies. During the 1970s, the direct employment programs were emphasized, but policy now focuses on the other two strategies.

New Concepts

Long-run Phillips curve
Short-run Phillips curve
Inflationary expectations
Rational expectations hypothesis
Nonaccelerating inflation rate of unemployment (NAIRU)
Fiscal substitution effect

Index